35/c

£15

(64)

A DRAMA OF POLITICAL MAN

Harley Granville Barker, *ca.* 1916

A DRAMA
OF POLITICAL MAN

A Study in the Plays

of

Harley Granville Barker

by

MARGERY M. MORGAN

SIDGWICK & JACKSON

LONDON

First published by Sidgwick & Jackson Ltd. 1961
© *Margery M. Morgan* 1961

PRINTED IN GREAT BRITAIN
BY CHARLES BIRCHALL & SONS, LTD.,
LIVERPOOL AND LONDON

PREFACE

This book is an attempt to do justice to the work of a very interesting and commonly underestimated playwright. Granville Barker's original plays, including some not published, have furnished the basic material for study; his translations of foreign plays have not been considered, as they make a further subject in themselves; and his non-dramatic writings have been discussed only as they shed light on aspects of his art as a dramatist. The biographical approach has been kept to the necessary minimum: the facts of his life and his career have been considered at length elsewhere. His theories and techniques of acting and production, though far from exhaustively treated, are examined here in order to complete the account of his dramaturgy. However, the bulk of this study concentrates upon a severely limited body of material, and the weight of comment that is offered may need some justification. It is provided partly by the type of drama that Barker demonstrably set out to create, which depends very considerably on effective detail and requires meticulous preparation from producers and actors. For the rest, the conception of the critic's task, which lies behind this book, has determined the use of a thoroughly exploratory method.

It is commonly held that nothing which is not boldly presented on the surface of the dialogue counts in a play, as it is unlikely to be perceived in performance. This book proceeds on the assumption that submerged meanings are a source of power in the theatre, even when the actor is not consciously aware that he is conveying them, or the audience of receiving them; and, conversely, that the play in which the words conceal no depths is inevitably a weak thing. Dramatic dialogue need not be written in verse to have the potency of a poetic language: that is one of the great discoveries of modern drama. Every line spoken by an actor from a stage can turn from speech to symbol. The true dramatist, knowing that, allows for it and chooses his words with as much deliberation as the poet. Dramatic criticism is accustomed to allow for this in the plays of Shakespeare; but reluctance to consider the words in other plays has been one aspect of the neglect of drama in England, which is only now being remedied.

Yet a dramatic text makes demands on the reader's imagination which are slightly different in kind from those exacted by other literary forms. A dramatist's mastery of his craft has to be measured in terms of his awareness of the relations between the different elements in a performance—play, producer, actors, physical theatre and audience—and his ability to manipulate them. The ideal spectator, which the critic aspires to be, thus has to look all round the play, borrowing the eyes of the experts, recognising when just this effect has to be got by just these means and only these, or when the potentialities are less limited; but entering, too, into the emotional experience which the rhythm of a good production would evoke. The present study cannot claim to have achieved so comprehensive a view; the critic's equipment is simply not adequate to the rigours of the task; but even a fitful attempt at such a view seems, in present circumstances, worth making.

Genius in drama, as in other arts, is not finally a matter of craft, but of vision and quality of emotion. Nothing is more difficult for the critic to convey, as his method of magnifying and translating effects into intellectual terms can easily destroy the delicate balance of the original. Granville Barker's quality can be suggested by establishing the range of his awareness and the depth of implication in his work. One function of the Notes to this book is to extend, by comparison, the argument that Barker was sensitive to the deepest currents of feeling in his age and had a more than intellectual grasp of traditional political philosophy. The development of the discussion in the body of the text is independent of these Notes, however, and they tentatively indicate a line of approach by no means fully pursued; so they have their proper place at the end of the book.

Chapter III is substantially based on an article, "The Early Plays of Granville Barker," by Frederick May and the present writer, in *The Modern Language Review,* vol. li (1956). The Editors of *M.L.R.* have kindly permitted its inclusion here.

The Voysey Inheritance, Waste and *The Madras House* were revised by Barker for editions after the first. Unless the contrary is stated, the texts discussed and quoted in this book are the final versions he chose to publish.

From *The Marrying of Ann Leete* onwards, Barker employed a method of dramatic punctuation which involved the frequent, and increasing, use of three dots (two in the original edition of *Three Plays*) to indicate the phrasing of the dialogue for the actors' delivery: the breaking up of speeches into separate, short intonational units, 'little tunes', requiring great flexibility in the use of the voice. In many instances, perhaps most, no perceptible pause is intended, but the actor has to suggest—and the reader may understand—that new thoughts are crowding up behind the words, as they are uttered. The use of the three dots has been retained in this book, and extended to replace the two dots of the original *Three Plays*. When a quotation from the plays is given in abridged form, the omission of matter is indicated by three dots enclosed in inclined square brackets. An example may be helpful:

> I have an almost unbounded faith in the ultimate perfectability of man [. . .]. But mind you . . . the freer the democracy the firmer must be the guiding hands.

* * *

The writer of any such work as this accumulates many more debts than can briefly be acknowledged. But the opportunity cannot be missed to record gratitude to the following for generous help: Granville Barker's first wife, the late Lillah McCarthy, O.B.E. (Lady Keeble), Sir Lewis Casson, Mr. Robert Farquharson, the late Herbert Thomas, the late Laurence Housman, the Rt. Hon. Sir Cuthbert Headlam, Bt., Mr. Alec Clunes and Mr.

Michael MacOwan. A note of special appreciation is due to Mr. C. B. Purdom for making available to me much of the material that passed through his hands during the preparation of his book on Granville Barker and for some interesting discussions. I am greatly indebted to the Trustees of the Granville Barker Estates, Messrs. Field Roscoe & Co., for permission to quote freely from Barker's published and unpublished writings; to the Public Trustee and the Society of Authors for permission to quote from the writings of G. B. Shaw; and to the other holders of copyright, to whom acknowledgment is made in the Notes. I have received much help from friends and colleagues: Dr. J. M. S. Tompkins, Reader in English at Royal Holloway College, and Mrs. J. D. Ottaway, who patiently read and criticised the first draft of this book; Miss J. C. Scourse and Miss B. P. Legge of the Department of Music, Royal Holloway College, whom I consulted on Barker's adaptation of musical forms; Dr. Harold Brooks of Birkbeck College, many of whose thought-provoking suggestions and references have been incorporated in the Notes; Miss D. M. Gillam and Miss D. Rayner. Mr. Frederick May of the University of Leeds has a special property in this book: my study of Granville Barker was begun in collaboration with him and continued with his advice and encouragement; many of the lines of thought followed here originated with him; his collaboration in the final writing would have saved the work from many faults and short-comings. Dr. P. M. Ball has generously given time and care to compiling the Index.

Finally, it is my pleasant duty to record that the publication of this book has been aided by a grant by the Council of Bedford College (University of London) from the Una Ellis-Fermor Memorial Fund. This was the first annual award from the Fund (for 1960-61), and I am especially pleased that the name of my former teacher, remembered with great admiration and love, should be associated with my work.

Margery M. Morgan.

Royal Holloway College
(University of London),
Englefield Green,
Surrey.

For
R. J. and F. M.

'. . . *the theater is the political art par excellence; only there is the political sphere of human life transposed into art. By the same token, it is the only art whose sole subject is man in his relationship to others.*' (*Hannah Arendt,* The Human Condition.)

Contents

CHAPTER I

'*There are more ways than one of Reading most Epitaphs*'

(A)

Harley Granville Barker* has two reputations to-day: as the greatest of English theatrical producers; and as a Shakespeare critic of many insights. As a dramatist he is largely undiscovered. Yet in 1902 Bernard Shaw wrote to Henry Arthur Jones:

> How do you get on with Granville Barker? Do you realise that he is a great poet and dramatist who feels towards us as we feel towards Sheridan Knowles? His *Marrying of Ann Leete* is really an exquisite play. I truckle to G.B. in order to conciliate him when he is forty. . . .[1]

The tone of these remarks is only half-frivolous. Seven years later, Barker published a volume of *Three Plays*, one of which had not been seen in the theatre because of the Censor's ban. A review in *The Bookman* testifies to the stir this made in some quarters:

> One discerning critic, speaking of *Waste,* said it proved what *The Voysey Inheritance* had led some of us to suspect, that in Mr. Granville Barker we possess 'a dramatist in a class by himself—the first class'.[2]

Shaw protested, after Barker's death in 1946, that the obituaries had not said nearly enough of his work as a playwright and recorded his own opinion that: '. . . his original contributions to our dramatic literature are treasures to be preserved.'[3]

Every age is responsible for inflated critical judgments, of course,

---

* Granville Barker adopted a hyphenated form of his name after 1917. The form without the hyphen is used throughout this book, except in quotations.

1

and there is no *a priori* reason for giving great weight to Barker's Edwardian reputation. However, as a key figure in a period of dramatic activity unequalled in England for well over a century, he challenges curiosity. The twenty years from 1890 to 1910 are traditionally viewed as a time of theatrical renaissance in this country. As well as Shaw, Barker and Galsworthy, many lesser playwrights were at work, Wilde, Pinero, Jones, St. John Hankin and Maugham, Barrie and Masefield among them. William Archer compared the new drama and the old[4] and observed many signs of fresh inspiration and bold creative experiment. The dramatists were turning away from old conventions and trying to formulate the experience of modern man. The English theatre was once more open to the fructifying influence of a various European drama and was taking its place once more in the main stream of European tradition in the arts. Directly and indirectly it contributed to the birth of a vital Irish theatre, too.

Granville Barker, more than any other single figure, was responsible for the re-establishment of drama as the principal artistic form of the age and for the restoration of civic authority to the theatre. The ideal relation between stage and public, towards which he worked, was such as had existed in the Greek city state, and his own plays do homage to it. Although his achievement is forgotten outside a fairly specialised circle, it certainly prepared the way for the recent theatrical revival, which was one of the more cheering aspects of the 1950s, associated to a considerable extent with Barker's old theatre, the Royal Court. The presiding genius of this latest renaissance has been Brecht; but his influence has been grafted on to a native stock, in which his doctrine of the function of theatre in quickening the political consciousness of subject man was already anticipated. For the theatre of Granville Barker was itself a scion of Ruskin's gospel that art and social responsibility are truly indivisible.

In histories of the drama, Barker is usually treated—and dismissed—alongside Galsworthy as a disciple of Shaw.[5] This is doubly misleading. Neither Shaw nor Barker was anything like as closely allied to Galsworthy as they were to each other; and, furthermore, their mutual relationship was less that of master and pupil than of partners of very different temperaments in a happy and fruitful marriage. They lived and worked for over ten years in close mental association, constantly interchanging ideas, criticising each other's plays before they were put into production, drawing upon common material for their writing, even experimenting with similar techniques. Yet both worked in recognition of the difference in their gifts and modes of perception and the very different qualities of theatrical experience that they could offer to audiences. It is true that a knowledge of Shavian drama is essential to the serious student of Barker's work; a truth much less generally recognised is that a knowledge of Barker's plays may contribute a good deal to the understanding of Shaw. For instance, Barker's *Madras House* and Shaw's *Misalliance* abound in deliberate crossreferences; Barker starts off with a theme borrowed from *The Doctor's Dilemma;* but, in turn, the principal symbols and terms of reference employed in *Misalliance,* together with certain aspects of technique, are drawn from *The Madras House.* Even when their partnership in the theatre was over, Shaw drew heavily upon Barker's last play, *His Majesty,* in the process of composing *The Apple Cart.*[6] Of the plays between, *The Voysey Inheritance* and *Major Barbara* can illuminate each other, as can *Waste, The Secret Life* and *Major Barbara,* or *The Secret Life* and *Heartbreak House.* Shaw was fond of comparing his own drama to the music of Verdi and Barker's to the music of Debussy. To some tastes, Debussy—or Barker—will always be the more congenial.

There are few critical procedures more barren than the praising of one writer at the expense of another, on the false assumption that comparison can yield an absolute assessment of the work of either. In fact, these two playwrights are complementary to each other in their virtues. Put in the most general terms, the central effect and power of Shaw's drama arise from the forcible separation of intellect and compassion, through the determination to think with objective clarity on all human issues; in Barker's drama, on the other hand, thought and feeling are closely and subtly related in a dominant mood which is reflective. Shaw's method is to turn all private experience into a public concern; Barker's is the more introvert way of exploring society: his work has as large a scope as Shaw's, but everything in it is referred back to the sentient organism, the single human being, whose inner life reflects the buried consciousness of his age.

Frank Vernon summed up the quality of Barker's art in 1924:

> ... as original author he contributed a new and strangely beautiful sense of intellectual, always intellectual romance to the naturalistic play.[7]

'Romance' had a meaningful content in the England of Granville Barker's youth, as one of the terms in which the mythology of the Age was commonly expressed.[8] He certainly absorbed something of the neo-romantic experience which occupied the *fin de siècle*. It remained with him to the end of his writing career as part of his own subjective reality; and he had to grapple with its meanings and paradoxes in the process of self-liberation that was his way in art.

'The writing is on the wall. Rome fell; Babylon fell; Hindhead's turn will come,' prophesies the comic would-be assassin in *Misalliance*. Since the first World War, western civilisation has come increasingly to accept the idea of its own decline. The symptoms have been read and identified with the classic signs of cultural decadence. How far the interpreters are observers with no influence upon the appearances they consider, how far they themselves help to create meaning and direction in the outer world, is a familiar platonic debate. Certainly this discovery of the twentieth century was first made in the nineteenth, only gradually seeping through into general consciousness: Carlyle hailed the process of disintegration at work in a commercial society; Wagner made the *Götterdämmerung* newly significant to the imagination of the late nineteenth century; Karl Marx gave scientific authority to the premonition of catastrophe which might, or might not, be followed by the millenium.

The *fin de siècle* mentality gradually asserted itself, apprehensive of the end of an age, as an individual may be apprehensive of personal dissolution; and the approaching end of a long reign intensified the mood in England. The Pre-Raphaelites had emerged and made way for the Æsthetes, and art, as if surfeited with imperial prosperity and industrialism, turned back to an imaginary past and then grew increasingly subjective: the orthodox faith of

Victorian materialism in the march of progress was counter-balanced by the retreat of the artist; utilitarianism was challenged by an all-sufficient aesthetic; art was elevated into an autonomous universe of private images and sensations, within which—the traditional symbol of the tower was much favoured—the artist could imagine himself inaccessible and deny an actuality to which he was sharply hostile; on the one hand, art opposed its simpler Utopias to the increasing practical complexities of modern society; on the other hand, a reaction from the robust commercial vigour and scientific positivism of the objective world took the form of a deliberately morbid cult of decay and corruption, a cult of the ultimate refinements of sensation and the extreme languor of passivity. The *fin de siècle* Decadents issued an elaborate invitation to destructive forces and went through a compulsive enactment of the ritual of decline. Half-aware that their strange posturings *were* ritualistic, they adopted the mask and the mirror among their chief emblems, assumed histrionic personalities and fancied that they could turn their own lives into works of art.

One mirror in which the nineteenth-century *fin de siècle* chose to find its image was the end of the century before: in the luxury of the French court on the eve of Revolution, in its sporadic satanism and affected pastoralism. Socialists of all varieties looked back to 1789 as opening the first Act of a drama whose climax still lay ahead. In art, the anarchism that had flowered into the earlier Romantic Movement was more recently detectable in Baudelaire's assaults on society, and in the less formidable attacks of his English disciples, chief among them being Oscar Wilde. The mood of the age was, perhaps, most intensely captured in Russian nihilism. Tolstoy, in his later writings and the gestures of his later life, offered a radical indictment of minority culture and all that Æstheticism and *Symbolisme* stood for. When Aylmer Maude's translation of Tolstoy's *What Is Art?* made its appearance in 1898, it joined Ruskin and Morris in rejecting an effete art and condemning the society that produced it. Shaw had already hailed Ibsen as the prophet of a new drama which would make social responsibility its motivating impulse; in his own imagination, Wagner's Siegfried and Nietzsche's Superman were figures of specifically political significance.

The cult of decadence thus merged imperceptibly into the anticipation of a New Age, and it is difficult to deny to either aspect of the time the description, neo-romantic. Indeed, they are the thesis and antithesis of the same phase of human consciousness.

In various of its manifestations, neo-romanticism spilled over into the present century. Its climactic social manifestation came in the violence of the first World War and the Russian Revolution of 1917. Its chief literary manifestations, in England, include the work of Yeats and Eliot and D. H. Lawrence, of Joseph Conrad, the pathologist of romance; and the plays of Granville Barker belong to this company, as well as to Shaw's. Yeats, writing within the scheme of his mystical view of history, expressed the idea that: 'Birth-hour and death-hour meet,' at a climax of the historical process. A major conflict—the most desperate—on which Barker's plays are based, is between the two views of the one event which may be death or birth.

The fact that Barker is traditionally regarded as a social dramatist, and not a political dramatist at all, indicates how little the nature of his work has been understood. Two of his unpublished plays, *The Weather-Hen* and *Agnes Colander,* are indeed social plays, with no significant political dimension. All his published drama, however, is infused with an understanding of the nature of politics that is essentially classical in origin. His heroes reach, or fail to reach, the fulfilment of their moral being in the public realm; if they seem to move within a domestic circle, still their decisions are made in awareness of their political significance. In the course of the plays they prove, or fail to prove, their possession of the political virtue of honour. The authority that honour bestows allows them to grasp power.

Political and social drama are, of course, sometimes combined. This has been made possible by the blurring of the distinction between political and social in modern consciousness, which has been interestingly discussed by Hannah Arendt.[9] She offers a useful definition of society (a modern phenomenon): 'that curiously hybrid realm where private interests assume public significance.'[10] The notion of politics as a function of society was popularised by Marx; an older view informs Aristotle's definition of man as a political animal. The contrast is between anonymous political action, which is more truly a behaviour, and the highest creative activity of the individual, whereby new impulses and potentialities are injected into the life of mankind. It is a distinction significant for drama: whereas a play of political society properly has no hero (e.g. Hauptmann's *The Weavers*, or even *The Cherry Orchard*[11]), a political drama in the classical sense is essentially heroic (Shakespeare's political plays belong to this type). In certain of his plays, Barker combines the two views: *The Marrying of Ann Leete* and *The Voysey Inheritance* are the most notable examples; yet, even here, it is the critical decision of the individual hero which renews political virtue in the society.

Granville Barker deals with politics in terms of politicians, who are also men, not in terms of abstract policy. In thus acknowledging the Aristotelian doctrine of politics as a natural function, he also reflects the attitude of his contemporary and fellow Fabian, Graham Wallas, who made this indictment of recent political theory:

> The thinkers of the past, from Plato to Bentham and Mill had each his own view of human nature, and they made those views the basis of their speculations on government. But no modern treatise on political science, whether dealing with institutions or finance, now begins with anything corresponding to the opening words of Bentham's *Principles of Morals and Legislation*— "Nature has placed mankind under the governance of two sovereign masters, pain and pleasure" . . .;[12]

and Wallas deplored the tendency to 'separate the study of politics from that of human nature' as harmful in its effect 'both on the science and conduct of politics'.

Similarly, Barker is interested in society, not as an abstraction, or non-human institution, but as an inescapable dimension of individual life. It is invoked in his plays as the objective form of that sense of race which, for most men, is a yet stronger element in human character than personal egotism, and which has been recognised as the *raison d'être* of all political organisation. Far from confining himself to the topical, Barker is even chiefly concerned with society as it spans and transcends time and becomes civilisation, still a living thing, communicating with the future as with the past.[13]

In such a view, the individual is not dwarfed, as in the work of Galsworthy, into a victim of circumstances; though only a fragment of a greater life, he appears in Barker's vision as the determining agent and vital source of all social values, as the true unit of history. Part of Barker's intention as a dramatist was undoubtedly to render political thinking and political behaviour in terms of basic human experience; to reveal the state as indeed 'Man writ large'; and to interpret political man to himself. Thus he presents the decline of civilisation as an experience with which his characters have individually to wrestle, and which the more heroic of them in some degree transcend.

The dramatist's interest in the political theme was in itself enough to save him from the shallower excesses of *l'art pour l'art*. The cult of sensation could not have satisfied his strongly developed intellect. Philosophical truth seems to have been from the first a more attractive quarry to him than self-sufficient beauty. On the other hand—and this again distinguishes him from Galsworthy—he held no brief for polemical, or propagandist art. Art for life's sake was his choice, most openly stated fairly late in his career, in a discussion of Tolstoy, but to be read throughout his plays in unmistakable terms. Ruskin's phrase, 'There is no Wealth but Life', can be heard echoing through several of them, perhaps most audibly in *The Voysey Inheritance* and *The Madras House*; and it is more life, or a renewal of life, that the main characters seek.

Barker's characteristic blending of naturalism and symbolism is significant of his rejection of too limited a view of man, too impoverished a form of life. It is also one aspect of his challenge to the convenient definition of man as a creature of divided consciousness, living two lives, an inner and an outer. Some would have that historical necessities have rendered this definition convenient: that the rise of the highly organised industrial society in fact tore the life of human communities away from its natural roots and drove into inward isolation—if it did not totally atrophy—instinctual feelings and the values they engender; such was Blake's understanding of things, and such was Lawrence's, reflecting Nietzsche's view of the divorce between civilisation and instinct. The struggle in which Barker's heroes are engaged is a struggle back to wholeness and the reconciliation of the worlds within and without. Whether life is renewed in them or fails them, the gain or loss is more than personal: it is so much added to one side or other of the balance between hope and despair of the good society, hope and despair of the survival of society at all.

His total output as a dramatist is not large, even allowing for the possibility that some manuscripts of plays, finished or unfinished, have been lost or destroyed.[14] Not only the variety of his interests, but the nature of his drama must be accounted responsible for the small number of plays that he has left, youthful experiments apart. He was a slow and painstaking writer, and his inclination was to revise his work over and over again. The original composition of *The Voysey Inheritance*, for instance, occupied his mind during the years 1903-5, and the work exists in two distinct printed versions[15] and a typescript, different again, that with minor cuts and revisions was the basis of the 1934 Sadler's Wells revival of the play. *The Secret Life* was written over a period of four years, *His Majesty* over five years. Both *The Madras House* and *Waste* are extant in two published versions, the revision of *Waste* amounting to a complete re-writing. There are even two versions of *The Weather-Hen*, both unpublished.

Writing straight ahead, he told William Archer, sounded like something one might hope to do in heaven. Each play, as he wrote it, was an attempt to express the entirety of his consciousness and contains, more or less implicit, the total experience of its predecessors. Thus images, and even quite common words, when carried over from one play to another, carry with them the inwardness of meaning and emotional colouring acquired through their use in the earlier dramatic context. The plays have a superficial smooth coherence, certainly, which an audience will receive easily enough on a first hearing; but their content is not quickly exhausted.

Barker had the kind of self-critical mind that composes minutely, caring for perfection of detail, enjoying subtlety; and with it went a power of control that could hold an abundance of material in unity. Shaw's comparison of his own plays to the opera of Verdi, Barker's to the music of Debussy, recognised the great technical difference between a loosely composed drama, that depends upon pace and energy and flamboyant performance to carry its faults, and one in which a delicate romanticism of feeling is combined with a precise sense of organic form, and in which the 'rightness' of the details, single notes or words, is capable of giving exquisite pleasure to the performer and the alert listener. Indeed, Granville Barker's style shows a kinship, however indirect it may be, with the tradition of French drama that is considered to originate with Marivaux and appears again, in variant form, in the plays of Alfred de Musset.[16] Grace and point characterise it, intellectual finesse balancing a sentiment at once pervasive and elusive. His writing consistently preserves a tension and close texture that Shavian dialogue only rarely offers. Here is a warning of greater difficulty to be encountered: a complexity that requires to be probed and that yields up its full meaning only gradually.

In his handling of the naturalistic convention and his extension of its significance, Granville Barker owed much to a careful study of Ibsen's technique. Such a general indebtedness has commonly been recognised. It is less often acknowledged that Ibsen's later plays, with their greater poetic content, influenced him more profoundly than did the more obvious social dramas. The relationship of his work to that of Maeterlinck, another Continental dramatist championed and translated by William Archer[17] and a leader among *symboliste* playwrights, has been generally unremarked; but it is demonstrable and suggests the eclectic nature of his approach to dramatic technique: he was little concerned with battles over dramatic principles, or the contradiction of one theory of drama by another. He was prepared to learn from anything good of its kind. So it is misleading to think of him as the disciple of any one dramatist, or any one school; the origins of his dramatic method are less simply traceable, and the range of experience his plays embrace is greater in consequence.

Throughout his career, he made it sufficiently plain that his chief master was not Ibsen and not Shaw, but Shakespeare, the greatest of eclectics, whose work he studied from the different viewpoints of actor, producer and scholar. His apprenticeship to Shakespeare, which began in his childhood,[18] had no such issue as the pseudo-Elizabethan archaism of so many modern imitators from Tennyson to Gordon Bottomley, or Christopher Fry. The blank-verse medium, Shakespearian rhetoric and superficial effects did not tempt him to direct imitation. For the treatment of political man in the terms of the theatre, Shakespearian drama offered him the supreme model, of course. But whatever enlightenment for his work he could gain from Shakespeare, he took in unfailing awareness that he was himself writing for another age and quite another theatre; he had his own task, to which he was compelled by the nature and problems of his contemporary world, and though he might share a theme with the great Renaissance dramatist, the validity of his work depended on its being worked out in terms of modern consciousness. The Machiavellianism which enters into the conflict in several of his plays is not that of the sixteenth century, though it may have amused him to be drawing upon a source that had proved fruitful for English drama before. In a similar way, having studied how Shakespeare turned to artistic account the material conditions of the Elizabethan theatre, he pursued some equivalent of the advantages gained, recognising that the same methods would not always secure the same effects in a theatre physically appropriate to naturalism and a naturalistic tradition of acting.

Indeed, he learned nothing more valuable from Shakespeare than these general lessons: that the dramatist is dependent all the time on the medium of an actual theatre and the living actor, with his particular histrionic equipment, and forgets these facts at his peril.[19] He discovered the advantage of a theatre in which every property was necessarily a symbol, and the desirability of making every aspect of the theatrical spectacle subserve the life of the play and the disciplined emotions of the actor. He further recognised—as Henry James failed to—that the key to dramatic power is not afforded by the playwright's simplifying of his vision; on the contrary, it was precisely the depth of resonance in thought, feeling and imagery, which gave to a play of Shakespeare's a life to outlast an indefinite number of performances and interpretations. In his *Preface to King Lear*, he contended:

> We need no more expect to receive—lapses of performance and attention apart—the full value of a great drama at a first hearing than we expect it of a complex piece of music. And what preliminary study of the music, with its straiter laws and more

homogeneous material, will effect, study of drama will not. A play's interpretation is an unrulier business, and we must face it rather as we face life itself ... it is the business of the dramatist, doubtless, in turning actuality to art, to clarify all this. ... But if he aimed only at its clear statement he would produce no illusion of life at all. ... Abundance of power ... there must be, and a certain waste must be allowed for ... though we may lose at the time in fullness of understanding, we shall gain in conviction.[20]

Observing that Shakespeare had to rely almost exclusively on dialogue to evoke all the richness of his dramatic world, Granville Barker set himself to discover the technical means whereby dialogue could be made to contain so much. In discarding verse rhythms and the temptations of an obtrusively poetic style, he made a necessary concession to the theatre of naturalism, but was able to rely on the compensating advantages of the contemporary theatre, especially the resources of modern lighting to create changing moods. 'The passionate pun,' declares the hero of *Waste*, 'is a feature of great literature,' and his author boldly follows Shakespearian example in the sometimes comic, but oftener serious, play on words in his dramatic texts. The use of echoes, of recurrent and cumulative imagery, of multiple reference and a subtly working allusiveness, all features of mature Shakespearian style, is also to be found in Barker's dialogue. He made his own experiments with syntax, seeking richer and more complex effects than the logical clarity of straightforward prose, and he relied much on deliberate ambiguity, which accomplished actors could make histrionically fruitful. Other dramatists than Shakespeare have experimented in the rhythms of dialogue and discovered the expressiveness of what is left unsaid; but in these things, too, his great Elizabethan predecessor was an obvious model for Barker's practice. Prose playwright as he was, Granville Barker still took into account the fact that Elizabethan drama at its most potent had a musical character difficult to separate either from its poetic expression or from its dramatic form and, especially in his last plays, he strove to capture a similar quality in his own writing, though by means derived ultimately from Wagner rather than Elizabethan sources.

Barker ascribed his true discovery of Shakespeare to William

Poel. In 1930, he wrote to him:

> ... such light as has shone for me on W.S. dates from an earlier
> day on which you came to York Buildings to see me and shook all
> my previous convictions by showing me how you wanted the first
> lines of *Richard II* spoken.[21]

Barker's achievement as a producer of Shakespeare is commonly
defined as the translation of Poel's theories into practicable terms
of theatre.[22] Perhaps the most important effect gained was the
restoration of a truer relationship between actor and dramatist than
had prevailed in the Victorian theatre and the re-establishment—
in defiance of all scene-painters—of the actor as vital centre of the
theatrical performance. It meant essentially a return to such primitive virtue as Henry James had recognised in the Italian theatre
of the 'nineties:

> ... the nudity of the stage ... and in the empty space the histrionic
> figure, doing everything it knows how, in complete possession ...
> the direction is right, and it has the superiority that it's a human
> exhibition, not a mechanical one.[23]

What seemed to Gordon Craig the most treacherous element in the
art of the theatre, the flesh-and-blood being that is instrument as
well as executant, but without the precision of a mechanical instrument, was to Barker its chief value, a channel for the fullest
and most vital communication possible. In the texts of his plays,
he allowed always for the dimension which the living actor would
add in the theatre, a dimension that the reader has to supply from
his imagination as best he can. So a necessary preliminary to an
understanding of Barker's work as a dramatist is some consideration of the acting technique that he favoured, the way in which he
trained actors who worked under his direction, and his general
understanding of the nature of their task.

* * *

(B)

Before any closer examination of his dramaturgy is made, however, some outline of Granville Barker's life may be helpful. Accounts of him are often reducible to legends, in which he figures as the Lost Leader and his second wife as a sinister enchantress. This view was first popularised by his fellow-workers in the Edwardian theatre. Bio-criticism has tended to portray him as the Man who Gave Up: one with a streak of weakness, too easily seduced by comfort, riches and respectability; a snob, who kept his origins in obscurity, cut himself off from his old associates and even tried to cover the traces of his theatrical achievements, when he was accepted into high academic, or aristocratic, society; a political renegade, who fell out of the company of Fabians into Conservative darkness. The faults of the man have, as usual, been read into his work. In these circumstances, a simply factual account may be best, while judgment is reserved until study of his plays has yielded a more intimate view of his mind.

He was born at Camden Hill, Kensington, in 1877. His father, Albert Barker, described himself as an architect, but seems to have practised his profession rather irregularly and precariously. His mother was seven years older and seems to have been the more forceful personality. She was the grand-daughter of Augustus Bozzi Granville, a pioneer in medicine and hygiene, a Vice-President of the British Medical Association and Fellow of the Royal Society. Born in Milan in 1783, he had left Italy in 1802 to avoid conscription by the French and, after some adventurous years, settled in England and adopted the surname of his English mother. He retained the reputation of an Italian patriot, and his many published writings include pamphlets on the cause of Italian unity. He twice visited Russia; he was for years a close friend of Joseph Bonaparte, ex-King of Spain, and an acquaintance of Louis Napoleon; and he could remember meeting Godoy and Bolivar. A man of immense energy and fiery enthusiasm, he died only five years before Harley Granville Barker was born and was certainly a vivid figure in Mrs. Barker's memory and a source of family pride.[24]

Mrs. Albert Barker herself was a professional reciter, a drawing-room entertainer, who early determined on a stage career for her son. He was sent to a fashionable Kensington school, so that he might acquire the right accent and manners,[25] and from quite an early age he would appear in a sailor suit to supplement his mother's programmes with such pieces as 'The Wreck of the Hesperus'. When he was thirteen, he made his first theatrical appearance at Harrogate and then went to Margate, where he was placed with Sarah Thorne's repertory company, while his mother took local engagements. Henceforward his formal education was confined to a professional apprenticeship, a description appropriate enough to the thorough discipline in their art that Sarah Thorne undertook to give to her young charges. It was at Margate that Barker first met Gordon Craig, then guest-actor from Irving's Lyceum. With this training behind him, he proceeded in the conventional way to find engagements with various reputable touring companies, among them Ben Greet's Shakespeare Company, in which he met Lillah McCarthy who was later to become his wife; and he played several small parts in undistinguished London productions.

According to Miss Horniman, he was an understudy during Florence Farr's season at the Avenue Theatre in 1894, which she financed:[26] an historic season which first presented Shaw and Yeats to West End audiences, through *Arms and the Man* and *The Land of Heart's Desire*. The part of Mary Bruin, in Yeats's play, was acted by Barker's early love, Winifred Fraser, who had played Hedwig in the Independent Theatre production of *The Wild Duck* and was later to play two of his own heroines, Ann Leete, and Baptista in the unpublished *Miracle*. His engagement at the Avenue Theatre was undoubtedly influential in fixing his eyes upon new developments in the contemporary drama and introducing him to actors sympathetic to them.

He had to wait until 1899, however, for the two events which marked him out as a young man with a future of some promise in the theatre: *The Weather-Hen*, which he had written in collaboration with Berte Thomas, an older actor, first met in Sarah Thorne's Company, received a matineé performance at Terry's Theatre on 29th June and, in consequence of its effect, was transferred to the evening bill; then, in November of the same year, he played Richard II in a production by William Poel.

The Weather-Hen was the only one of five plays, that Barker and Thomas worked on together, ever to be produced. Their collaboration appears to have begun before 1895 and to have continued at intervals until the century ended. The first play to be written, *A Comedy of Fools*, was destroyed, and over the last, a dramatisation of *Henry Esmond*, the partnership broke up. No manuscript of *Henry Esmond*, finished or unfinished, is known. The texts of two of the plays are now in the British Museum, the third at the Lord Chamberlain's Office, and they afford most valuable evidence of Barker's aims as a dramatist, the nature of the technique that he evolved, and the growth of his mind.

The foundations of a number of valued friendships were laid in this period. With Mrs. Patrick Campbell's Company, Barker acted in a short run of Gilbert Murray's melodrama, *Carlyon Sahib*, and met the author again when, with William Archer, he attended the first meetings of a committee to discuss the plan of establishing a National Theatre. Archer himself, the influential theatre critic and translator and champion of Ibsen, was much struck by the promise of *The Weather-Hen* and seems to have become a kindly mentor to the young actor-dramatist from about this time. In 1900, Barker's performance as Robert in *The Coming of Peace*, a translation of Hauptmann's *Friedensfest* by Janet Achurch and C. E. Wheeler, brought him a very favourable notice from J. T. Grein (who had founded the Independent Theatre), helped confirm his standing among the reformers of the English theatre and, in Dr. Wheeler, gave him another scholarly and cultivated friend, with whom he was later to work on versions of Schnitzler's plays.[27] The same year, 1900, saw him on the council of management of the recently founded Stage Society, producing for it a number of plays, acting in others, including, in July, Bernard Shaw's *Candida*. The two men had met before this,[28] but it was now that the close association began that was to last until Barker's second marriage, which introduced a distance between them lamented by Shaw to the time of his death.

Such men as Murray, Archer, Wheeler, Shaw made a formidable band and led to further and varied contacts. All, even Murray, an absurdly young professor, were considerably senior to Barker; he sat informally at the feet of them all and learned from them with great rapidity. In an age of self-education, it is understandable that he was never ready to condemn the practice that took children from school and placed them in the theatre at an early age. A voracious reader, even in his days at Margate, he was certainly directed to fresh interests and guided in his tastes to some extent, through these associations. To Archer and Wheeler he certainly owed an extension of his awareness of what was happening in European drama; to Murray, an introduction to Greek drama and a more informed interest in Greek philosophy; to Shaw, among many incalculables, an extension of his acquaintance with political philosophy, a heightened sense of the vital and enthralling nature of practical politics, and the encouragement of a lively interest in music, especially in the Wagnerian music-drama. All this was valuable equipment for a budding dramatist who already had the advantage of direct knowledge of the stage and the actor's business; it ensured his freedom from the severe limitations, set by more recent theatrical tradition in England, upon the matter and themes available to the dramatist and generally considered appropriate to his medium.

He was continuing to write plays: *The Marrying of Ann Leete,* the earliest which has been published, was performed for the Stage Society in January 1902, having been written in 1899; a three-act play, entitled *Agnes Colander,* survives in a typescript dated January 1901; a one-Act piece in verse, *A Miracle,* though impossible to date accurately on present evidence, seems to have been a product of the first years of the century. At the same time, he was finding himself as a producer: of Maeterlinck and Yeats, Brieux and Maugham and then, in 1904, of Euripides, Shakespeare and Shaw. There followed the seasons at the Court Theatre, 1904-7, in which Barker as Director established Shaw's theatrical reputation, gave to the London theatre new standards of acting and production, encouraged a new school of playwrights, among them St. John Hankin, Galsworthy and Masefield, and produced their work alongside that of Ibsen, Hauptmann, Maeterlinck and Euripides. The tremendous impact of this management upon the cultivated public is reflected in Wilfred Scawen Blunt's response to *Hippolytus,* first produced at the Lyric Theatre and later introduced into the programme at the Court:

> I have never seen a tragedy like this. ... At the end of it we were all moved to tears, and I got up and did what I never did before

in a theatre, shouted for the author, whether for Euripides or Gilbert Murray I hardly knew.[29]

It was indeed a theatre that put the service of the author first.

The work of Shaw proved most popular with the audiences, and his name came to dominate the repertory. Consequently, those who disliked his anti-romantic approach tended to equate the whole Court Theatre movement with it, though it was an unenlightened criticism that identified Shaw and Galsworthy as dramatists of the same kind. In fact, a study of the programmes reveals a more catholic taste in the Director, which audiences were not so ready to share. However, the generally revolutionary and re-vitalising effect of the whole enterprise could not be denied, and Desmond Mac-Carthy could fittingly enough preface his book on the experiment[30] with the quotation:

> TOUCHSTONE. Wast ever at the Court, shepherd?
> CORIN. No, truly.
> TOUCHSTONE. Then thou art damned.

For this undertaking and its successors at other theatres Granville Barker wrote his three best-known plays, *The Voysey Inheritance*, *Waste* and *The Madras House*. He continued as undisputed leader of the new theatre in England until the 1914-18 war quenched serious public interest in the drama entirely.

In his successive managements, culminating in the famous Shakespearian productions at the Savoy, 1912 and 1914, he was associated with his actress wife, Lillah McCarthy. During the war they were divorced and Barker married a wealthy American novelist and poet, Helen Huntington, with whom he was later responsible for a number of English versions of Spanish plays. These events were followed by his retirement from active work in the theatre and a measure of withdrawal from some close associations of earlier days. They have been the subject of much acid comment and indignant hostility. Amid all the fury, Barker's first wife, though perhaps the most deeply perplexed person, was less bitter than others less intimately involved.

The fact that he was no longer in the theatre partly accounts for the neglect of the last two plays he completed, *The Secret Life* and *His Majesty*. For some years he lived the life of a country gentleman and supplied introductions to the Players' Shakespeare that made the basis of his later series of *Prefaces to Shakespeare*. He was for a time a Reader at Liverpool University, and a number of special lectures and lecture courses, given in various parts of the world, are among the texts that he published in the later years of his life. To him perhaps more than to any other single person we may attribute such bridging of the gap between the academic approach to drama and the theatrical as there has been.

In 1930, he and his wife went to live in Paris, and from 1937 to 1939 he was Director of the Institut Britannique. His connection with the English theatre was briefly renewed in 1934 and 1936, when he participated in new productions of *The Voysey Inheritance* and *Waste* (the first in collaboration with Harcourt Williams, the second with Michael MacOwan), and again in 1940, when he produced *King Lear* for the Old Vic, in association with Lewis Casson. He returned to Paris before this last production opened, —in time for the German invasion. The Granville Barkers escaped through Spain to England and then proceeded to America. Barker regarded himself as an unofficial cultural ambassador for England and worked officially for the British Information Service.[31] He was also an Honorary Professor of Yale and, in 1943-4, a visiting lecturer at Harvard. When the war was over, he and Helen returned to Paris, where he died in 1946, aged sixty-eight.

CHAPTER II

Naturalism and the Art of Acting

Miriam ... explained, as if it were a discovery of her own, that there were two kinds of scenes and speeches: those which acted themselves, of which the treatment was plain, the only way, so that you just had to take it; and those which were open to interpretation, with which you had to fight every step, rendering, arranging, doing it according to your idea. Some of the most effective things ... were of the former sort; but it was the others she liked best.

(Henry James, *The Tragic Muse*.)

Recognition of the categories of 'explicit' and 'implicit' is fundamental to Granville Barker's dramatic theory. It is an actor's distinction, which he found more meaningful than the essentially literary division of dramatic kinds into poetic and prosaic, or even naturalistic and symbolic. The relation between actor and playwright in the theatre has often been one of rivalry, or even antagonism. Barker, having tried his hand at writing plays at the same time as he was serving his apprenticeship as an actor, acquired early a sense of the true interdependence of the two functions, the nature of the debt that actor and dramatist owe each other, and the limits of the power each may exercise, if the art both serve is not to suffer. In the *Prefaces to Shakespeare*, the Bradleyan concentration on character, character as vital personage rather than symbolic counter, corresponds to the actor's focus of interest and balance of emphasis in approaching a play. Barker's conception of drama rests firmly upon his sense of what acting is and what the actor can do. He judged the greatest dramatists to be those who exploit the power of the actor to the greatest extent.

By the time that he came to write *The Exemplary Theatre* and
the lecture, *On Poetry in Drama,* he could cite Chekhov as the
supreme modern practitioner of the implicit style, who demands
an imaginative collaboration from the actor to supply the rever-
berations and nuances that are the essential stuff of the play, without which it is incomprehensible. He does not seem to have known
Chekhov's plays before 1914, when he visited Moscow, and so only
the later phase of his career as a dramatist can have been influenced
directly by the Russian writer. Towards the end of the nineteenth
century, it was Ibsen and Maeterlinck who were challenging actors
in western Europe to evolve new refinements of technique and
offering them opportunities for creative collaboration.

The way of Ibsen seemed, in the England of the eighteen-
eighties and 'nineties, to be the way ahead dramatically. In an essay
on "The Coming of Ibsen",[1] Barker looked back, when he was a
Fellow of the Royal Society of Literature, upon the excitement or
dismay with which actors of those days received the demands of
the Norwegian dramatist. The strictness of the naturalistic convention which Ibsen evolved, and the economy of his dialogue,
did not allow the player to rely on any *'gros moyens'*. At the same
time, the interest of his mature plays resided so little in their outer
action and intrigue, so much in character psychology, that they
could not hold the attention of audiences unless the characters were
made to live on the stage. Melodrama, farce and poetical rhetoric,
which had been the staple of the nineteenth-century English
theatre, were poor disciplinary preparation for this new task. The
finest acting of the century had been evolved for the great theatres
that, by their physical dimensions, demanded rhetorical methods
and encouraged spectacle; Irving's hostility to the Ibsenists was no
surprising reaction from one whose imagination was trained in
terms of grandeur.

It was the smaller theatres, where greater intimacy was possible,
that first produced a style of acting appropriate to the drama of
contemporary life, cup-and-saucer comedy. In the 'sixties, the
Bancrofts and their playwright, Tom Robertson, established an
art whose virtue lay in a quality of factual truth and fresh observation of life. It was still a very limited art, however: Robertson's
characters are without depth or subtlety, and little poetic insight

3

has gone to the making of his plays. The Bancrofts could offer their successors a lesson in how to move about a realistically cluttered Ibsen drawing-room, how to adapt speech and style generally to the box-set. But the greatness of Ibsen's drama rests upon other elements than the simple portrayal of everyday life; had Irving been able to penetrate beyond the accidentals of this art that he so disliked, he might have recognised a quality more akin to his own.

In retrospect, the quarrel between the theatre of beauty and the theatre of truth may seem rather futile and wasteful, though it was probably necessary. Ibsen's naturalism and the symbolist drama, in which Maeterlinck and Yeats are major figures, and to which Gordon Craig's concept of theatre is allied, were equally in reaction from rhetoric, superficial emotionalism and 'ham' acting. They offered genuine alternatives to different temperaments; but, in their finer achievements, each drew perceptibly nearer to the other. Symbolist producers going to the extreme, approved by Yeats, of immobilising their players on the stage, were not really diverging so far in intention from the naturalistic producers, of whom Barker was to be one, concerned to reveal the undercurrents of thought and feeling whereby the characters of an Ibsen play live. *On Poetry in Drama* makes a point that is applicable to Ibsen and Maeterlinck and Shakespeare, irrespective of the different schools to which they may be assigned:

> ... as the aim of his *[the dramatist's]* art grows finer and its practice more mature, we are likely to find him relegating action to the background and economising in every sort of doing so that his characters may be able less disturbedly to *be* what they are ...[2]

Interpretative acting is in fact indispensable to Ibsen as to Shakespeare, though the two compel the actor to make his contribution by very different means. For significant naturalism, the means of the Bancrofts had to be extended and informed by a greater degree of such sympathetic imagination as allowed Irving, defiant of physical handicaps, to make even a Matthias, in *The Bells*, an embodiment of profound experience.

Barker's allegiance to naturalism did not come about without consideration of alternatives. When he did adopt it for his mature expression, he was ready to enrich it with elements from other sources. The earliest plays he produced professionally were Maeterlinck's *Intérieur* and *Mort de Tintagiles*, with Fiona Mac-Leod's *House of Usna*.[3] Such dramatic manifestations of *l'art pour l'art* were clearly not uncongenial to his taste. When Yeats was looking for a suitable producer for a Stage Society performance of *Where There is Nothing*, it is not surprising that the choice ultimately fell on Barker.[4] Among his first plays written outside the collaboration with Berte Thomas, the tiny verse drama, *A Miracle*, belongs indubitably to the type of Maeterlinck's little plays for marionettes and the fairy-tale mediævalism of Yeats's earliest dramatic efforts. The Christmas production at the Court Theatre in 1904 was *Prunella*, by Barker and Laurence Housman, which was to have a successor in *The Harlequinade*, written in 1913 in collaboration with Dion Clayton Calthrop.[5] Both were individual explorations in the vein of *commedia dell'arte*, implying recognition that a healthy theatre must have room for many conventions of drama; and *Prunella*, especially, courts an atmospheric delicacy. Beneath the surface of Granville Barker's later, more ostensibly naturalistic plays, the values to which these earlier interests testify are still pursued.

The basic distinction between representationalism and symbolism corresponds to a recognised dichotomy in human life. In its particular form of naturalism, representational drama is closely associated with the later nineteenth-century growth in the prestige of science and the rise of sociology. For this art analyses men and presents characters in terms of heredity and environment, as creatures moulded by the past and by social relationships; the retrospective method, which is so marked a feature of Ibsen's plays, is one manifestation of this general approach. Whatever its variant forms, the naturalistic convention is most appropriate to the depiction of social existence and the objective entity of form and manners which is created by any human group; it reveals the face that a man wears towards his fellows, whereas symbolist art is primarily concerned with elemental, or superhuman, reality and the private world of individual experience, whose values cannot be verified by the common measure of men's senses. There is, of course, nothing fortuitous about the approval given by Marxist communities to naturalism, which tends to reduce the importance of individualist values in favour of social values.

The extreme theory of naturalism as offering a *tranche de vie* comes infinitely near to contradicting the very idea of art. However, Barker at no time fell into the heresy of supposing that drama could be a mere transcript from the meaningless disorder of life. He understood and asserted that: 'A play's dialogue is an incantation, and the actors must bewitch us with it'.[6] The words must have 'a more than rational power', since there is no living art in which the divinity of the symbol does not reside with a vivifying truth beyond factual accuracy.

For Barker, as for Ibsen and Chekhov, a modification of the naturalistic mode was necessary to communicate his complex vision. It corresponded to an undeniable truth of experience and one sharply distinguished in the consciousness of his time: the quarrel between naturalism and symbolism was a rendering in other terms of the quarrel between scientific materialism and religion, between the philosophy of progress and the philosophy of permanence. Since the Industrial Revolution, art has had increasingly to choose between the deliberately fragmentary, minor statement and acknowledgment of the social automation as a dominant aspect of humanity, behind which the 'secret life' might still be discovered.

The great dramatists of the modern world have accepted the situation, but given their work a larger truth by retaining at its centre the contradictions of consciousness: so Chekhov reveals the paradox of the ultimate loneliness of man in a destiny that is common to all; so Ibsen counterbalances the impoverished and destructive conception of truth that possesses a Gregers Werle with the truth of a Hedvig's creative imagination, ranging free in the forests and oceans of a timeless world; Pirandello plays off against each other the social comedy and the tragedy of Man, the rigid logical patterns that the mind imposes on experience and the strangeness that the universe assumes when the pattern is shattered; in Strindberg's finest 'naturalistic' play, *The Father*, the characters take on the immense proportions of myth, as the mind obsessed challenges the dull and blinkered vision of sanity. In naturalism thus enlarged is revealed not only the extent to which man is the creature of social relations, but the way in which he may elude their defining grasp. The conflict between the two modes of existence is an abiding theme within the various themes of Granville Barker's plays: the naturalistic surface of his drama is a reflection of the ineluctable encroachment of society upon individual existence; but other recognitions move constantly beneath that surface.

'It is in the soul,' Maeterlinck held, 'that everything happens.' In a famous passage,[7] he claimed to find the deepest tragedy in the spectacle of an old man sitting idle in a chair. In time he discarded the theory of 'static drama', as Yeats did also. And indeed action is not banished from Maeterlinck's little plays, but only limited and subdued to reveal the more shy and secret movements of the soul and to allow mood its domination. Even so, these plays are too precious to be long sustained. The characters exist in feelings too tenuous to be plainly stated. The result is a drama at once elliptical and implicit, but also somewhat flimsy and monotonous. The nature of what happens in the soul may be more truly revealed if the dramatist can penetrate to it through the context of appearances. Maeterlinck's art has its graver limitations: the fairyland, in which some of his plays are set, is suggestive of a retreat into childish imagination; the concentration on the passive response to experience is anti-heroic, in that the characters do not grapple with life in an effort to bring it nearer to the forms of their desire.

*   *   *

When greatly moved, modern civilised man probably gazes into the fire and says nothing, as Yeats remarked.[8] A major challenge that the naturalistic dramatist accepts is to make this very inarticulateness expressive. He is able to accept it precisely because it is in the power of an able actor, rightly trained, to move an audience deeply, even while he does no more, to all appearances, than Yeats assumes. It is no magic art, though a difficult one, that can realise the implications of the most fragmentary utterances, or of silence itself, and project to an audience moods so vivid as to seem palpable. Barker more than once attacked an academic criticism of Shakespeare that seemed convinced, though it never dared say so, that the master-dramatist had in his greatest plays set impossible tasks for his actors.[9] The protest has the authority of an expert statement; there can be heard in it, too, a defence of the dignity of what was once his own art, and an echo of the intelligent and sensitive actor's desire for abundant opportunity to exercise his special gifts.

Bridges-Adams, in a broadcast talk, has recalled Granville Barker's own playing of Marchbanks in *Candida*:

> You believed his name was in the peerage. You believed he had been sleeping on the Embankment. What is more, you believed he was a real poet, capable of flights beyond anything the author had given him to say.[10]

Able himself to supplement the dramatist's work in this way—and Shaw's plays, he recognised, are largely explicit—, he wrote consistently for actors who could do the same. No dramatist has ever more invited collaboration, and imaginative collaboration, from producer and actors. The corollary of this is that his plays will hardly ever 'act themselves', and that paucity of ideas in producer and players is sure to betray them.

He allowed, of course, for the fact that it may be necessary for the actors' ideas to be initiated by the producer. Though Max Beerbohm, after reading *The Exemplary Theatre*, sent its author a series of cartoons of the Theatre of the Future,[11] in which bespectacled ex-seminarists act Shakespeare's lovers to an empty auditorium, Granville Barker was in no real danger of confusing the actor's equipment, or his manner of study, with the scholar's. He might wish to sit the Court Theatre players round a table and make them discuss the play and their parts, as Stanislavsky did, and as many others have done in imitation; but, in practice, he was ready to compromise, letting his actors start moving about as soon as the play had been read.[12] He was perfectly familiar with the phenomenon of the actor who can convince his audience by a fine performance in a part and a play that he has not begun intellectually to understand; and he accepted it. There have been intellectual actors, and Irving seems to have been one; but intellect was never among the qualities that seemed to Barker essential to acting. He put the matter clearly in the *Preface to Othello*:

The actor ... neither mere mouthpiece nor mere puppet ...
interprets a character—the material the dramatist gives him—in
the terms, more or less disguised, of his own personality. He cannot,
strictly speaking, know more of the character than the dramatist
has told him, and this, though it be the essential part, can never be
much. But he must seem to know much more, and in many ways,
if we are to think of the two as one. Yet this need be but seeming.
He need acquire no knowledge but apparent knowledge, cultivate
in this respect no ability but to seem able, nor need he build up,
of this composite personality demanded, anything but a painted
façade. Note that it is not a question of trivial knowledge or poor
ability, ... but of knowledge and ability merely reflected as in a
mirror ... [13]

The mirror, he explains, may have to reflect what lies beneath the
surface and make apparent, but still only apparent, processes of
mind. He goes on:

The actor's is, above all, the faculty of sympathy; found physically
in the sensitive ear, the receptive eye, the dancer's body that of
itself responds, emotionally in the tears or laughter ready at call,
and intellectually in a capacity not only seemingly to absorb some
product of another's thought, but to reproduce the effects of understanding it without necessarily having understood it in the
least ... [13]

As one might expect, Barker draws a clear distinction between
the way in which the actor gives the substance of an inner life to
the character, as the play is staged, and the procedure of the unscrupulous actor, who distorts an author's intention in order to
display his own personality. This latter process he calls 'impersonation' and sees as respectable only in the Music Hall artist. An
actor may use impersonation to pass off a bad play, or a particularly
thin character, on an uncritical audience; so it is inevitably a leading feature of the 'actor's theatre', in which there is a dearth of
good dramatists.

For Barker regarded the good dramatist as the actor's chief ally
in his struggle for artistic self-discipline. He never doubted that
emotion was the very essence of theatre, allowing that a great
dramatist might create 'an Antony and Cleopatra or a Lear and
Cordelia, characters full of meaning to be interpreted ... and call-

ing besides for as much outpouring of emotion even in a single
scene as might leave a strong man prostrate'.[14] But he was aware
that the actor of such rôles must still use his emotion, as a means
under his control, in the service of the playwright's more objective
vision; and he recognised many qualities of emotion, 'severely controlled and refined into humour or deepened to meditation',[14]
appropriate to an Alceste or Célimène, a Rebecca West or Peer
Gynt. Hence his respect for Chekhov: giving the actor far greater
opportunity than most dramatists did also involved keeping him
more strictly in his place. Of Chekhov's drama, compared with
Ibsen's, it could be said: '. . . the lights were still more broken,
and the audience might only learn enough of the actor to illuminate
some quite impersonal theme.'[15]

In his various accounts of the process of assuming a character,
Granville Barker betrays knowledge of the theories of Stanislavsky.
He observed the Moscow Art Theatre at work in 1914.[16] Yet undoubtedly he and the great Russian producer, faced with similar
dramatic material, had been moving in rather similar directions
before direct influence of one on the other was a possibility. It
can be said that Barker never employed such autocratic methods
as were Stanislavsky's until quite late in his life. To make
the plays of Maeterlinck theatrically effective certainly called for
the projection of delicate feeling akin to what Chekhov required, and it is quite possible that Barker was commenting on
his own experience and a discovery made to some extent independ-
ently of any foreign influence, when he discussed the crucial stage
in the process whereby the actor divests himself of his ordinary
personality and becomes identified with the character.

He thinks of it as involving a partial lowering of the threshold of
consciousness, a forsaking of the familiar self, 'a desperate business,' until the powers of response—thought and feeling as much
as tone and gesture—remain active as if without principle, unable
to answer to the call of the usual personality, ready to be called into
the service of another image, another—though temporary—concept of the self. The letting go of normal control, he stresses, does
no more than supply a necessary condition:

. . . unless the quiescence of the conscious mind helps the receptive, sub-conscious, emotionally expressive self to be only the more keenly alive—and, even when in complete physical quiescence, to be actively alive—the method fails.[17]

He took, as a classic example of what might be achieved by some such means, the performance of Olga Knipper Chekhova as Madame Ranevsky, in *The Cherry Orchard*. This is how he described it:

> It will be remembered how, in the third act, Madame Ranevsky comes out of the ballroom to hear of the sale, asks but a couple of brief questions, and then stays listening till the curtain falls, never speaking another word . . . The impression left on me by Madame Tchekov's silent performance was that she had played a chief part in a long and strenuous scene. As she had. But how was the effect produced? . . . As far as I remember, Madame Tchekov sat down at the table as the curtain fell, and that was all . . . It might be to the point to argue that Madame Tchekov reaped at that moment by entire passivity what she had sown in action during the rest of the play . . .[18]

But he is inclined to attribute the effect largely to the 'sub-conscious activity' that preparation had induced in the performer during that scene.

Actors who worked in Barker's productions have given testimony of his practice.[19] Thorough discussion of the play, around a table or moving about a stage, was one way of ensuring that the style of a production would be as homogeneous as possible, that a real *ensemble* would be created. In a way inconceivable to Mr. Vincent Crummles, the individual actor was never allowed to forget his place as a member of a company corporately responsible for bringing the play theatrically to life; Barker even went so far as to declare that there should be 'no solitary study at all'. In so far as the producer directed the discussions, the imaginative conception of the production would be his in the first place; but his cast had to participate in the imaginative process for the final unity to be as rich and vital as possible. Modification of one rôle entailed a shift of balance in the entire production. He did not approve of the actor's learning his lines except gradually, as the play and his rôle were explored with the rest of the company. The intention was to avoid the stultifying effect of imposing on any aspect of a production an interpretation and a pattern worked out in detail; instead, the aim was a process of growth, in which the original conception was continually enriched and deepened, imperceptibly changing all the time like a living organism.

It is obvious that Barker worked on the assumption that the audience at any performance receives much more than it is conscious of receiving. In the later nineteenth century, the English theatre had learnt from the Saxe-Meiningen Company the importance of authenticity in setting and costume as an aid to conviction. Strindberg had protested against the theatrical custom of painting such things as shelves and kitchen utensils on a backcloth; Granville Barker insisted that a pair of genuine Chippendale settees must be procured for the 1936 production of *Waste*. The audiences would probably have been content with imitations, but the real thing may well have made a difference to the actors' imaginative response; that shade of difference in the actors' consciousness would affect the audience subconsciously. The more complete indentification of the actor with his rôle was the end in view, identification in depth, to which the whole personality contributed. Barker's care as a producer for detail of every kind, which corresponds to the care he took as a playwright, betrays his belief that the slightest negligence or falsity weakens the play's hold on an audience.

On these assumptions, the many months, even years, that a permanent, subsidised company may spend in the study of a play and preparation for its production are not time wasted: at the end, it may live in performance as completely as in its author's imagination; and the one production may survive a generation of playing. Such were the conditions of work that Barker envied the Moscow Art Theatre; they depended on the recognition of the art of the theatre as serious and creative, and on the dedication of actors and producer to their work; except in an age of wealthy patrons, they must depend on public recognition of some considerable social value in art. In the absence of the ideal conditions, he did what he could to raise English theatrical standards to the point at which the need for such conditions might begin to be appreciated.

We know the kind of hint that he would throw out to his players in order to share with them his image of their parts, to help them place the characters socially and grasp the quality of feeling and psychology basic to them. There is a well-known story, existing in more than one version, of how Barrie parodied the method in his demand to an actor: 'I want you to come on like a man whose brother has a chicken farm in Gloucestershire.'[20] The printed texts of Barker's plays offer in their directions[21] many examples of the kind of remark that, made to an actor, might prove fruitful. The Huxtable sisters, in *The Madras House*, are sketched individually, but also thought of as a group, showing '*to a casual eye the difference between one lead pencil and another, as these lie upon one's table after some weeks' use; a matter of length, of sharpening, of wear*', the limits of individuality set.

The verbal direction is not the only means of evoking from the actor the desired response: in the description of the scene for the one-Act play, *Farewell to the Theatre*, comes the remark:

> *The newest thing in the room and quite the strangest seeming there is a photograph on the mantelpiece of Edward's daughter, and that has been here nine years or so, ever since she died. A pretty child.*

Neither the photograph nor the child has any place in dialogue or action; the author has no piece of 'business' in mind; but for the building of character that small property has as much value as the actor is capable of realising, a measure of his imagination and his intuitive understanding of human beings. The audience may notice that sole token of a personal life in the fustiness of the lawyer's office; it can hardly have any further direct meaning for them. But indirectly, through the actor, they may comprehend all that the dramatist intends it to betoken.

Such details as this—and the play-texts are prolific in them—indicate how greatly Barker was concerned that his characters should be built up from the material of naturalistic psychology, and how much more essential to drama he thought the projection of character and feeling than any transmission of facts. A company, rehearsing over a considerable period in the way he envisaged, might embody the whole inner depths of a play without being analytically aware of how much their acting included. In his own plays, he does not merely allow for the intuitive and subconscious element in the exchange between actor and audience, but encourages its extension. The realisation that a single human action may have an infinitude of meanings is reflected in the many-faceted design of his plays. A richness of experience, implied within the dialogue, may baffle the reader, but is a source of power to the sensitive actor. *On Poetry in Drama* considers the type of character-effect, towards which the art of the implicit tends, and comments on the flexibility of dialogue-style that it requires:

> ... it is a question not merely of what a man thinks he knows about himself ..., but, added to this, and by far the more important, the things about himself he does *not* know ... We need a language, then, capable of expressing thought and emotion combined, and at times, emotion almost divorced from thought.[22]

There is recognition here that the fundamental appeal of drama is to common humanity, that a play's intellectual content, however great, must still be rooted in that ground and conveyed, implicit, through the medium of shared experience.

Making the actors discuss the play and their rôles certainly developed an approach critical and objective in some degree. The parts of Granville Barker's histrionic theory most difficult to follow occur when he is trying to explain the place of critical intelligence in the assumption of character. He seems to have recognised a moment when it might interfere disastrously with the process: the crucial moment, when the normal conscious self became quiescent and the actor entered—as a reward of much toil—into the skin of his part. Yet he was aware of a danger remaining: that the player might still be carried away beyond calculation by the power of his own emotion, unless he retained an alertness, a residual element of detachment from the character. Norman Marshall, writing in *The Producer and the Play* (p. 92), has identified this alerting of the critical faculty during the actual performance as the aim of Brecht's doctrine of alienation, as it applies to the player. *The Exemplary Theatre* puts the matter thus:

> Through the sensitive channel which the interpreter has now become will flow unchecked the thoughts and emotions generated in the part's studying ... and at each fixed point the interpreter must consciously control and direct them. He must never let this side of the part's playing escape his quite conscious control. ...

But to the rest he need only sub-consciously attend. To demeanour, tones, gestures and the like he need now oppose no mental bar.[23]

Writing to John Gielgud, Barker could take understanding of his meaning for granted: '. . . at the full rehearsals . . . learn to "let yourself go" and only keep enough self-consciousness to enable you to correct faults (well, you know all about that duplicate consciousness which only an actor, and a *real* actor, seems to understand).'[24] There is some general reflection here, though, of that struggle between emotion and the executive intelligence that is a necessary part of all artistic creation. The taut energy that might be produced in the struggle especially interested him.

How to prevent somnambulist performance and how to keep the acting fresh were among the chief problems that occupied Barker as a producer. He was struck by the device of a bow-shaped bridge used in Reinhardt's production of *A Comedy of Errors*, at the Deutsches Theater in 1910:

> It is not too easy to negotiate; you slip and stumble if you're not careful, so that it gives the impression of bustle, of scramble, of hurry, and always it must look a necessary scramble . . .[25]

This kind of obstacle, as he explained to Michael MacOwan, when supervising the 1936 production of *Waste*, prevented the actors from falling into automatic routine or making meaningless effects. With his concern for harmony in a production went a precise attention to emotional detail. MacOwan has related how, in the rehearsals of *Waste*:

> No sooner would an actor feel that he had settled into the mood of a scene, or a speech, and thought he saw smooth water ahead, than Barker would point out that a particular speech or a sentence was outside that mood, that something new must be brought in . . . and every moment was to be made tinglingly alive.[26]

Every speech was to be treated as a graph of constantly varying ' "little pieces", shades of thought and feeling'.[27] This, of course, is the method of impressionism, and its practicability has been tested and proved by other producers, among them Stanislavsky and, rather differently, by Gaston Baty for the *théâtre du silence*.

It is a method particularly appropriate to a drama in which the action is less a matter of strongly plotted, well-marked outbursts and large movements than of a more organic and gradual development.

Doubtless, it is only in the supreme performances of theatrical legend that the actor is emotionally present and concentrating throughout, striking a vital contact with his audience all the time. It is very rarely that either actor or audience is capable of anything like such sustained intensity. For the most part, occasional moments of genuine projection of feeling must serve to persuade an audience that the emotional interchange is continuous,—a possibility, if the actor is sensitively alert enough to register his audience's response and so recall it to concentration when need be. The scenes which he relives emotionally, the scenes in which he acts automatically, merely simulating emotion, are likely to vary from one performance to another. In a long run, there must be very many occasions—and they are perhaps the majority—when all is simulation. Barker's championship of repertory and his fierce opposition to the long-run system were doubtless intensified by his sense that the type of drama in which he was most interested depended peculiarly for its effectiveness on the actors' concentration during performance, and on genuine and directed 'subconscious activity'. Any device which might serve to reduce the actor's emotional absence from his part to a minimum was justified.

Barker's letters to Gielgud are much occupied with suggestions of how to retain freshness in a performance that must go through many repetitions. One letter declares:

> I believe the solution may lie in doing the things separately at first, sitting round a table—*if* you have a company accustomed to working with you and to follow—and one day working out the sense, and the next singing the music, and then, when first you go on the stage doing nothing but the movements (the words merely muttered). Then when all three are so fixed in the mind that you don't have consciously to think of them—but not till then—letting the whole thing rip.[28]

It is a passage which betrays the source of much of Barker's technique as actor and producer and gives the clue to the means whereby he achieved the effect of a rhythmical whole, for which his productions were much admired. For there are echoes here of some of the ideas in which William Poel was fertile.

Granville Barker played Richard II for Poel in 1899 and Marlowe's Edward II for him in 1903. It is not likely that these experiences taught him much about the building of a character by the method of psychological realism; character interpretation in Poel's productions was erratic in quality and was not free from the effects of his eccentricity.[29] It has been thought that the German company led by Andresen and Behrend, which visited London in the 'nineties, at the invitation of J. T. Grein, and played Hauptmann and Sudermann, offered Barker a model for *ensemble* playing which gave full value to naturalistic characterisation.[30] What Poel gave him was an exciting idea of style, a sheer technical discipline, together with a liberation from the conventional nineteenth-century approach to staging. He further encouraged him in the belief that the human voice and the words it speaks are far more important to drama than any visual element.[31]

The Exemplary Theatre complains that English actors of this period had, for the most part, only one acting style and that truly appropriate only to the *pièce-bien-faite* on the French model, a drama of intrigue. The style which William Poel developed was applied by its originator mainly to Elizabethan and Jacobean plays, but Granville Barker found in it invaluable elements to sustain artifice as a chief source of delight in the drama of modern life.

The older man submitted all his players alike to his peculiar discipline, in pursuit of an ideal of stylistic consistency. 'Irving is wonderful in his own way, but it isn't mine,' he said firmly; it was between two ways of achieving beauty in the theatre that he distinguished. Sir Lewis Casson has said of Poel's way:

> His first step was to cast the play orchestrally. He decided which character represented the double-bass, the cello, the woodwind, so to speak, and chose his actors by the timbre, pitch and flexibility of their voices, far more than from their experience or even their skill. Before starting rehearsals he had worked out (within fairly wide limits) the eventual sound of the whole play, the melody, stress, rhythm, and phrasing of every sentence; and for the first three weeks of a month's rehearsal the company sat round a table, as in a school class-room, and 'learnt the tunes' from him by endless

repetition in a strongly marked exaggerated form; so that at the end of, say, two weeks the whole play had become as fixed in musical pattern as if written in an orchestral score.[32]

He insisted that an actor should be able to '*hear* more colour in speech than the average and be able to express it, using . . . a range of 2½ octaves'. Poel even carried his idea that the dialogue of a play should have a self-sufficient existence as a musical composition to the extent of assigning to women certain male rôles, including the part of Everyman, in his famous production of the mediæval morality, because the timbre of the female voice gave him the quality of sound that he wanted. The 'little tunes' ensured that the actors' speech was inflected to a degree far surpassing that of normal English speech and, perhaps surprisingly, had the effect of making it easier for an audience to grasp the sense of lengthy passages spoken at great speed; monotony was certainly avoided.

* * *

'All art constantly aspires to the condition of music,' Walter Pater declared, and he considered it an observation important enough to reiterate. It was, indeed, a commonplace of French *Symbolisme* and English Æstheticism, most strikingly expressed in the aesthetic theory of Mallarmé. Gautier put theory into practice by writing a poem and calling it '*Symphonie en Blanc Majeure*', Whistler by painting Harmonies and Symphonies; George Egerton entitled two volumes of stories *Keynotes* and *Discords*; Max Beerbohm, reprinting an article written for the *Pageant* as the conclusion to *Works*, called it *Diminuendo*. Lip-service—it was often nothing more significant—to the idea of the transposition and fusing of the various arts was a *fin de siècle* craze.

Pater had in mind the movement of the other arts away from the limitations of conceptual thinking; but the musicians themselves were sometimes to be found developing the conceptual expressiveness of their work. Wagner had achieved the triumph of making music a flexible instrument of his thought by his elaboration of *leitmotiv* structure. Debussy, in *Pelléas et Mélisande*, subdued musical to dramatic effect by a more extensive development of *recitative* than had ever before been attempted in opera. He was met half-way by Maeterlinck, who had already used repetition and echo to achieve emotional effects of a subtlety comparable to that of music. Chekhov dissolved a greater drama more poignantly into the harmonies of the sister art. In 1902 and 1907, Strindberg was to substitute musical form for argument, or straightforward narrative development, in his *Dream Play* and *Ghost Sonata*.[33] Thomas Mann, importing *leitmotiv* structure into the novel, carried the fashion a stage further, though to an effect perhaps more generally formal, or even poetic, than strictly musical. Among theatrical designers, Craig and Charles Ricketts, Craig's disciple in this respect, explored the theatrical possibilities of Whistlerian colour-harmonies, and Craig developed the idea of stage lighting as the visual equivalent to a musical accompaniment, underlining the changing moods of the drama.

The practical lesson that the spoken drama is music, which Barker learned from Poel, was thus reinforced by general artistic tendencies. The effect on his own dramatic writing, as well as on his productions, was to encourage him in an endeavour to create an over-riding rhythmical structure, that would give closer unity to a play and enhance the organic quality of the action. In producing Shakespeare, he aimed at an unbroken musical line from end to end of the Act; in modern plays, including his own, at an antiphonal effect. He sometimes uses musical forms in his plays as precisely as Strindberg does: throughout much of *The Marrying of Ann Leete*, at the beginning of the revised text of *Waste*, and through the first Act of *The Madras House*, the dialogue is composed in discernible musical patterns and determines the rhythm of performance accordingly. More conventionally, he sometimes employs actual music to set a mood, or as a general key to his dramatic themes; a single phrase may anticipate a dramatic climax, or give warning of the course that a scene is to follow. In his last plays, an attempt is made to fuse dramatic development with a musical development that gives to the individual Acts the character of movements in symphonic compositions.

* * *

The stylised quality that naturalism takes on in his work is evident in such technique; and the greater part of what he says about his chosen subjects is only accessible through due attention to the style; the musical character and the symbolic values of his work are very closely associated. The general end of all Barker's attention to form is dramatic concentration and sharpening of focus. Sir William Rothenstein claims[34] to have initiated Barker's awareness of how a stylised setting could underline the tone and approach of the most strictly naturalistic play. (Certainly, the Note on the Costume, which accompanies the typescript of *Ann Leete,* in the British Museum Library, and has not been published, shows little consciousness of how much the visual aspect of the play might contribute to the total meaning; when he wrote that, at the very beginning of the century, Barker had still, it seems, a great deal to learn about the art of production.)

The novelty of an uncluttered stage, where the presence of every property was dramatically justified, went far to earn for his Shakespeare productions the epithets, 'tidy' and 'hygienic'.[35] They might have been applied with equal appropriateness to the trim hedges of his setting for *Prunella,* or the formal avenue of yews in *The Sentimentalists.* Here was a challenge to eyes over-familiar with Victorian Gothic and the lavish realism of such producers as Beerbohm Tree; the shock it dealt was part of the impact of an individual mind that valued exact perception, respected the symbolic power latent in everything on the stage, abhorred confusion, and was more responsive to form than bright colour.

St. John Ervine, whose tributes to Barker are grudgingly paid, admits to a vivid impression, surviving forty-five years, of how the trial scene in *Justice* was made the more tense for the accessory detail in the production: as the scene progressed, the lamps in the court were lit, unhurriedly, one by one, until the climax was reached in a blaze of illumination;[36] P. P. Howe remembered the dropping of a book, audible in the hush.[37] A favourite device of Barker's productions was to focus a scene from an unusual angle in what yet seemed the simplest of settings. Even the otherwise undistinguished *Helena's Path* gained something like distinction in the scene of the cricket-match, with its representation of 'one line of trees behind another, foreshortened very boldly',[38] and in that other scene of 'a summer garden seen from an original angle by moon and lantern-light'.[39] In several of his own plays, Barker provides for such mixed, or contrasted, lighting. The techniques by which the artists of the cinema were to give an edge to visual naturalism were similar enough to these. The angle of vision and the light, like the selection of detail, are part of the substance of communication, images of the invisible.

Most of his plays reflect Barker's consciousness that the physical stage was more than a convenient place for plays to be mounted; he regards it as another element in his dramatic vocabulary to be bent to his purposes and made expressive. He certainly found the conventional box-set constricting and wearisomely over-used in the theatre of his day. He had a stage specially constructed for his production of *The Dynasts*: a slightly raised inner stage, two side entrances, two quite steep flights of steps down, converging at a lectern, with a raised seat either side of the main stage for the chorus. He was convinced that Greek plays needed to be acted in the open air (though the English climate so rarely made it possible), and he produced *The Trojan Women* and *Iphigenia in Taurus* in the Adolph Lewisohn Stadium in New York and in the Yale Bowl. He did not despise the mechanical inventions, or re-discoveries, of the modern theatre, when convinced of their use-fulness, and employed a revolving stage for *Androcles and the Lion*. Nearly all his own plays, starting with his early experiments, allow for some difference in stage levels, if only the difference be-tween the floor of the hall and the short flight of steps up to the dining-room, in the last Act of *Ann Leete*. Time and again, he demands the division of the stage into well-marked acting areas. This kind of experiment is carried furthest in *The Secret Life*, which comes nearest to demanding the freedom, variety and flexibility that the Elizabethan theatre offered its dramatist. Barker approved a movable proscenium as a most desirable feature for any National Theatre building; and Act III of *His Majesty*, at least, repudiates the proscenium decisively.

The virtual rejection of the box-set as a constant feature of the stage has a general significance. The box-set had come into the English theatre with naturalism and, in time, had become its in-variable associate. By relegating it to the position of one resource among many others, Barker was demanding liberation for the whole naturalistic form to allow within it the freer and more dynamic working of imagination. His whole technique was similarly directed.

CHAPTER III

Experiment and Achievement

During the period of Granville Barker's dramatic apprenticeship, the chief names in contemporary English drama were Henry Arthur Jones, A. W. Pinero and Oscar Wilde; W. S. Gilbert was a veteran figure, though with many years of achievement still before him. It is possible to find some reflection of each of these writers in Barker's early work, together with an awareness of the greater genius of Ibsen, not simply transmitted through the first three. (Even the disapproving Jones had absorbed something of the Norwegian's influence.) However, a considerable individual talent is already apparent in the earliest surviving play in which Barker had a hand, *The Family of the Oldroyds,* written when he was eighteen. Some of his first attempts show a surprising power; but no quality in them is more impressive than the artistic integrity that compels a faithful working-out of his themes, in defiance of conventional thinking and considerable technical difficulties. He experimented because he had to, in the interests of what he had to say.

In all five of Barker's early unpublished plays extant, the central character is a woman. There may be in this an indication of the nature of his sensibility, but it also mirrored general contemporary consciousness to some extent. It was the time of the discovery of the New Woman and the identification of her with the revolutionary ferment making itself felt in many departments of life and thought. The young dramatist is not content with the superficialities of the topical theme: the demand for the political and social equality of women with men. He is interested in the woman's

achievement of self-reliance and human maturity and in the liberation of her natural qualities and powers. The question of the
equality of women and men in sexual matters concerns him, as it is
fundamental to that liberation. Following Ibsen, he shows himself
aware, as Lawrence was later to be, that the nineteenth-century
marriage ideal must be broken to allow the woman to fulfil her total
humanity and so make way for some new and richer association
of the sexes. These plays challenge the dichotomy between the
ideal woman and the nocturnal woman, the natural wanton,
of which the Decadent mentality was peculiarly aware. What the
heroines of the plays enact is fundamentally the rebellion of
offended Nature, or some neglected truth of life, against the
stultifying artificiality of civilisation.

It is possible to generalise about the content and method of the
five plays, irrespective of the fact that three of them are the result
of collaboration. Although Berte Thomas was nine years older than
Barker, the dominant personality expressed in *The Family of the
Oldroyds, The Weather-Hen* and *Our Visitor to Work-a-Day* is
certainly the younger man's. There can be little doubt that he was
responsible for the choice of themes. Thomas has stated that his
own part in the work was increasingly that of a secretary and that,
as he wrote down the dialogue of *Our Visitor*, he understood hardly
a word of it.[1]

When the two first met in the summer of 1891, in Sarah
Thorne's stock company at Margate, Herbert Thomas was a recent recruit to the theatre, though already twenty-two; 'Berte' was
a version of his christian name then considered modish for stage
use. At the end of six months, Granville Barker returned to London
and Thomas was engaged with other companies. It was some time
later, when the latter also was acting in London and enjoying a
modest success, that the playwriting collaboration began. Thomas
was already the author of one play, produced at Margate, and this
fact seems to have prompted Barker's suggestion that they should
see what they could do together. The first play they wrote, *A
Comedy of Fools*, was judged unsatisfactory, and the two copies
were destroyed. The partnership was resumed in 1895-6, after
Thomas's return from an American tour with Tree, and there followed in order: *The Family of the Oldroyds, The Weather-Hen*

and *Our Visitor to Work-a-Day*. *The Weather-Hen* appears to
have been written in 1897 and received professional production
two years later; among Barker's papers is a revised version of this
play, made in the light of the criticism the production received.
Our Visitor was finished by the spring of 1899.[2] The collaboration
broke up during work on a dramatic version of Thackeray's *Henry
Esmond*, of which no text is known. Whether Barker completed
the work on his own or not, something of what he learned from
Thackeray certainly went to the making of *The Marrying of Ann
Leete*, the earliest of his published plays.

*   *   *

The nineteenth-century quarrel between rationalism and faith is
the background to *The Family of the Oldroyds*. Already the organisation of the dramatic plot corresponds to the demands of theme;
what happens has its clearly marked philosophic implications as
well as its general human value. The heroine, Tessa Oldroyd, is
Anglo-Italian, as Granville Barker liked to think himself. She is
the illegitimate child of a novelist, Clement Oldroyd, come of a
family in which religious scepticism is a conscientious tradition,
and an Italian Contessa, figure of passion and licence, who is already dead when the play opens. On the verge of womanhood,
Tessa falls in love with Sir Noel Cherrington, a reformed rake,
who is himself in love with her cousin, Naomi Dare. In this situation, she discovers no restraint upon her desires and freedom of
will, except her love for her father which he, embittered by the
faithlessness of Tessa's mother, returns with a repressive sternness.
The issue of the conflict within the girl is self-destruction, but
within the structure of the play the suicide carries the weight of
a partial, not a final statement; it is modified by the pattern
of character and attitude against which it is set. A grasp of dialectical form is already evident in the bare bones of the play: in
the shadowy figure of the Contessa, balanced by Clement Oldroyd,
passion is confronted with reason; strict puritan morality, in
Naomi, Ruth and Robin Dare, with worldliness, in Sir Noel, and
free-thinking, in Clement and Tessa herself; the stern justice of
Naomi is opposed by the charity of Ruth and of Max Oldroyd,

Clement's brother; Tessa's pursuit of freedom, which leads to destruction, is balanced by Robin's, which leads to innocent fulfilment; Luke Heryett, the clergyman who marries Ruth, is a figure of blindly conventional goodness, modified by association with the hypocritical rascal of a sexton, Grinnidge; and, central pivots of the thematic structure, Max and Clement Oldroyd embody the good and the evil in intellectual detachment, the acceptance and the rejection of life.

The end of the play has something of the form of Henry Arthur Jones's re-assertions of conservative values, but the distribution of sympathies makes for a different effect. Max Oldroyd, poorly realised as a dramatic character, holds the balance of judgment and represents a divergence from Jones's view: a trust in natural piety and in the power of life to make and re-make itself; and the linking of Tessa's impulse to freedom with Robin's, and with the natural emotions of youth, implies an essential nobility and creative potency in the rebellious spirit.

The whole family sufficiently reflects a wider society for Tessa's drama to convey the burden of a hidden disintegration of the social order. The family of the Oldroyds, in its alliance with the Dares, is the embodiment of English puritanism, the still uncorrupted tradition of Tanner's Lane, with its doctrine that every man must find his own religion, that no other man's is good enough for him or will serve his need. The most interesting thing in the play is the nature of the dramatic relationship between Tessa and her father. It is quite skilfully delineated, so that the human bond of agonised love lends its emotion to the symbolic relationship. For Tessa's tragedy contains the more subtle tragedy of Clement: his failure to surmount the experience of his betrayal in love, his consequent distrust of natural impulse and affection, his denial of any natural innocence, and his assumption of ironic detachment as a defence against life. This is the first instance of a type of dramatic relationship to be found in several of Barker's mature plays: the two central characters, usually father and child, representing inverse aspects of one truth.

The play is a medley of received impressions and reminiscences, a new structure, certainly, and conveying an individual view, but composed of many ready-made, imperfectly adapted elements.

Rebecca West is the Ibsen prototype of characters in Tessa's dilemma, though there is a much closer similarity in drawing between this Anglo-Italian girl and Hilda Wangel (at first, the Hilda of *The Lady from the Sea*). Tessa is the most convincing of the characters, nevertheless; personal insight has gone to the comprehension of a dramatic symbol, so that the borrowed form remains flushed with life in its new context. Luke Heryett, played upon by Grinnidge, recalls the duping of Manders by Engstrand, in *Ghosts*. But the pervading atmosphere of the play is by no means purely Ibsenite: the relationship of Tessa with her father and her dead mother is treated more in the manner of Sudermann;[3] the Dare family and Luke Heryett, in their narrow piety and over-concern for purity of life and conscience, might be creatures of Jones's drama; some of the passages on social morality have a Wildean, or possibly Shavian, ring; there is also apparent a similarity of conception between Clement Oldroyd and Sir Austin Feverel, although the immediate impact made by the two characters is rather different.[4] The too frequent substitution of literature—or drama—regurgitated, for freshness of observation is one sign, perhaps, of a very young man's sense of his insufficient human experience.

In some ways this is certainly immature work, the product of a bookish, but untutored, mind. Beside the genuine insights into character and experience are traces of a rather fevered imagination, nourished on exotic and melodramatic fare. The errors of taste and judgment in it may well have been necessary to Barker's self-education as a dramatist. There is much crudity in technique, only too probably reflective of plays in which both authors had acted: Tessa, hidden in the curtains of a window-seat, overhears Naomi murmuring a letter aloud; a similar device is used at the catastrophe, when Tessa, again concealed by curtains, her presence unknown to either of the others, overhears her father talking to Sir Noel and then stabs herself. But at least—it is a common virtue of plays written by actors, sometimes the only one!—the authors are throughout writing for a solid, actual stage, the structure of which is made to convey meaning, as it begets incident. Certain episodes, such as Tessa's outburst against the way that Clement treats his horse, or her tearing of her hat, when he has objected to the roses with which it is decorated, are at once psychologically convincing and dramatically expressive. The beginning of a search for a style of dialogue adequate to dramatic purposes is here, too. Experiments in the compression and fragmentation of speech, sacrificing logical syntax to vigour and point, are continued in Barker's manuscript alterations to the typed copy of the play.

*　　*　　*

In its content, *The Weather-Hen* is the least ambitious of the three plays; it is also the one finished product of the collaboration, showing the greatest degree of restraint and control. In theme one of the multitude of variations on *A Doll's House*, it yet follows in the native comedy tradition of Robertson and Pinero at their best.

The heroine, Eve Prior, having drifted into a marriage that offered her security, is tempted to escape from its failure and the bankruptcy of her happiness by running away with Dicky Battye, a boy considerably younger than herself, who is chivalrously in love with her. The plan is checked, and she is saved from social and moral self-destruction, by the intervention of an old friend and fellow-actor, James Ferguson, who enlists the help of the boy's father. The shock of the check and Ferguson's appeals to her native honesty and sense of justice awaken Eve to genuine responsibility and test her power to stand alone. At the end of the play, Ferguson departs for Canada and Eve prepares to join a touring theatrical company, in spite of the evident sympathy between them.

There was some objection, when the play was produced, that the authors had gone out of their way to avoid the obvious 'happy ending', but their response was merely to state more clearly in the revised version the motives originally implied: 'You don't want your freedom—you're not fit for it. You want another protector,' exclaims Ferguson, when Eve suggests that *he* take her away from her husband, 'I love you—but I'm no use.' The infringement of the social code, though it enters into consideration, is treated rather cursorily: it is not from the conventional sin that Ferguson wishes to save Eve, but rather from a selfish care to preserve conventional virtue at the expense of realities, the boy's freedom and ultimate happiness. The deadly sin is to hold back from full self-commitment, and the choices are made in no narrow social context, but between what makes for life and what for death. In this sense, the play is a celebration of the tenacity of human courage and the power of spiritual regeneration; for what takes place in Eve is not moral discovery only, but a renewal of life. There is no mechanical referring of an unanswered question to the audience, in the end; the leaving of the play open is here—as it will be in *The Marrying of Ann Leete*—a positive statement of the destructive irrelevance of form, the tragic implications of formulation, and the necessity of yielding to the flow of life.

By this time, the two dramatists had learnt the value of ironic detachment, expressed in its crudest form here in the introduction of farcical situations alongside elements of potential tragedy, notably in the scene of the arrival of Dicky's parents at the cottage in Staines to which he is bringing Eve, and in the subsequent encounters. They had discovered a still rarely tapped spring of humour in the clash of subjective and objective views of experience: a humour that restores balance and health, as the views are reconciled and emerge in a delicate comedy at which one must smile but can never laugh, so mixed is the ridicule with sadness, or anguish, or the simple dignity of accepted humiliation. For the realism of this play depends less on setting, action, or even character, than on absolute fidelity to the truth of mood and feeling, to the shifting and impure quality of most emotion.

The dialogue strikes a balance between naturalistic and evocative. It is elliptical, laconic, ironically ambiguous. The more highly stylised and fanciful effects are reserved mainly for the scenes between Eve and Jim Ferguson, when time, that measure of external action, seems suspended and the emphasis is thrown on their half-hidden consciousness.[5] A device which Granville Barker was later to put to considerable use is employed in the revised text to point the thematic value of the action: it is the use of words in significant counterpoint. 'Dicky,' says Eve, in Act II, 'is a man of honour,' and Ferguson retorts: 'When you're discarding one social code, I think it's more honourable not to trade on another.' At the close of the Act, when he threatens to stop the planned elopement, she protests:

EVE. You have no right to interfere with my affairs—because

I was fool enough to be honest and write to you. It's not honourable.
JIM. I'm not troubled with honour.

His response implies an inversion of stock romantic values and
stock dramatic treatment such as the writers of the *grotesque* plays
(*e.g.* Chiarelli, in *The Mask and the Face*, and Synge, in *The
Playboy of the Western World*) were to pursue; and Eve's paradoxical 'fool enough to be honest' belongs to the same complex of
ideas and images as produced Wilde's epigram, 'The truths of
metaphysics are the truths of masks.' When he came to write his
last play, *His Majesty*, it was Ferguson's attitude and the image
of the mask that Barker chose for his central themes.

The Weather-Hen has not yet done with the word, 'honour'.
That last passage has given it a double edge, and we are prepared
for the full irony of its occurrence in Act III:

DICKY. What can I do?—you won't trust me.
EVE. I have trusted you.
DICKY. You've told our secret to a man I didn't even know.
EVE. Yes.
[. . .]
DICKY. You'd better have let me be to you, just like any ordinary
blackguard.
EVE. Do you want me to?
DICKY. No, I don't. I respect you far more than I love you:
though I love you too. But it wouldn't be any use their interfering
then.
EVE. I must do as you wish.
DICKY. Do you love me?
EVE. I'm very fond of you.
DICKY. Unless you love me I don't think it would be right. I
love you enough—at least I hope I do.
EVE. I don't love you.
DICKY. But you want to be free from Prior?
EVE. Yes.
DICKY. And to marry me.
EVE. (*Doesn't answer.*)
DICKY. It's an honour to be made use of.
EVE. I've never lied to you about this.
DICKY. Oh, no—.
EVE. Nothing binds you to me, Dicky.
DICKY. My honour.
EVE. (*With an hysterical crack in her voice*) Oh, how funny.

Behind all the play's argument about honour there lie the Shakespearian definitions, of course. But here Dicky's words, 'I respect you far more than I love you: though I love you too,' are his unconscious echo of Lovelace:

> I could not love thee, dear, so much,
> Lov'd I not Honour more.

The woman's virtue is being measured by the old, high, masculine standard; and condemnation is implied by the antithesis between her demand for freedom and Dicky's assertion of the responsibility that binds him.

*   *   *

In the explorations of *The Weather-Hen* some reviewers saw irresponsible cleverness, and its novelty lays *Our Visitor to Work-a-Day* open to the same charge. Barker—it is hard to believe that any of the dialogue is not his—seems carried away into a tortuous subtlety of expression that goes beyond the demands of the particular dramatic necessity and stiffens into mannerism. Yet the impression of power survives; and the element of brash virtuosity is subordinate to a genuine and sustained attempt to find a dynamic language that might give to naturalistic drama the dimensions of poetic experience.

The action is mainly interior, and the dramatists have tried to capture the meaning they see in the life-process itself, the 'world-work' to which the text alludes. They are not at all moments successful in fusing the literal and symbolic: we remain conscious of two levels. In literal terms, the plot is slight and rather banal, concerning a marriage of youthful impulse between Griselda Green-hayes and Evelyn Gurth, poet and medical student, which, tested, reveals its insufficiency; Griselda discovers her love for an old friend, Dr. John Greatorex, while Evelyn, in London for 'hospitals', has an abortive affair with Vivien Lomax, John's former wife or mistress; the play ends with Griselda, renouncing John, awaiting Evelyn's return. The whole drama takes place in John's surgery, out-of-hours, and the effect is of a truly oppressive confinement. Through the unpainted upper window can be seen a bleak wall across the street and, twice a day, the heads of passing factory workers. For this is the ugly industrial town of Cardoxeter, mentioned among the *dramatis personae*. A freer world, the natural world of growth and blossom and fruit, is invoked in the dialogue; but Cardoxeter is 'work-a-day', the drudgery of physical existence unenlightened by any sense of purpose beyond the appeasement of bodily hunger, and the dust heap from which every creative principle is absent; the Edens of instinctive happiness must fail there, as Evelyn's and Griselda's fails.

Against this background, and from autumn to late spring, Griselda's spiritual growth continues, an inner experience, looking outwardly like passivity. It begins in mourning for the death of her father. (There is a hint of the dead man's skull beneath the roots of many of Granville Barker's flowers, and this is only the first of a number of instances in his work, when new life stirs secretly within the experience of death.) The wintry conditions of disillusion and heartbreak nurse the growth further, until the blossoming comes with her love for John. This is the 'travailing of change'.

It is from the recurrent imagery in what otherwise seems mere conversation that the course of the inner action and its significance are to be gathered. This is itself so tenuously allusive that the most careful reading can only very slowly probe out the meaning. If the thread of comprehension is not to snap, half-quotations have to be completed and the meaning of whole sentences—often already concentrated in the original—recalled at the signal of single words, *e.g.* 'jigmaker' (Hamlet's 'O God, your only jig-maker'); 'grasp' and 'reach' (Browning's 'Ah, but a man's reach should exceed his grasp, Or what's a heaven for?') in the following:

> Such guardians of the God-like as we—are we? Our grasp through disabuse, our reach fails through disuse; degeneration.[6]

The twisting of syntax in the interests of an artifically pointed prose rhythm recalls the later style of George Meredith, who has surely contributed to the imagery and thought of the play, too.

Barker was undoubtedly an admirer of Meredith, the generally acknowledged master of the English novel at the turn of the century: the New Woman, as she appears in the dramatist's work, owes many of her features to the ideal that Meredith's heroines represent; and he chose to produce Meredith's unfinished dialogue, *The Sentimentalists*, at the Duke of York's theatre in 1910, thus giving P. P. Howe occasion to remark:

> ... Mr. Granville Barker should have completed it. The rising of the curtain on the trim early-Victorian garden is comparable with the rising of the curtain on the Georgian garden in *The Marrying of Ann Leete*. The same charming people in beautiful dresses talk the same literary talk with the same air of detachment.... But no one who reads *Waste* can be in any doubt as to how influenced Mr. Barker has been by the dialogue of Meredith.[7]

In retrospect, we may perceive a Meredithean quality in the style of *The Weather-Hen*, also.

The dialogue of *Our Visitor* is theatrically impossible. Actors, very carefully schooled, might make what is happening comprehensible in emotional terms and terms of character, but they would have hard work to free the dramatic movement from the literary burden it has to carry. A play, as Barker later realised, must have a surface coherence that is fairly easily grasped, or the dialogue will puzzle, distract, and eventually alienate the audience altogether. *Our Visitor* is a *Finnegan's Wake* that came early in its author's career: a failure in communication, but a worth-while struggle to say in his own way what he had thought out for himself of the manifold paradox of human existence: the responsibility that is prison and freedom; the desire that is fleshly lust and the yearning for perfection; the earth which means death, yet is also the material of creation; the sense of extreme degradation and infinite potentiality, the tug of animal nature and the tug away from it. He was exercising his intellectual sinews in preparation for his mature work, which easily subordinates an equal concentration of meaning to the movement of human experience in the drama.

The character of Vivien Lomax is interesting evidence of the element in Barker's art that is traceable to the imaginative world of the *fin de siècle*. The contradiction between matter and spirit is most obviously embodied in her. (It is also present in the confrontation of Greatorex, man of science, by Yeo, the priest; while

among Evelyn's books are found 'Swinburne and the Materia
[Medica] cheek by jowl'.) Vivien is half-whore, half-nun, a
butterfly—'wings not faded yet,' who collects boots for the Sisters.
The romantic ideal of woman and its converse are at war in her;
it is for Griselda to reconcile them.

* * *

A Miracle and *Agnes Colander*, which Barker composed without any collaborator, represent the two contrary aspects of his art
which he was to bring most completely together in *The Secret
Life*. The first is his only play in verse (if we except *Prunella* with
its light verse of so different a kind, possibly attributable to
Laurence Housman). *Agnes Colander,* on the other hand, is the
play that most nearly conforms to the type of social drama which
the period associated with Ibsen. It is more closely related to *The
Weather-Hen* than to any of Barker's other plays, but is more
homogeneous in style. The presence of a Norseman among the
characters and a line of Norwegian in the dialogue give scarcely
needed confirmation of the origins of the piece.

In one respect *Agnes Colander* has dated more obviously than
any of Barker's other plays, apart from *The Family of the Oldroyds*: it assumes a background of sexual manners and values
that has vanished, an obsession with sexual purity that is wholly
of the late nineteenth century. The play proceeds, however, to test
the conventional attitude objectively. It is concerned in part with
purity as mere social convention, an aspect of respectability, but
also seeks to identify the real value that gives its compelling power
to the ideal; and the dramatic development is essentially a process
of liberation from the confusion of temporary manners with abiding truth. 'The lilies and languors of virtue,' indeed, provided the
exotic and unnatural obverse of the *fin de siècle* mysticism of sins,
as the Tennysonian figure of Sir Galahad shadows Dorian Gray.
If Barker had not tackled this theme when he did, his honest grap-
pling with the contemporary situation, as he saw it, would have
been handicapped from the start.

The two main characters, Agnes and the young man, Alec, are
variants on Eve and Dicky in *The Weather-Hen*. Agnes, it is true,

gives the impression of a stronger-minded and more mature personality than Eve, and Alec is less of a bumpkin than Dicky occasionally seems. When the play opens, Agnes is working as a painter in her London studio, having already left her husband. She is despondent at the failure of her work and aware that this proceeds from some lifelessness in herself. Having reached the conclusion that, while she is nothing but a painter, she will never be able to paint, she is in danger of drifting back to her husband. A message from the latter, however, precipitates her decision to become the mistress of her fellow-artist and good friend, Otho Køje. The second Act is set in Brittany and reaches its climax in Agnes's quarrel with Køje, who is obviously susceptible to other women and sees no reason not to be. Act III confirms her decision to leave him and return to her work in London, but is chiefly significant in its presentation of the enlightenment that gradually comes to her, revealing the outward and inner aspects of her situation and bringing understanding both of her own nature and that of *l'homme moyen sensuel* (Barker's Don Juan). Bitterness gives way to the reflection that Køje is 'a loveable man', part child, part brute, who requires no more of any woman than that she should be his mistress and his housekeeper. Reflecting that so many women would be 'glad of the place', she admits to having always reached out for something more—and failed to find it.

She and Alec, it is indicated in Act I, made a compact of chastity for their mutual help, at the time when she left her husband. The curtain-lines of Act I make it clear that these two are the characters in which the theme is most fully realised:

> AGNES. It comes to me—how one hammers eternally at the door of this sex question.
> ALEC. I think the door is always open. People who have passed through we annoy. Those who have avoided it we shock. But the question is put to everyone of us, so it's no use pretending that it isn't there.

The mark of the rhetorical theatre is in that recognition of the presence of the audience; but it is also the admirably honest declaration of a dramatist who will proceed to find his own answer, sheltering neither behind the pretence of sophistication nor the defence of orthodoxy.

In the second Act, Alec arrives in Brittany, and the dramatist contrives to keep the two characters still in step:

> ALEC. . . . since you chose to throw yourself away—I have done likewise—why not?
> AGNES. Are you married?
> ALEC. Are you?

That brief exchange turns Agnes's challenge back upon herself and nerves her for her critical decision; the countering of question by question, half-suggesting irrelevance, anticipates one of the play's key epigrams: 'Marriage is precisely a means to prevent one seeing deep into the sex question.' By this time, Barker knows when understatement can be effective and a superficially inconsequent line can bear the manifold significance of a large part of the action. At the climax of the Act he gives such a line to Agnes—and to the actress, her opportunity:

> OTHO. But Alexander is what it pleases him to call respectful to womanhood—which means that he doesn't understand it.
> (*There is a moment's pause, then she speaks with the bitterest irony.*)
> AGNES. I have much to thank you for, Otho.

Much indeed: not only the disappointment of Alec's lapse and his present unhappiness, but her own humiliation, and a fragment of bitter understanding that will go to the making of new strength.

Act III brings further help from an unexpected source through the character of Mrs. Marjoribanks, the representative of polite society, who speaks much of the time in the accents of Wilde's drama, but is not simply a figure of stage convention. An intelligent woman, she is frank with herself, admitting that she accepts society's current values for safety's sake; and she can be frank with Agnes, when learning that she and Køje are not married:

> As woman to woman, I like you—If there were another civilised soul in this place I should cut you dead.

It is she who forces Agnes to recognise the commonalty of her womanhood, even as she tries to persuade her to stay with Køje:

My dear, I've seen some downfalls ... to the unmentionable—
haven't you? And weren't they just like us—before—and after?

Alec comes on, later in the Act, with essentially the same argu-
ments, but Agnes is readier to meet them, and the similarity serves
to mark how far she has travelled in thought. To his conventional
suggestion that a woman who is not held firm by some man will
inevitably drift to disaster, she opposes the self-reliance that she is
finding within herself. It is the form that a new kindling of life is
taking in her and enables her to teach Alec her new and profounder
faith: in the power of life to surmount moral failure. She adminis-
ters the lesson with a vigorous good sense: 'You'll be a better man
than ever you were if you'll only stop wishing yourself an
opinionated boy again;' and there is a healthy good humour in her
leave-taking of Otho:

> AGNES. I'm going.
> (*There is a pause—he stares at her without a word.*)
> In about an hour. I'll order some lunch first. Will you eat it with
> me?
> OTHO. (*Severely*) You are very cruel and unwomanly.
> AGNES. Am I?

The play has made its way out of the solemn falsities of convention, literary and dramatic as well as social, to this lively truth
to the nature of things. (There are profounder truths, and some
of them find their way into Barker's later plays.) In the lucidity of
its thought and the pointed economy of its style, *Agnes Colander*
is closely akin to the more complex *Marrying of Ann Leete*. It
could be argued that in the firmness with which it handles all its
characters, it at least equals that play.

*   *   *

Whereas *Agnes Colander* is about the everyday world in which
men have to live their lives, *A Miracle* is a small pseudo-mediæval
drama about the acceptance of death and the abrogation of self. It
is set in the darkened tower where lives the pure-spirited and loving
Baptista, a hunchback, away from the eyes of men. 'No mirror is in
the room,' she declares, 'Lest I should grow to hate myself and

die.' The beautiful Margaret, a dramatic projection of the author's search for the meaning of life in the thought of death, seeks out Baptista, her opposite in fortune and in character. Though the world seems at Margaret's feet, a consciousness of the barrenness of her living, inability to love and emptiness of virtue, have brought her premonitions of dying. Out of her own life of dreams, Baptista is able to supply the other's need; and it is *her* death that makes the climax of the little play, restoring to the other the quickening power of human sympathy.

A Miracle was produced by the Literary Theatre Society, in setting and costumes designed by Ricketts, at a matinée on 23 March, 1907.[8] The precise date of its writing is unknown; Barker had had it by him some time, when Winifred Fraser asked him for it to complete the Society's programme. It has the weaknesses of its *genre*: the remoteness of the allegory from actual life makes it insubstantial; the characters are shadows of ideas, unparticularised and incapable of engaging any strong sympathy; the very little that happens is illustrative of the author's thought rather than issuing out of the life of the characters. What is more, Barker's verse, as Max Beerbohm pointed out in a review of the performance,[9] is not powerful enough to give intensity to the parable and secure the immediate hold over the audience that is necessary to the success of so short a piece. This is, perhaps, intrinsically the least valuable of the dramatic texts that Granville Barker left. Yet it is interesting as evidence of his study of Maeterlinck and a desire to include an introspective, lyrical quality in the range of his drama.

Incidentally, it proves him thoroughly justified in his adoption of naturalism for the main body of his work; his dramatic imagination certainly operated more happily in the discipline of its more complex material. In all his major plays, however, the subjective world, the private universe in which men live as in a dream from which they cannot escape, offers its challenge and supplies its values to the world of actuality. The allegory of an exchange of life, or vicarious sacrifice, most simply presented in *A Miracle*, haunts some of Barker's later writings, most notably *The Secret Life* and the story, *Souls on Fifth*. In it is implied the intercourse of the two worlds, the two modes of human existence, which is part of the stranger and richer vision that the later plays oppose to the values of sanity and health and power for survival that are the matter of celebration in *Agnes Colander*.

*   *   *

In conception and organisation, all these early plays are impressive. *Agnes Colander* shows that Barker could write a simple play for William Archer to understand and enjoy, one that was quite practicable for the theatre of the day, yet illustrates the author's concern always to probe for understanding. The others, in varying degrees, demonstrate how much more he wished to express. They anticipate the prolific quality of thought and interest in his mature drama and contrast most strikingly with the flimsy and mechanical material of contemporary theatrical fashion. The fact that they go direct to English life, and reflect the traditions and values of the English mind, is not the least sign of a fresh vitality that they offer. In all except *A Miracle*, where the form offered a special problem, Barker is clearly aware of the essential difference between a play and a narrative: story is subordinate to dramatic shape, reflecting the rhythm of developing feeling; and the dialogue is predominantly dramatic dialogue, conveying conflict and the urgent human meanings that break now and again into incident.

CHAPTER IV

The New Dawn

The Marrying of Ann Leete can be taken as an eighteenth-century costume play about political corruption and the decay of a noble house. The plot, as distinct from the form and technique, is simple and conventional enough. Carnaby Leete, an able, but venal, turncoat politician, is approaching a crisis in his career. With a hope of office not too distantly in view, he has left the Whigs and is negotiating an alliance with the Tories. He regards the personal lives of his three children, Sarah, George and Ann, as legitimately at the service of his ambitions. Sarah's marriage to Sir Charles Cottesham cemented an earlier deal with the Whigs; George has disappointed his father's expectations by marrying a farmer's daughter; Ann remains, and Carnaby looks to advance his cause with the Tories by marrying her to Lord John Carp. By the end of Act I, the plan is well on the way to fulfilment; early in Act II, Lord John asks Ann to marry him. However, the girl then becomes the observer of her brother and sister, as crises arise in their respective marriages: Charles Cottesham's proposal for a legal separation from his wife (another political manœuvre), and the birth of twins to George's wife, Dolly.

Ann's observation is part of her fast-travelling experience and it precipitates the crisis: an act of rebellion, which implies a social revolution, for she asks the gardener, John Abud, to marry her. The unconventional alliance is celebrated in the last Act; Ann leaves her home to share her husband's cottage and humble way of life; Carnaby, his approach rejected by the Tories, is a sick and broken man, but fighting to his end; Sarah accepts the termination of her marriage and prepares to retire from the society she has loved; for George there is the prospect of a common happiness and the status of a gentleman-farmer. Some early critics were troubled by what they considered the improbability, or unnaturalness, of Ann's marriage.[1] Their bafflement was certainly the result of over-literal interpretation and an attempt to make the play fit completely into a familiar dramatic category. In fact, the drama is delicately suspended between plausible actuality and metaphysical image.

The technical audacity of the opening should jolt any audience into realising that here is something new, which requires concentrated attention. When the curtain goes up, the stage is in almost total darkness, rent by a girl's scream. This is theatricality of the most blatant sort. Two running figures enter. The play has begun with a rape. But there is hardly time for the effect to be made and the conclusion reached, before Barker disrupts both with the first words of the dialogue:

> LORD JOHN. I apologise.
> ANN. Why is it so dark?

He has skirted the disaster of the *wrong* effect as closely as possible, only swerving at the final second from melodramatic Sardoodledom into the idiom of 'the polite world' (the phrase comes later in the play) of Meredithean comedy.

The impression of that first moment is likely to remain, although it is not followed up in any obvious way in what now ensues. Far from playing an artistically irresponsible trick, however, Barker has alerted his audience to receive a meaning deep within his play that will eventually shatter the comedy of manners. For *The Marrying of Ann Leete* is, at its core, more poetic, more romantic, and concerned with a more central human experience, than a cursory reading of any passage of its dialogue would suggest.

* * *

At the present day, it is known only to a reading public; and it often proves baffling to those who are not very practised readers of plays. The principles of narrative, or logical, continuity and

smooth syntactical development have been set aside in favour of a
style of speech that is truly nothing but notation for actors, and
extremely accomplished actors, at that. An example taken at random
from Act I will serve our purpose:

> CARNABY. Sarah, when Sir Charles leaves Brighton . . .
>   SARAH *rises but will not move further.*
> CARNABY. *[Sweetly threatening.]* Shall I come to you?
>   *But she goes to him now.*
> CARNABY. By a gossip letter from town . . .
> SARAH. *[Tensely.]* What is it?
> CARNABY. You mentioned to me something of his visiting Naples.
> SARAH. Very well. I detest Italy.
> CARNABY. Let's have George's opinion.
>   *He leads her towards* GEORGE.
> GEORGE. Yes?
> CARNABY. Upon Naples.
> GEORGE. I remember Naples.
> CARNABY. Sarah, admire those roses.
> SARAH. *[Cynically echoing her father.]* Let's have George's
> opinion.

The broken syntax avoids statement, but arouses curiosity. Nothing that is said seems to mean very much in itself; but what *is* conveyed is an impression of something going on, for which the dialogue is a cover. The oblique and cryptic quality of their utterances is calculated to suggest that the minds of these characters are furiously occupied. They are using words falsely, in order to communicate sentiments that cannot be openly admitted. The fact that they understand each other shows them up as conspirators.

There is a tussle of wills going on. Carnaby's first, uncompleted sentence waits for his daughter to obey a sufficiently indicated wish. 'Shall I come to you?' is a slight flick of the whip. Sarah's hesitation and compliance give warning that she intends to resist, but also that she is afraid of her father. Her reception of the word, 'gossip,' betrays her fear of a scandal. (It is later revealed that she has compromised her reputation with Lord Arthur Carp.) Carnaby is playing with her, very smoothly, but venomously. He sees that his point has been taken and, with a merely apparent shift of ground, alludes to the fact that she did not accompany her husband to Naples. Sarah's 'Very well' is an acceptance of challenge; she will defy the accusation with a bold front to the world: 'I detest Italy.' But the whole line constitutes an admission to her father. So George is called into consultation: 'Upon Naples;' that is, upon Sarah's behaviour and, particularly, its political dangers. George is not quite sure whether he wants to play: 'I remember Naples' is non-committal. Perhaps irritated by this, the tyrant in Carnaby speaks openly now in the peremptory order: 'Sarah, admire those roses.' He intends to speak seriously to George; meanwhile, she may as well occupy herself in concealing what is going on from the others on the stage (Ann, Lord John). He can afford the punning acknowledgment that this is all *sub rosa*. But Sarah thinks that she may have an ally in George. Is he going to play Carnaby's game, or isn't he? Are the two men together going to dispose of her so high-handedly? There is a specifically feminist element in her rebelliousness: 'Let's have George's opinion.'

The delivery of all this cannot afford to be ponderous. The actors must be mentally and physically on their toes. As for the pauses, mishandled, they would produce a sagging tension; like hesitations in a piece of music, they must be part of the rhythmical line of the whole passage.

Theories of dramatic dialogue were in the air, at the end of the nineteenth century. A passage in Strindberg's Preface to *Miss Julie* (itself reflecting the theories of Zola) is so apposite as to make one wonder if Barker had read that manifesto of naturalism:

> I have avoided the symmetrical and mathematical construction of the French dialogue, and have instead permitted the minds to work irregularly, as they do in reality, where, during conversation, the cogs of one mind seem more or less haphazardly to engage those of another, and where no topic is fully exhausted. Naturally enough, therefore, the dialogue strays a good deal as, in the opening scenes, it acquires a material that later on is worked over, picked up again, repeated, expounded, and built up like the theme in a musical composition.[2]

Barker had a stylistic model nearer home, in Meredith's dialogue. Yet a similarity of theme between *Ann Leete* and Strindberg's play is suggestive of direct relationship; for Julie, also, is an aristocratic young woman who stoops to love a servant, and both dramatists identify the unconventional alliance that they present with the theme of the movement of classes.

It could be said of the dialogue of *The Marrying of Ann Leete* that 'the cogs of one mind seem more or less haphazardly to engage those of another'. The lines of Barker's text stray about, yet present a musical character in their verbal repetitions. The words dance about, interweave from speech to speech, linking into a pattern lines that seem in isolation abrupt and staccato. The single speech is not a self-sufficient unit; instead, the dialogue falls into paragraphs; and the impression of the characters as moving within a group over-rides any sense of their separate individuality.

As the play begins in darkness, the ear is likely to be the more alert, in order to supply the want of sight, and more receptive then to musical effects:

> LORD JOHN. I apologise.
> ANN. Why is it so dark?
> LORD JOHN. Can you hear what I'm saying?
> ANN. Yes.
> LORD JOHN. I apologise for having kissed you . . . almost unintentionally.
> ANN. Thank you. Mind the steps down.
> LORD JOHN. I hope I'm sober, but the air . . .
> ANN. Shall we sit for a minute? There are several seats to sit on somewhere.
> LORD JOHN. This is a very dark garden.
> *There is a slight pause.*

The first line, 'I apologise,' is the equivalent of the first statement of a subject in a musical composition. It is repeated in extended form: 'I apologise for having kissed you. . . .' The second voice introduces another subject, which the first voice repeats in variant form, at the close of the short passage: 'Why is it so dark?'—'This is a very dark garden.' A hint is given in 'Mind the steps down' that the characters may be moving in a dance measure. The evasive replies, or counter-questions, are like slight movements away from the centre, but held always within its orbit. With the pause, the first figure of the dance is completed.

Now the characters move into the second figure, returning at the end of it to positions taken in the first:

> ANN. You've won your bet.
> LORD JOHN. So you did scream!
> ANN. But it wasn't fair.
> LORD JOHN. Don't reproach me.
> ANN. Somebody's coming.
> LORD JOHN. How d'you know?
> ANN. I can h e a r somebody coming.
> LORD JOHN. We're not sitting down.

Considered in terms of sound, the two voices have now exchanged their subjects: of the themes heard in the first passage, Lord John's 'Can you hear what I'm saying?' is now taken up in Ann's emphatic 'h e a r'; and Ann's original 'Shall we sit for a minute . . .' is now echoed in Lord John's response, 'We're not sitting down.' This second stanza, also, offers its almost exactly repeated phrase: 'Somebody's coming;' 'I can h e a r *somebody coming.*'

A third voice now enters, and we are launched on a new passage, longer and more elaborate than either of its predecessors. It opens:

> GEORGE. Ann!
> ANN. Yes.
> GEORGE. My lord!
> LORD JOHN. Here.

It works back round to this, at the close:

> GEORGE. . . . . Ann, shall we return?
> LORD JOHN. She's not here.
> GEORGE. Ann.

The words, 'bet' and 'scream', the first and second subjects of the stanza before, are sounded again in this movement, combined now with 'kissed' from the first stanza. Recalling the iteration of 'I apologise', there is a more elaborate statement and repetition, both by the one voice, here:

> ANN. I had rather, my lord, that you did not tell my brother why I screamed.
> LORD JOHN. I kissed her.
> GEORGE. Did you?

ANN. I had rather, Lord John, that you had not told my brother why I screamed.

The staccato phrasing of Ann's 'Shall we sit for a minute? There are several seats to sit on somewhere', is audible once more, as she says, again with the insistent sounding of one note: 'He betted it because he wanted to bet it; I didn't want him to bet it.'[3] So the two shorter stanzas that have gone are united into a whole with this. In such deliberate and extended patterning of the dialogue, Barker has moved beyond Meredith.

The impression of a contrived analogy to courtly dance is confirmed in the words that recall Ann's 'Mind the steps down' and now signal the arrival of two more persons on the scene:

> MR. TATTON. Three steps?
> SARAH. No . . . four.

So the play is launched on its formal and even ritualistic course. Again and again we have the impression of characters taking their partners and entering into the measure. One example from the first Act is the formal quarrel between Carnaby and Lord John, through which they prompt each other with cues. The changing of partners, during the dance, may be illustrated from Act II, when the gardener, Abud, having been interviewed by George, turns to Ann and goes through the same moves over again with her, though in a variant order. The repetition of themes is not always verbally exact, and to that extent this method of composition is not strictly musical. Yet there are sufficient verbal echoes to increase the hearer's awareness of recurrent motifs and to intensify his perception of the replacement of a straightforward logical sequence by a rhythmical movement to and fro. And the fact is significant that, within the choreographic design of the play, the characters move rather like marionettes, the life in them subdued to the ordered and predetermined motion of the dance. The counter-movement—the more conventional outer action—is, by contrast, rather jerky: a fault to be mastered in later plays.

*   *   *

Until the last scene, *The Marrying of Ann Leete* has the nature of a long ballet, or masque, analysable into a succession of dances, showing variations in style and tempo, and imposing a severe discipline upon the performers. In Act I, the dance of courtship alternates with a dance of antagonism: Carnaby Leete assumes the rôle of the possessive father, jealously defending his daughter's honour against Lord John Carp's attempts on it, in an ostentatious masquerade, through which he tortuously pursues a political advantage; and the verbal duelling, feint, thrust and parry, is conducted to the climax of a challenge to an actual duel, a climax in mime, a ritual gesture, as Carnaby strikes his opponent across the face with a twist of bass, left behind by the gardener.

It is possible to analyse Acts II and III into a sequence of *pas de deux* and *pas de trois*. The pantomimic quality evident at the climax of Act I re-appears in Act III, at the main climax of the play, in an emphatically symbolic action, when the young gardener sets down his tools, emerges from the background, where he has been working almost unnoticed, and carries the sick Carnaby from the centre of the stage up the steps to the terrace and so off.

The setting remains unchanged from the beginning of the play to this climax: there are two stage levels, representing a terrace, bordered with rose trees, twin flights of broad steps leading down from its corners to a grassy space with a fountain in the centre. Such a set demands graceful movement from the actors and invites decorative groupings and the plotting of intricate, visually satisfying chains of moves, along both levels and up and down the steps; the dance rhythm was surely not intended to be verbal only. In the fourth Act, two indoor scenes are sharply contrasted. The first, the scene of a wedding in the great house, is an animated Hogarth painting, colourful, noisy, public, a grotesque *ensemble*. Barker keeps this scene constantly in flux, with single figures and groups making eruptive entrances and, as abruptly, pouring off; and he gives to the whole movement the character of a dance of death.

The final scene of the play falls outside the pattern of the dance. The insistent rhythms are stilled. Only two characters appear, Ann and the gardener, who are still and seated for much of the time. The interior of a tiny cottage appears on the stage, and it is the condition of a greater intimacy than the play has previously allowed. The whole visual scene is drained of colour by the method of lighting: it seems to be illumined by a single candle. The place is dark and cold, in the wintry night before a new dawn.

The change in dramatic style for the last scene is essential to the communication of theme. As Act I advances, the sun rises. The light grows gradually brighter, while the meaning of the first incident, prompting Ann's scream, is clarified; though what is now offered is its daylight meaning, matter-of-fact: behind the kiss there was a bet, and the gesture of love was a betrayal of innocence. The first treachery is made cloak to another, as Carnaby proceeds to conduct a political intrigue under the pretence of exacting satisfaction for insult. Throughout the Act, nothing is done, and little is spoken, without a political, or diplomatic, intention. The action is played out according to the formal manners and insincerities of the 'polite world'. One of the key ideas of the play emerges through the recurrence of the words, 'game,' 'sport,' 'play'. 'Tell me the rules . . . for next time,' says Ann, looking back in enlightenment on the events of Act I. Her father, in that first game, holds the ace and calls the suit; and he conducts the action to the culmination of the duel: the eighteenth-century's formalised, cold-blooded game of love and death, the game of honour.[4] This is the ballet of the polite world, which moves, when the time comes, into the *danse macabre*. The extreme artifice of the convention Barker employs fosters a realisation of what is false in the life of that world. With the last scene, there is an escape from artificiality to the simpler truth of human nature.

*   *   *

The precise period of the play is the time of the French Revolution and the contemporary English revolution in taste and sentiment, which became the Romantic Movement. The aristocratic house of the Leetes is an old one, already fallen somewhat into decay; in its name, Markswayde, may be heard a punning allusion to Karl Marx.[5] For this is the first of Barker's plays to be primarily concerned with the growth of society as a living organism, and its action represents the natural process whereby civilisations decline and new ones emerge. Yet the form and style of the drama are more closely allied to Æsthetic art than to the new scientific and socialist realism.

Intellectual maturity tends to precede full human maturity in our society; and Barker, twenty-one years old when he wrote this play, in 1899, was not then ready to explore his subject of the society moving towards disintegration with the directness that he was later to employ. *The Marrying of Ann Leete* is recognisably a young man's play, product of an integrity of thought and imagination, to which actual experience of the world contributes little. To say this gives the general measure of its limitations. The young dramatist chose to write a pastiche, exquisite and artificial; a composition not too distantly related in manner to the verse of Austin Dobson, to Max Beerbohm's *The Happy Hypocrite*, Aubrey Beardsley's illustrations to *The Rape of the Lock*, or the famous contents page of the first number of *The Savoy* (1896). (Indeed, Carnaby Leete bears the marks of close relationship to Beardsley's disdainful, masterly and unexpectedly mercurial John Bull, armed with a pen, elegantly cloaked and garlanded.) The pastiche convention at first seems to belie the topicality of Barker's theme and even to typify the retreat of art from life, offering prettiness— damning word!—rather than beauty. It is doubtful, however, if he could have succeeded so well with a theme of such dimensions by any other means available to him at that time.

Some genuine eighteenth-century drama persisted in the contemporary repertory, and there was a vogue for the pseudo-historical play of the period, too. Barker had already made the abortive effort to dramatise *Henry Esmond*, in collaboration with Berte Thomas. It is likely enough that he carried over his sense of period manners and speech into this new play, written for the same kind of contemporary actor, accustomed to move through the pattern of the minuet, or gavotte, and able to bring a disciplined elegance to artificial manners and stylised speech, which would be a distancing and cooling medium for theatrical emotion. Thackeray may have suggested the possibility of a costume drama which would be serious, apparently anti-romantic, avoiding the merely lush. The characters of *The Marrying of Ann Leete* will not serve as flattering, over-size reflections of the audience in fancy dress and, confined as they are by the spare dialogue, they do not lend themselves easily to egoistic display in the acting. Subdued to the necessities of the play as a whole, they are such broken lights, serving to illuminate an impersonal theme, as Barker later recognised Chekhov's characters to be.[6]

To convey the essence rather than the illusion of life was the aim. If no vitalising spark is introduced, nothing is more stale and wearisome than pastiche; the term is, consequently, pejorative in common use. *The Marrying of Ann Leete* succeeds and is important, because its form is controlled and adapted by a constantly alert intelligence and a tension is maintained between the stylised medium and something dynamic and fluid in the content.

The reduction of the dialogue to a succession of brief, fragmentary utterances, in which certain words and phrases recur insistently, has the effect of giving to the reiterated words a greater emotional resonance than they would have in a context of greater explicitness. In this respect, the dialogue of *Ann Leete* is reminiscent of Maeterlinck's echoing lines and similarly constitutes a delicate and subtle notation of the course of unexpressed feeling. Simple monosyllables emerge as key words and echo in the mind in isolation, out of any syntactical context: 'dark,' 'light,' 'ghost,' 'rose,' 'air,' 'rain,' 'world' are chief among them. Out of the imprecise and very general response that they arouse in the hearer's consciousness, something that we may call the mood of the play proceeds. This symbolist technique prepares the way for the action to pass, at the play's climax, almost completely beyond credible actuality and to take on a primarily symbolic identity. It is the vehicle of a melancholy and sensitive, but subdued vitality that is neo-romantic and decadent. It is appropriate that what is probably the most satisfactory and appreciative account of the Stage Society performance of the play, in 1902, should have been written by Arthur Symons.[7]

Through its blending of tenuous feeling with pointed finesse, *Ann Leete* recalls the short plays of Musset and Rostand's *Romanesques;*[8] and it has its native *locale* in their *pays bleu*, with its deceptive resemblance to a period setting. Against this background move characters that are, for the most part, only masks. Yet the central characters, lightly sketched though some of them are, are not stock figures responding to stock situations according to formula; they are exploring figures of the author's creative reverie.

The very obliqueness and unobtrusiveness of the play's allusions to historical events indicate the dramatist's desire to keep the action imprecisely localised. He might have tried to write a play directly about the French Revolution, a study of the social crisis in western civilisation at the point when it was first most clearly manifested. As it is, Carnaby Leete's sigh, 'My poor France!' (Act III) is the strongest hint given. Granville Barker's precise subject could not be expressed in specific historical terms: what he set himself to say was at once too generally philosophical and too individual in its implications. His play is concerned with an inner crisis: a universal reality, but an intimate reality, too. For Barker, also, sees everything that happens as happening in the soul and casting its shadow in external events. The process at work in the seemingly impersonal great occasions of history is approached, in this play, through the consciousness of a young girl: the human significance of revolution and the blind movement of social forces are probed through the experience that leads to, and follows from, Ann Leete's critical decision.

The historical drama, as usually conceived, has a strong narrative interest, as it attends to the shaping of outer events. In Barker's variant of the type, the narrative element is subordinate to the shifting of mood; and it is by the mood, rather than explicitly, that the major part of the play's statement is made. Here is a kinship to Chekhov's art; and *The Cherry Orchard*, in particular, is most interestingly close to this play in theme and certain aspects of method and symbolism. It is an instance of one of those remotely conceived correspondences that accidents of time so strangely bring forth. Maeterlinck, from whom the two dramatists, Barker and Chekhov, certainly learnt, was an artistic link; the similar awareness shown by the Englishman and the Russian testified to their participation in a culture that spread across Europe at the time: *fin de siècle* England and Russia in transition had both received the prophecies of Marx and Tolstoy.

The garden of Markswayde and the Cherry Orchard alike represent the beauty of an aristocratic culture, a costly luxury, now in decline. The desire for escape and the fear of exile, hope and despair have warring possession of the characters in both plays. Like the sale of the Cherry Orchard, Carnaby Leete's announcement, 'Markswayde is to let,' signifies the close of an era; and in both plays the young depart in search of new life, yet uncertain of finding it, or of the form it will take. The dance in Chekhov's play has its counterpart in the wedding reception at Markswayde, the sense of dissolution and the frenzy of approaching death hovering about each; the parasites and the new country *bourgeois* are there, in each, ready to dismember the spoil. The difference in the power of the two works is related to the fact that *The Cherry Orchard* is not pastiche, but approaches life direct. Yet two other details of presentation are curiously analogous: the opening of both plays in the pregnant atmosphere of the darkness just before dawn, the extinguished candle serving as an accessory visual symbol; and the ambivalent response of Carnaby, in the one play, and Lopakhin, in the other, mirroring the double value of the climax as end and beginning.

The imagery of darkness and light is relevant to Ann's personal drama and to the social theme of the play. It is there in the darkness and gradual dawn of Act I and in the note of darkness struck twice in the first passage of dialogue (quoted on p. 61); it is implied by the branched candlestick, 'its lights out,' brought by Mr. Tatton 'for a link', and again in the final scene, where the darkness is less of death than of the wintry earth, holding the seeds of new life. Abud raises the candle to light Ann up the stairs; and the gesture and the token of birth and continuity balance the earlier symbolism of the dead branches: the light extinguished; the family tree, or tree of life, withered. A verbal imagery of light is to be found in Act II, in Parson Remnant's definition of 'pellucid': 'letting light through'. In that context, it is the rain, for which the parched earth waits, that is 'pellucid'. At the climax, which comes later in the same Act, Carnaby uses the word with increased force:

> CARNABY. Take me indoors. I heard you ask the gardener to marry you.
> ANN. I asked him.
> CARNABY. I heard you say that you asked him. Take me in ... but not out of the rain.
> [. . .]
> ANN. If we two were alone here in this garden and everyone else in the world were dead ... what would you answer?

6

ABUD. *[Still amazed.]* Why . . . yes.
CARNABY. Then that's settled . . . pellucid.

Carnaby is delirious from the wound received in the duel. The disturbed mind serves the dramatist as a vehicle for a preternatural clarity, a clairvoyance, that focuses the symbolic value of the scene: the recovery of Eden, the return of fertility. Ann's proposal of marriage to the gardener is a token of a liberation from false and outworn values: 'I don't believe in you, Papa,' she has just declared. Yet, in his heralding of the rain, Carnaby seems to express his own relief at the breaking of an evil enchantment which has lain upon the whole garden and upon himself: 'Take me in . . . but not out of the rain.' This is the place where light and darkness, life and death, meet. The power that is passing and the new power, coming into being, share the illumination of wisdom. The complex dramatic relationship between Carnaby and Ann thus holds the central position of interest in the drama.

*   *   *

Carnaby Leete is an anticipation of the elder Voysey. Both are representations of the histrionic personality that covers a destructive criticism of society. In neither can a detached observer trace adequate rational motives to account for the elaborate chicanery that undermines order and stability; it is the real principles of society, as opposed to the professed, that are laid bare in the nefarious activity of each. Both characters show a natural superiority to their dupes that, confronted by what it profoundly despises, finds subtly insulting expression. Both are egoists, generally merciless even to those for whom they have some affection. Carnaby, however, is more penetrating in self-knowledge, and he is denied Voysey's zest in the game of treachery; liberated more completely, in his thought, from the assumptions of his class, he is nearer the end of things in his search for value and discovery of vanity. He is able, as Voysey is not, to lower the mask; he wears the habit of his world more loosely; and his revenges on society are more deliberate. Ann's marriage and the reception held at Markswayde serve as expressions of his strange irony. This is one manner of suicide, carried out with a final contemptuous flourish. There is power in him, even at that point in affairs, to move the puppets, arrange the scene, realise his fantasy, and turn what is effectually his end into a dramatic occasion. Barker's drama contains no more impressive figure.

Carnaby's recognition of the principles of 'the polite world' is most clearly revealed in an exchange with Sarah, in Act II:

> CARNABY. Fight for your honour.
> SARAH. You surprise me sometimes by breaking out into cant phrases.
> CARNABY. What is more useful in the world than honour?
> SARAH. I think we never had any . . . we!

The world's estimate is in terms of utility, of what can be bought and sold, as Ann's innocence is bought and sold in the two kisses she receives from Lord John. 'It's time for me to vanish from this world,' declares Sarah to her lover, Lord Arthur Carp, in the last Act, 'because I've nothing left to sell.' It is a transparent fiction, this so-called honour, that exists in the eyes of the world, a matter of public prestige and reputation that can be established or denied arbitrarily, in a game of chance, by a public demonstration. Carnaby's willingness to exploit this 'honour' is indicated in his threat to Lord John: 'You'll value that kiss when you've paid for it.' As late as the last Act there comes a reminder of the virginity that is an economic asset:

> MR. CROWE. Damn *you*, sir . . . have you paid him to marry the girl?
> *[. . .]*
> CARNABY. *[. . .]* This is a maid's marriage, I assure you.

Sarah has become wholly a creature of the polite world, feeding on prestige, flattered vanity, the pleasures of the town and its artificial excitements, including the illicit love affair that relieves boredom, yet avoids passion and the self-commitment passion exacts. She has another refuge, also: 'Why, who doesn't love sport!' is her rallying cry in Act I, softened in her later protest to the lawyer, Mr. Tetgeen: 'I am a little fond of play.' It is a more innocuous counterpart to the deadly sport with lives which is the one passion that rescues Carnaby from sophisticated *ennui*. The name, Lady Cottesham (based on *cot, cottage* and *sham*), hints at Sarah's nature and the dramatic function that Barker intends her to fulfil: a being of false impulses and failed motherhood, no longer capable of choosing simplicity, she is a foil to the truth that is in Ann and Ann's choice. At the climax of the action, Ann speaks a curse upon this sister, whose character and fate have been shaped by the lost honour of the Leetes. The curse on her family and its whole world is gleefully recorded by the drunken chaplain, Tozer, at the wedding celebrations: 'Damn you all!'

True honour is a secret thing, guarded as in the heart of a rose: the symbol with which Ann is identified.

In the first three Acts, the fashionably dressed and powdered figures move about the old and rather formal garden: a grassy patch, with a fountain in the centre, sunk below a balustraded terrace and bordered by rose trees. The dialogue draws attention to the fact that there is stagnant water in the fountain and the roses are over-blown. The gardener continues to move silently about his work of trimming the rose-trees, so directing the visual attention of the audience. The rose is the traditional flower of the Earthly Paradise, which has also its pool of Narcissus, or well of truth; but this Paradise is a Waste Land, in which Carnaby is to walk, its king, with a green wound in his arm.

For him, the association of the rose is, characteristically, classical: 'Emblem of secrecy among the ancients.' Secrecy, as he speaks the words in Act I, appears as an attribute of intrigue, but Sarah soon extends the range of the rose image to include the enfolded life:

> LORD JOHN. I suppose she, or any young girl, is all heart.
> CARNABY. What is it that you call heart ... sentimentally speaking?
> SARAH. Any bud in the morning.

The innocence of youth, the hidden promise of the innermost life, must pass away, it is implied, by a natural process of time and change; the freshness of spontaneous feeling ceases to be adequate as a response to the experience of life.

At the beginning of Act II, Parson Remnant returns a book that

he has borrowed: 'Ballads by Robert Burns . . . a very vulgar poet!'
Barker seems to be counting on his audience's thinking first of the
'red, red rose'. He is certainly using consciously one of the primary
symbols of the romantic attitute, associated now with the ideas
of passion and natural vigour: the challenge that wildness offers
to cultivation, passion to reason, peasant strength to aristocratic
refinement; and in the hint of the revolution of sentiment is an
undertone of social revolution.

The emblem of the rose was much favoured by the artists of the
'nineties: Yeats took his Secret Rose from the Alchemical tradition; Lionel Johnson seems to have valued the same symbol for its
meaning in Catholic tradition and as used by Dante (also the
source of Eliot's 'rose garden'). By the time *The Marrying of Ann
Leete* is completed, these connotations also are gathered into the
total symbolism. Abud, who threads his way through the first three
Acts, is a significantly named figure of the integrity that Ann ultimately chooses. He is a reminder of Rousseau's myth of natural
virtue; 'à Dieu,' Carnaby makes his epigram on his daughter's
wedding, 'she enters Nature's cloister,' and the concepts of the
noble savage and the dedicated virgin are united. Ann's flight from
civilisation is, indeed, in the very pattern of romantic escape. In
action and dialogue, however, the dramatist is concerned to re-
define the romantic approach and romantic values. Ann's spiritual
journey acquaints her with the debasement of romance that
counterfeits truth and also with the limitations of the simple
romantic vision.

*   *   *

The word itself is appropriated by the Leetes' neighbour and
guest, Mr. Tatton, in his response to the news that Lord John has
asked Ann to marry him: 'I guessed so . . . give me a bit
of romance!' The association strikes Ann by its incongruity and is
in her mind still, when she replies to her sister's felicitations:

> SARAH. . . . . I wish you all the happiness of courtship days.
> GEORGE. Arcadian expression!
> ANN. I believe it means being kissed . . . often.
> SARAH. Have you not a touch of romance in you, little girl?

ANN. Am I not like Mr. Dan Tatton? He kisses dairy-maids
and servants and all the farmers' daughters . . .

Tatton is the simple sportsman, not very intelligent, not very sensitive, living to amuse himself, yet not brutalised, not degenerate. At worst, he is the dupe of the society to which he belongs. To Tatton's view, that first kiss concealed a bet; the more subtly treacherous intrigue is beyond his imagining. 'Tatton is honest,' is the verdict of Carnaby, in whose vocabulary 'honour' and 'honesty' are carefully dissociated.

The life of instinctual pleasures has another champion, much lower in the scale than Tatton: the contemptible Tozer, chaplain to old Lady Leete. Without honesty and without human dignity, brutalised by unrestrained indulgence, he chants his creed in the words, 'Marriage means enjoyment!' The disgusted Dr. Remnant adds his gloss, in the language of polite society: 'I have found in my own copy of the prayer book no insistence upon a romantic passion.' When Tozer claims to be 'a gentleman . . . by nature', Sir George Leete offers a prompt comment: 'Lie down . . . you dog.' In Tozer is seen the underside of an intellectual culture, from which the veneer of manners has been removed; but he also indicates the state man is reduced to, when he equates animal and natural, appetite and love. Here is warning that the Nature to which Ann returns is of another order.

The romantic return to simplicity is reflected in the play in two forms. It may seem, superficially, that George's marriage to Dolly, the farmer's daughter, is an anticipation of Ann's more extreme, but similar, defiance of society in marrying the gardener. (It *is* such an anticipation, in so far as the playwright is concerned to make Ann's marriage more credible to the literal mind; and the establishment of an earlier association between Dolly and Abud bridges a social chasm that might otherwise seem impassable.) When the news of the birth of his children comes to her brother, Ann recognises from his reponse the distinction between real and unreal and the wholeness that comes with submission to the power of life. But his marriage otherwise has a radically different meaning from hers, signified in the contrast between the marriage partners of their choice: the commonplace Dolly, who aspires to rise socially, and

Abud, sufficiently undefined as a character to carry the symbolism of Adam unfallen, a figure of content, who challenges the acquisitive society with his belief that: 'The less a man wants, Miss, the better.' About the union of Ann and Abud there clings a numinous quality;[9] it is the rose, beside the 'wayside flower' (the natural choice with no spiritual enrichment) which George has plucked. Barker is concerned with something more than a deliberate reversal of the upward and onward movement of progress, in accordance with Tolstoy's doctrine and Morris's; the conclusion he was to draw in a preface to Tolstoy's plays is apposite here:

> ... it may be ... that the simple life, even as its fruits in art, is like the kingdom of God, within us, and not to be counterfeited elsewhere.[10]

Elements of romantic—or neo-romantic—feeling enter the play with occasional hints of the supernatural. The theme of the *revenant* is recurrent and evocative of an atmosphere of dream, or of the twilight between life and death or between two civilisations. The word, 'ghost,' is used (with undoubted reminiscence of Ibsen) four times: at the beginning, when George comes out into the darkness to find his sister ('. . . what ghost or other bird of night or beast . . .?'), later in the same Act, when the revellers look at each other in the light of the newly risen sun ('What ghosts we seem!'); and finally twice when Sarah is reluctant to return to her 'happiness' ('I'm tired of that world . . . which goes on and on, and there's no dying . . . one grows into a ghost . . . visible . . . then invisible [. . .] the painted ghosts were very ill to see').

Other lines create a similar *frisson*, as when Carnaby lays his mask aside:

> CARNABY. . . . Ann, I first saw your mother in this garden . . . there.
> ANN. Was she like me?
> SARAH. My age when she married.
> CARNABY. She was not beautiful . . . then she died.
> ANN. Mr. Tatton thinks it a romantic garden.
> CARNABY. [*Pause.*] D'ye hear the wind sighing through that tree?
> ANN. The air's quite still.

CARNABY. I hear myself sighing . . . when I first saw your mother in this garden . . . that's how it was done.

The romance known to Tatton is dispersed, at that; but a sense of invisible presences remains, in the sadness and weariness. The slightly eerie and melancholy sense, as of a spirit passing, comes again, when Carnaby remarks: 'How still! Look . . . leaves falling already.' The effect obtained is very close to that which follows the mysterious sound in the air, heard in Act II of *The Cherry Orchard*: it is strangely disturbing, ominous; the stillness communicates the characters' state of waiting for an end yet to come. It is the romantic nostalgia for death, the mood of decadence, that Carnaby voices and the whole episode implies. They are themselves the ghosts, until Ann breaks the spell upon them, time and the seasons resume their flux, and all that is decayed can die.

The wedding scene is also the scene of the obsequies of what Markswayde has represented; the wedding dance is also a *danse macabre*. The grotesque partners who focus attention on this last aspect of the scene are Lady Leete, Carnaby's mother, decrepit, blind, deaf, an animated corpse, and her grinning chaplain, whose grace is 'Damn you all!' and whose belief is only in Hell. The mixture of pathos, terror, indignity and farce, that characterises the dance, is summed up in his sudden, drunken cry: 'Silence there for the corpse!' The harmless, gaping crowd that invades Markswayde, under Carnaby's ironical eye, is the masquerade equivalent of a rabble of bloodthirsty pillagers. The potential violence in the scene is symbolised in the pistol that Carnaby levels at Abud. The jealousy, iconoclasm, parasitic greed and ambition, which are fuel for revolution, are present; and the innocence of Mr. Prestige's remark, 'One could hang bacon here!' awakens reflections of a more startling nature.[11] As it is, there is a negation of order in the violation of established barriers of rank and taste that the strange assembly represents, and in the outraging of good manners. Tozer presides as a lord of misrule, and his glee sounds a dionysiac note of destructive passion: a prelude, it may be, to the birth of a new order.

A mood of resignation possesses Sarah and her father, an ability to let life go which is denied to egoism. Sarah, to herself a rapidly fading ghost, admits: 'It's time for me to vanish from this world;' and, in Carnaby's imagination, the image of the spectre is fused with the idea of dying light: 'Lately, one by one, opinions and desires have been failing me . . . a flicker and then extinction.' The note of doubt is audible in his voice for the first time, as he seems to comprehend Ann's motives and even to participate in the course she takes:

> CARNABY. It doesn't matter.
> GEORGE. Smile. Let's be helpless gracefully.
> CARNABY. There are moments when I'm not sure—
> GEORGE. It's her own life.

When Ann goes to her father to say good-bye, he admits, in effect, the justice of what George has said, in words that are intimate and gentle in their restraint:

> CARNABY. *[Quietly, as he kisses her cheek.]* I can do without you.

This is an abandonment of possessiveness and its stranglehold on life in favour of a gospel like Abud's, 'The less a man wants, Miss, the better.' Nothing could be further from the manner of his dismissal of George, in Act III:

> CARNABY. The begetting you, sir, was a waste of time.

The affection between father and daughter, at this point, reemphasises their dramatic relationship as complementary figures, enacting together a single complex process. The principle of continuity is as inherent in Barker's vision of human life as is the principle of man's social existence. So now Ann takes up and continues the search Carnaby has left and turns his destructive criticism of the old into a positive assertion of the new. When she is content to live, he can be content to die.

The theme of imprisonment within the self is one that Barker's later plays explore more fully, but it is certainly emergent in *Ann Leete*. It is implicit in Carnaby's 'polite' allusion to the woman's imprisonment in marriage: 'I have always held that to colour in the world-picture is the greatest privilege of the husband.' It is more fully realised in his detachment and scepticism, which correspond to a sense of limitation; for he has found nothing greater than himself to believe in. A gesture and related image reveal his sense of this; his usual irony seems partly laid aside, as he talks to Dr. Remnant:

> Ours is a little world, Parson . . . a man may hold it here.
> [*His open hand.*]

It is the disappointed remark of a ruler who has found himself the slave of his circumstances. When Sarah exclaims, 'Papa . . . your food's intrigue,' his response is: 'Scold at society . . . and what's the use'; and his musings review the marriage of convenience of which he was born, the marriage of convenience that he made himself, and the issues of rank and wealth that have come to nothing.

Both Ann and Sarah use metaphors of capture. The idea of escape is first introduced in Act I, when Sarah urges her sister: 'Never run away.' Ann takes it up, when Lord John has made his proposal:

> ANN. . . . . Sally, don't let me be forced to marry.
> GEORGE. Force of circumstances, my dear Ann.
> ANN. Outside things. Why couldn't I run away from this garden and over the hills . . . I suppose there's something on the other side of the hills.
> SARAH. You'd find yourself there . . . and circumstances.

Carnaby's identification of the escape from the established order with escape from self ('You have no more right to commit suicide than to desert the society you were born into') confirms the force of the description, 'a runaway,' applied to the heroine in Act IV. From society's point of view, escape is indistinguishable from exile: 'Banished to a damned hole in the provinces' is Carnaby's contemptuous gloss on Sarah's notion of leaving the polite world. The paradox prepares for a shift in the symbolism of the garden of Markswayde, after the climax, so that Ann's ten-mile trudge away from it, in the pouring rain, appears as both a journey from the

Waste Land and an expulsion from Paradise into the world of toil and mortality. The verbal echoes of 'curse' and 'damnation', heard earlier in the play, have been further preparation for the reversal of values in the final scene.

Barker had already tried to communicate the experience of the mind's awakening and progress to maturity through the character of Griselda, in *Our Visitor*. He succeeds more completely now. 'Wisdom cometh with sorrow, O my sister,' was George's prophetic comment, and the mood of the scene at the cottage conveys directly the sense of loss and gain inextricably intermingled, as the greedy desire for happiness, such as life cannot give, yields to acceptance of the burden of knowledge, a fruit paid for in terms of life. It is beauty, not prettiness, that this last scene offers: a beauty touched with the poignancy of mortality.

Acceptance, content, is as strong an element as sadness in the unusual mixed mood. Abud contributes to it a tentative, shy hope, an innocent, sensitive pride, an inarticulate wonder; in Ann, the clarity of mind that led to decision is accompanied by a willed submissiveness and feelings still numb from hurt, withdrawn and frozen, like the bulbs in the wintry soil that Abud shows her and that she turns from indifferently. In the bare cleanliness of the place, the two are alone, strange to each other and subdued by the strangeness; the chill of winter is in the trembling of Abud's hand and in Ann's shrinking from his kiss. The key is turned in the lock; there is no going back; the escape 'over the hills' has ended in this narrow cell: prison, bed, cloister, grave, the narrow future to which they are now committed.

The light of a single candle hardly disperses the shadows. This is no occasion for vivid emotion; they are in the place of reflection, quiescent. 'God help us both,' says Abud. They sit hand-in-hand. 'I'll do my part,' says Ann, 'something will come of it.' This seems the negation of romantic feeling, yet implies a metaphysical spaciousness to counterbalance the apparent bondage to stern circumstances. It is a resolution, not a solution, that the end of the play offers: an opening out of life to undefined possibilities.

One of the frankest acknowledgments that the eighteenth-century setting and costumes are mere illusions of the dramatist's fantasy comes in Act II:

ANN. I want to take people mentally.
GEORGE. You want a new world ... you new woman.

Progressive thought, in the eighteen-nineties, looked to the 'new woman' to determine the new direction that civilisation was to take. When Ann invites her new husband to sit down and then delivers herself of the meaning that this marriage has for her, we may catch an allusion to another new woman, Ibsen's Nora Helmer. Yet Barker seems deliberately to have reversed the last scene of *A Doll's House*: Ann's marriage is beginning, not ending; she accepts the door locked upon her; and she has chosen the traditional womanly part of sacrifice and patience. (Only the intelligence and responsibility of the choosing are not traditional.) The new womanhood with which Barker is concerned is evidently different from what most of his contemporaries understood by the phrase.

The figure of Ann in its original setting of the garden, which is *her* garden, and her brother's comment, 'Wisdom cometh with sorrow, O my sister,'[12] together recall a passage in the *Song of Solomon*:

A garden inclosed is my sister, my spouse; a spring shut up, a fountain sealed. (4.12)

Her vulnerable youth and innocence acquire the value of a holy virginity full of promise: '... à Dieu,' says Carnaby, 'she enters Nature's cloister.' The rose of romantic passion and of the secret heart is identified with the rose of the Virgin and the *rosa mundi* (which Barker will remember again in Queen Rosamund, whom he associates, in *His Majesty*, with the heart and its foolishness and with the intangibles that call out men's devotion); and the scene in the cottage dimly foreshadows a messianic birth. In her union with Abud, who is innocence—not the innocence of ignorance, from which she has emerged, but that of a profound and clear-sighted integrity, which her choice implies—, honour is restored to the woman and her new world, generating the power to bring into being a new order of life. The initial scream out of the dark before dawn was the scream of childbirth, as well as of rape.

A critic has recently written, in interpretation of Yeats's *King of the Great Clock Tower*:

The consummation of virginity lies in its 'desecration', just as the consummation of the divine order lies in its reconciliation with the fallen world.[13]

It would serve as a comment on the finished statement made by *The Marrying of Ann Leete*.

*   *   *

Since the notion of a bet is introduced pointedly in *The Secret Life* and supplies one of the early verbal motifs in *Waste,* it seems probable that Barker's decision to use the bet as his starting-point for the action of *Ann Leete* has a special significance. Of course, it is appropriate to the eighteenth-century social background of the play. But the frivolity suggested by the recurrent references to 'game' and 'sport' and 'play' has a residual similarity to the recklessness of Ann's marriage. At the moment of climax, she throws the dice in a great gamble; and the issue is still undeclared when the drama ends. In fact, the bet appears to be a major symbol, which looks forward from the first moments in darkness to the meaning implicit in the climax, the decisive step.

The last decades of the nineteenth-century saw a rediscovery of Pascal by French thinkers and by William James, who examined the doctrine of *le Pari,* the wager, in *The Will to Believe,* published in 1897.[14] James used Pascal's argument of the gamble of faith upon the existence of God to lead up to his own pragmatic conclusion:

> Our passional nature not only lawfully may, but must, decide an option between propositions whenever it is a genuine option that cannot from its nature be decided on intellectual grounds . . .[15]

Has the darkness at the beginning of *Ann Leete* any quality of that darkness of ignorance that surrounds the natural man and necessitates the gamble of faith? Certainly it is Ann's 'passional nature', *le cœur,* which prompts her self-commitment.

CHAPTER V

The Reconciliation of Opposites

When *The Marrying of Ann Leete* was performed by the Stage Society in January 1902, Barker's friendship with Bernard Shaw was already secure. In September 1901, Shaw had written to Mrs. Patrick Campbell, suggesting that Barker might translate for her Rostand's *La Princesse Lointaine*, as his style was particularly well suited to the creation of a delicate 'fairy' atmosphere.[1] In the first Court Theatre season, *John Bull's Other Island* and *Candida* were counterbalanced by Maeterlinck's *Aglavaine and Sélysette* and also the Christmas production, *Prunella,* by Laurence Housman and Granville Barker. This suggests that fantasy was still a favourite form with Barker, and it may be a sign that his mind had not yet reached full maturity, or liberated itself fully from the hold of late nineteenth-century neo-romantic fashion.

Laurence Housman declared it impossible for him to disentangle his own contributions to *Prunella* from Barker's; the collaboration seems to have been as complete as possible. It is not so very far from the awakening of Ann Leete in her garden to the breaking in of life upon Prunella in hers. As for Housman, the nature of his writing at this period is exemplified by the whimsical fairy-tale, 'Blind Love,' which had appeared in *The Pageant* for 1897, and the play, *Bethlehem,* for which Gordon Craig had designed setting and costumes in 1900. To the temperament of each partner in the collaboration a Pierrot play about the fools of love offered congenial expression.

In a private letter,[2] Housman stated that he and Barker worked together upon six or seven plays after *Prunella*. His autobiography,

The Unexpected Years, makes it clear that these included: *The Chinese Lantern;* the scenario for an entertainment called *The Pied Piper of Hamelin*, which was to have been acted by children and survives in manuscript among Barker's papers; and the text of a light opera for Liza Lehmann, based on *The Vicar of Wakefield* and brought almost to completion. But *Prunella* is the only published work which Barker allowed to stand under his name as well as Housman's, a fact which points to a sense of the special nature or degree of his contribution to this play. It is certainly an essential document in the record of his development as a dramatist.

Prunella is more than a piece of whimsy. Desmond MacCarthy called it 'a real Pierrot play',[3] implying justly that the meaning of the traditional characters was not lost in a simply nostalgic or decorative use of fancy dress. The dramatists were offering their audiences a form of entertainment almost identical with the basic nature of theatre, but rarely met on the modern English stage. In content, however, *Prunella* is as genuinely Edwardian as St. John Hankin's one-Act classic, *The Constant Lover* (1908); indeed, Hankin's Cecil and Evelyn are as surely identical with Pierrot and young Prunella as they are with Adam and Eve.

In the Barker-Housman version, Pierrot is a mummer, belonging to the tribe of irresponsible outlaws that has always been for the respectable a source of fascination and distrust. Guardians and worshippers of fantasy, they are to be feared for their power to lure men out of safety and sanity into an unpredictable world. To Prunella, Pierrot brings revelation of what has been lacking in her Dutch Garden. Pretty enough after its fashion, it is a neat and formal place, a timeless Kate Greenaway garden, setting for a perpetual Kate Greenaway girlhood, safe and sweet and innocent, orderly and fragrant dreamland of the Victorian mind at its least intense. Excitement and uncertainty have no place in it, and its virtues are admittedly a little dull: propriety and reasonable moderation above all; and such things have a way of ruling out transforming experience. There Prunella has to learn her lessons which map out the universe for her, denying any reality beyond the bounds of human knowledge, or any mystery in human behaviour inexplicable in terms of a narrowly defined morality of right and wrong. Fancies and speculations are stamped out; and even the moon, perennial symbol of human dreams, is robbed of romance. But, youth being naturally sceptical of the wisdom of age, Prunella quickly adapts herself to the entry of the man-in-the-moon himself through the hedge, when her dragons of aunts are nodding in sleep. When, in the second Act, he comes to serenade her, the statue of Love within the garden comes to life and her mother's story renews itself in her: awakening to womanhood, she prepares to follow her enchanter into the world of adventure, joy and love that he promises.

So the theme of escape is enacted in this play as in *The Marrying of Ann Leete*, only to reach a similar conclusion. In the original form of the play, the ending of youth's dream is presented only retrospectively, in the last Act. For the 1930 production, the dramatists wrote a new Act which portrays the coming of change more directly and with more elaboration, but alters the original significance of the play not at all. Fantasy is Pierrot's life, he appears serious in nothing, and in nothing can he be constant. His love is the love of Don Juan, heartless and hollow; and, though he hides it under his powdered mask, the sourness and cynicism of absolute egoism have their part in his personality and cast a black shadow: the sinister Scaramel (a fusion of Scaramouche and Sganarelle, servant to Molière's Don Juan). The gaiety of Pierrot's eternal cherry fair of a world soon palls for Prunella, who is fully human and so capable of suffering; the careless joy of youth and first love grows faded; and the insufficiency of the earthly paradise is proved once more. The search for reality and a nourishing truth drives her from her make-believe lover.

With Act III (Act IV in the 1930 version),[4] the play is transposed into a different, a minor key. Into the timelessness of the Pierrot play there now breaks the sense of time running out, high summer turning to late autumn and life fleeting away too fast for those who would enjoy its fruits. Even Pierrot, it seems, can become middle-aged, melancholy, and he returns to the Dutch Garden seeking the Prunella he has lost, as he would seek a lost vision. Faintly to be discerned behind Pierrot and Prunella, in this last Act, are the distant forms of Peer Gynt and Solveig. 'The single effective antiphon to the long canticle of egoism'[5] was later to be Barker's description of the words in which Solveig resolves Peer's

search for his true self: 'In my heart; in my faith; in my love.'
Such is the burden of this play's ending, as dream and reality fuse
and Pierrot is redeemed.

Music, dance and masquerade make up much of the fabric of the
play; indeed, the new Act of 1930 contains one scene that is wholly
pantomime. These dramatic means are nicely scaled to the general
conception. The style of dialogue, too, light verse woven out of the
commonplaces of language and literary echoes not quite de-
generated into clichés, fits the nature of the play exactly, the sophistication of its verbal fancy maintaining throughout the consistently pleasing level of minor art. Except for Pierrot, Prunella
and Scaramel, the characters are all choric, essentially dancers.
The part of Scaramel is all on one note and has interest only in
reference to Pierrot. The period colouring apart, Prunella is nothing but generalised girlhood, 'Any bud in the morning' (in the
words of Sarah Cottesham). The main lines of Pierrot's character,
as much as his costume, are laid down by tradition. All are predominantly images, held within the total convention like metaphors
in a poem, and with no more power to disrupt it. In *Prunella*,
Barker had a medium which offered, even more nearly than the
pastiche of *The Marrying of Ann Leete*, an equivalent to the conditions that the pastoral offered to the sixteenth century.

It is what the living actor is made to contribute that gives the
piece power to absorb and convey the experience that Ibsen evokes
at the end of *Peer Gynt*. Associated with both the main figures are
realities of feeling that it is the actors' business to suggest and that
make the specific work of art out of the conventional lines of idyll
and make-believe. Some of the early audiences, it seems, were inclined to find Granville Barker's playing of Pierrot too harshly
astringent; and it is possible to see in this character's cynicism and
bitter disillusion an anticipation of the frame of mind of some of
his later heroes. The savagery, balancing the pleasing fancy, is
clearly maintained in the additional Act of the final version.

*   *   *

In his entry into the management of the Court Theatre with
J. E. Vedrenne, whose concerns were only with the business aspect

7

of the undertaking, Barker was certainly encouraged by the support of both Shaw and William Archer. The former was then the author of eleven published plays, only one of which had been given public production in a West End theatre, and he had very recently been disappointed by the inability of the Irish Literary Theatre to put on a play written especially for them, *John Bull's Other Island*. For him, the taking over of the Court meant a stage for his drama at last. It was on the suggestion of Archer, it seems, that Barker produced Gilbert Murray's version of *Hippolytus*, in May 1904, at the Lyric Theatre, a production that was to be revived during the first of the Court seasons. The two men, with Murray, had been members of the first unofficial committee working for the foundation of a National Theatre, and 1904 saw the private printing and circulation of the *Scheme and Estimates for a National Theatre*, on which Granville Barker and Archer had worked together. In his biography, *William Archer*, Charles Archer included a letter[6] in which Barker wrote to consult the older man about the idea of taking the theatre for a six months' experiment in repertory, designed to encourage a new drama. In one significant sentence he states:

> Our actors—and worse still our actresses—are becoming demoralized by lack of intellectual work.

It is likely enough that the young actor-producer saw before him an opportunity of carrying further the preparations for the National Theatre by gathering together and training a body of actors who could help him demonstrate to the general public the lines on which such a theatre might be run and the quality of the fare it could offer.

This motivation partly explains the new direction in which he himself, as a dramatist, was soon to turn. *John Bull's Other Island*, written for a National Theatre, had the marks of a work addressed to a nation, to an audience of citizens: it took as its subject current affairs of state and aired them in public spectacle and debate. This was the dramatist assuming his democratic function; and the nature of the audiences that the play drew and delighted soon made it clear that the fact was recognised. Political and propagandist drama had established its claim to public attention.

However, the new enterprise was experimental as well as demonstrative. Writing years afterwards, in *The Exemplary Theatre*, with his own former aims as a producer surely in mind, Barker was to make a point that can be regarded as central to his whole career in the theatre:

> Who is to say . . . that a Platonic dialogue or the like is not a possible play—given suitable interpretation and suitable audience? The one cannot be developed without the intelligent sympathy of the other.[7]

He did not in fact produce a Platonic dialogue, but he proved that shavian drama could be highly effective in the theatre, when the critics had been sceptical of its being drama at all; he was to produce to keen appreciation the actionless *Sentimentalists* and Hardy's epic drama, *The Dynasts*, as well as the 'static' drama of Maeterlinck and the peasant tragedies of Masefield; he was eager to try his powers on a play by Henry James, undiscouraged by the novelist's earlier failures in the commercial theatre;[8] to all intents and purposes he made a frontal attack on late nineteenth-century notions of what constituted a play by establishing Greek drama within the modern theatre—for the *Hippolytus* began a series of such productions that was to continue at intervals into the first World War. By disciplining his company and by every attention to detail in rehearsal and presentation, and also by cultivating a regular and discriminating audience, he endeavoured to control the conditions for what can be regarded as a succession of critical experiments, designed to establish just how far the scope of drama extended and so to liberate it from the deadening limitations of recent convention in style, composition and material. In his own playwriting practice he had been an experimentalist at least as early as the composition of *Our Visitor to Work-a-Day. Prunella* and *The Harlequinade* were attempts to discover what old, half-forgotten, or at least unfashionable, traditions of the theatre might still have to contribute to a richer modern repertory. In *The Voysey Inheritance* he set himself to pursue a question on which Shaw might well have started him thinking: What is dramatic action, and is unity of action essential to an effective play?

To the casual eye, *The Voysey Inheritance* could hardly seem more different from *Prunella*. It is probably the most generally known of his plays to-day, and the reason is not far to seek: it helped to establish the naturalistic play of family life as the most popular form in the English theatre and, consequently, is the least disturbing to the expectations of the average theatre-goer of to-day. The *avant garde* reaction against this convention began several decades ago, and sophisticated taste proceeded to dismiss *The Voysey Inheritance* along with its sentimentalised and watered down descendants.

Topicality has been a major factor in the partial swing back to naturalism, shown first in the acclaim given to *Look Back in Anger*; and the changes that have taken place in English society since 1905 make it more difficult to perceive that the similarity between John Osborne's play and *The Voysey Inheritance* is more significant than anything that either has in common with *Dear Octopus;* they are pioneering, where the other moves contentedly along a well-beaten track. The background of Jimmy Porter is very different from the background of Hugh Voysey, but the two figures have essentially the same value: negative, anarchic protest, the impotent kicking of a protracted adolescence against the orthodoxies of an older and still dominant generation. A quality of lively truth and a fresh critical view of the English scene marked out each of these plays when new; *Dear Octopus* took much the same material for observation, but the author's eye was distinctly more jaded.

The great difference between *The Voysey Inheritance* and *Look Back in Anger* is in form: the latter is structurally spastic, whereas *The Voysey Inheritance* is among the firmest and most complex dramatic structures to be found in the English language. It is a difference that reflects the distinctive choice of hero in each of the plays: not Hugh Voysey, but his brother Edward, the positive pole of the drama, is the hero Barker finds interesting. The narrative element of the fiction, together with the presence of well-defined character-types, constitutes the strongest appeal of debased, or insignificant, naturalism for an unsophisticated audience. Barker's refusal to get on with a story and his placing of a character who goes beyond any broadly conceived type, at the centre of the drama, are major tokens of his concern to express a personal vision.

While making his experiment in dramatic form, he retreats somewhat in the matter of dialogue, writing more explicitly, even rhetorically. A new quality of energy enters his work, as the looser writing permits a faster playing pace. That he was deliberately extending his own range by exploring the possibilities of Shaw's method, is clear in the pronounced farcical element, in the adoption of progress through digression as a principle of the dramatic structure, and in the founding of the comedy on paradox and the reversal of conventional judgments.

It is surprising how often the fact that *The Voysey Inheritance* is primarily a political drama has been overlooked. (This, of course, makes it quite different in kind from *Dear Octopus*.) Not only does it offer a satirical indictment of capitalism from the socialist viewpoint, the Voyscy family serving to represent bourgeois society, but the challenge which the hero faces is similar to that offered to Barbara Undershaft and Cusins, in *Major Barbara*:[9] the philosopher is called on to emerge out of his private idealism and pursuit of private virtue, in order to accept responsibility for public justice and power over the material world.

Three sources can be identified which seem to have contributed substance of major importance to the play.[10] It is very likely that Ibsen's *Pillars of Society* furnished a hint for one aspect of the situation. Consul Bernick, the most respected and apparently soundest of the 'pillars' of his community, is discovered to have founded his success and reputation upon a fraud, practised in order to save the family business; Voysey, the prosperous solicitor, has similarly been 'living on a lie', and his self-justification resembles Bernick's in various details. The second probable source is perhaps less expected, but is more fully suggestive of the central dramatic conflict on which *The Voysey Inheritance* turns and may have made a greater contribution to the complex argument. This is Book I of Plato's *Republic*.

Socrates questions Cephalus upon the origin of his riches, whether inheritance or personal acquisition, and receives the reply:

> In the art of making money I have been midway between my father and my grandfather: for my grandfather . . . doubled and trebled the value of his patrimony, that which he inherited being much

what I posses now; but my father Lysanias reduced the property below what it is at present: and I shall be satisfied if I leave to these my sons not less but a little more than I received. (Revised Jowett trans.)

Socrates is concerned to discover what gives money its value to the possessor and observes that 'the makers of fortunes have a second love of money as a creation of their own, resembling the affection of authors for their own poems, or of parents for their children'. The enquiry into the nature of justice is pursued through consideration of the responsibility given to those who administer the property of others; for Polemarchus grants that the just man is to be preferred when one wishes to place money in trust and keep it safe. 'That is to say,' counters Socrates, 'justice is useful when the money which it supervises is useless.' The definition of justice as consisting in 'speaking the truth and paying your debts' has already been propounded and laid aside. Now the dialogue proceeds:

> ... he who is a good keeper of anything is also a good thief? ... Then if the just man is good at keeping money, he is good at stealing it.
> ... justice is an art of theft; to be practised however 'for the benefit of friends and for the harm of enemies',—that was what you were saying?

A little later, Socrates introduces the alternative paradoxes of apparent honesty, which may be false, or genuine honesty, which may not seem so. These correspond to the opposition between the characters of Voysey and his son, Edward, which is central to Barker's dramatic structure; and Edward's discovery of the nature of justice is, in fact, the dramatist's ultimate theme.

The whole of this Book of *The Republic* seems to have been in Ruskin's mind, when he wrote *The Crown of Wild Olive*. He is particularly concerned to develop the argument of intrinsic value and states some of Plato's points in his own way. The Introduction asserts:

> ... the wealth of nations, as of men, consists in substance, not in ciphers; and ... the real good of all work, and of all commerce,

depends on the final intrinsic worth of the thing you make, or get by it.

This is the general doctrine which underlies the scene between Edward and Hugh, in Act IV of *The Voysey Inheritance*. Voysey's attitude to his business, including the illegal part of it, is the sign of a psychology that Ruskin mentions in his section on 'Work':

> ... all healthily-minded people like making money—ought to like it, and to enjoy the sensation of winning it: but the main object of their life is not money; it is something better than money.

This same section has previously defined 'play', going on to declare: 'The first of all English games is the making of money ... no one who engages heartily in that game ever knows why.' References to the playing of games are scattered through the text of *The Voysey Inheritance*, though they seem at first less artistically deliberate than in *The Marrying of Ann Leete* and usually arise with perfect naturalness from the realistic context; there is a much frequented billiard-room in the Voysey family house; the room, its table and the cues often enter into the characters' conversation. The dramatist's insistence on these things gains a precise significance if related to Ruskin's comparison of the City to 'a huge billiard-table without the cloth, and with pockets as deep as the bottomless pit; but mainly a billiard-table, after all'.

English socialism was still very conscious, in 1905, of its debt to Ruskinian economics, and Barker was doubtless exploiting the fact, in order to convert a chain of literal references into an allusive imagery. Set against this background, his use of the term, 'pockets,' in this play, seems already to anticipate an association—and antithesis—with the symbol of the womb, which becomes habitual in Barker's later work. It may well have had its origin in Ruskin's chief indictment of capitalism: that it filled the money-bags and frustrated the womb of creative labour.

*   *   *

The play begins with a situation which immediately engages the attention and promises amusing developments: the unscrupulous lawyer, who has been living and bringing up his family in luxury on the trust monies and investment funds of his clients, decides that the time has come to explain to his morally upright and idealistic son the nature of the business in which he is a partner and the nature of the inheritance that is to come to him. This makes a neat parable of capitalism as it is viewed with horror by the pure-minded doctrinaire socialist. Edward's conviction, 'It's not right,' is not only that of the gentle Fabian, however; like Vivie Warren before him, he is the innocent embodiment of the deluded moral consciousness of respectable society that does not recognise the real principles on which its prosperity is based. Edward's lesson is to be that the economics of capitalism are the economics of gambling and that the crimes of fraud and theft, in this society, are only extensions of the most respected legitimate activities of money-making. With immense confidence and pride in his achievement, Voysey proceeds to open his son's eyes and seeks his approval and co-operation.

In Act II, the narrative plot thus launched is checked, in order that the Voysey family may be displayed at home with its intimates and that the argument may be extended. The dissolving scene, created by the restless movement of characters off and on, is a feature of this Act adopted from the wedding-scene in *Ann Leete*. Here Major Booth Voysey, a pompous ass whose bullying is rendered harmless by his stupidity, the first need of whose nature is to be impressing his personality on others, precipitates the general turbulence, as his booming voice sounds above all other conversation to give an effect of meaningless din. He stalks down his victims with a billiard-cue. It is the nearest thing to a rifle that conventional domestic life allows him, and symbolises the self-assertive masculinity of an apparently patriarchal society.

Though the dialogue now seems to wander about in the same unsorted confusion as the characters, it does in fact give to the themes introduced in Act I a larger frame of reference: power, the idea of the gentleman, honour, morality and religion, art, the acquisitive instinct, games of chance and skill, marriage, the dependence and independence of women, the cost of things (tangible and intangible), impulses and principles, Oliver Cromwell and gardening, all are brought in. The grown-up children squabble and have to be controlled as if still in the nursery; the 'children's tea-fight', which the Vicar is to talk over with Mrs. Voysey, is a comic comment on the scene, in which an echo of the 'Boston Tea Party' may be heard. The parallel between the household and the *polis* is as old as Plato and, though Aristotle denied its validity, has persisted in modern times; it had been given new life by Ruskin. As a direct portrayal of life in a prosperous Edwardian middle-class home, Act II of *The Voysey Inheritance* is remarkably full and accurate; the political satire has been firmly related to a vivid and substantial social context.

In the final minutes of the Act, Barker returns to the subject of Voysey's fraudulent dealings, first obliquely, in an ominous conversation between him and his old friend, George Booth, then directly, when Edward announces his decision to stay with the firm.

Act III, though in the same setting as Act II, is a contrast to it in mood, being ushered in with preternatural hush and solemnity, as the characters return from Voysey's funeral. It is a contrast also in its physically static quality, the dialogue being conducted round a table. Edward, prepared for a crisis, announces to the whole family how matters stand; but, when each member has made his self-centred response and Edward himself has talked over the situation with Alice Maitland, all is left outwardly as it was, and the curtain comes down. The hero is condemned to do penance for his father's sins by devoting his life to keeping the firm going and putting the worst cases right.

Some of the topics raised in Act II have been discussed again and more directly applied to the dramatic situation, the ideas of Law and principle being chief among them. A more important feature is the serio-comic tension achieved through the association of the trappings and figures of awe and grief—the black-clad, weeping maids, Mrs. Voysey in her widow's weeds, the exhausted and heart-broken Honor, the scared, white-faced schoolboy, Christopher,—with the still predominantly comic note of the dialogue, vehicle for the dramatist's assertion that it takes more than death to kill Voysey. The element of genuine sorrow prepares, however, for the clearer emergence of the play's serious preoccupations. Edward Voysey, drawn in subjective terms to be acted sensitively, is never, even in Act I, a comic character; and in Act III he takes and holds the centre of the stage unchallenged, for the first time. He is still there, and with more authority, in Act IV; and with the re-assertion of the native quality of Barker's drama, which Edward—no shavian character[11]—represents, the play takes on a new tautness.

Act IV is composed of three successive duologues, the second of which is strikingly different in style from the other two. The scene is once more the solicitor's office, opening with a significant variation on the beginning of the play: Edward's manner, as he arrives in the morning, and his clerk's manner to him are a melancholy, devitalised reproduction of the scene in his father's day. The three duologues confront Edward with three successive demands: for two hundred pounds, Peacey's annual hush-money; then, in anti-climax, for 'five bob', so that Hugh may buy himself some lunch;[12] and finally George Booth's demand for all his securities, which he has decided to withdraw from the firm. The crash, it seems, has come: the long-postponed climax of the action.

Yet it is the episode with Hugh that marks the thematic climax of the play. He is the most vehement critic of society numbered among the characters, and his completest indictment of it comes in this Act, flowing out in comic exaggeration that is an expression of vitality and carries the scene along at a much more rapid tempo than the hard cut-and-thrust of the preceding and following duologues allows. This episode was the most substantially revised of the whole drama, in 1934,[13] and the re-writing has the effect of making the contrast sharper, as well as lightening the tone of the diatribe:

> HUGH. ... I want five bob. I left home without a penny. I've walked.
> EDWARD. From Highgate?
> HUGH. Yes ... by Hornsey and Highbury and Hackney and Hoxton. And I must have some lunch.
> EDWARD. I can manage five bob ...
> (*He puts them on the table.*)
> HUGH. And Upper Holloway and Lower Holloway ... and Pentonville ... and Clerkenwell ...
> EDWARD. I don't know any of them.
> HUGH. Nobody does ... except the million people who live

there. But that's London. And I also, my dear Edward, want it destroyed.

EDWARD. We are warned that . . . under certain circumstances . . . it may be [. . .]. And what about the people who live there?

HUGH. Why should they live there . . . or anywhere? Why should they live at all?

EDWARD. Well, they've their work to do . . . most of them. Incidentally . . . much as I love your society . . . so have I mine. And this morning I'm rather busy.

HUGH. Aha! There's the fatal word. We don't work, Edward, not one in a thousand of us. Work is creation. Is that what an outworn civilisation requires of us? Obviously not. It asks us to keep busy . . . and forget that to all these means there is no creative end at all. We've to keep our accounts straight . . . as you have to now . . . to keep the streets clean . . . and ourselves clean. . . .

And so it goes on, offering a contrast of characters by no means unimportant in the drama at this point and focusing the central question of ends and means. 'Five bob' is honesty's modest yield.

With Act V the play returns to the Voysey home at Chislehurst and the superficially anarchic style of Act II. In the first moments, George Booth arrives to tell Edward of his decision not to prosecute and to offer an alternative that the young man greets with bitter derision. The entry of Honor with a basket of Christmas gifts—for this is Christmas Eve—frightens the old man away, and it seems as though the outer action, never very efficiently developed, were now slowing to a complete stop. George Booth does not appear again before the play ends and the bankruptcy, public exposure, trial, imprisonment, which seemed to threaten in Act I, in Act III and at the end of Act IV, are no nearer—and no further away—, when the last Act is complete.

A new situation and subject are now introduced, not as an underplot so much as a substitute plot, as if to keep the play going, though the unity of action is broken. The prospective separation of Hugh and Beatrice Voysey becomes the centre of attention, though its relation to the theme of capitalism and to old Voysey's methods of conducting his business is tangential only. The break helps to subordinate the main story to the theme by making that story less important in the total pattern. The digressive dialogue has, in fact, prepared for a digressive structure. The understanding that is reached between Edward and Alice Maitland at the end of the play, and that holds promise of a future of marriage and hope, rather loosely counterbalances the disagreement between Hugh and his wife, but is itself the climax of a true subplot and the only narrative element in the play that is rounded off in conventional fashion.

The divorce of Hugh and Beatrice is as far off, at the final curtain, as the trial and imprisonment of Edward; both are possibilities of the situation, with which this play is not concerned as actualities. For the limitation of dramatic movement is a feature of the dialectical drama, as Barker has chosen to write it. With the exception of Edward, the characters, though they may be gradually revealed, do not change and grow. If their personal situations undergo alteration, they do so outside the dramatic structure, as the death of Ethel and her child are contained within the drama only in a silence from which facts may be deduced, the quality of the silence being relevant, the facts strictly not so. It is the balance of stresses that gives the play its form, a form that seems to have as much in common with architecture, or even sculpture (a critic once compared it to a Lutyens monument),[14] as with the progressive, moment by moment, form of drama. The characters are so placed as to offer parallels and contrasts to each other, and most of them have their allotted positions within not one group, but several, each group in its turn balancing another. The interweaving and combination of the play's various themes and lines of argument contribute further to the intricacy, but also to the firmness and balance of the whole.

The elements into which society may be analysed are clearly represented. There congregate at Chislehurst persons who speak for the Army, the Law, the Church, the gentlemen of England, masters and servants, Commerce and Art. The primitive tribal division between male and femal societies, surviving so faithfully in the middle-class of the period, is unmistakably drawn, and between the two ranks some interesting correspondences are indicated: Beatrice straightforwardly counterbalances the Major, as Emily does Hugh; more subtly, Edward, also used up by his family, corresponds to Honor. The different couples offer typical variations on the theme of relations between the sexes. At the centre is the antithesis offered by Edward, the idealist, and his father, the opportunist, an antithesis which is repeated on a slightly smaller scale, and with some variation, in the relationship between Edward and Alice. George Booth and Peacey, the confidential clerk, unite with Voysey to form a group which illuminates the organisation of capitalist society.

Both George Booth and Peacey are parasites. The former inherited a fortune that, he thinks, has never diminished; he has 'never needed to take the bread out of other men's mouths by working', and has found in money his chief pleasure and consuming interest; it is he who gives to money its absolute value, fed with all the wasted potentiality of his life.[15] His significance is explored further: his wealth has enabled him to live always in comfort and irresponsibility; it has made him an egotist and, by current standards, a gentleman, the highest virtue which he can claim, with dubious right, being harmlessness. The irony in his reference of the ideal of the gentleman to himself emphasises the falseness of the morality that supports his self-esteem. George Booth becomes, within the play, the measure of what is 'respectable'. His creed is one of easy compromise or, in terms whose full ambiguity it takes the total evolution of the play to reveal, the 'practical ideal.'[16] His appeal is always to legality, the ready-made abstraction, not the reality of experience and vitality.

As a representative of unearned profit, the negation of the creative principle on the economic level, George Booth is a crude enough exaggeration, but Barker does not make the mistake of leaving him such an abstraction. His old-bachelor ways, his attachment to Voysey and, most of all, his grief and doubt on learning that he has been robbed, humanise him. Some dim perception of the nature of reality breaks upon him as, to the best of his poor ability, he tries to master the crisis: 'I don't understand . . . because your father . . . But I m u s t understand, Edward . . . ;' 'I'm sure I'm more grieved than angry. But it isn't as if it were a small sum. And I don't see that one is called upon to forgive crimes . . . or why does the Law exist?'—but he turns aside.

The structure of Act IV, beginning with Edward's treatment of his clerk's demand and ending with his treatment of his client's, enforces the analogy between Peacey and Mr. Booth. In the dialectical scheme, Peacey is the figure that enables Barker to make the logical reversal of judgment on George Booth and Voysey. In his double attitude to the latter, acquiescent and censorious, the clerk is a comic image of the self-righteous, but fundamentally irresponsible, social conscience; according to one view, which is Edward's, he is the criminal that society breeds, the blackmailer, prepared to benefit as Voysey's tacit accomplice; according to his own view, however, he is a lesser reflection of George Booth, the 'respectable' gentleman, whose ways he copies and whose protestations he anticipates. The ambiguity of Voysey's own relationship to society is thus underlined: his adoption of its real economic principle of the lucky bag, or the game of pool, allows him cynically to exploit his society in the very process of conforming to it.

The character-scheme does not remain a matter of bare bones; it is clothed and vitalised by realistic detail and, in some instances, by the drawing of temperamental affinities, clashes, variations. Touches of family likeness give the whole community a homogeneity. Thus Major Booth Voysey and Hugh take after their father in the flamboyancy with which they present themselves to the world. The Major proves to be a hollow caricature of old Voysey's masterfulness; the old man's practice of deception has borne fruit in this son, without knowledge of the world as it is, or knowledge of himself. Force without brain, the fault in him is a deficiency, rather than a corruption of spirit and consequently, though an irritating character, he is not an entirely unattractive one. Hugh has reacted from both father and brother; for Hugh's self-dramatising manner is the deliberate exaggeration of the gibe against oneself. 'Hugh's tragedy,' says Beatrice, in the final version, 'is that he is just clever enough to have found himself out . . . and no cleverer.' Like Edward, he is an idealist and the only member of the family who makes the gesture of offering his money to aid the task which the other has undertaken. But Hugh remains where the Edward of Act I stood, a theoretical critic, who declines to enter the struggle:

> You say this is the cry of the weak man in despair! I wouldn't be anything but a weak man in this world.

He is the ineffectual artist whose only answer to the state of things is destruction. (But the zest for life that he has inherited from his father is, in counterpoint, an implicit answer of more positive value).

The marriages of Booth and Emily, Beatrice and Hugh, present opposite extremes. The meek Emily accepts her husband's public bullying, secure in the knowledge that in sly ways she can manage him as if he were a baby in her care; Beatrice, on the other hand, has had openly to direct her marriage and keep it solvent, and she has not liked the experience. Both marriages are varieties of unbalance, suggesting possible relations between strength and weakness, alternatives of power and submission, and thus are relevant to Edward in his dilemma: to deny the world or accept its challenge, mastering it while appearing to serve it. Hugh and Beatrice are more essential foils to the hero than the other two, as the greater prominence given to them in the last Act makes clear. The false opposition of idealism and practicality, which they represent, sets off the true synthesis which Edward is to achieve; his union with Alice Maitland is the seal upon it. All the more effective for the absence of any allegorical meaning is the tacitly offered parallel of the happy, mutually confident affection between Voysey and Mrs. Voysey, testimony as it is to the genuine virtue in the old swindler.

It is in this respect that Trenchard, the least amiable of all the Voyseys, is furthest removed from his father. The dramatist's device of building up suspense for the entrance of a major character, only to disappoint expectation, is an ingenious method of drawing attention to the importance of Trenchard in the underlying scheme of the play. Supremely efficient, but negative, even dehumanised (the Major's oracular comment, 'No heart, y'know! Great brain!' is surprisingly apt), Trenchard has openly quarrelled with his father and been disinherited. The cause is not far to seek. 'Oh . . . why is it so hard for a man to see clearly beyond the letter of the law!' old Voysey exclaims, when Edward condemns his behaviour as 'not right'; but Trenchard could never desire such a manner of vision. Indeed he is the embodiment of the legality to which George Booth appeals: legality divorced from moral values, the keystone of the prevailing system. Disinheritance cannot wipe out natural kinship, however. Voysey's repudiation of legality has itself been made in the manner of legality. His bitterness towards Trenchard is his only betrayal of self-disgust; for it is an aspect of himself, the outwardly conforming image, inwardly meaningless and dead, that he sees reflected in his eldest son. 'What was he after all but a fraud?' asks Alice Maitland, pondering Voysey's nature after his death. It is left for Edward to try to bring the world to terms with the living sense of justice that he finds within himself.

Though Edward is part of the family group, the character has an interest and importance that detach him from it and make the play as much his play as it is a drama of milieu. Indeed, he is the society individualised, self-conscious and responsible. He is on the stage for nearly the whole of the lengthy play, and the main justification for the reducing of outer action is that it makes possible greater concentration on the inner drama of his conversion. It is this which supplies the unfaltering dramatic movement in the play, for Edward is represented as maturing in understanding and experience, scene by scene. Except, perhaps, in Act IV, he cannot be said to dominate the play; it is his father who does that. But it is Edward who is identified with the final paradox on which the drama turns: the paradox of the 'honest cheat'.[17]

'We do what we must in this world,' is Voysey's excuse, as 'Scold at society . . . and what's the use' is Carnaby Leete's. Voysey is intellectually less tortuous than the earlier character, with a full-blooded enjoyment of life that contradicts the disillusioned view of affairs that he holds. He has the ability to leave business behind at the office, to departmentalise his consciousness, as he advises Edward:

> You must realise that money making is one thing, and religion another, and family life a third . . . and that if we apply our energies whole-heartedly to each of these in turn, and realise that different laws govern each, that there is a different end to be served, a different ideal to be striven for in each . . .[18]

It is this idea that the whole play, in its complex structure, opposes, and it marks Voysey's limitation: that he sets blinkers upon his mind. The rhetoric in which he indulges is the mark of the self-deceiver, established by Ibsen as the sign of this type of character; though Voysey's self-dramatisation seems to be limited to his professional identity. His greatest strength is one that neither Carnaby

Leete nor Edward shares: the genial warmth of his nature in response to life, which gains him the confidence of his clients and, coming to be appreciated by Edward, enables him to explain to George Booth:

> MR. BOOTH. ... We were friends for nearly fifty years. Am I to think now he only cared for me to cheat me?
> EDWARD. *[...]* No ... he didn't value money quite as you do.
> (First version.)

In the original version of Act IV, Hugh obliquely pointed the moral of his father's life in a Ruskinian assertion: 'I remember once giving a crossing-sweeper a sovereign. The sovereign was nothing. But the sensation I gave him was an intrinsically valuable thing.'[19] Money-making has been the expression of Voysey's abundant vitality; delight in his ability has given money its value for him. The real value which leads Edward to continue with the firm during his father's lifetime and after his death is, as he confesses to Beatrice, human affection, the bond between him and his father. It establishes a much closer connection between the two figures than Shaw implies between Vivie and Mrs. Warren. Once again, Granville Barker has made the relation between father and child the central symbol of his play, as it is also the emotional centre.

If Edward, in the course of the action, changes to the point where he unites the contradictory values of idealism and pragmatism, there is also a hint that the contradictions may be transcended in old Voysey's consciousness. The Will he makes can be regarded as his last confidence-trick to ensure the continuing prosperity of the firm. More subtly still, it is his confidence-trick played on Edward, binding him to his task and so leading him to wisdom. (It is here that Voysey's gambling takes on its most Pascalian aspect.) Edward prefers not to think that his father foresaw George Booth's withdrawal of his securities, as that suggests to him a callousness towards his own fate; but this marks one of the limitations in the hero's awareness, which the play as a whole transcends.

Indeed, by the end of the play, Voysey has become something more than a naturalistic character and—like Carnaby in this, too,

8

—emerges as a figure summing up the playwright's ironic vision. (Ultimately, it is to this clairvoyance that his name, in its combination of *voir* and *see,* is chiefly appropriate.) After his death, the spirit of Voysey seems to haunt the play, its presence betrayed in the thoughts and words of the other characters; but now it is endowed with a prescience denied to the conscious mind of the living Voysey, seen in Acts I and II. As everything that happens is connected by the others with the old man, it comes to seem as though he had predetermined the entire action, from the moment when, like some interfering god, he made his (unnecessary) revelation to Edward and demanded that first decision which started the change in his son. So his father's portrait smiles down on Edward, at the close of the play, while his approval is spoken in the voice of Alice.

*   *   *

Despite the fact that Barker has relegated narrative to a place of minor importance in *The Voysey Inheritance,* none of his other dramatic writings has more of the quality that is generally associated with the realistic novel. Insistence on the literal value of the characters, made effective by his portrayal of them as human beings with affections and aversions, in sympathy with others, or grating upon them, is a major factor in building this impression. In the case of Voysey himself, Barker succeeds in giving to the character something of the dimensions of an actual human being, by keeping the contours fluid and including in the portrait the contradictions, the mixed and never completely definable motives, which belong to life. The other characters voice different interpretations of the old man and his career. So he remains alive and changing, still able to dominate the play, in the last Acts, as he is reflected in their continuing speculations. The truth, or the degree of falsehood, in his story of the inheritance from his own father, of his own early career and the way in which he saved the firm, his motives in disclosing the situation to Edward or in seeing that Mrs. Voysey's money was safe, the nature of his thoughts on receiving George Booth's hint that he was unlikely to leave his business in Edward's hands, his intentions in drawing up his Will, these matters are all left undefined finally. Ibsen's method of giving depth to a character who does not actually appear in the drama,[20] and building up interest in him, through the retrospective probings of the characters on the stage, has been adopted and extended.

Another feature of the naturalistic fabric of the play is the amount of anecdotal detail it contains, even concerning minor characters. Around the periphery of the drama is a wider world. In it live the Pettifers, Lady Mary, old Thomson, the physiologist (given a name only in the final text), Mrs. Colpus, Denis Tregoning's father, as well as Edward's grandfather and Peacey's father and son, the unseen clients and other clerks in the office. Mrs. Voysey reads, and writes letters to, *Notes and Queries* and *The Nineteenth Century* on such subjects as the first umbrella-maker, the Chinese Empire and, of course, the family of Oliver Cromwell. This is indeed a *tranche de vie* artificially isolated on the stage. The character of Trenchard is so completely inessential to the action plot that, despite his appearance during Act III, his reality remains more nearly on the level of those who are merely alluded to in the dialogue, as for the most part he is himself. Much the same might be said of Ethel, that she and her story seem to exist more outside the play than in.

Especially in the scenes set at Chislehurst, the dramatist continually brings back attention from abstract and general considerations to the details of everyday living: the arranging of the roses in their vase (the actor's sense of the usefulness of a carefully selected piece of 'business' for the revelation of state of mind is also to be traced in this and perhaps in most of the other details, too[21]), the making up of the fire, the clearing of the table, sewing and mending, hunting for lost objects, surveying the garden, attending to a blocked ventilator, packing Christmas presents. All this, together with the flurrying stage movement, compensates for the meagreness of the outer action and counterbalances the element of discussion. Such is the common fabric of life, indeed, but the strength and firmness of the dialectical scheme prevent these appearances from ever dwindling into insignificance, while the impression of the life of a household reflects its own reality back upon the various members that it holds in its unifying frame. The solidity that such detail gives and the strong fabric of meaningful connections are, together, the justification of the considerable length of the play. Desmond MacCarthy's judgment is worth recalling in this connection:

> The most remarkable feature of *The Voysey Inheritance* is the skill with which the interest in a single situation is maintained through four acts; that this is a sign of fertility and not poverty of imagination all who have ever tried to write know well.[22]

Even in the detail in all its restlessness, the discipline of proportion is maintained; perspective is established in the drawing of character from the slightest reference to a client, through the flat characters and the characters presented partially, but with a depth more than superficial, to Voysey, now flat, seen only from the outside, now in the full depth and shadow of implied thought and feeling, and to Edward who, throughout, requires to be subjectively acted. The differences are reflected in the style of the dialogue, varying as it does between inflated rhetoric and the spareness and reticence of quietly intimate talk. The variation serves other purposes, too: psychological, as the two styles distinguish the genuine human being in Voysey from the fraudulent financier and Edward's quiet strength from the assertive bluster of his brothers; and rhythmical, as it allows for alternations of swift and slow pace, the acceleration in the central episode of Act IV being, perhaps, the most striking example in the play. The discipline which serves the artist is itself expressive of aspects of this theme: the community which defines the conditions of individual existence; the grip of tradition on personality; and the outward limitations that it imposes on freedom of choice and creative living.

*   *   *

Granville Barker keeps his audience in mind of the fact that a professedly Christian society is his subject. The Vicar is on the stage, in Act II, to receive George Booth's appeals for support on the subjects of morality and religion; readily, subserviently, he gives it. The hostility expressed in this portrait of a churchman is unequalled elsewhere in Barker's writing. It conveys his revulsion at the betrayal of the religion of Christ by official Christianity's acquiescence in capitalism. (Like Ruskin's, Barker's socialism has a religious basis.) By the broadest of strokes, the true nature of Colpus's Christianity is revealed: 'What will Colpus . . . what will all the other Christian gentlemen demand?' exclaims Edward in comic distraction, 'Pounds of flesh! Pounds of flesh!'

But the reminders of Christianity are not in the play only for the purpose of satire. Hugh's remark, '. . . to all these means there is no creative end at all,' and a brief passage later in the same scene:

> HUGH. . . . .You've no right to let your life be brought to nothing.
> EDWARD. Does my life matter?
> HUGH. But of course.
> EDWARD. *[the iron in his soul.]* That's where we differ,[23]

these take the play deeper in its search. And, following them up, we find that *The Voysey Inheritance* is not only an indictment of society; it belongs alongside the dramatist's earlier work in being also an exploration of the nature of reality. Among the small naturalistic details that are included in the play are recurrent references to Voysey's garden, the roses, the celery, the strawberry beds, the position of a tree; in Act II, he picks up and examines some apples on a dish. The literal details are caught up and transformed into something else, when Mrs. Voysey, whose deafness sets her apart from the other characters and permits her to speak inconsequentially, talks to herself, or to anyone who will listen, at the end of that Act:

> This is a very perplexing correspondence about the Cromwell family. One can't deny the man had good blood in him . . . his grandfather Sir Henry, his uncle Sir Oliver . . .
> *[. . .]* and it's difficult to discover where the taint crept in *[. . .]*
> I believe the family disappeared. Regicide is a root and branch curse. . . .

There can be little doubt that Barker, introducing the word, 'correspondence,' was indulging in his favourite device of the pun. With the metaphor, 'root and branch,' the tree so casually mentioned earlier stands before our minds with the force and absurdity of a symbol.

The playwright adds a touch of comic embroidery to the family tree, growing in the garden of civilisation, by two references to Ethel and Denis as birds building (or should it be 'feathering'?) their nests. But Ethel dies, and her child with her; the Voyseys are good at 'nursing fools' money', but not at nursing life, and the comic note grows sad. The family, it is remarked in the last Act, seems to be dying out, as though cursed in its turn; and thus, to the ideas of right and wrong, so bandied about in the dialogue, there attach themselves the profounder implications of good and evil. The inheritance of the play's title and the recurring figure of the policeman, image of Law, take on another dimension. It is not only by his family and capitalist society that Edward is condemned to his desk and the drudgery of his daily work. When George Booth says, 'You may be put in prison,' he gets the reply:

> I am in prison ... a less pleasant one than Wormwood Scrubbs. But we're all prisoners, Mr. Booth.

The chain that Hugh accuses him of clanking 'with the best of them' is the chain of the generations and the universal human bondage, within which we are members one of another; the Voysey inheritance—like its counterpart (usually hereditary disease) in Ibsen's drama—is original sin, or that common heritage of guilt and error that humanity has accumulated and that no-one can put aside. The idealist, who in Act III was still prepared to plead that his hands were clean, has had gradually to discover the unwanted knowledge of good and evil and the weight of human responsibility.

Barker has taken up again the theme of honour employed in *The Weather-Hen* and *The Marrying of Ann Leete*. Carnaby's ironic question; 'What is more useful in the world than honour?', is implicitly asked in this play, too. The elder Voysey daughter, at the beck and call of everyone, was christened Honor; '...and what have we always called her?', asks Hugh, 'Mother's right hand! I wonder they bothered to give her a name.' The question of values has special pertinence in this connection, and a variant of Carnaby's ambiguous words can be heard in George Booth's phrase, 'practical ideal.' What distinguishes the 'honest cheat' from the 'fraud', the whole fabric of the play suggests, is just the manner of 'use' to which his honour is put. Edward has learnt to accept the truth of his father's statement, 'We do what we must in this world,' but has not given up the struggle to do more and to reconcile means and ends.

* * *

Through the final episode, in which Alice Maitland promises to marry Edward, Barker endeavours to close his play on a note of affirmation and hope. In fact, having conducted his argument successfully to its conclusion and transformed Edward convincingly from a prig to a wise, if rather melancholy, man, he falls short of the effect he intended in the final scene. The fault seems to lie in his insufficient development of the character of Alice for the major dramatic function assigned to her. She is the most sententious character in the play, proclaiming the commonplaces of shavian morality. It is plain that she was intended to represent the 'practical ideal', but she is too consistently right to be dramatically tolerable. Her common-sense and conscious, rational power seem insufficient to meet the demands of Edward's ultimate question: 'Does my life matter?' Alice belongs to a more purely sociological type of play than Barker's sensibility could long be confined within.

A letter he wrote to Rudolph Kommer, Max Reinhardt's impresario, who translated *The Voysey Inheritance*, provides interesting evidence of how he himself regarded the play:

> Dec. 18, 1913.
>
> You write me the most interesting letter and there is much to be said. If I were writing Edward Voysey now I dare say I should write him a little different, but then I am not, and though you may patch up the details of a play years after writing it I am sure you must never patch up the characters. I too am sick of the eternal feminine drawing him upward on and on, but after all Alice does not do that in the last scene (as a matter of fact she is far more masculine than Edward is in the usual sense of the term). No, honestly, you have got hold of the wrong end of the stick there. He is the idealist and she is the practical person. If I had developed her more it would have been in the direction of making her considerably more like old Voysey in unscrupulousness. At the worst she interprets Edward to himself.[24]

The last remark suggests that perhaps he had not progressed beyond the point of interest in Alice for Edward's sake to interest in her for her own sake. Later in the same letter comes a verdict that points us forward:

> I do believe in *The Madras House*. It is far more universal than *Voysey* and incidentally far better written.

CHAPTER VI

Political Tragedy

Other plays, novels and films have found popular material in stories like that of *Waste*, concerning a politician at the height of his career, who is destroyed by the scandal of his adultery with a married woman. Two notorious episodes of the 'eighties had brought such topics into prominence: the fall of Sir Charles Dilke, despite his protestation of innocence, when he was cited in a petition for divorce; and the Parnell-O'Shea case.[1] In its popular treatment, this makes a romantic tale of All for Love and the World Well Lost, a debased form of the *Antony and Cleopatra* type.

In Barker's version, certain anti-romantic elements are immediately obvious and provoked hostile reactions from some critics. Thus there is great insistence on the Bill for the Disestablishment of the Church, with which the hero is concerned, and much detail of the cross-bench politics that give him his chance of power.[2] Trebell is no dashing romantic hero, carried away by generous enthusiasms; instead, he seems temperamentally cold and tightly self-disciplined. The 'heroine', Amy O'Connell, is shallow and frivolous, so inferior to Trebell in quality that it is impossible that he should have any serious regard for her. Their relationship is a casual sexual contact from which both subsequently feel revulsion; appallingly, it results in the conception of a child. When Amy has died, after a back-street abortion, a coroner's inquest threatens the exposure of Trebell.

These elements do not make for a pretty play. The dramatist does not even exploit their sensational qualities, but he does require from his audience a mature capacity for sympathetic identification with characters far from admirable, or even ordinarily likable. His play is a reminder that the tragic hero may have only one virtue, if he has that to a supreme degree.

Discussion of *Waste* is complicated by the fact that the play exists in two very different versions. Twenty years after it was first composed, Granville Barker re-wrote the text for a projected staging which did not in fact come until 1936. The prefatory letter to H. M. Harwood, printed with the second version in 1927, obliquely reiterates the comments on what is possible in revision, that the dramatist had already made more fully to Kommer à propos of *The Voysey Inheritance*:

> When we agreed you should revive it, I never thought of reading it through. Did you? I said lightly that one or two alterations might be needed. Then, later, I turned to the job—and this is the result. I doubt if one scrap of the old dialogue survives; the story and the characters are here, that is all. So it is a thing I had—dramatically —to say twenty years ago, said as I'd say it now. But now I'd have something different to say.

It is plain from this that the theme, as well as 'the story and the characters', is constant in the two versions.[3]

A great deal of what is to be said about *Waste* applies equally to both texts, and that simplifies the critic's task. In some respects the author's intention is more effectively executed in the revision; but an examination of the original version usually reveals the same elements, at least in embryo. Changes in the dialogue have sometimes affected the emotional response that the characters arouse. Thus the Tory political hostess, Julia Farrant, is more critically presented than in the original. Similarly, though the original moral judgments upon them are not waived, the later Amy O'Connell is drawn with more of compassion and Trebell has undergone an intellectual mellowing, bringing him nearer in type to the later hero of *The Secret Life*, Evan Strowde. Superficial alterations made the play more topical for an audience of the year of the General Strike, which had seen a Labour Government take office; an audience that had long taken universal education for granted, was now familiar with universal adult suffrage, and had ceased to regard Church disestablishment as a burning issue.

Certain modifications of technique and structure have been made for æsthetic reasons: the whole nature of the exposition is changed; discussion of the Bill of Disestablishment and of the education question has been greatly reduced; the development of events at the climax is subtly altered; and the motivation and meaning of Trebell's eventual suicide are clarified. The later text is undoubtedly the work of a more mature craftsman, as well as a more mature human being. A full comparison would reveal that the writer who had retired from active work in the theatre remained no less aware of the exigencies of stage performance than he had been in 1906; but such comparison will not have place in this chapter.

The view of a Britain governed by a country-house oligarchy is retained, and there is no radical change in the presentation of the position of women in society and public life. In fact, the relation between the two societies—of men and of women—and the spectacle of a powerful aristocracy are fundamental to the drama, part of the necessary symbolism in which the dramatist's idea is embodied.

* * *

The playwright has again made his imagined world as concrete and circumstantial as may be. A whole political situation is contained, at least in allusion, within the play: the balance of power between rival interests of class and sect and party; the temper of a given moment of time; the condition of public opinion and the topics with which it is occupied; the framework and machinery of English democracy; and the inconsistencies, alliances and incompatibilities of men; their personal aims, ambitions and temperaments. *Waste* is no simple documentary drama; but actualities are the medium in which the politician works and, as such, they claim their place as part of the essential subject of this play.

Barker had already attempted to present political intrigue in *The Marrying of Ann Leete,* but as a subsidiary feature of the drama, illuminating the character of Carnaby and indicating the corruption of the society he represents. In *Waste* the political tactics, which contribute largely to the outer action, come nearer to giving the measure of the complexity of a modern political society and the chaos of forces out of which policy emerges: the practicable compromise. Horsham, the leader of the Tories, puts his point-of-view succinctly:

> I have to match you all with ... and against ... each other, so that from the heat of your differences a little power to do something may, if possible, result.

This view of the statesman's task, which demands all his ability to reach however slight-seeming a result, provides a background to Trebell's heroic stature.[4]

By outlining the Bill of Disestablishment, which his hero is expected to steer through a Cabinet and then through the House, Barker brings the politician's daily work within the range of his drama. In the first text of the play, the Bill is discussed in Julia Farrant's drawing-room, in Act I; then, in Act II, between Trebell and his old friend, Dr. Wedgecroft; and finally expounded more formally to Cantilupe, a wary political ally of High Church leanings. It is thus a constant element, by which variations of attitude and approach are measured: Trebell's professional interest in his work is set beside the personal meaning it has for him; policy as it reflects the mixed opinion of a group is weighed against policy as the creation of the individual, directing mind; simple discussion and explanation are contrasted with the oblique diplomatic approach, designed to bring round a potential opponent. Here is a means of indicating the various types and degrees of relationship that go to make the sum of the political life of a human community.

Shakespeare, in his political plays, among which the major tragedies may be numbered, certainly gave Barker his model for the presentation of affairs of state as the larger aspect of human experience. A passage in 'From *Henry V* to *Hamlet*' has an illuminating relevance to all the author's own mature plays, but to none more than *Waste*:

> Shakespeare might answer that his Elizabethans felt the need and responded to the art of personal expression more than we do whose minds are full of science and machinery and of all sorts of things, actual and speculative, that cannot be reduced to terms of human emotion. 'Though can they not be?' he might add, 'and must they not be at any rate brought within the range of it, if you are really to comprehend them?'[5]

In *Waste* is recorded an attempt to bring within the range of human emotion the political activity of the highly organised modern state, in which human issues seem most completely de-humanised.

Letters written during the period of the original preparation of the play refer to it by an earlier title: *The Statesman*.[6] In 1906-7, *Major Barbara*, Shaw's dialectical drama of Christianity and Machiavellianism reconciled by the philosopher-king, was included in the repertory of the Court Theatre. Barker, writing for the same audience a drama on the same scale, seems also to have had *Il Principe* and Plato in mind. The direction of his thought is indicated in a brief passage from the first Act of the original text: 'I think a statesman may be a little inhuman,' says Julia Farrant, using the permissive auxiliary, and she is taken up by her mother: 'Do you mean superhuman? It's not the same thing, you know.'

The plot of the play serves to focus the commonplace that the morality of a politician's private life may be different from what he publicly professes. But the dialogue and general development carry the thought further and question whether the morality proper to public affairs may not indeed have to be nobler than private life necessitates. The crisis turns on the question of whether Trebell can, in the face of scandal, be included in Horsham's Cabinet. Within this reverberates a deeper consideration: whether any man is fit to be a statesman; or whether humanity can survive, in view of natural flaws that leave it ill-adapted to control power in the modern world. Through Trebell's self-questioning, the dramatist explores the difficult concept of true political vision, not inhuman, not superhuman, yet reaching out beyond narrow and selfish concerns to comprehend human society as a living thing.

*   *   *

Waste was originally intended for inclusion in a continuation of the Court Theatre seasons in a further period of repertory at the Savoy. The first performance was announced and rehearsals were completed, when the Lord Chamberlain banned the play. The official reason given for this act of censorship was the presence in the text of references to abortion. Barker was given the option of making verbal alterations which would obscure the cause of Amy

O'Connell's death. Despite the financial loss it meant to his company, he refused. He was not a playwright to introduce material arbitrarily into his work without careful weighing of its potential significance; and he certainly intended the title he eventually chose for the play to direct attention towards 'that balked scrap of being', as surely as to the destruction of Trebell's career and the annihilation of his work. The abortion is, indeed, the crucial symbol.

There is some reason to suppose that a passage from *The Republic*, which follows the discussion of the breeding of guardians for the ideal state, lingered in Barker's mind and confirmed his decision to use this particular squalid and pitiful instance:

> Anyone above or below the prescribed ages who presumes to beget children for the commonwealth shall be said to have done an unholy and unrighteous thing . . . his child shall be the offspring of darkness and strange lust.
> . . . And the same law will apply to any one of those within the prescribed age who forms a connexion with any woman in the prime of life without the sanction of the rulers . . .
> . . . after that we shall probably allow them to range at will . . . *accompanying the permission with strict orders to prevent any embryo which may come into being from seeing the light.* . . .

But the death of Amy and the child she had conceived also recalls the implied death of Ethel and her stillborn child, in the immediately preceding play; what was there a subsidiary comment now moves to the centre of attention.

Within both *The Voysey Inheritance* and *Waste* can be traced an awareness of contemporary public concern over apparent symptoms of national decline, and in particular the fall in the birth-rate, an anxiety which reached its climax with Sidney Webb's articles in *The Times*, in October 1906, on the results of a Fabian Society questionnaire on birth control. 'What are men to do when this is how women use the freedom we have given them?' exclaims Justin O'Connell in the play; but Trebell goes deeper in a retort to Blackborough, his chief enemy in the Shadow Cabinet:

> You know we're an adulterous and sterile generation. Why should you cry out at a proof now and then of what's always in the hearts of most of us? (First version.)

The symbolism of the Waste Land that civilisation may become had appeared in *The Marrying of Ann Leete*; in the present play it is identified with the sterility within the individual life: the source of civil corruption and political futility.

* * *

In striking contrast to *The Voysey Inheritance* with its movement of the single character through a static field, *Waste* is a play of violent conflicts juxtaposed to quieter conversation-pieces. The crises of life, conventionally accepted as the most fit material for drama, are invoked to make their tremendous and disruptive impact on character and situation: birth and copulation and death, the three things which Trebell admits to have the power of arousing authentic emotion, are the events on which the action turns. The intimacies, covert and obscene, of private life—an illicit affair, an illegal operation, unacknowledged primitive impulses at work within the highly civilised, the irrational fears and superstitions underlying a sophisticated manner, the sicknesses and corruptions of body and mind—force their way through the smooth surface of well-regulated social existence and continue their work in the battles of diplomacy and the jockeying for social position and political power. The sharp contrasts offered in Acts I and II—between the drawing-room discussion of affairs, with which the play opens, and the love-making of Trebell and Amy; then between the episode in which Amy reveals the fact of her pregnancy to her former lover, and Trebell's exposition of his Disestablishment Bill to Cantilupe—lead into the splitting of the Tory caucus, in Act III, over the adultery and consequent death of the woman and the child she refused to bear: to the detachment of the statesman is opposed the challenge of the human situation, raw and crude.

The introversion of the tragic theme is accomplished in the last Act. After Trebell's virtual expulsion from political life and the collapse of the policy he represented, he makes his judgment upon himself in the only world left to him: the solitude of his own mind. Barker was probably consciously following a pattern laid down by Ibsen, in whose work *Rosmersholm* offers the clearest example of the withdrawal of the whole social and political context, towards the end of the play, to leave only the drama in the soul of the two main characters. What happens in *Waste*, as in *Rosmersholm*, is not a simple rejection of the political issues as no longer interesting, but a penetration beyond them to their sources in the depths of human personality. Barker may also have had in mind the development of *Antony and Cleopatra*; for *Waste* likewise challenges, in its final Act, the anti-romantic verdict of 'All for Lust, or the World Ill Lost', invited by the whole earlier part of the play. Now the full significance of Trebell's Bill for the drama emerges: the relation of Church and State portends also the relation between work and faith, temporal and eternal, which the hero discovers; the idea of Disestablishment points towards the liberation of spiritual power, which makes part of the paradoxical meaning of his suicide.

* * *

Only a close scrutiny of the play can demonstrate how Barker, in a markedly philosophical drama, avoids the effect of dogmatic statement and brings his theme to dramatic life with superb stage-craft.

Act I consists of two scenes, separated only by a dimming of the lights. The term, intrigue, might be applied to the matter of both: in the first, the characters are concerned with political intrigue, publicly conducted by Julia Farrant; in the second, the sordid intrigue of a sexual affair contributes an oblique comment on the first and introduces the drama of the individual, the microcosm, in which the macrocosmic theme is to be reflected.

The first scene is a general conversation-piece, revealing the attitudes and inter-relations of characters and introducing the dominant themes of the play. The audience has several moments, after the curtain goes up, and while Julia plays Chopin's Prelude, opus 28, number 20, in which to observe the setting and the group of figures on the stage. Apart from the young Walter Kent, just down from Oxford, it is a group of women, in this first view of the select minority that governs England: the Edwardian alliance of birth and wealth, intellect and professional politics, constituting an oligarchy of the privileged. The drawing-room, on a Sunday evening after dinner, is a not inappropriate background to throw into relief the arrogance informing a system which allows the conduct of a nation's business to take place over billiards or golf, as part of a week-end's relaxation.

The arrogance is sensed, and dramatically emphasised, by Mrs. O'Connell, the one member of the group who is certainly outside the select circle of approval. The dramatic movement, in the first part of the Act, is provided by her sly skirmish with the others. Attack is her self-defence and her weapons, that she wields with a half-concealed impudence, are charm of manner and a pretty wit. 'Poor partridges . . . with nobody but nobodies left to shoot at them,' she gibes, when the prospect of a September dissolution of Parliament is discussed. It is the critical voice of vulgar humanity, the unprivileged, sounding within the citadel of culture and high-mindedness.

The particular Chopin Prelude, which Barker has directed to be played, hammers away at a single solemn theme ('God save the King', interprets the first line) as the play itself is to do. Allusions to Bach and the fugue, in the first passage of dialogue, further suggest—if we remember the method of *Ann Leete*—that contrapuntal technique and a very concentrated, pithy style are being used in the revised text, at least.[7] Barker introduces his voices briefly, one following another, in this first passage, as if in canon. The third voice, speaking of the 'reply', may hint at the Subject-Answer alternation of fugue (cf. George Leete's phrase, 'Ann, shall we return,' in one figure of the 'dance', and the following entry of Tatton and Sarah with the words, 'Three steps? No . . . four.').

Walter Kent, leading in with ' "God save the King" ', introduces the subject and counter-subject which are to be developed; Julia's '*polite* reply' glances at the State and its politics; then the antithesis between feeling and thought, heart and head (of which Church *v.* State is one variant), rings out again and again in: 'Chopin'—'John Sebastian,' 'moonrise'—'starlit,' 'emotional'—clever,' as a beginning. Amy's words, 'And I'd been wondering what was missing,' are the climax of the fugal Exposition, focusing attention on her. Lady Julia's move across the stage may have been intended to mark the equivalent of an Episode. Then with 'Dear Lucy, are you doing it for a bet?' (Pascal's wager once more?), Amy starts again to call in the other voices, one by one. At the same time, the playwright is acquainting the audience with his characters:

> WALTER KENT. Oh . . . was that "God save the King"? I'd have stood up.
>
> LADY MORTIMER. Thank you, my dear Julia.
>
> LADY JULIA. Thank you for listening, mamma. That's the polite reply, isn't it?
>
> FRANCES TREBELL. Chopin for a finish, Julia . . . after John Sebastian!
>
> LADY JULIA. Allow us that much emotional indulgence.
>
> WALTER KENT. Romantic moonrise into a starlit sky.
>
> LADY DAVENPORT. Five marks to you for an epigram, Walter.
>
> WALTER KENT. Don't be so frightfully surprised when I say something clever.
>
> FRANCES TREBELL. I prefer the stars.
>
> AMY O'CONNELL. And I'd been wondering what was missing.
>
> LADY JULIA *finds herself a chair; it happens not to be very near* MRS. O'CONNELL.
>
> LADY JULIA. Don't you like Bach? Why didn't you say so?
>
> AMY O'CONNELL. I respect the old gentleman . . . but he makes me feel a demi-semi-quaver of a creature.
>
> LADY JULIA *catches sight of a book—a quite severe-looking book—upon* LUCY DAVENPORT'S *lap.*
>
> LADY JULIA. Lucy . . . were you reading while I played?
>
> LUCY DAVENPORT. No, indeed, Cousin Julia. But I keep hold of it . . . it soaks in up the arm.
>
> AMY O'CONNELL. I spent half a fugue trying to make out the title.
>
> *The book is handed to her;* LUCY'S *arm at full stretch will just do it.*
>
> Walter Bagehot . . . the English Constitution. Bagehot and Bach! What company I'm in! Dear Lucy, are you doing it for a bet?
>
> LUCY DAVENPORT. No; it's good stuff.
>
> AMY O'CONNELL. So all the authorities declare. Yes . . . and one ought to be able to say: I've read Bagehot. You can say that, Julia, can't you?
>
> LADY JULIA. I can . . . even truthfully. But I don't.
>
> AMY O'CONNELL. And Frances has lectured on Bagehot.
>
> FRANCES. No. Mathematics were my bread and butter.
>
> AMY O'CONNELL. And Lady Mortimer will tell us that she once saw Bagehot plain. And I'm sure he was plain.
>
> LADY MORTIMER. Yes . . . he used to come to my father's house . . . with Mr. Richard Hutton . . . when I was small. They had long beards . . . which frightened me.

AMY O'CONNELL. That's better. Now, Mr. Kent ... what's
your contribution?

WALTER. I have been lectured on Bagehot ... and examined
on Bagehot. And it never, please Heaven, can happen again.

LUCY DAVENPORT. Shame!

AMY O'CONNELL. Well ... if I'd only thought of it I might have
put all you clever, well-brought-up people in the shade by protest-
ing loudly at dinner to the distinguished statesmen each side of me
that I'd never even heard of Bagehot! Though I have ... oh, yes,
in my hot youth, I have!

LADY JULIA. Who did bring you up, Amy?

With this, the culmination is in process. What follows is a monologue from Amy, only briefly interrupted by other voices. Though
its ostensible matter is autobiographical, the themes already heard
are further developed within it. The last line before the scene is
dissolved by the entrance of two new characters, 'I wish the
country's salvation were so simple a matter,' brings the dialogue
right back to the linking of religion and the state that "God save
the King" introduced. The whole section needs, of course, to be
delivered with the precision and absolute, unbroken rhythm of a
Bach fugue. Analysed in terms other than musical, the passage
marks out the metaphysical perspectives of the drama to follow:
from the stars to the frightened child and the 'demi-semi-quaver
of a creature', from Mathematics to bread-and-butter, in the plain
man and his relation to God and King. Julia's 'even truthfully',
following swiftly upon Lucy's 'good stuff', may contain the
briefest of passing allusions to the Platonic Ideas. The topic of
education is brought in, first by Lucy's 'Five marks ...', then more
directly, towards the end of the extract; and what follows links it
with the question of the position of women and the education
appropriate to them. In the original version, the talk is more
obviously concerned with those two features so prominent in the
argument of *The Republic*: the education of the governing
class and the right of women to engage in politics as equals with
men. In the revision, those disciplines for the statesman which
the Platonic dialogue reviews, music, arithmetic and astronomy,
which leads the mind heavenwards, are among the themes con-
trapuntally introduced; and Amy is soon to link 'mathematics and
morals'.[8]

The women characters presented (no new ones, apart from a maid, are introduced later in the play) suggest the range of alternatives open to women in this society. Julia Farrant is 'a power behind the throne', the able woman greedy for command and obtaining it through her private influence on men. Lucy, the young woman, seems to be following in the same path, more straightforwardly and innocently. Frances Trebell is the female variant on her brother's nature, though aware from the start of the aridity in her intellectual life, which he comes only gradually to perceive in his own. Lady Mortimer (the same character is called Lady Davenport in the first version) and Amy O'Connell represent more traditional forms of womanhood. The old lady does not appear again in the play; her presence in the first Act, with her quality of serene and humane wisdom, is a gage of the reconciliation to come at the close of the drama.

*   *   *

Amy is the chief element in the scene that is alien to the thought of *The Republic*. She is certainly no personification of love, but is employed by the dramatist to invoke the principle of love. The phrases, 'emotional indulgence' and 'romantic moonrise', with the Chopin Prelude to which they are applied, and the effect of moonlight visible through the uncurtained windows of the room, help suggest the value that her character is to contribute to the drama. They are reminders of *Prunella*, as the sight of Amy, '*nunlike*,' with white lace draped about her head and shoulders at the beginning of the second scene, is to reflect an affinity to Ann Leete, the dedicated virgin of Barker's romanticism. By such accessory effects, he gives a poignancy and delicate grace to a character that he usually presents with an objectivity merciless to her lack of admirable qualities. Amy has the physical beauty of a romantic heroine. In the battle of contrasted personalities, her ignorance and imperfect taste, the triviality of her interests and purposes, are paraded so as to throw into relief the virtues of the others. Yet, in the process, their undoubted superiority is made to seem very slightly complacent, their dispassionateness takes on a tinge of indifference to the rest of the world, and the contempt that lurks in their restraint with her is turned back against them to reveal the narrowness of their exclusive culture and a littleness of spirit in them.

Of all the characters, Amy has the nature of the victim in most marked degree (though Trebell himself will finally take on the rôle). 'There's something of the waif about her' is Frances's comment in this first Act, and it is as a waif-like figure that she haunts the later part of the play. The ruthlessness of the political society is nowhere more uncompromisingly revealed than in the unsparing epitaphs that its masters pronounce upon her. 'A worthless woman!' is O'Connell's contribution; 'The little trull!' is Trebell's; Horsham, detached as he always will be from human passions, enjoys expanding the statement:

> I always found her a detestable little woman . . . . A harlot at heart!
> How much better then . . . for all concerned . . . just to be a harlot.

Such men are schooled to the statesman's disregard for the petty and trivial fate of the individual in the vaster scheme of life. But already and subtly, in his very first scene, Barker is making a point central to the action: the moral advantage which the unprivileged always have over the privileged, as foolish things confound the wise. 'My wonder,' Trebell comes to reflect, in the first version of the text, 'is at the power over me that has been given to something I despised.' The same perception informs Frances's words, in the revised text: 'What was she but a bit of base pleasure to you?' But the base things, as St. Paul further observed, have a way of bringing to nought the princes of this world.[9]

Amy tells something of her past and background, in a dressed-up account. The matter of what she has to say about herself underlines the precariousness of her position: the Edwardian society woman, living apart from her husband, the solitary 'womanly' woman in a man's world, without the support of family connections, birth or wealth, to lend her prestige. So, with a slightly piquant malice, she makes a taunt out of her disadvantages:

> . . . But if I'd only been sent to Cambridge instead . . . and been lectured at by Frances, perhaps, on mathematics and morals . . . what a very different woman I should be! More like Lucy . . . though never so nice. Or I might have gone in for politics and been

a power in the land *[. . .]* a power behind the throne . . . like Julia.
But, of course, never so powerful.

They are too well-bred to acknowledge the gibe; and she can do
them no harm, surely.

*   *   *

The entry of Russell Blackborough breaks up the conversation,
introducing a new factor, a masculine force of personality, that the
atmosphere of the drawing-room cannot subdue to itself. With this
figure, so different from Amy, the playwright carries further his
criticism of the fastidious aristocracy. In Julia Farrant's attitude
to this other guest is already implicit the contempt and dislike that
her husband and Horsham will between them express in Act III:

> FARRANT. And what sort of very private life has he led, I wonder.
> HORSHAM. I should suppose that his relations with the gentler
> sex have always been business-like . . . most business-like. The
> social scandals of the Industrial North do not, however, penetrate
> to our sophisticated world. . . .

But, as Amy knows, the nice people are not really so very nice;
and the fact emerges that Julia herself, in most business-like
fashion, had invited Amy expressly as an amusement for Blackborough and because 'A house-party needs just a dash of . . . her
sort of thing'. (An imagery of prostitution, procuration and sex-
degeneracy is half-submerged in numerous passages of the play
and supplements the main action in its comment on the disordered
society.)

However, Blackborough is a character that Julia can ill afford to
despise, an omen of the future, already far too secure in his grasp
of power to be troubled by the opinions of those who need his
money and the industrial interests he controls. 'I will not be called
an intellectual snob by Mr. Blackborough,' she asserts, when he
has gone; but she is not unaware of the real menace he offers to
her kind.

Blackborough's rhetoric, exaggerated for Julia's benefit, is
rather ludicrous; his robust contempt for the democracy which

gives him his opportunity is a distorted caricature of the attitude of Julia's world; yet, though his words must seem off-centre, delivered in his tone and expressing so anti-heroic a character, they convey an aspect of the total truth that the play is gradually to reveal:

> ... the statesman's task is the accommodation of stubborn fact to shifting circumstance ... and in effect to the practical capacities of the average stupid man. Democracy involves the admission of that.

An echo of the Platonic indictment of democracy may be heard in that, and it reveals the source of the character's personal strength: his freedom from illusions.

With Blackborough's departure, the scene relapses once more into quietness. The others drift away, until only Julia, Frances Trebell and Lady Mortimer remain on stage to complete the exposition and build up expectation towards the hero's first entrance. Their talk suggests that he is the key figure in the situation, enigmatic in his isolation from party interests and personal attachments, and a potential saviour from the forces that Blackborough represents. Then the three women also go off, and the lights are lowered.

* * *

It is in the most intimate of relationships that the aloof statesman eventually appears. The dimmed lighting and the empty stage, upon which he and Amy enter as from the garden, are intensifying factors in the scene of passion that follows. In this scene, from which all the subsequent violence takes its origin, Barker strips the sexual relation of all its usual modifying, non-sexual factors, friendship, mutual respect, common interests and likenesses of temperament, such things as Frances will appeal to in her desperate last Act struggle to hold her brother to life. Amy is flirting, amusing herself, making little provocative advances and retreats, but working herself in deeper than she realises. Trebell goes through no such parade, but watches her, still and intent, self-confident and predatory, restraining all but the slightest indications that the excitement of the chase is gaining possession of him. The advent of the butler, come to lock up for the night, whips up passion in both and precipitates Trebell's triumph and Amy's yielding. Apart from recurrent verbal reminders of the play's political concerns, this might be a critical scene from any commonplace well-made play. There can be no mistaking it for a love scene; it is too evident that the man despises the woman and that she has not begun to understand his nature.

When despair breaks through Amy's guard, in Act II, to let the truth come pouring out, she admits to the antagonism that underlay this earlier encounter:

> I don't really like men . . . that's the silly thing. But you've to fool them . . . or they'll fool you.

It is not simply lust that drives Trebell. His attitude to the woman is one manifestation of the sense of mastery that has come to him in his political career. It is the form of hubris that leads to his self-betrayal. His sex expresses itself in the force of will that bends life to itself. Although she scarcely realises it, Amy is subject to him: the instinctive, vulnerable creature, born to submit and be sacrificed. Yet she expresses desire for one power, the power to make the man suffer, which is ironically to be granted to her as a consequence of her death. In kind, the power of suffering, associated with the weak woman, offers the antithesis to the more obvious dominance of force.

During the discussion which takes place between Wedgecroft and Trebell in the original version of Act II, the former raises the question: 'A priestcraft of women too?' adding, 'There's the tradition of service with them.' But he provokes from Trebell a sour response that anticipates Constantine Madras:

> Slavery . . . not quite the same thing. And the paradox of such slavery is that they're your only tyrants.

It is probable that Barker intended Amy's fate, and the events it sparks off, to contain recollections of the slave religion of Christianity, its sacrificial doctrines and theology of victory through defeat. The theme of male against female, touched lightly in *The Voysey Inheritance*, is probed more deeply here.

*   *   *

Trebell is on the stage throughout Act II. There is no provision for any break in the playing, but the dramatist uses the device of the ringing of a telephone bell as a warning of the approaching end of each of the three episodes that compose the Act; it is a simple means of setting the audience on the alert for a new twist in the action. There can be no doubt but that the continuity and compression of the three episodes into a whole heighten the ironic contrasts between them and increase the effect of a swift, inexorable development in events.

The Act opens in a mood of exhilaration. The setting is Trebell's new study, light and airy, and fit background for his abounding hopefulness and energy in the face of his new, big task. Walter Kent, now Trebell's secretary, echoes the almost boyish excitement that lends impetus to the hero's unguarded talk with his sister and his old friend, Dr. Wedgecroft. The replies of the others, they are amused to observe, offer little check to Trebell's enthusiasm. He offers an explanation to Wedgecroft:

I am in love with a Bill for the Disestablishment of the Church of England ... and for doing sundry other more interesting things.

Thus is recalled to the audience the scene that is past, in which he refused to apply a word meaningless to him, this same word, 'love,' to a personal relationship. Indeed, he responds much more humanely to his work than he did to Amy, and consequently shows up in a more attractive light.

Before he leaves, Dr. Wedgecroft counts his friend's pulse. Balanced and sane himself, with a warmth of feeling to counterpoise his scientific mind, he serves to measure the deviations of others, Trebell especially, from the true. His comment, 'I've never seen you thrilled or rattled,' prepares for the central episode of the play, the interview with Amy, in which the whole situation is to be violently reversed and the issues of life and death fought out. The static nature of this preliminary scene is designed to make the subsequent rise in tension all the steeper.

Frances has already gone, and Wedgecroft is about to go, when Amy arrives. The new scene is ushered in with the weighted, symbolic action of her throwing of the note, whereby she has drawn Trebell's attention, into his huge, new waste-paper basket, the 'statesman's companion', as it was designed to be. It is a signal for concentration before battle is joined.

As soon as the man and the woman are once more alone together, Amy's hysteria, at first severely controlled, adds its pressure to the urgency created by the time limit (for Lord Charles Cantilupe is expected in a very few minutes). Her too long suppressed fears find relief at last in an uninhibited utterance which reveals a very different creature from the elegant woman of fashion; and profound embarrassment at the public stripping of the civilised being to reveal a shameful ignorance and crudity is likely to be the first intense reaction of an audience:

> You think I've had lovers . . . besides you. It's not true . . . whoever has told it you. I've been near enough to the edge of it. I don't really like men . . . that's the silly thing. But you've to fool them . . . or they'll fool you. I did do one thing that wasn't quite right before I was married . . . though nothing happened [. . .] Still . . . being a Catholic and confessing now and then does help keep you straight. Though you can't confess everything. And what do priests know about marriage anyway? They oughtn't to . . . .

So it pours out, the more shameful for Trebell's failure to comment on any of it. It is in this passage, indeed, that the playwright reaps the fullest benefit of the extreme polish of the opening scene of the play; the contrast between the two views of Amy is a painful one.

The rest of the episode consists of a succession of further emotional climaxes, interspersed with slight, temporary lulls. Between the bursts of self-revelation from Amy, Barker employs the different tenseness of understatement, checking the flow of passion with such terse exchanges as:

> AMY. And that'd smash you.
> TREBELL. At the moment . . . yes.
> AMY. I'd be so sorry. Still, you'd marry me.
> TREBELL. That is the usual thing.

About that hangs the particular blank hopelessness which belongs to failure of communication.

Amy works up from 'He might have killed me . . . not that I'd mind much. Or he might kill you' to 'I'd sooner kill myself', almost immediately reiterated more shrilly and determinedly: 'I'll kill myself sooner.' It is not fear of scandal, but something more fundamental, less easy to comprehend at once, that prompts this absolute, passionate denial: revolt against her sex, against the men who would tame it and subdue it to the order they frame; against generation, time and mortality, the very nature of things. The fundamental ambivalence of the play emerges here and will not again desert the figure of Amy: sign of the diseased society, she expresses also the unending protest of the soul against the limitations of life, which leads at last to the choice of death.

Trebell's response to this storm of emotion is a concentration of quiet reasonableness. A stage direction has already drawn attention to an echo, in Amy's phrase, 'Say something,' of Trebell's words to her in Act I. A new irony arises now from a further interchange of rôles: whereas it was he who, in the previous Act, brought the charge of 'cant' against her, the word is now Amy's. By such touches Barker underlines the value of the present scene as a grim counterpart to the mock struggle of their courtship. It is Amy's turn to charge the other, justifiably, with a retreat from actuality:

> I'm in trouble . . . I'm in danger . . . and you talk platitudes to me!

—though they are platitudes which serve the author's further purpose as clues to the meaning of the fate that awaits Trebell himself:

> We choose and think we've chosen wisely . . . then by some grace we blunder on a better thing. Then comes the test. Have we a sense of it . . . and the faith to go on into the unknown? [. . .] My dear, my dear . . . beauty or brains, what are they worth . . . if we've not enough life in us to pay Life on demand?

The woman's passion seems temporarily exhausted in her repudiation of such talk, and it is once more in understatement that the relevance of those words, '. . . if we've not enough life in us . . .,' to her present condition is ominously borne in upon an audience:

> TREBELL. If that's the truth . . . let's start from that. . . .
> AMY. I don't see what use the truth is. I wish I were dead.

There is a deadly logic in the apparently casual sequence of her sentences. Her failure to recognise that truth may be life-giving is what condemns her. The lines also foreshadow the difference between the two deaths that the play is to contain: Amy's, inadvertent, yet expressive of despair; and Trebell's, deliberate, yet obscurely hopeful.

The telephone rings, and the announcement of Cantilupe's approach heightens the last and tensest climax of the whole conflict, when Amy takes up again a metaphor she has used earlier ('. . . don't question me . . . and steady me . . . as if I were a beast being broken in!') and, giving it a further grim twist, flings it at Trebell:

> AMY. . . . I'm a sick beast . . . unclean . . . cancerous.[10]
> TREBELL. Hold your tongue, will you . . . before you believe what you are saying! You unhappy woman . . . if life only seems like death to you!

But there is no release yet. Amy pulls herself together, on the advent of Lord Charles, covering the turmoil of her feelings with the social mask and the conventional phrases of apology and compliment. Nothing is resolved; the struggle is just perforce abandoned; and the dramatist discovers an audacious solvent for the tense mood in the anti-climax of Walter Kent's gaffe, as Amy turns away into his room:

> WALTER KENT. It's as if the big room had had a baby . . . I tell Miss Trebell.
> AMY. Quite! How witty of you!

There is a distinct drop in temperature, before the next scene works up, slowly at first, to its different pitch of intensity.

* * *

Barker seems once more to be forcibly arresting the action, while he places the two men on either side of a table and sets them to discuss impersonal matters.[11] But their talk is far from idle. This is the one scene, in the revised play, where the provisions of the

Disestablishment Bill are discussed in some detail, and the only
scene where the themes of the tragedy are debated formally and
in abstract terms, yet with an eloquence at once appropriate to the
situation and, in the context, very moving.

With an adroitness that he did not need to bring to bear on Amy
in Act I, Trebell proceeds to court the favour of Cantilupe. It is a
difficult task, demanding a concentration of all his powers. This is
the cause nearest Trebell's heart, his 'love', and represents the
point of fortunate destiny towards which all his life seems to have
moved. An ironic light is cast over the scene by the omen already
given that his ambitions may be doomed through his association
with Amy; and the personal emotional situation just revealed lends
its quality of strain and urgency to the discussion. Trebell does not
appear distracted by his fears of what Amy may do, but his un-
hesitating search for her, as soon as he has shown Cantilupe out,
suggests that his thoughts have never left her. It is an indication
to the actor that Trebell's mental alertness must convey the pitch
to which he is strung and that the eloquence with which he
addresses Cantilupe must carry a double burden of passion: it
is not only the latter's potential opposition that has to be fought
off; Trebell is also fighting off a more intimate dread. Every successful turn that the debate takes is a reprieve from fate.

Cantilupe's characteristic style of speech, very formally phrased
and non-conducive of emotion, slows down the opening of the
scene, until his discovery of some sympathy of ideas with the other
man brings about a cautious relaxation, and the pace increases to a
brisker measure. Even at its most business-like, the talk has a way
of touching on the deeper concerns of the play. For all his spirituality, Cantilupe is a shrewd critic of idealism:

> Every big Bill in my time has had its one provision which the Press
> would unite to praise and all Parties promise to support ... in
> principle ... upon a first reading. Yet it seldom survived Com-
> mittee. I have wondered if it ever was meant to. Not quite per-
> versely, I have sometimes opposed it from the start.

And that also is an omen, as well as a debating point.

Barker allows his various characters to contribute their fragmentary and circumscribed glimpses—now conflicting, now con-

firming—of the total truth contained in his choice of Trebell as hero. We have had Blackborough's share. Now Cantilupe expresses the tragic paradox on which the drama turns, as he diagnoses, in words of manifold relevance to the play's various themes, the spiritual state of the civilisation that Trebell represents:

> ... the master-fallacy of a godless age ... the belief that the things we do can be better ... or other ... than the thing we are.

Cantilupe's is not the heroic character, and this truth, which he can perceive, does not challenge his personal existence, as it will challenge Trebell's. As he stands aside from the age he denounces, in the security of his orthodox faith, so he will stand aside from Trebell and any Cabinet that would include him, only to find at last that he has betrayed his own values through his claim to immunity.

Cantilupe's temperament and manner supply the conditions which make acceptable the elevated prose, in which Barker allows his hero, at this interim stage, to proclaim the faith that his mind holds. It is an almost lyrical medium and communicates the rarefied sense of beauty that attaches the idealist to his ideals. Lord Charles listens and responds briefly, though with interest, while Trebell soars to a peroration, far above the squalor implied in the recently past scene with Amy; it may be a defiance of that and the threat it holds:

> .. For I believe in vocation ... and in the calling of voices from that hill, however confusedly [...]. Once we're through with youth's appetites and illusions, what does our carnal life hold for us? The past becomes a picture-book. The moment as it passes can't be very interesting [...] for we live it ignobly chained. But the future! That we create ... selflessly ... out of ourselves ... We can be honourably happy there[...]. I have strange visions of your churches, Cantilupe ... and of week-day praises to God. Of Cathedral cloisters busy with dispute. And of every parson in the country turned scholar and school-master ... with his soul really set upon eternal things [...]. It may be our civilisation's last chance too. You Churchmen shall write us a creed for our children to believe. You shall sanctify their new world for them or perish.

(In the event, it is through Amy, not through Cantilupe, that

Trebell is to discover the sanctifying creed.) It does not need the printed direction which accompanies this speech (*'he has, in a sense, ceased to speak to him'*) to show that the dramatist is here presenting his equivalent of the great Elizabethan soliloquy, in which the profounder concerns of the play are gathered up and offered through the medium of the hero's consciousness.

It may be remarked how the words, 'That we create ... selflessly ... out of ourselves,' suggest a subconscious awareness of Amy, suggest also that Trebell's mind is turning to find a meaning in generation, a wonder at the extension of life that it gives, the discovery that she has failed to make. The irony is piling up: 'Once we're through with youth's appetites ...',—but Trebell is hardly through with the consequences of his appetites; '... the future!'— but the future of his personal dreams is doomed; he has yet to discover that the 'eternal things' do not belong to the future any more than to past or present. Drily, Cantilupe can hint at an intellectual arrogance, an ill-based confidence, in the other's attitude, and he has the last word in the discussion:

> ... the hells of this world are paved, don't you think, less with good intentions than with high ideals.

When the door is opened for Cantilupe's departure, Wedgecroft is found waiting on the landing, watch in hand, a reminder of urgencies other than his own:[12] there is to be no relaxation of suspense until the curtain falls. Amy has gone and left no word, but here is a message from Brampton, who wants to see Trebell at once about the finance of the Bill, and in the room is Lucy, requiring to be talked to civilly. In the final moments of the Act, the happiness and clear hopefulness of Lucy and Walter, now engaged to be married, restore a calmer mood, but also deepen by contrast the darkness that has gathered about Trebell since the Act began. The pride of the young couple in their association with his work is a poignant reminder of his own exultant confidence, so short a time ago.

*   *   *

The dramatic action leaps over some of the incidents which

would be climaxes of narrative: Trebell's decision to join the Tories, which falls into the no-man's land between Acts I and II; and now the death of Amy, announced to the audience with the shock of fact accomplished, in a casual question from Cantilupe near the opening of Act III; and the shot with which Trebell ends his life, in the final Act, will not be heard at all, the lights being dimmed upon his preliminary slamming of the door. The fact that the inner climaxes do not always coincide with the outer is part of what the play has to demonstrate. The hero will make the point explicitly in Act IV:

> I once heard four doctors ... Gilbert among them ... disputing the moment, the exact moment, when they'd a right to say: This is death. I thought the corpse ought to know ....

Towards the end of the play he will talk of himself consistently in the past tense.

Act II is composed from materials that suggest the conventional *scène-à-faire*: the confrontation of husband and lover over the dead body of the wife; and the rejection of the statesman by his colleagues, at the zenith of his career. Yet, in the revised version at least, the scene does not materialise as expected: Trebell's attention fastens on O'Connell only briefly; and the rejection of the statesman is determined at a moment when at least two of the figures on the stage are unaware that anything of importance is happening. Barker forces us to look under the surface for the more significant part of the action.

The *Preface to Julius Caesar* puts the rhetorical question:

> ... do not these three sorts of men, the idealist, the egoist, the opportunist, stand with sufficient truth for the sum of the human forces which in any age will be holding the affairs of the world in dispute?[13]

The three typical disputants appear together in this Act: Trebell, the idealist (Cantilupe and O'Connell are lesser variants of the type); Blackborough, the egoist; Horsham, the opportunist. Egoist and opportunist, little as they like or respect each other, combine in the work of destruction. As Horsham's failure to recognise any absolute value leaves him a tool of the meaner, less scrupulous character of Blackborough, so a defect in Trebell's idealistic nature, his disregard of human frailty—symbolised by Amy—has prepared the way by a self-betrayal for the climax of the play.

It is significant that this climax is reached in an Act containing no woman character: in the 'man's world' that is associated with the more obvious forms of power. In general organisation, Act III balances the first part of Act I. This is another drawing-room scene; again the interest is dispersed over the whole group and the dialogue carefully orchestrated for a variety of voices. The room bears the impress of Cyril Horsham, as Julia Farrant's drawing-room bore hers. Barker uses a simple device to give outward shape to the Act: to the group on which the curtain rises he adds, at intervals, O'Connell, Blackborough, then Trebell himself, so marking more forcefully the rising tension, until the climax is past; and the subsequent relaxation is also gradual and marked by the dispersal of the characters: first O'Connell, then Trebell, Blackborough, Farrant, one by one, until Horsham and Cantilupe are left to go off together at the end.

The figures on which the curtain rises are engaged in the desultory talk of those who have no more to say to each other, yet are kept waiting for some new development. The gloom is a little relieved by Horsham's acidities, but even he is appropriately subdued in the presence of bereavement, when O'Connell is shown in. Each in turn tries his particular method of approach to bring the Irishman round to their point-of-view, rather as each of the other characters had encountered Amy, in Act I; in much the same way, the composite portrait of this group is built up.

O'Connell's personality freezes sympathy. The cold passions of hatred and denial govern it. Like Cantilupe, he dissociates himself from his age and its doings; but his indifference to individuals and society alike is not only intellectual. Cantilupe's humane qualities are shown up by contrast, when O'Connell's fanaticism speaks:

> Is the fate of the two of them worth a lie? For your time breeds such . . . and will . . . till its corruption burst.

This might be a caricature of Trebell's own ruthlessness in pursuit

10

of truth; but the metaphor is also a grim, obscene repetition of Amy's horrified protest at the life within her:

> I'm a sick beast . . . unclean . . . cancerous!

(The lines recall the imagery of disease and corruption employed in *Hamlet*.) The power of death, which Amy first invoked, hangs about O'Connell, too, and distinguishes from Trebell's the spiritual arrogance that can assert:

> Our souls are in constant peril. That is not troubling me.

His faith, like the thirteenth-century studies that occupy him, has become his retreat from life.

Blackborough's entrance interrupts the scene, but he remains a silent witness of proceedings, portentous in his stillness, until O'Connell has given the promise they want and the time comes for his own attack to be launched. The noise and evidence of a physical tussle at the door brings the sharpest shock yet, in this politest of settings, and is followed by Trebell's unexpected entry. The rest are transformed into a hushed audience for the meeting of the two men whose private lives have been dragged into this small version of the political arena. Barker doubtless intended to contrast the Irishman's religious fanaticism with Trebell's sceptical temper—and the lover of the past with the lover of the future; but there are curious similarities in the two characters, also, which make credible the fact that it should be Trebell himself who finds the right words to persuade O'Connell; significantly, 'truth' is the dominant one:

> What she was to you . . . you know. Tell the truth of it to-morrow.
> She has had to die to trap me. I'll tell the truth of that if need be.

At once, the fanatic fire blazes up in the Irishman. He can agree to this cryptic reflection on the worthlessness of Amy and the barrenness she brought in her train. Yet the promise that he quickly gives is at variance with what Trebell has just asked:

> I shall say nothing to-morrow that will compromise Mr. Trebell.

But such an evasion of truth, it is soon clear, will have no power to save the statesman.

Trebell does not even thank O'Connell, but turns quickly away to the others and the harder battle that is still to be fought. O'Connell has only to listen for a few minutes, in order to reach the conclusion:

> No, sir, you were right . . . I can do nothing for you.
> And had revenge been what I wanted . . . could I be leaving my interests in better hands?

He goes. But this is still only the beginning of a process that will pursue the conflict and the vengeance at last into the recesses of Trebell's mind. Already the hero is thinking in terms of sin and atonement and, as he talks to Cantilupe, seems to be seeking spiritual help more than political support. In words that expose the strain that he is labouring under, he moves a stage further in his struggle towards the light:

> Oh, I can repent . . . the thing done . . . and the folly of it. But the thing that I am . . . to repent that is to die.

The true climax of the Act lies there, in that sudden anticipation of the catastrophe. The full revelation of the truth of his own nature is what will kill Trebell; such is the tragic experience that this play recognises.

Blackborough has made his position clear. Abruptly, recognising that the decision now lies with Horsham alone, Trebell leaves the company to settle matters in his absence; and the alliance begins to disintegrate as, restraint removed, tempers at last escape. An unexpected attack upon Cantilupe is the first move in the renewed campaign that Blackborough prosecutes with a drive, a brutal concentration of force, that has been only hinted before this. Horsham's last chance of holding them all to the Bill and to Trebell, already weakened by the defection of Cantilupe, is lost when Farrant lets slip: 'If Trebell doesn't come in, Brampton won't.' For what better could Blackborough desire than such ruin of a Cabinet and a measure that he has never liked? He has only to hint at the impossibility of checking the spread of such a scandal as this, involving Trebell, and he can relax with satisfaction into the deadly contempt of:

> ... put him on the Bench. You've a reputation as a cynic. The Divorce Court ought to be vacant soon ....

Like Trebell, he leaves before Horsham declares his mind; he does not need to wait.

The conflict is over, and the three remaining can relax. Horsham can let go the reins, as he retraces with the others the scene that has been played and points out to them the false and irretrievable moves that each made. There is a general slowing down of the movement, continued when Farrant also has left, and the cousins, Horsham and Cantilupe, turn from the business that has occupied them all this time to make a gently, teasingly ironic end with their private family concerns:

> She'd been his mistress undoubtedly ... and their later relations were unspeakable [...] if she tries to sell that picture all these old stories will be raked up.

It is a coda that recalls in its effect the end of Act II of *The Voysey Inheritance*, which left old Mrs. Voysey murmuring to herself about the family of Oliver Cromwell.

*　　*　　*

Though he appears only in Act III, Horsham is to be counted as one of the play's major characters, in whom Barker's emphatic denial of Julia Farrant's '... a statesman may be a little inhuman' is most forcefully concentrated. It is a type rarely portrayed in the English theatre: the mature sophisticate, to whom all experience has become primarily intellectual, who protects his nervous sensibility through an acquired ability to distance and objectify whatever threatens it with hurt. This is what makes Horsham efficient; it also leaves him without passionate convictions, but only aesthetic perceptions of harmony and propriety: 'Oh ... why?' is his response to Farrant's protest that he would not have spoken to O'Connell after his Sinn Fein activities, 'but for this;' on hearing that the Coroner is a Plymouth Brother, he is detached enough to indulge his aesthetic disgust, *'his eyes upturned to the classic Adam ceiling:'*

> Why do not the members of that distressful sect abandon a designation which does so suggest gin-drinking?

His care for manners, prestige, respectability, as much as anything, is the sceptic's refuge from destructive despair. It is apparent in his strange frivolity, which enables him to talk of his work as a game, dismiss the fate of Amy, the fate of Trebell and the failure of his own political aspiration from his mind with no undue regret:

> ... at sixty-five I am tempted to try this rather imaginative stroke ... and I fail. I'm not surprised. But the calculation was such a nice one ... such a combining of incompatibles! What a triumph ... and how amusing ... to have brought it off! Would you post this, then, in the corner pillar-box as you pass?

His want of principle leaves him—as he himself recognises better than anyone—only the instrument of other forces. He puts it to Farrant:

> You take, I think, a romantic view of my office, and, consequently ... though I don't complain ... an unromantic one of me. What authority will make men abler ... or more honest ... or less selfish than they are?

The words are a counterpart of Cantilupe's criticism of 'the belief that the things we do can be better ... or other ... than the thing we are'; but Cantilupe's condemnation is turned by Horsham into an excuse. (Trebell will emerge as a true romantic hero in offering an answer to Horsham's question; for the authority of a new-found faith is what his suicide will assert.)

The notation of the character, as distinct from the conception, is rather more helpful to the actor in the second version. One of his chief tasks is to reconcile the diversities and contradictions from which the figure is built and that, finally, make it comprehensible: the genuine courtesy and considerateness that Horsham shows to his secretary, Saumarez, and the caustic virulence of his comments on Brampton ('... his scabrous little chats with the dozen or so young women whom he honours with his senile attentions'); the sympathetic imagination to be glimpsed when, thinking only of the human fear and agony, he exclaims of Amy, 'Poor woman!' and the fastidious contempt of his later verdict on what he chooses to consider her harlotry. A direction is illuminating: '*A little snappishness is a safety-valve;*' the verbal calumnies of such unexpected force are a release from the strain of diplomacy and, for the actor, a means of conveying that strain. Horsham's silences, his abstractions, his alertness are all aspects of his finesse. Such is the channel in which his vitality runs, contrasting sharply with Blackborough's bludgeoning methods of destruction. (His name, punning on 'whore' and 'sham', reflects Trebell's comment on "an adulterous and sterile generation'; it may be compared with 'Windlesham' in *The Madras House.*)

* * *

In the course of Act IV, the words, 'past' and 'done', which have already been pointedly used in the play, acquire fresh significance. Barker's use of them seems to be informed by reminiscence of the words Shakespeare gives to Antony: 'Things that are past are done with me.' In its superficial sense, that statement could have been applied by the Trebell of Act I to himself, in his impatience of cant and shades of emotion. When the political world, which has been his only world, casts him aside, he has to find a new meaning in 'past' and 'done': one corresponding to the sense of illimitable possibility which lives alongside the note of doom in the Shakespearian context.

Walter Kent's lament for his hero will be: 'Oh, the waste of him ... oh, the waste ... the waste!' The young man is not himself aware of the relevance of his cry to the inner drama. That is pointed by a backward glance to Trebell's idea, introduced into his discussion with Cantilupe:

> The blood of the martyrs you've made ... that also has been the seed of the Church.

The end of the play will covertly assert the value of what is not done and the potency of the promise unrealised and hopes disappointed which make up the greater part of history and most individual lives.[14] Such things escape the net of time, as Amy has done in her blind instinctive choice, as Trebell does in his deliberate following after her.

The paradox of the shattered blade, from which a victorious weapon is forged, sounds at the opening of Act IV, when the Siegfried sword motif, whistled by Dr. Wedgecroft, calls Trebell to the window.[15] His room, with the curtains drawn back to show darkness outside, is already a promontory beyond the public conflict; and the effect of isolation is intensified when Wedgecroft, the last friend, has come and gone. Before he departs, he unintentionally recalls the events of Act II:

> WEDGECROFT. . . . I'm thinking of your job, not of you. You must keep fit for it.
> TREBELL. I told her that.

Here is a fleeting glimpse of Trebell's consciousness of Amy's fate as a mirror in which he chooses to read his own. 'Pull the door to, hard, would you? The lock's loose or something,' he advises his friend. There has been some business about a door in every Act. It is hardly possible to impose any symbolic interpretation on such incidents as the scuffle at the door of Horsham's room; the dialogue does not invite it. Yet it may be that Barker was deliberately preparing for this moment and this utterance: the presage of Trebell's escape.

Frances, like enough to her brother in the directness of her questioning and the brutal accuracy of her comments, is not yet to be told more than the public facts about Amy:

> TREBELL. An unwelcome baby was on the way. She went to some quack [. . .].
> FRANCES. [. . .] The little fool! The little runaway!

But it will not do to give her verdict a value in the scheme of the play which does not take into account how like it is to Sarah Cottesham's observation on Ann Leete. Meanwhile, Trebell stands apart, watching, not assenting:

> FRANCES. Fear of life . . . the beginning of all evil.
> TREBELL. Is it?

It is the question of a man whose mind is at work, taking no certainties for granted, searching for new values, and perhaps beginning to find them. His very reticences carry weight in this situation to which the drama has come:

> FRANCES. Is this all you know?
> TREBELL. It's all I can tell you for the moment.

It is the veiled response of one travelling far and fast.

The action is suspended, the lights dimmed, to represent the night in which Trebell thinks his way through to understanding. In the clarity of the morning light, which reinforces sanity, brother and sister talk again. As they talk, they open the pile of letters that has arrived. Any one, the audience knows, may prove to contain Horsham's message ending the suspense, ending the respite that ignorance has allowed; and so the moments borrow a critical intensity from the mechanical task. Frances is now told the rest of Amy's story and, for an instant, seems about to deflect the onward-driving course of the fate that holds her brother:

> FRANCES. If you'd loved her . . . only a little . . . she might have found courage to face it.
>   *At this he turns to her in sudden poignant uncertainty.*
> TREBELL. D'you think so?

However, when the suggestion has been made, it takes its place alongside the other abstract truths that the dialogue has offered, and Frances comes back to the specific case: 'No. We are what we are, I suppose.' It is Trebell's sentence, as well as the last verdict on Amy, and he greets it with the phrase he had used in Act I, that Amy later cast back at him: 'Then don't let's cant.' The web of correspondences is nearing completion.

The letter comes to the top of the pile, is read, put aside for another. Deadening the agony with automatism, Trebell goes on reading aloud. By the time Frances has taken in the import of what has happened, he is, as the cliché puts it, dead calm, the intellect passing its judgment on the whole finished situation:

... I'm done. I've come to the end. Walter will finish the letters.

When Frances questions the meaning of these words, his reply has for the audience an ambiguity which again marks the situation that, seeming to close in finally, is yet in another sense beginning to open out:

> FRANCES. To the end?
> TREBELL. As far as I can see.

It is still contrary to his nature that he should be able to understand and pity the dead woman as a suffering human being, in her own right. Only in relation to himself, only as ideas with which he has to come to terms, are she and the unborn child present to him. Of the two, it is the child, Frances perceives, the thing of no being and no actuality, which chiefly obsesses him. He has always lived among abstractions, and it is an abstraction that brings about his intellectual conversion, the only kind possible to the man he is.[16] His mind is now occupied with the idea of revenge, passed on to him by O'Connell. He glances back at Horsham and the rest:

> Oh ... I could still make a show of success. Have my revenge on them too! A barren business.

He rejects the futility of that mechanistic notion of guilt and punishment, except as it relates to self-conviction and self-punishment and to the destiny men carry within themselves. So he applies it to his relationship with Amy:

> And if this new power coming to birth in me has been killed now ... as wantonly as she denied life to that child ... ! I'd rather like to think Fate could be so subtle in revenge.

Alive to his intention, Frances bends her powers to hold him to life, as he had done with Amy. She uses the imagery of spring and the return of fertility, and it makes a distant counterpoint to a remark by Wedgecroft in Act II:

> I'd begun to wonder about you. I seem to have watched so many rivers run into the sand.

This is what has happened, after all; but the imagery of renewal prepares the audience to receive the hope implicit in the play's end.

Now, when the death of the unborn child seems to have cut off the future beyond his personal future, the idea of an eternal value, voiced to Cantilupe in a quotation from Donne ('On a huge hill/ Cragged and steep, Truth stands . . .'), is transformed to a living reality for Trebell. So, out of the enlightenment of the whole man, he tries to convey to Frances, could she but grasp it, the meaning that his suicide will hold:

> What's a week [. . .] or a year . . . or ten? Who'd bargain for life on such terms . . . even if he could? Time's no measure, is it, of the things men have made honourable?

That earlier quotation continued more pragmatically ('. . . and he that will/Reach her, about it and about must go'); and honour, as *Ann Leete* and *The Voysey Inheritance* have already asserted, has its indispensable political use.

Unable to believe what she knows, Frances leaves her brother at last to exchange greetings with the maid, who has come to clean the room. Bertha's enquiry about his holiday, like the appearance of Lucy at the end of Act II, marks the tremendous compression of experience in the play, the precipitous descent from the beginning of Act II to this point, when Trebell goes out of the room and shuts the door decisively behind him.

The main part of the brief final scene is acted out between Frances and Julia, come to condole, as Cyril Horsham's envoy. Grief brings the once arid-seeming Frances to simple and plain-spoken comment on the society Julia represents:

> . . . you've just got to be greedy, haven't you, of the things you need from the people who can help keep you where you are.

Wedgecroft is present throughout the scene, uncompromising, humane, but offering no word of comfort. Still business-like, he is a figure of the life that goes unostentatiously on; but he is also a figure of anger and the power for change that lies in anger. Walter Kent's lament, which concludes the play, is more vehemently angry; and the cry which sums up the ambivalence of the tragic concept continues to echo as the curtain comes down:

I'm not grieving . . . I'm angry *[. . .]* I'd like to go through the streets and shout that he's dead . . . that they've lost him and wasted him, damn them! *[. . .]* Oh, the waste of him . . . oh, the waste . . . the waste!

The musical foreshortening of the phrase gives a formal close to balance the fugue with which the play opened. Kent, Barker has contrived to hint, may be a young Siegfried. But that is another story.

*   *   *

William Archer, in *Play-making*, records that Barker took the first notion of the plot of *Waste* not from the Parnell or Dilke sensations, but from another topical *cause célèbre*, involving the suicide of a soldier.[17] Archer gives no specific details, but there can be little doubt that he was referring to Major-General Sir Hector MacDonald,[18] 'Fighting Mac,' as he was popularly known, a talented and courageous Highlander, who had risen from the ranks and, in March 1903, shot himself at the Hôtel Régina in Paris, when a scandalous accusation threatened to put an end to his career. That the dramatist's imagination began to play about this nucleus of a suicide, adding the rest of the plot later, is borne out by a letter he wrote to Gilbert Murray in 1909:

> I think what Butler has to say about *Waste* is most just and true. The worst of it is faults of execution, not conception. I have him all right in my head. The man of no religious ideas who when he gets one at a great crisis in his life is so superstitiously possessed by it that it drives him monomanical and kills him.—That's all right I believe—but I've not done it! ! ![19]

Though the finished play is much less simple than that comment would seem to imply, the straight statement confirms our interpretation of the crisis of *Waste* as a religious crisis and the whole action as relevant to the religious idea.

On its appearance in 1909, the play was extravagantly hailed as the twentieth-century rival to *Hamlet*. The comparison can be justified on grounds of theme. Modern criticism has absorbed the Hegelian concept of a tragic moment in historical progress, when the ethos of a passing age is at war with an opposing ethos, before the new synthesis emerges. It is recognised that Shakespeare presented such a moment, in the transition from the mediæval world to the modern, through the troubled consciousness of his Prince; the tragic experience which Barker identifies with Trebell is essentially of the same kind.[20]

This is a justification for the prominence of the Education issue in the play, especially in the first version. 'I've watched the Education fever take England . . .,' declares Lady Davenport, in the first scene. Some of the force of that uncompleted statement can be recaptured from a contemporary lecture by Professor Gilbert Norwood on "Euripides and Mr. Bernard Shaw" (delivered in 1912). This represents the Education Act of 1870 as the main historical turning-point of modern times, dividing the early twentieth century from the middle of the nineteenth, as if they were different worlds. A mid-twentieth-century audience, familiar with the course of world-warfare, may be slow to recognise how central the issues that concern Barker's politicians were to the Edwardian period. If we substitute for universal education the related idea of modern democracy, it is easier to appreciate the particular political challenge with which the dramatist was occupied.

'I grew up,' Trebell explains to Cantilupe, 'in the late nineteenth-century neo-Polytechnic belief that you couldn't take God seriously and be an F.R.S.' He speaks for an age that, having adopted materialism as a sufficient faith, was now finding a need to look beyond it. Ellesmere, we are told, is his 'pocket borough': uncomfortably Lilliputian in its metaphysical dimensions.[21] His dryness, austerity, devotion to work and lack of ready human sympathy reflect the dominant spirit of late nineteenth-century intellectual life. His heroic quality is identifiable as a ruthless intellectual honesty, the honesty of the Victorian agnostic, carried to its extreme. The tragedy that the play uncovers belongs to that narrow virtue: uncompromising, it leads to destruction, and yet through it Trebell finds not only an end but a kind of salvation.

The play's intricate and far-reaching argument has the unity of a philosophical system; this is the basis of its supremely 'well-made' quality. In the inexorable working-out of this tragedy of the man to whom life is thought, Barker has produced a model of tragic form, almost too academically complete. Within the action, many dualisms move towards a final resolution: principle and compromise, time and eternity, power and weakness, fulfilment and waste, interwoven with the central antithesis of scepticism and faith. The religion of progress has left its trace in Trebell's care for the future, and in the fact that it is the unborn child which eventually claims him.[22] Otherwise, he seeks a neo-platonic way of mastering 'this world of power that our secular minds have made'; and, in his debate with Cantilupe, he speaks for Platonic idealism against the religion of Christianity.[23] The conflict takes variant form in his relation to Amy. Here it is the elements of reason and love that clash, as they must, even to the destruction of the embodying forms, before their values can be reconciled. The dialectical pattern and the conflict between the spirit of philosophy and Christian feeling correspond to Hegel's way out of the *impasse* of rationalism to his final synthesis.

It is sometimes argued that suicide, as it implies an evasion of life, is an inadequate end for a tragic hero. Trebell's suicide, however, is the logical consummation of his tragedy: a self-judgment, as there is no other Judge; an assertion of self-responsibility, by one who recognises that Man must look within himself for divinity. (In the same way, the suicide of Ibsen's Rosmer and Rebecca is their willing fulfilment of what classical drama would have represented as the divine sentence of doom upon them.) It is also an act of consent, releasing the future, by one who—like Hamlet—foreshadows it, but is destined never to enjoy it.

* * *

If we regard it as a social play, *Waste* has a claim to be considered as important a study of the Edwardian governing class as *The Voysey Inheritance* is of the professional middle-class of the period. Its surface authenticity is derived from the author's first-hand observations of the society depicted.

Barker served on the Executive of the Fabian Society from 1907 to 1912, though his attendance at meetings became increasingly irregular; his own lectures to fellow-members were usually on some aspect of theatre, but he chaired other meetings, more specifically political.[24] Through his acquaintance with the Webbs, he was introduced to statesmen and to the recognised intelligentsia, people of the calibre of Sir Oliver Lodge and Bertrand Russell. He had many opportunities to acquire insight into the actual forces at work in politics and the intricacies of political technique. The statesmen now formed part of the established audience for his productions, and some of them attended his luncheon and dinner parties,[25] H. H. Asquith, A. J. Balfour and Winston Churchill—three of the century's Prime Ministers—among them. The deliberations of the National Theatre Committee gave him further opportunity of meeting men of affairs, such as Lord Esher, financiers and academics. His grandfather, Dr. A. B. Granville, had been at home in such society; Barker himself was to keep a place in it for the rest of his life. In the spring of 1910—this takes us beyond the first writing of *Waste*—, he was at Newbuildings, discussing prison reform with Churchill and being offered a parliamentary seat (a polite attention!), during a week-end when Irish affairs were very much in the air; for his host, Wilfred Scawen Blunt, had a confidential communication on the matter to make to the young Home Secretary.[26]

It is understandable that the dramatist should have wished to turn such new experiences and observations to account, in his endeavour to bring English society as a whole within the compass of his theatre's art. The portrayal of the Tory Shadow-Cabinet, in *Waste*, has indeed a startling air of actuality. A group very like that of the 'Souls' moves about Julia Farrant. Trebell's career and political character show marked similarities to Asquith's. However, Asquith's reputation for cynicism is transferred, in the second version of the play, to Horsham:

> BLACKBOROUGH. . . . put him on the Bench. You've a reputation as a cynic. The Divorce Court ought to be vacant soon.[27]

And there is a reflection of Balfour's temperament in Trebell's cold and austere idealism.

Our Partnership contains an account of a visit Barker made with Sidney and Beatrice Webb to Lord Milner. It has a special interest as part of the background of *Waste* and of those early criticisms of the play which confused the consciousness of the hero and the consciousness of the author.[28] Beatrice quotes a comment made by Barker on the disappointed imperialist, which struck her by its perceptiveness:

> A God and a wife would have made Milner ... into a great man: without either he has been a tragic combination of success and failure. 'He would have been made by being loved,' summed up G.B. as we rode away.[29]

CHAPTER VII

Woman and Empire

MRS. HUXTABLE. And have you left the Army long, Major Thomas?
THOMAS. Four years.
MRS. HUXTABLE. Now what made you take to the Drapery Trade?

So Hercules was enslaved among women. The lion-hearted hero spinning for the Queen of Lydia, like Samson shorn, is a comic figure to an unkind eye. Such terms as Mrs. Huxtable has at her disposal quickly reduce his moral situation to absurdity; it is an absurdity that the whole elaborate *jeu d'esprit,* which is *The Madras House,* is concerned to exploit.

This is a Don Juan play. The view of the tyranny of sex, which Tolstoy offers in the horrifying terms of *The Kreutzer Sonata,* is here translated into comedy. None of its clarity is lost in the process, and Granville Barker supplied his own insight into the contradictions and torments of sexuality in modern civilised life. So we need not be too surprised to find that his farce is in truth tragicomedy. The evasion of sexual realities that seems to go alongside keen analysis in Shaw's best-known Don Juan play, *Man and Superman,* is not practised in *The Madras House.*

Time is deliberately flattened out, in this new play. In effect, Act I is a presentation of any Sunday morning in the home, at Denmark Hill, of an elderly and prosperous tradesman with a large family of unmarried daughters, while Act II depicts any day at the premises of Roberts and Huxtable, a drapery store in Peckham, and Act IV shows any evening in Jessica Madras's discreetly

148

luxurious drawing-room; the typical now supplies the chief dramatic interest. In Act III, where a climax is expected, a particu-
larised event does take place: the Madras House, a Bond Street
emporium, is sold; but the business transaction is completed in a
few seconds at the end of a conference of directors who have preferred to let their talk range widely, in the manner of a shavian
disquisitory play. If outer action is now almost entirely excluded,
it is not in order to give more prominence to the moral revolution
accomplished in the hero's nature, after the manner of *The Voysey
Inheritance*. Instead, Granville Barker might be challenging his
audience to find any development within the consciousness of Philip
Madras that the term, 'inner action,' might be stretched to cover:
in the first moments of Act I is announced his intention of retiring
from commerce and standing for the L.C.C., and the end of Act IV
merely re-affirms that intention; it has not been called seriously in
question at any point between.

The various Acts, each with its own setting to which the play
never returns, are laid out as if side-by-side for the mind to note
analogies and contrasts. The drama has a broadly defined shape,
which rises to a climax of spectacle and excitement in Act III, as
play and characters soar away in an effervescence of fantasy, and
then quietly descends again to the intimate style of the final scene.
In the way of argument, Act IV must certainly follow the rest, for
it reviews the evidence of the preceding Acts and draws conclu-
sions from it. Otherwise, *The Madras House* can be regarded as
a sequence of loosely attached entertainments which combine the
theme of sex with the theme of the commercial society. But, as one
Act follows another, a panorama of that society is unfolded: its
masters, servants and dependants, their domestic and business relations, the gradations of social status and wealth within the extreme limits of the upper and lower middle-class in imperial
England.[1]

The choice of hero is related to the general nature of the dramatic experiment. Philip Madras is essentially an observer-charac-
ter, often a silent witness of the main business of the scene. The
other characters represent the circle in which he lives: his father,
Constantine Madras, founded the Madras House; Major Thomas,
his friend, is the agent of the American who buys the business;

Philip is himself on the board of directors of both the Madras House and the subsidiary establishment of Roberts and Huxtable, and he is thus the employer of the work-people who appear in Acts II and III; Mr. Huxtable is his maternal uncle; Jessica Madras is his wife. It is not a happily united society: Philip's father and mother are separated; the Huxtables have sided with Amelia Madras in the family quarrel; while Jessica extends the barest tolerance to both her husband's parents. Philip's personal situation is thus one of conflicting strains that the course of the drama does little to resolve. And the part he takes in the shaping of such events as do occur amounts to nothing very significant: persuading his uncle to attend the meeting of directors, attempting to settle the troubles of the staff at Peckham, warning his wife against flirting with his friend. The things that happen make some impact on Philip's mind, but none on his character or destiny. The hero is, in fact, not a man of action and not the author's mouth-piece so much as the author's eye, focusing upon the significant appearances. Through Philip, Barker directs the response of the audience to the play: detachment, more than emotional participation, is the attitude, appropriate to comedy, that he wishes to establish in them.

To make an effective drama, substitutes had to be found for the usual conventions of development, which would hold the interest of the audience. Prominent among those that the playwright has found are: a use of caricature that testifies to the influence of Shaw, a close-knit and provocative argument, a rococo extravagance of design, and a style of dialogue that defeats *longueurs*, even while seeming to cultivate them. Theme and the elaboration of theme are now central features in a satirical drama, but the communication of intellectual pleasure, not instruction, is the playwright's primary aim. The means whereby the exposition and elaboration of theme are contrived are also the principal sources of amusement.

*　　　*　　　*

The household at Denmark Hill, which provides the subject for the first Act, consists of the elderly, successful and semi-retired Huxtable, his formidably respectable wife and their six unmarried daughters, also for the most part rather elderly, the difference between them being, as the dramatist says:

> ... *to a casual eye the difference between one lead pencil and another ... a matter of length, of sharpening, of wear.*

They return from church to find visitors: their cousin, Philip Madras, subtle, sophisticated and intellectual, and his friend and business associate, Major Thomas, a stranger to the Huxtable ladies and much the simpler personality of the two. Before the visitors can talk to Mr. Huxtable, as they have come to do, they are compelled to run the gauntlet of what the family recognises as polite conversation. A brief specimen will suffice:

> PHILIP. Do you like this house better than the old one, Clara?
> CLARA. It has more rooms, you know.
> MRS. HUXTABLE. Do you live in London, Major Thomas?
> THOMAS. No, I live at Woking. I come up and down every day as a rule. I think the country's better for the children.
> MRS. HUXTABLE. Not a cheerful place, is it?
> THOMAS. Oh, very cheerful!
> MRS. HUXTABLE. I had thought not for some reason.
> EMMA. The cemetery, Mother.
> MRS. HUXTABLE. (*accepting the suggestion with dignity*) Perhaps.
> CLARA. And of course there's a much larger garden. We have the garden of the next house as well.
> JANE. Not all the garden of the next house.
> CLARA. Well, most of it.

That is small talk transcribed as it might be spoken, with an accuracy merciless to its triviality, its stiltedness, its embarrassments, its complete lack of interest for all the participants, the self-consciously dutiful questions, the unnaturally constrained answers. The dead hand of propriety is on it all. In order to keep panic-filled silence at bay, the speakers revert to the same few topics again and again and are more and more possessed by the automatism of their talk with every repetition. (The effect achieved is an anticipation of Ionesco's method, though Barker carefully refrains from the distortion which brings the other's plays closer to the experience of dreams than of waking life.) This dialogue is calculated to bring an audience near to hysteria, in which exasperation, mirth and mental horror strive against each other. Whether any particular audience will be more amused or appalled must depend largely on the bias of the production; the text itself keeps a very precarious balance between the two moods.

The effect of stylised naturalism is not everything, in this first Act. The method employed in the revised text of *Waste*, whereby motifs which bear upon the meaning of the action are interwoven in the dialogue to form a continuous pattern, is used here also, but to very different effect: a fantastic growth out of the accuracy of observation and bareness of statement. 'Woking . . . not a cheerful place, is it?' The dramatist is launched upon a game, one that has much in common with the psychologist's techniques of association. The questioning form of Mrs. Huxtable's comment sends the mind burrowing for half-remembered information, and to the cemetery the memory may add those other remarkable features of the Woking scene, the Mosque and the oldest crematorium in England. The relevance of these suppressed associations is confirmed later in the play.

Act III is set in the Moorish Room at the Madras House and is dominated by Constantine Madras, who explains to the entranced American, Eustace Perrin State, that he has become a Mohammedan. A more intricate pun is contained in the concealed allusion to the crematorium. The passage quoted begins the process of linking this motif with others, improbably diverse. Talk of the garden takes the Huxtable daughters to the balcony:

> JULIA. Do you notice how near the Crystal Palace seems? That means rain.
> PHILIP. Of course . . . you can see the Crystal Palace.

But the balcony is also a way of reaching the conservatory, the Huxtables' domestic Crystal Palace, where Jane finds a dead frog and the Cineraria blooms,[2] flower of the burial urn, reminiscent of the cemetery and crematorium, too, that hothouse of death. A direction refers to the conservatory as '*the glass house of death*', and the description is reflected back upon the Crystal Palace. In Act IV, Constantine refers to 'this civilisation of yours . . . half-factory and half-hothouse'.

By that time, a whole system of antitheses has been built up: the references to town and country, garden and conservatory have introduced the ideas of nature and civilisation, culture and preservation, simplicity and exotic luxury. Already in the passage quoted, the crossing of the lines of conversation, by juxtaposing 'garden' and 'cemetery', presents the opposition of growth to death. The association of Crystal Palace with Mosque and crematorium anticipates the contrast between cold and heat that is to be played upon in Act III, which opens (in the Moorish Room) with lines that momentarily suggest that the conversation of Act I has never stopped:

> MR. HUXTABLE. A perfect barometer, as you might say—when your eye gets trained to it [. . .]
> MR. STATE. Is it really? The Crystal Palace! What a fairy sound that has!

Here the change from the original reading ('But what a sound that has.') ensures a swifter recognition of the icy palace of the Snow Queen, where hearts are frozen and the splinter of glass distorts vision to make deathliness seem beautiful.

Every so often contrasted images are turned round and revealed to be identical. So the symbolism of the Crystal Palace, the palace of industry, the great show-place and monument to imperialism, may be identified with that of the Madras House itself; and thus the basic idea of the commercial empire emerges, defined in terms of death and sterility, hot sensuality and Turkish despotism, coldheartedness and calculation; it is ready to be further associated, in Act IV, with the 'museum', that is Jessica's drawing-room, her refuge from life amid the culture of past ages. The basis of the whole elaborate mesh of correspondences is perceptible in the word 'conservatory' itself, a misnomer that suggests petrifaction, preservation, rather than the fostering of life.

These associations, puns and symbols are the framework of the dramatic structure. Single aspects of separate motifs interlock with others and generate new meanings, until the text can be regarded as an intricate system of intersecting circles, a frenzy of ordered movement, in which each gyring unit preserves its balanced relation to the rest.

The characters make a similar pattern. The most obvious Don Juan is Constantine Madras, who reveals himself as simply an exaggerated version of Major Thomas, the common man of the play. Yet the meaning of Don Juan which Barker earlier presented in Pierrot—coldness of heart—is finally traced to Philip, the monogamist, through the inflated figure of Eustace Perrin State, the virgin, though *their* philandering is with ideas and their seductions are to their own opinions. Even Jessica Madras and little Miss Yates play out their different female versions of the Juan rôle. Here again, contrasts merge at intervals into a common identity, and Don Juan is revealed as a symbolic figure of humanity, alien to none.

State's interest in place-names and their associations is confirmation of the deliberate element in the reference to Woking and suggests that the other place-names in the text may be similarly significant. Indeed, the appropriateness of the Huxtables' choice of Weymouth for their summer resort is emphasised by Mr. Huxtable's reference to George III, though it is left for the audience to trace the parallel between the Misses Huxtable and the clutter of unmarried princesses (and, perhaps, between the scandal of Princess Sophia's child and the shocking conduct of Julia Huxtable). Weymouth is described by Constantine as 'a *cockpit* of haphazard lovemaking'; by a simple pun, Peckham, where Huxtable's drapery store is situated, contributes further to the farmyard imagery in the play; *Denmark* Hill offers a variant pun, alluding slily to the financial jungle, at the same time as the dialogue reminds us that Ruskin lived in this locality. *Bond* Street is a suitable locality for the Jew's paradise, the 'industrial harem', in which Constantine keeps his female slaves. Illusions of grandeur haunt the minds of many of the characters, betrayed partly by their talk of royal figures. Mr. State associates Denmark Hill with Queen Alexandra; through his naming, Constantine recalls the last great Roman Emperor, though to his wife, Amelia, he seemed 'a fairy prince' and to State he brings thoughts of Disraeli.

It is not necessary to identify every allusion, grasp every pun, elucidate the mention of Woking, or recognise Hercules in the Drapery Trade, in order to follow the play and its argument and enjoy much of the comedy. Whenever recognition of such devices does take place, it increases delight; and this is the final justification of the method. The profusion of puns and comically associated ideas focuses attention on a relatively limited number of themes; and the trick of recognising them in their variant forms and combinations is quickly acquired.

This comic method recalls the technique of multiple puns which was employed in *Our Visitor*. Barker may well have been encouraged in his belief that audiences could respond to it, by the thought of related devices that had proved themselves theatrically in his boyhood, in the work of W. S. Gilbert and the burlesque tradition that Gilbert inherited. Barker's article, 'Exit Planché—Enter Gilbert',[3] abounds in examples. He points out that the following would be very flat, if the references were not appreciated:

> Each evening you may see him sitting so,
> Under that *linden when the sun is low*!
> On close inspection, too, you'll also see
> His noble *eye, sir, rolling rapidly*,[4]

or again:

> The lock upon the door at the first landing,
> The only Locke upon my understanding.[5]

His own punning is less simply mechanical than this, more akin to Gilbert's allusive technique, which requires that the whole original context should be remembered. This may be illustrated from two brief passages. The first, from *The Palace of Truth*, is straight burlesque of the opening of *King Lear*:

> PHANOR. . . . Your verdict, come!
> ARISTAEUS. I'm blunt and honest. I can't teach my tongue
> To lie, as Zoram here, and Chrysal do.
> I tell the truth, sir. If you want to know
> My estimate of what you've given us,
> I think your poetry contemptible . . .

The second example, taken from *The Princess*, is neater and funnier. Burlesque of Tennyson is combined with Shakespearian parody here. Exact quotation of Hamlet and Horatio leads into more general reminiscence of Juliet's Nurse and Capulet, too:

> HILARION. I think I see her now!
> (*Looking through a telescope.*)
> HILDEBRAND. Ha! let me look!
> HILARION. In my mind's eye, I mean—a blushing bride—
> All bib and tucker—frill and furbelow!
> How exquisite she looked as she was borne
> Recumbent in the monthly nurse's arms!
> How the bride wept!—nor would be comforted. . . .
> And I remember feeling much annoyed
> That she should weep at marrying with me;
> "But then," I thought, "these brides are all alike!
> Cry on, young lady—brides are bound to cry.
> You cry at marrying me? How much more cause
> You'd have to cry if it were broken off! . . . ."

The general inadequacy of burlesque lies in the fact that the laughter evaporates, leaving no residue of thoughtfulness. The point may be worth making, however, that the best burlesque technique can be traced right back to the young Shakespeare. J. R. Planché himself attempted a free adaptation of Aristophanes' *The Birds,* produced at the Haymarket Theatre in 1846, and Gilbert emulated the Aristophanic function, if on no very high level, and embroiled himself with the Lord Chamberlain in his attempt. The burlesque writers in fact regarded their art as a potential vehicle of political satire.

But the true modern Aristophanes was, of course, G. B. Shaw. *The Madras House* obliquely acknowledges its close relation to the plays that the older dramatist was writing at this period. Shown into the Huxtable drawing-room to await the family, Philip continues an argument with Thomas:

> Very well then, my dear Tommy . . . what are the two master tests of a man's character? His attitude towards money and his attitude towards women.[6]

A major part of *The Doctor's Dilemma* is an exposition of substantially the same text:

> SIR PATRICK. There are two things that can be wrong with any

man. One of them is a cheque. The other is a woman. Until you know that a man's sound on these two points, you know nothing about him. (Act II.)

The view of Don Juan that Barker presents in Philip Madras was anticipated to some extent in one of Shaw's first plays, *The Philanderer*, which reveals its hero, Charteris, as a mental and emotional vivisectionist.

Shaw's *Misalliance* had its first performance in the repertory season at the Duke of York's Theatre on 23rd February, 1910, and *The Madras House* was introduced into the programme on 9th March. The two plays were in fact written side-by-side. As the story runs,[7] Shaw attended a reading of the first draft of Barker's new play, then went away, smiling, and wrote *Misalliance*. His decision to introduce a Turkish bath into the scene, as an arbitrary symbol, preparing for all the fantasy to come, was undoubtedly influenced by the symbolism of Mosque and Moorish Room and the 'turban of the Turk', organic to the structure of *The Madras House*. The citations of authority, 'Read Mill. Read Jefferson,' 'Read Tennyson,' 'Read Whatshisname' (*alias* Nietzsche, or G. B. Shaw), to which John Tarleton is greatly addicted, offer a variant on the conversational habits of State, whose appearance on stage is anticipated by a telephone conversation, in Act II of Barker's play:

> PHILIP. Yes? Well? ... Who ... Mark who? ... Aurelius. No. I've not been reading him lately.

Misalliance may fairly be regarded as Shaw's first example of the political extravaganza form, only partly foreshadowed in the earlier *Getting Married*. Both he and Barker were at this time evolving an art of the preposterous as a medium for fundamentally serious comment on human life and the political organisation of society.

Barker's association with the Fabian Society must again be given some credit for the choice of subject and many of the ideas in the play. There were Fabian philanderers, among them Hubert Bland, who was to be Shaw's model for Hector Hushabye. More significantly, *The Madras House* was written shortly after the occurrences

that Edward Pease summed up as 'The Episode of Mr. Wells'.[8]
H. G. Wells had challenged the Fabian Old Guard on many fronts
and came near to disrupting the Society. Where precisely Barker
stood in this debate is not certain and perhaps not important; Pease
erroneously attributes his entry into the Society to Wells's influence;[9] but the Old Guard seems to have been behind his election
to the Executive. The novelist's insistence that the Fabians should
draw up a policy for the reform of marriage and the family, giving
official support to his scheme for the endowment of motherhood,
was resisted; his general indictment of Fabian methods and organisation started a lively uproar; the struggle over policy became a
struggle for power; and private feelings, inflamed by Wells's
attempts to proseletyse for free love among the women members of
the Society, added to the conflagration.[10] At last the originator of
the trouble retired in disgust to write *The New Machiavelli*, including in it his satirical portraits of the Webbs, as Altiora and
Oscar Bailey.

The questions that Wells put to the Fabians provide the chief
ostensible concerns of *The Madras House*: the surplus women,
the unmarried mother, polygamy, in relation to imperial power
and prosperity and to the economic and industrial system, which
is represented as determining the waste, the anomalies, the sordid
little tragedies. The Madras House itself represents at once commercial prosperity and the oriental attitude to women, the pam-
pering of slaves. Meredith's Diana is assigned a *bon mot*: 'Men
may have rounded Seraglio Point: they have not yet doubled Cape
Turk;' the feminist metaphor is never far from Barker's consciousness in this play. The six Huxtable daughters, the employees of
the drapery store, Philip's wife, Jessica, and his mother, Amelia
Madras, are all carefully chosen variants on the theme of tyranny.

Unmarried, homekeeping, the Huxtable girls are half-comic,
half-pathetic slaves to Edwardian middle-class respectability and
its domestic ideal. In his directions, the dramatist explains:
'EMMA ... *would have been a success in an office and worth perhaps thirty shillings a week. But the Huxtables don't want another
thirty shillings';* financial security sets the seal upon their futility,
of which Act I is so cruel a distillation. Their mother treats
them still as irresponsible and rather troublesome children; and

to her monumentally humourless domination they all, even Emma, dutifully submit. 'Julia,' Mrs Huxtable calls, 'won't you catch cold on the balcony without a hat?' The evocation of Juliet, only comic at the moment, offers a dispiriting contrast when Emma gigglingly confides to Philip the story of how her thirty-four-year old sister nursed a matinée idol's collar, returned from the laundry by mistake: 'And when mother found out she cried for a whole day. She said it showed a wanton mind.' Philip's unsmiling reception of the tale throws into relief the unawareness and subjection of mind, that condition the traditional respectability enslaving these women. Mrs. Madras, the deserted wife whose only glory is her injury, belongs by right in such a setting, where negation, disinclination and resentment are idealised as 'duty'. 'I'm sure I don't know why I come and stay here at all,' she protests, 'I dislike your mother extremely;' but that is surely reason enough for such a character, to whom a petty martyrdom is life.

*   *   *

Act I would seem to contain all the ingredients to make a truly depressing spectacle. ' "Ah, repetition—recurrence: we haven't yet, in the study of how to live, abolished that clumsiness, have we?" ' is the complaint of Gabriel Nash (alias Oscar Wilde) in James's *The Tragic Muse*. ' "It's a poverty in the supernumeraries that we don't pass once for all, but come round and cross again, like a procession at the theatre. It's a shabby economy that ought to have been managed better. The right thing would be just *one* appearance, and the procession, regardless of expense, forever and forever different." ' *The Madras House,* Act III excepted, implies a like criticism of life, in its presentation of the ordinary and typical. But Granville Barker has managed his procession with an ingenuity that extracts an effect of considerable variety from some very small change. Artifice intervenes to allow the comic mood to prevail over the ugliness and pathos; and the spirit of fantasy moves in the stagecraft as well as in the dialogue.

The playwright makes the most of a scene crowded with furnishings and ornaments to suggest a superfluity of persons, and he even resorts to packing his characters on to the balcony and into the

corner of the conservatory, features that add to the general clutter
of the set. Mr. Huxtable's private consultation with Philip has to be
conducted to the accompaniment of Jane and Julia, locked out upon
the balcony, tapping the glass, and is invaded by Laura, precipi-
tately entering through the door. The daughters form a chorus,
repeating one after another the absurd little ceremonies of greeting
and farewell, punctuating the Act by repeated handshakings, recurrent collisions in the doorway, dartings on and off.

The element of dance, introduced into *Ann Leete*, enters here
again. This time Barker exploits 'repetition—recurrence' so as to
punctuate Act I with choric passages. The main themes are introduced in a Prelude that presents Philip Madras and Major Thomas
with the Huxtables' maid: Holy Communion, food, money, the
Army, charity, revolution and talk are the subjects touched on
here and that will be returned to again and again, before the play is
over. Then the family returns from church, and the various members enter in their ones and twos and proceed to introductions:

> JULIA. Oh, what a surprise!
> PHILIP. Yes, we walked down. Ah, you don't know ... Let me
> introduce Major Hippisley Thomas ... my cousin, Miss Julia
> Huxtable ... and Miss Huxtable.
> JULIA. How do you do?
> THOMAS. How do you do?
> LAURA. How do you do?
> JULIA. Have you come to see Aunt Amy?
> PHILIP. No, your father.
> JULIA. He's walking back with her. They'll be last, I'm afraid.
> LAURA. Will you stay to dinner?
> PHILIP. No, I think not.

In another moment Emma arrives, and it all has to be gone through
again, but in more concentrated form:

> PHILIP. Hullo, Emma!
> EMMA. Well, what a surprise!
> PHILIP. You don't know ... Major Hippisley Thomas ... Miss
> Emma Huxtable.
> THOMAS. How do you do?
> EMMA. How do you do? Will you stay to dinner?
> PHILIP. No, we can't ...

and his explanation again sounds the words, 'father' and 'walk', from the preceding passage; indeed this whole section is composed out of elements heard just previously. Soon it is the turn of Mrs. Huxtable, whose majestic entrance is heralded by three ringing phrases:

> JANE. You? Mother!
>   *She has turned to the hall, and from the hall comes* MRS. HUXTABLE'S *rotund voice*, "Yes, Jane!"
> JANE. Cousin Philip!

There follows the culmination of the greetings heard so far:

> MRS. HUXTABLE. What a surprise! Will you stay to dinner?
> EMMA. (*Alive to a certain redundancy*) No, Mother, they can't.
> PHILIP. May I introduce my friend ... Major Hippisley Thomas ... my aunt, Mrs. Huxtable.
> MRS. HUXTABLE. (*Stately and gracious*) How do you do, Major Thomas?
> PHILIP. Thomas is Mr. Eustace State's London manager.
> THOMAS. How do you do?

There are nine sets of introductions scattered through the earlier part of the Act, and they reach a climax in a lively round, the pattern being reduced to the barest essentials:

> MINNIE. How d'you do?
> THOMAS. How d'you do?
> CLARA. How d'you do?
> MINNIE. How d'you do, Philip?
> PHILIP. How d'you do?
> CLARA. How d'you do?
> PHILIP. How d'you do?

The lengthened phrase makes a small central climax, calling the fourth person into the chain. The bowing and hand-shaking, the advancing and retreating figures belong to a visual dance that matches the dancing rhythm of the lines.

The other trivial themes recur in similar fashion: the question of dinner is mentioned seven times; there are six distinct references to taking a walk: five times the attention of the visitors is drawn to the Crystal Palace; the weather, inevitably, is a recurrent topic. Even the tiny incidents that occur seem to fall into a regular pattern, as when Clara bursts out of the conservatory:

> CLARA. Jane, that Cineraria's out.
> JANE. Oh!

and then Jane has her turn:

> JANE. Minnie, your frog's dead . . . in the conservatory.
> *Minnie pales.*
> MINNIE. Oh, dear!

Even when conversation is more continuous, it is inclined to take a question-and-answer form that is musical in effect and also suggests setting-to-partners. On several occasions it slows to a dead stop (as a section ends), and there is a sameness about Mrs. Huxtable's notions of how to get it re-started: 'Not in the Army, then, Major Thomas?' is followed after an interval by: 'And have you left the Army long, Major Thomas?' 'Have you been away for the summer, Major Thomas?' is varied by: 'Do you know Weymouth, Major Thomas?' Another character is drawn in with: 'You think more of Bognor, Amy, I know;' and then Philip takes over the lead: 'Do you like this house better than the old one, Clara?' Mrs. Huxtable resumes it almost immediately: 'Do you live in London, Major Thomas?'

In the central part of the Act, especially when Mr. Huxtable takes the stage, the rhythms are less insistent. But the unmistakable effect of a dance (bringing in everyone, this time) returns towards the end, with the farewell hand-shakings:

> PHILIP. Good-bye, Clara.
> CLARA. Good-bye, Philip.
> MR. HUXTABLE. You really won't stay to dinner?
> PHILIP. Good-bye, Laura.
> THOMAS. Thanks, no. We meet to-morrow.
> *The general-post quickens, the chorus grows confused.*

The figure is repeated at greater speed, with five more good-byes. There is a pause, while the group sorts itself out, and then a final burst of chanting:

EMMA. Good-bye, Major Thomas.
PHILIP. Now good-bye, Emma.
THOMAS. Good-bye, Mrs. Madras.
PHILIP. Good-bye.
THOMAS. Good-bye.

Drama is on the verge of becoming another art.

This is very brittle comedy, almost inhuman in its presentation of characters so subdued to the mechanism of politeness. However, glimpses of stronger individuality are offered, with touches of feeling that is not stylised. A close-up view of Emma lends a more convincing reality to the whole group of daughters. Even Mrs. Huxtable is briefly revealed as a troubled human being, when she tries to explain her attitude to Constantine Madras, apologetically, just before Philip leaves. But it is the three male figures that make the vital centre of Act I and testify, in their conversation, to a life that extends beyond the limits of Mrs. Huxtable's domain.

Amid all the cruelly precise satire, the father of the family, Huxtable himself, is a point of attraction, with his congenial humanity and late-awakened savouring of the oddity of things. Unsafe and unsettled, while the others are secure in their bonds, he is aware of the discomfort of coming truly alive:

> I do not know what's coming over me *[...]* I'd never been ill like that before ... I dunno how it is ... you get thinking ... and things which used to be clear don't seem so clear ... and then after, when you start to do and say things that used to come natural ... they don't come natural ... and that puts you off something ....

In the play's careful balancing of attitudes, this questioning bewilderment is complementary to Philip's sententiousness.

* * *

The industrial living-in system supplies the material for most of the second Act. Barker's study of it may again owe something to Wells, who wrote of it in *Kipps*. But the dramatist's evocation of respectable near-poverty surely owes its authenticity to personal experience. It is worth recalling that his boyhood was passed in a family that clung to middle-class society, while its most regular income was earned by his mother's performances as a *siffleuse*. The hysterical fit, which occurs during Act II of *The Madras House*, is a protest against sexual privation; but it speaks equally for those who live in constant panic lest they should lose a precarious social status and, with it, the remnants of their human dignity.

Though the living-in system is attacked, especially in the presentation of Mr. and Mrs. Brigstock, who are most obviously the victims of that employers' method of economising on wages, still it does not carry attention entirely away from the theme which dominated Act I. The economic factor determining the fate of women and the relation between the sexes was suggested in the first Act; it is now moved to the centre. Barker does not present living-in as an unmitigated social evil; indeed, he avoids extreme cases. Mr. Huxtable is a benevolent employer, who doubtless houses and feeds his work-people well and protects them from the hazards of loneliness as, equally at the cost of freedom, he does his own daughters at Denmark Hill.

The rôle of Mrs. Huxtable passes, in the industrial context, to Miss Chancellor, the housekeeper at Roberts and Huxtable's. She, too, is a pillar of respectability, upholder of the system from which she has been able to reap the satisfaction—happiness let it not be called!—of authority over lesser beings. Mrs. Brigstock, the wife whom the Third Man in the Hosiery cannot afford to acknowledge and live with, brings Julia Huxtable to mind, in her hysteria of frustration; if her unreasoning jealousy and foolish pride are comic, it is with a comedy like that of Amelia Madras, at once acid and saddening. The symbolism of the conservatory remains relevant: 'No, I've no children,' Mrs. Brigstock replies to Philip's enquiry; 'How can you save when you have children?' she adds. Sterility— the point is made once more—is a condition of civilisation. But the virginity of the Misses Huxtable and the provident barrenness of Mrs. Brigstock are both challenged by the most vital character in Act II: little Miss Yates who, to the scandal of the respectable, is expecting a child and declines to have a husband.

Miss Yates is Philip's main antagonist in the first half of the Act, and she is tacitly contrasted with his wife, Jessica, the woman who dominates the second half. The acting-part of Miss Yates is a relatively small one, but its importance is unsurpassed. By the time the play is over, all the other characters have been exposed as ultimately negative or passive in their response to life; she alone makes a positive assertion. Her decisiveness is the repository of hope.

It is not economic necessity alone that enslaves Miss Chancellor and the Brigstocks; their ideals make, perhaps, more effective chains. 'Are we beasts of the field, I should like to know?' Miss Chancellor exclaims, 'I simply do not understand this unladylike attitude towards the facts of life;' and Mrs. Brigstock echoes the sentiment: 'I'm sure I hope I've said nothing unbecoming a lady . . . I didn't mean to.' The devotion of the female Huxtables to their duty is there to be recognised. When Jessica Madras appears, in the second half of Act II, the play's gallery of female portraits is complete, and the ideal whereby these others live is at last realised, in the choicest bloom that the hothouse has to offer. The dramatist's comment on Jessica is disingenuous and gives an edge to his critical reservations:

> *Is not the perfect lady perhaps the most wonderful achievement of civilisation, and worth the cost of her breeding, worth the toil and the helotage of—all the others?*

Jessica has grace and sophistication, as well as beauty and unostentatious wealth; she is intelligent and sensitive, with cultivated tastes, caring genuinely for painting, music and poetry. She is not only the finest flower of womanhood, but a representative of aristocracy, the virtues and achievements that are the glories of a civilisation. Yet there is an element of greed in her nature and a determination to keep her social advantages, which responds quickly to the least threat. Otherwise, she is rather bored by an existence that, in its very different way, is as futile as that of her husband's dowdy cousins. When weary of the enclosed world of art, Jessica amuses herself by flirting with Major Thomas—an exquisite feminine philandering that will never come to anything.

Since the play was written, the ideal of the lady has almost entirely vanished. The ideal of culture which Tolstoy had attacked, 'the gospel of beauty,' as the play calls it,[11] has not yet entirely

gone; but the play's criticisms were prophetic. As Constantine
Madras puts it, in Act III:

> An effete empire is yours, gentlemen . . . and the barbarian with
> his pick and shovel and his man's capacities is over its frontiers
> already.

D. H. Lawrence's *White Peacock* appeared in 1911, and the work-
ing-class assault on the ideal was fully launched.

*   *   *

The tocsin of social revolution is to be heard at intervals in Act
III. It is in this Act that Constantine makes his first, much anticipated appearance: 'the gentle Mohammedan' of Jewish origin, who
combines a Turkish uxoriousness with a Turkish contempt for
women; and the figure of imperial splendour who, like his great
namesake, has retreated eastwards from the barbarian hordes.
Thoughts of the French Revolution are casually evoked in the
directors' discussion with State, most particularly in the anecdote
of la Belle Hélène, the Parisian *cocotte*: 'What should she see but
Madame Erlancourt . . . one of the old guard;' 'She fetched in out
of the Bois the ugliest little gamine she could find . . . put her own
hat on its horrid little head . . . sat it at her table and stuffed it with
cakes.' Hélène's thrifty asceticism recalls Madame de Maintenon,
but the cakes bring to mind Marie Antoinette; 'the Bois,' 'the Pré
Catalan,' the buttermilk, and the fish-basket, worn as a hat, become,
in the context, images of false simplicity and prepare for the mention of the toy farm with which Windlesham, the manager of the
Madras House who tells the tale, beguiles his leisure and refreshes
his spirit, as the court of Louis XVI distracted itself with pretty
pastoral play. State drives home the point by saying to Constantine,
'But you were for the Old Régime,' and his talk of 'the Fall', has
the music of revolution in it, as well as an echo of the story of Eve.
In the early moments of the first version of the play, Philip commented: 'There's something wrong with a world, Tommy, in
which it takes a man like me all his time to find that it's bread people
want, and not either cake or crumbs.'
  Through the anecdote of la belle Hélène, the ideal of beauty,

for which Troy might honourably burn, is identified with prostitution: 'Quite la haute cocotterie, of course,' and, as such, not too distantly removed from the ladylike coquetry of Jessica. The two themes of commerce and the relation between the sexes are here brought together with an emphatic snap. The insistence on the metaphor of whoredom, carried through Act III, is intellectually uncompromising, but is rendered less offensive by the fantasy which laps it round. It is Constantine who applies the image most deliberately, and his words are acceptable for the most part as the exaggerations, or paradoxes, of satire. Most of the customers of the Madras House are 'kept women', its founder explains to the pleasantly scandalised State, 'Kept by their husbands. Or somehow kept . . . in return for what they are, not for what they do . . . by Society;' referring to one of the dresses on display before them, he stigmatises 'a community in which five men of ability and dignity are met together to traffic in . . . what was the number of that aphrodisiac that so particularly attracted Major Thomas?' Speaking of the nice women, Julia Huxtable, or Jessica Madras, who yet trick themselves out to attract male attention, he uses a language whose offensiveness is less easily absorbed by the comic mood:

> Let him but veil his leering, my dear Harry, and the lousiest beggar's tribute is but one more coin in the pocket of their shame.[12]

Even in this Act, within the superb blandness and self-confident audacity of Constantine, the sour misogyny of the professional amorist makes itself heard. Sex antagonism and the motives of contempt, spite, resentment and suspicion emerge here and in Act IV as the emotional basis of social relations. Indeed, within the laughter of *The Madras House*, lurks a savagery that breaks cover from time to time. Raw feeling, driven by desperation beyond niceness, was to be heard in the first Act anecdote of Julia, who 'gets hysterical when her headaches last too long'. The same note was sounded more forcefully by Mrs. Brigstock in Act II:

> No, I've no children [. . .] But if it was his child this hussy was going to have and I thought God wouldn't strike him dead on the spot, I'd do it myself, so I would . . . and he knows I would [. . .] I

> lie awake at night away from him till I could scream with thinking about it. And I do scream as loud as I dare . . . not to wake the house. And if somebody don't open that window, I shall go off.

Philip's sophisticated presence intensifies the embarrassing effect, in both instances. He is gravely, even sensitively, censorious of the pressures which so outrage human dignity, but remains emotionally detached. Through him, the dramatist ensures that his audience will respond thoughtfully to the moral shock received, and not be carried away in a flood of pathos. There is a continuity of mood, however overlaid, between the naturalistic presentation of the Brigstocks, in Act II, through the fantasy of Act III, to the once more naturalistic, and graver, final Act.

There is no communication between the male and female figures in Act III; for the mannequins are French, not speaking or understanding English: they have but to beguile the time for their masters, who are seated at ease, waiting to begin the serious business of their conference. For the first time in his drama, Barker has separated dialogue sharply from the visual interest of the scene, and the separation heightens the hallucinatory effect. The setting, commercial art's idea of the exotic, '*all about as Moorish as Baker Street Station used to be in the days of the old sulphurous Underground*' (Don Juan's hell?), is a riot of visual absurdity, mocking at the staid and soberly attired business-men in their 'Moorish' chairs about an oval table, also 'Moorish'. The hat, imitated from la belle Hélène's improvisation, becomes the centre-piece and a further mockery. (Its appearance here was anticipated at the beginning of the play, when the Huxtable's maid took Thomas's sober hat and caught it on the door-handle, as she went out.) Constantine designates it, 'a cap of slavery,' the emblem under which this society marches.

The setting exerts a half-intoxicating effect upon the male participants in the scene—and upon the audience, too. Sobriety reels even further at the elaborate gyrations of the mannequins, which fascinate the eye in visual counterpoint to the gyrating extravagances of the talk. This time the directions indicate unambiguously the author's intention of presenting a species of comic ballet: '*a dance of modish dervishes*' is one pertinent phrase, and Windlesham, prancing about the posturing female dummies, speaks at one moment, '*pausing in the dance*'. Indeed, a greater dramatic exploitation of such fantastic accessories and a more even distribution of interest among the participants in the scene are two of the features that distinguish it technically from the Don Juan in Hell episode in *Man and Superman,* which may well have prompted Barker to place the lengthy discussion-scene at this point in his drama.

The ballet focuses more wickedly the themes of the debate it accompanies. The playwright implies his various parallels: if Roberts and Huxtable ran an 'industrial seraglio', the Madras House is certainly a fantastically decorated brothel; Windlesham is the ballet-master, but also the pimp, or the slave-trader putting up his girls for auction. He is the dancing-partner, too, and the dramatist plays on the popular English idea of the male dancer, as a means of establishing a dominant aspect of the Act: the parade of sexual grotesques.

While Constantine discourses of the 'softening influences' of women and bewails the decay of manliness, Windlesham moves about the stage as an example of the sorry condition (*blasé* is his own word) to which a lifetime in the drapery trade reduces the warrior. Nature has lost her dominion in Windlesham: '*a tailor-made man,*' the directions call him, adding, '*Impossible to think of him in any of the ordinary relations of life*' (and these certainly include the 'ordinary' sexual relation). The artificial creature speaks an appropriately artificial language, the debased patter of the salesman, interspersed constantly by snatches of milliner's French: 'Lucky the lingo's like second nature to me,' he comments. The remark incidentally glosses his effusive protest, 'Nature's my passion!' It is certainly a secondary kind of nature—and a contraceptive sex—that is represented by his farm: 'Just a toy . . . .' (The choice of word hints a pun on Touchstone's bauble!) In the character-plot, Windlesham, the degenerate, is most closely related to Eustace Perrin State, the eunuch, another appropriate guardian of the harem.

Of all the characters in the play, State is furthest removed from credible actuality. He is a caricature of the successful American, reminiscent of Hector Malone in *Man and Superman,* a purely comic exaggeration that, appearing only in this Act, contributes largely to its anti-naturalistic style and mood. He, too, speaks a language all his own, predominantly dithyrambic. But State is furnished with a subconscious personality that wrily modifies the impression of his self-confident exterior. Many of the idioms he uses betray this philosopher of commercialism. It is his complaint that 'the unknown and somewhat uninspiring name of Burrows upon an opposition establishment might *cut no ice*'. His business procedure involves telling competitors: 'Gentleman, come in, or *be froze out*.' It is fitting that he should be exclaiming over the Crystal Palace, when the curtain first rises on the Act. A favourite word of his, in the second version, is 'stimulus', with the implication of provocative and titillating sex dormant in it, and a 'cold cigar'—one of Barker's furthest ventures in obscene imagery—is his indulgence.

A sentimental bachelor, he relates how he has sought the poetry of the Woman Spirit in 'the virgin forest'; but his money-maker's touch has reduced it to dead wood, mere lumber. The 'canned peach' and 'the ready-made skirt' have also served their turn in inspiring and enriching him. (Barker is certainly playing here on the Edwardian and Georgian slang meaning of the nouns, as he does when referring to Thomas's partiality for 'rolypoly'—which barely conceals its relation to 'polygamy'.) More ruthless accents sometimes make themselves heard through the alluring style of the commercial advertiser: 'the middle class woman . . . think of her in bulk . . . is potentially the greatest money-spending machine in the world;' 'I gave some time and money to elaborating a mechanical moving figure to take the place of . . .'—and the sentence can be left incomplete, as the sight of another mannequin satirically supplies the missing allusion and emphasises the indecency, as with a music hall gesture; 'a real automaton,' he adds, 'the ideal figure.' He shrinks from the woman of flesh and blood, it seems, preferring to amass a museum of corsets. To Constantine, in the guise of 'fairy prince', Barker opposes this figure of the snow king, whose touch is death.

The poor mannequins are grotesques, too, bewitched victims of the commercial system: 'with a couch, y'know,' explains Windlesham, 'we might get a sort of mermaid effect out of some of them.' They are unexpected visual symbols of the curse of barrenness upon the Huxtable sisters, Miss Chancellor and Mrs. Brigstock. Even Miss Yates, though she has finally escaped undefeated, has been submitted to the devitalising process. A transitional passage in the second Act looked forward to Act III. As in Act II of *Waste*, Barker used the device of the ringing telephone as a formal indication of the shift from one scene to another, when the playing was continuous. Jessica came in, while Thomas was receiving the telephone call from State. The dramatist introduced, simultaneously, a variation on the purely verbal pun, a concealed reference to the telephone itself, as Miss Yates declared: 'I was always a chatterbox, madam.' The first hand in the costume department who, in the presence of a lady, is disciplined to *'become, indeed, a black-silk being of another species'*, was thus the first instance of the human being transformed into the machine, the functionary, by the evil magic of the commercial civilisation. And promptly, with another anticipation of what Act III was to reveal, Major Thomas complained: 'They've cut him off.' The conventional phrase contained the gist of what Barker presents directly in the character of State: the divided consciousness that does not recognise its own motives, the culture torn away from natural roots, the machine age with its secret token of castration.

(This recalls the climax of Jean Genet's *Le Balcon*, also set in a brothel of fantasy, a more recent attempt to combine the themes of sex and politics so as to reveal the sub-conscious mind of a civilisation. Barker's free use of obscenity in his play, especially in the form of the fundamentally serious *double entendre*, is possibly more Aristophanic in tone than Genet's.)

The presence of other characters in Act III introduces a purer geniality into the group. From the start of the play to the end of this Act, Thomas accompanies Philip Madras and represents ordinariness; he is the creature of simple instincts and affections, 'the mean sensual man' of the American's startling phrase. He fulfils the very necessary function of reconciling the audience to Philip who, for all his perceptiveness and moral rightness, repels any easy liking by his emotional detachment: 'a cold-blooded egoist,' Constantine calls his son; 'we ain't all so unattractive to women as you are' is Thomas's friendly gibe. The Major has an elder counterpart in Mr. Huxtable; and the two are, with Miss

Yates, the most completely sympathetic figures in the drama. In this Act, Huxtable shares with Thomas the function of awakening and setting-off the brilliance of the others. Beyond this, his receptivity to new truth is the dramatist's strongest means of ensuring his audience's receptivity to a new sense of justice. Starting far behind Constantine and Philip, Huxtable seems to be growing and changing, whereas they are caught and fixed in their attitudes:

> I like to take things as I find em ... that is as I used to find em ... before there was any of these ideas going around [...] Stifling their instincts ... it's a horrid way to talk. And I don't believe it. I could send for every girl in the shop and not one of em would hint at it to me [...] Not that that proves anything, does it? I'm a fool ...

The self-revelation is engagingly modest, amid the egoistic display of State and Constantine, and beside the cool self-containment of Philip.

Huxtable's reluctant, but genuine, affection and the adulation shown by State are dissimilar tributes to the man who pits his individuality against the organisation of society and gets away with it. Constantine's late entrance, the massively 'oriental' silence that he preserves through the first part of the discussion, and—when at last it comes—the force of his contradiction to everything that State has said, all contribute to a formidable portrait. State's preference for 'the spiritual side of facts' has already extended the range of the argument. Constantine launches a sweeping indictment of the religious and political condition of a society whose mirror is the drapery trade, in what amounts to a great monologue with interruptions. Like the shavian hero-villain, Constantine bases his wrong-doing on the highest principles: naturally promiscuous, he has adopted a religion that lends sanction to his promiscuity, while preserving his dignity and self-respect; and from within its stronghold he proseletyses the westerner, already resentful of insurgent feminism. Here, too, he takes the highest philosophical ground:

> From seventeen to thirty-four ... these are the years a man should consecrate to the acquiring of political virtue. Wherever he turns is he to be distracted ... by the barefaced presence of women?

The author's satirical eye is upon the defender of the rights of men, although he seems to carry all before him. In part, Constantine is a caricature of the conventionally despotic male; but the logic of his point-of-view is carried so far that it acquires a valid penetration of its own and recoils critically upon the very society he represents. So, like Voysey, he both embodies and challenges social evils, now with a proposition that is comically startling:

> Harry, you have six daughters, neither married, nor now with much hope to be. Even if you like that ... do they? You'd much better have drowned them at birth [...] How much pleasanter then for you ... and how much better for them ... if you could still find a man ready for some small consideration to marry the lot!

now with an accusation in which comedy and grimness are more obviously mingled:

> What is your Roberts and Huxtable but a harem of industry? [...] You buy these girls in the open market [...] once you've worn them out you turn them out ... forget their very names ... you wouldn't know their faces if you met them selling matches at your door. For such treatment of potential motherhood my Prophet condemns a man to Hell.

Barker gives more than one view of Constantine. His building up of the character is an instance of the transformation of a shavian model into something radically different in kind. Through the greater part of Act III, the character is allowed to impose a dignified, self-flattering portrait upon his eager listeners. When the high-speed polemical comedy has drawn to the end of its second great lap and the group is breaking up, Constantine goes on throwing out his comments, more disjointed now, to such as remain to hear. It is a transitional passage, leading gently back towards the naturalistic mode. A more intimate quality of feeling enters; the rhythm slows down; and the characters seem to dwindle to a more credible life-size. The king of men now appears as the old companion of Huxtable, linked to him in good-humoured affection, sharing his wistful imagination, not so free from a simple romanticism as his earlier apostrophe to State, 'my dear sentimental Sir', would seem to imply. The cadences of a familiar poetry creep occasionally into the dialogue:

MR. HUXTABLE. I must be getting back.

CONSTANTINE. Running away from me, Harry?

MR. HUXTABLE. *[in frank, amused concession]* Yes ... I was. Habit, y'know ... habit. *[...]*

CONSTANTINE We'll go together ... on a bus. D'you remember when the new shop opened how we loved to ride past and look at it ... from the top of a bus? *[...]* You should come and stay with me for a little at Hit ... not far from Hillel ... Hillel is Babylon, Harry

MR. HUXTABLE. *[curious]* What's it like there?

CONSTANTINE. The house is white and there are palm trees about it ... and not far off flows the Euphrates.

MR. HUXTABLE. Just like in the Bible. *[His face is wistful]* Constantine *[...]* You've said odder things this afternoon than I've ever heard you say before.

CONSTANTINE. Time was when you wouldn't listen, Harry *[...]*

MR. HUXTABLE. *[with sudden misgiving]* You don't repent, do you? *[...]* Katherine said this morning that you might have ... but I wasn't afraid of that. *[...]* of course you ought to be ashamed of yourself. Still ... well ... it's like the only time I went abroad. I was sick going ... I was orribly uncomfortable ... I ated the cooking ... I was sick coming back. But I wouldn't have missed it ...!

CONSTANTINE. *[in affectionate good-fellowship]* Come to Arabia, Harry!

It is an invitation to a land of dreams, whether to the fabled richness and magic of the land of Haroun al Raschid, or to a lost Eden. Constantine has in effect made his retreat to a simpler world, back into the cradle of civilisation: his chosen version of the return to nature. Sheer abundance in his innocent idea of the good: the potency and prolific opulence that the rivers symbolise and the growing wheat, enough to feed the entire British Empire. He is let off lightly at this point, as Huxtable's friendliness casts such a softer light upon him as Major Thomas's friendship casts upon Philip. It is left for Act IV to introduce a less merciful view of Constantine's romantic temperament.

There, Philip, discussing his father with Jessica, ventures his belief that vanity has been the motive force behind 'that fine and flamboyantly amorous career'; 'Nature's energy must be slacking', he muses. Such analysis reduces the superhuman impressiveness of the figure to more easily measurable terms and even suggests that the Constantine of Act II was unreal, a giant stuffed with sawdust. Jessica, who does not share Huxtable's affectionate regard for her father-in-law, promptly makes her criticism of the identification of good with natural fruitfulness:

> Let it slack! The way men allow Nature to befool them into swinging the pendulum ... they've no other notion ... between getting babies born and starting wars to destroy the surplus!

So the limitations of Constantine's philosophy and the naïve quality of his mind are fully exposed. Even the attractively vital Miss Yates, who approved of him sufficiently to conceive his child —it is inevitable that Act IV should reveal him as the seducer!— now rejects him.

When he appears in Act IV, he shows a surliness of temper unsuspected before, as, in the brief scene with Amelia, Barker contrives to catch the full quality of that married life the two spent together long ago: the quarrels, reproaches, tears, and absence of any mutual respect, the blunted sensibilities and dulled intelligence of the wife, the brutality of the husband. The memories that return to the Constantine of Act IV are sour ones; behind the imposing façade of Mahommedan righteousness appears the 'unworthy Baptist', passing through his 'little hells of temptation and shame and remorse'; instead of the pride of the sexual conqueror in the virility that has not deserted him, he confesses to Philip another, private vision of his old age '... of a loose lip and a furtive eye'.

In its variable nature and naturalistic complexity, this character is no such caricature as the dramatist deliberately offers in Eustace Perrin State. Read in the context of the entire rôle, even Constantine's share in the scene at the conference table demands to be played with some indication of the reality behind all the posturing; although he is making a deliberate public appearance, he gives some indication, even there, of another self, acknowledged in occasional remarks to Philip or Huxtable, but shadowed in reserve.

*　　*　　*

No flattering illusions hang about Act IV. At the first production of the play, audiences delighted by Act III found the last Act disappointing; the longer it went on, the cooler grew their response.[13] Expectation of something more in the style of the previous Act and slowness in relinquishing that expectation probably made for final dissatisfaction with the drama. A strain of bitterness, such as had not been evident in Barker's earlier plays, was now apparent. The action resolved itself largely into a succession of tense and cold exchanges, or quarrels that brought no relief. Not only did Constantine appear in the least attractive light, but a repellent quality was obvious in the other figures, too: not foolishness, but stupidity, was revealed as Amelia's chief characteristic; Jessica was disdainful, bored, with a temper quick to resent and very ready to wound; in Philip, a puritanical distrust of beauty and happiness combined with a rather priggish tendency to lecture the rest of the world. The satiric intention, when pursued simply by bringing to view in the coldest light the meannesses of human nature, was certainly less palatable fare than the earlier Acts had offered. The failure was not wholly in the audience's comprehension, however. It is hard to resist the conclusion that the play was finished too soon, before the last Act was adequately formed and vitalised in the author's imagination; the dramatic problem which he had set himself, in trying to write an almost actionless play, was not completely solved.

There were still a few ends to be tied in the play's slight narrative fabric: the meeting of Constantine and Amelia was foreshadowed in Act I; the business of Jessica's flirtation with Major Thomas had still to be cleared up; the revelation had yet to be made that Constantine was the father of Miss Yates's child. This last detail has an obvious contribution to make to the shape of the play, rounding the circle, but also providing an ironically fitting reversal of the conventional situation: in the 'asphalted dust-heap of a park at New Cross', the imperial tyrant and apostle of fruitfulness meets his defeat at the hands of the independent woman; denied responsibility for his own child, and denied rights over it, he can but echo Huxtable's sentiment: 'I've been made a convenience of' (which is traditionally the sentiment of the women Juan betrays). However, the defeat takes place off-stage and the report of it is no more than an incidental climax.

The last Act was certainly designed to bring home to the hero, Philip, the whole force of the drama already enacted; for the context is now narrowed to his immediate family: the relations of his wife and his mother, his father and mother, and his own relationship with each, are surveyed in turn and culminate in a final scene with Jessica, which reviews in most intimate form the entire question of man, woman and society. Some counterpoise was necessary to the dispiriting incidents that occupy the first part of Act IV; the view of life-as-it-is needed to be balanced with a vision of meaning in it. Barker clearly intended his final summing-up to be humanised as part of the variety of the marriage of Philip and Jessica. But, in the original version especially, the end of the play demonstrates once more the fatal interference of a didactic purpose with the process of imaginative gestation.

What is wrong with the first version of *The Madras House* is not that it suggests that the solution for the problems it has presented must be sought in the world outside the play, but that it has not fully achieved the indispensable resolution, in which the morality itself issues from the creative imagination. Shavian rhetoric, and the rhetoric of Constantine and State, is not didactic, but an overflow of the vitality of the character. In Philip, Barker presents a figure that cannot give full conviction to such rhetoric as he is now assigned: one in whom intellectual penetration is set off by human inadequacy, a character conscious of his own aridity and the dissipation of his energies in sophisticated doubts and hesitations. Aesthetically, this is the hero Barker approves here, the one most fit to his theme. At the end of the play, this hero seems to be given moral approval, too (for Jessica is an ineffectual opposition, there mainly to be converted); the necessary detachment of the author from the character is not preserved as completely as it has been hitherto.

Barker's socialism has its place in *The Madras House* as one aspect of his search for wholeness; it corresponds to his Christian consciousness that 'We are members one of another'. As in *Waste*, here again he occasionally relies upon an ambivalent statement to indicate a truth concealed beneath a falsehood exposed. So State declares:

Lift your head, broaden your horizon, and you will see, I think, that all human activities are one. And [...] that art, philosophy and religion can and should, in the widest sense of the term, be made to pay. And it's pay or perish, in this world.

The harsh accents of the money-maker can be heard in that, but beneath them is the author's comment on his attempt to bring the diversity of human activities into the scheme of his play. The sentiment is directly contradictory of Voysey's advice to Edward: 'You must realise that money-making is one thing, and religion another, and family life a third. . . .' We may recall the second landmark which the Huxtables pointed out to their guests: the chimney pots of Ruskin's house. That was evidently an early hint of the way that the play's argument was to go; for State's words express a Ruskinian attitude and even their phrasing is reminiscent of Ruskin, who wrote: 'To see clearly is poetry, prophecy and religion, all in one.'[14] Barker's criterion of judgment, utilitarian indeed, but not narrowly so, is also expressed in this speech of State's: commerce, in *The Madras House*, is not only an object of satire, but a reminder of the principle of value whereby good is preferred to evil, happiness to damnation; as Philip remembers that it may indeed profit a man to lose the world and save his soul.

The association of religion with the concepts of gain and distribution of goods, which culminates in State's 'pay or perish', begins with the maid's allusion to Holy Communion, when the visitors are shown in, at the rise of the curtain on Act I. Recurrent insistence that they should stay to dinner at Denmark Hill keeps the Sunday feast still in mind, and the first version of the text also contributes some Prayer Book phrases to this Act. The cineraria, which blooms in the conservatory, was originally an agapanthus. Barker's choice of that grotesque-sounding flower was undoubtedly determined by the pun on *agape*, which he could recognise in it. (The change to cineraria may have been made because the original pun was too obscure for audiences to catch, when nineteenth-century gossip that the Agapemonites of Somerset practised free love had been forgotten. Shaw, in *Too True to be Good*, risks labelling a part of the set, αγαπεμονε, but glosses it with the chalked legend: 'NO NEED TO WASTE THE ELECTRIC LIGHT.') *Agape*, as the antithesis of *eros*, would have offered a ludicrously ironical comment on the Huxtable virgins. As a reference to the early Christian love-feast, it would have been a comment on the general conduct of Act I: the recurrent greetings and affectionate leave-takings of the charitable sisterhood, with the scent of dinner on the air. As the occasion for the sharing of goods, the *agape* would have served Barker as his first—comically incongruous—symbol of Christian communism. The pun has been removed from the final text, but the ideas concentrated in it remain in other forms: in the burlesque analogy between the *agapemone* at Denmark Hill and the idea of polygamy, or polyandry, which Don Juan—male or female—champions.

Act IV opens with a brief discussion of bills and debts between Amelia Madras and Jessica; it is Barker's way of introducing the theme of 'pay or perish' in the Act where it is to predominate. In the final scene, Philip puts the matter quite explicitly to Jessica:

> If we can't love the bad as well as the beautiful . . . if we won't share it all out now . . . fresh air and art . . . and dirt and sin . . . then we good and clever people are costing the world too much . . .

Barker might have done better, artistically, to have left the notion simply as it is expressed in the story of the man on the train (quoted below, p. 181), supplemented with the ironic bite in Jessica's Malthusian reckoning of the price of prosperity ('. . . swinging the pendulum . . . between getting babies born and starting wars to destroy the surplus!'); but the desire to point every theme, and round off the play in every respect, won the day. So la belle Hélène is recalled and the Act III argument about the basic identity of the respectable woman and the *cocotte* is pursued to its logical extreme, in another passage from the final scene in its original version:

> PHILIP. . . . Jessica, do you feel that it was you that shot that poor devil six months ago? . . . that it's you who are to be hanged to-morrow?
> JESSICA. I don't think I do.
> PHILIP. That it's your body is being sold on some street this evening?
> *She gives a little most genuine shudder.*
> JESSICA. I hate to think about such things.
> PHILIP. [*Summing up.*] Then there's precious little hope for the Kingdom of Heaven upon earth.[15]

State proclaims his faith in the 'gospel of beauty'; it is a way of salvation that Philip emphatically rejects. A popular gibe against socialist principles, expressed in the mock-slogan, 'Nationalisation of women,' has been inverted to reveal the religion of socialism: faith in human community and mutual responsibility. When he first wrote the play, in 1909, Barker may still have had in mind Tolstoy's rejection of the idea of salvation through a minority culture and its art, as well as Ruskin's. When he came to revise the play, the simplicity of the original conclusion yielded to a more personal apprehension of his subject and his identification of it with his private obsessions and frustrations, lending a greater inwardness to the finished text.

There is evidence enough in the first text that Barker intended to focus the negative and ineffectual aspects of Philip's character at the centre of the drama, as he has done more clearly in the second version. Thomas makes his chaffing and valid criticisms of his friend at the beginning of the play (only slightly re-phrased later), and thus offers an obvious anticipation of the moralisings of the last Act:

> ... you've got what I call the Reformer's mind ... and got it badly, Phil;

and again:

> ... you'd think a lot clearer, Phil, if you didn't spell everything with a capital letter.

The insistence on the hero's coldness is present in both texts and warns of his kinship, however remote it may at first seem, to the impotent sentimentality of Eustace Perrin State. Philip's intellectual sophistication is as much a part of the sterile culture that the play exposes as is Jessica's fastidious refinement, the tradition and cosmopolitanism parodied in State's Latin tags and Windlesham's debased French.

Huxtable's new-found freedom is accompanied by a rejection of book-learning and, in the original fourth Act, Philip himself concludes: 'I must turn my back for a bit on artist and scholar and preacher ... all three.' In the first form of the play, that utterance seems no more than a variant on the shavian call to political action; but, in revision, Granville Barker deepened the potentially tragic core within the comic structure of his play: the artist's, or thinker's, torturing consciousness—vividly equated with the sense of physical impotence and barrenness—of the divorce between vision and reality, and the imprisonment of creative power within the mind. The freezing of the dramatic action is more than a novel trick; it corresponds to this ultimate theme.

The figure of the poet haunts the dialogue in both versions. It is there in the anthology pieces that State quotes to veil from himself and others the true nature of his actions and of the world he chooses to serve. To his Nottingham experiment of 'The ladies' department served by gentlemen . . . the gentlemen's by ladies . . . not a man under six foot . . . bronzed, noble fellows!' (an unconscious reminiscence of Rousseau's noble savage?) he applies the troubadour phrase, 'the Courtesy of Chivalry and the Chivalry of Courtesy,' befitting his conscious attitude of distant adoration, seeking no fulfilment. Looking into the future, Constantine remarks in the first text: 'There will be poets like you, Mr. State, to dream about women and to dress them . . . their bodies in silks and their virtues in phrases'; and, in the revised fourth Act, Jessica draws a similar parallel: 'You men parade in words just as fantastically as we do in our fashions.'

The point is made with greater emotional force in Philip's anecdote, which supplies a climatic passage in both versions of the last Act:

> D'you remember when I was very young and used to salve my social conscience by lecturing on Shelley to select little audiences in the slums? [. . .] Well . . . I remember once travelling in the train with a poor wretch who lived . . . so he told me . . . on what margins of gain he could pick up by standing incompetently somewhere between the cornfield and the baker . . . or the coal mine and the fire [. . .] I forget which. And he was weary and irritable and very unhealthy. And he hated Jones . . . because Jones had just done him out of a half per cent on two hundred and fifty pounds . . . and if the sum had been bigger he'd have sued him, so he would! And the end of Prometheus was running in my head: This like thy glory, Titan, is to be Good, great and joyous, beautiful and free . . . and I thought him a mean fellow [. . .] But when

he asked what was taking me to Canning Town[16] ... somehow I
was ashamed to tell him.

The ironic juxtaposition, emphasised by the contrasting rhythms,
is a token of the split society. It sums up Philip's situation within
the play, the observer's rôle and his sense of atrophied emotion
and inability to transform the material world.

In the 1925 text, Barker employs Philip more consistently as a
medium for self-criticism and presents the gist of his indictment in
the interview with Miss Yates:

> PHILIP. ... if you set out on this adventure believing all the
> conventional people tell you ... why, I'm not very happy about
> your prospects.
> MISS YATES. Oh, that's all right, sir. When you're up against
> it you don't bother about believing things or not.

As they face each other across the table, her freedom of action
makes his mere freedom of thought seem as much an irrelevant
indulgence as Jessica's treasured culture. Self-knowledge informs
his remark in the new fourth Act: '... as a visionary I'm all for
compromise'; there is a reiteration of George Booth's 'practical
ideal' in the ambiguousness of that, but the present phrasing also
communicates Philip's rueful awareness of his unheroic quality.

The image of the 'farmyard world of sex' finds its way into the
new Act IV. 'Have we won nothing nobler from the jungle?' is
Philip's rhetorical question. The dramatist has decided to end his
play with another image of civilisation that belongs alongside those
of the garden and the conservatory, alongside Windlesham's allusion to 'second nature' and Philip's more recent mention of the
man in the train, 'standing incompetently somewhere between the
cornfield and the baker'. The farmyard, too, is the half-way house
of compromise, the ignoble compromise of tameness or domesticity,
to which the noble savage is reduced in a human community that
sacrifices creative vitality to docile order.[17]

The quality of this view of society corresponds to Philip's disillusion. Between him and his father, in the revision, there exists
some degree of sympathetic understanding. They can afford to
drop pretences with each other:

CONSTANTINE. . . . Rebellion against nature brings no happiness, Phil.

PHILIP. What else is civilisation?

CONSTANTINE. And what better condemnation of about half of it?

PHILIP. *[with his ironic smile]* Well . . . I agree that this present stage of our moral progress is hardly suited to your simplicity of temperament, my dear father. A heart-breaking paradox . . . to find one's manliest virtues turned to mere weakness under temptation!

CONSTANTINE. You're a queer fellow, Phil. If I'd sat and turned all my vigour into phrases as you do . . . they'd have poisoned me.

PHILIP. That's a home thrust. Thoughts curdling into words . . . and into more thought and more words. Yes . . . it leaves one lifeless.

The pendulum swings between the two: the simple sensualist and the fastidious intellectual, the extremes of barbarous nature and sophisticated culture; there is no synthesis in sight. If Constantine's conception of the Good is insufficient, it seems that Philip also comes no nearer to the secret of creative living. The end of Constantine's journey, for all his dreams of Eden, is the 'asphalted dust-heap of a park at New Cross'; and no less, the play implies, is the measure of western civilisation's failure.

The final scene appears to imply that the only solvent of the complex problems of this world is love. ('I have come so to fear the pleasant sounding word,' Philip muses.) Yet the note of reconciliation is heard only very briefly; Philip and Jessica reach a moment of mutual understanding, but its precariousness is stressed in the author's final comment:

> *She pats his cheek, then kisses it . . . As long as he'll only see his visions in the domestic fire . . . !*

Little Miss Yates, who turned the tables on the exploiters, is forgotten now. Barker has proceeded from the criterion of the natural towards his definition of the good, as in *Our Visitor* and *Ann Leete* (and following Meredith again),[18] but more hesitantly, it may seem, than in those earlier, simpler plays.

Even so, *The Madras House*, whatever its faults, remains a testimony to the comprehensiveness of Barker's thinking and to his mastery of dramatic construction. He has succeeded in combining what are in effect different *genres*: of naturalism and fantasy. He has succeeded in holding the ramifications of his thought in tension, without the aid of the usual plot-framework. The progress of the drama is cumulative, bringing more and more diversity within its compass, until—the argument completed—the central figure, Philip Madras, is seen as the pivot of the whole, the character to whom all the themes are most pertinent.

CHAPTER VIII

Defeat

Between *The Madras House* and Barker's next full-length play, *The Secret Life* (for *The Harlequinade*, in conception, is more Dion Clayton Calthrop's than his), there intervened his divorce from Lillah McCarthy and his second marriage, his virtual retirement from the theatre, and the first World War. The relationship between these different events has been much disputed, and the search for the motives which led him to turn away from practical work in the theatre and to academic pursuits has overshadowed some accounts of his career as a whole. Whatever the truth of outward events, the nature of the inner experience through which Barker passed is sufficiently plainly to be read in his literary work of the war years and after. The revised texts of *Waste* and *The Madras House* truly belong to the later period, of course, and support the conclusion that the mixed experience of those intermediate years matured him and involved a deepening of self-knowledge and a keener, more disillusioned awareness of the outer world.

Granville Barker's theatrical existence had been precarious as the life of an actor, or producer, commonly is. He had often been out-of-work and in his earlier days had economised on food.[1] He is reputed to have pawned his clothes to pay the debts of the Vedrenne-Barker management.[2] Shaw's financial backing had gone some way towards making possible the various theatrical ventures and, as his letters to Barker reveal, Shaw was too shrewd a businessman to be prepared to throw good money after bad unless there was a fair hope of eventual profit. Charles Frohman's idealism ran

185

out even more quickly. Lillah McCarthy did more than her share of the courting of patronage which her husband hated. As early as 1907, Shaw could tell Gilbert Murray that Barker's disgust with the theatre was growing more acute. In 1910, he returned from a tour of German theatres with the conviction, Gordon Craig's before him, that his artistic future, if any, lay on the Continent. He was offered the directorship of a German municipal theatre and proposed to his wife that they should leave England and apply for German citizenship. In order to keep him in this country, Lillah McCarthy persuaded Shaw to write a new play (*Fanny's First Play*) and, together with Lord Howard de Walden, to put up the money for its production at the Little Theatre. Even then, Barker would not read the play and did not see it until the dress-rehearsal.

He spent a great part of 1911 in his home at Stansted, living quietly and writing, taking only a desultory interest in affairs at the theatre, leaving much of the responsibility for productions to his wife and to A. E. Drinkwater, his business manager. Disenchantment with the conditions and prospects of his professional life was certainly upon him, and a volume in his library, which passed through the Institut Britannique to the British Museum, suggests the direction in which his mind was turning: the spine carries the simple title, *1910*, and in the volume are bound together the articles and fiction he had published in that year. Then the generosity of Lord Lucas made possible the three famous Shakespeare productions and, with a twenty-five years' lease of the Kingsway Theatre taken, a degree of security for future work seemed to be offered to him. The outbreak of war took it away.

The war made no sense to Barker. He had no illusions and no convictions that could blind him to the ugliness and sadness of the facts. Lillah McCarthy remembered him as mentally paralysed in depression and fear, a simple fear of having to fight and be killed; by nature, she said shortly before she died,[3] he was very gentle and considerate and nothing of a fighting man. Asquith advised them that the war would not last long and that they would do best to go on with their work in the theatre. *The Dynasts* was produced on Moscow Art Theatre lines, in the winter of 1914 (Barker had been to Russia in the spring); then, on an invitation from the Stage

Society of New York, they went to America and there undertook a number of productions. Before they went, Granville Barker had insisted on giving up the lease of the Kingsway, being determined, it seems, that his career in the English theatre was at an end. His meeting in New York with Helen Huntington, whose husband was one of his backers, prepared the way for his full withdrawal from the professional stage; love for the woman contained also the hope of a new kind of life, when the old seemed to have come to an end.

* * *

The restlessness of the years from 1910 is reflected in the record of his literary activity. He wrote three one-Act plays: the farce, *Rococo,* in 1911, skilful enough, and incidentally a surprisingly realistic presentation of a lower-middle class domestic background, but of little general significance; *Vote By Ballot,* in 1914; and *Farewell to the Theatre,* in 1916. He followed an attempt in the short-story form, "Georgiana," published in the *Fortnightly Review,* in 1910, with another short *nouvelle, Souls on Fifth,* which appeared in book form in Boston, in 1916, and then in the *Fortnightly,* the following year.

The first of his English versions of foreign plays, the *Anatol* dialogues, was made in 1911 for performance by himself, with Lillah McCarthy and Nigel Playfair, at the Little Theatre. Of *Anatol* he wrote to Sir John Martin Harvey in 1929:

> ... the Schnitzler affair was—in a literary sense—rather an immoral proceeding. Not ten words of German do I know![4]

(He undoubtedly relied upon the interpretations of his friend, Dr. C. E. Wheeler, as he was later to rely upon his second wife's knowledge of Spanish in his work on the plays of Sierra and the Quintero brothers.) His collaboration, in 1913, with Dion Clayton Calthrop on *The Harlequinade,* a revised version of a text originally Calthrop's alone,[5] was also undertaken as part of the business of providing plays for a repertory, though it is additional testimony, also, to Barker's own interest in *commedia dell'arte.*

He dramatised *The Wrong Box* (R. L. Stevenson and Lloyd Osbourne) for production in New York under the title of *The Morris Dance.*[6]

Having joined the Red Cross, he was commissioned to write a book as propaganda for the war effort. So from America he went to France and, to the embarrassment of the organisation, wrote *The Red Cross in France* which, even in its published form (and copies are now very rare), reflects something of the fear and suffering that he saw and looks forward to the kind of war its author understood, the war that would come after the war and be fought against a more secret enemy. Much of the book is written in dialogue form, because 'for me, it is easier to write'.

Among Barker's unpublished manuscripts there also survive from this period a short sociological study, *The Bigamist*, some notes towards a play called *The Committee*, apparently based on an incident involving the National Theatre Committee, and a much more substantial body of notes, including two completed Acts, for a long play, originally entitled *The Village Carpenter* and later, *The Wicked Man.*[7]

Always a slow and painstaking writer, Barker did not, in fact, succeed in bringing one serious imaginative work of any length to completion between 1909 and 1923. What he did achieve is not without interest. In his failures is still to be seen the direction in which his mind was moving and the development of his imagery. And in a few of these pieces there resides, if only on a small scale, a quality that cannot be simply and immediately dismissed with the verdict of 'failure'.

At first it looks as though Barker was tempted in these years to try his hand at non-dramatic writing, but in effect he remains a dramatist in all these pieces. As in *The Red Cross in France*, so he was to use the dialogue form unexpectedly, and perhaps inappropriately, for an article in *The Times* on 'The Spirit of France' (19 July, 1938) and for chapters of *The Exemplary Theatre*. His preference for first-person narrative is demonstrated in *The Bigamist*, as well as in the short stories, and this suggests that it may have been the actor's approach through subjective realisation, and hiding behind the mask of character, which was particularly congenial to him. Even in a sociological study, the man he is concerned with takes on the life of a character, with an individuality that defeats the author's apparent intention.

The typescript survives in a folder labelled: 'Prison Studies. / No. 1 (1910) / *The Bigamist.*' It is doubtful whether any more studies in this projected series were written. The date supplies a hint that the example of Galsworthy's *Justice*, and even possibly a direct suggestion from Galsworthy, may have had something to do with the composition of this piece. 'Barker has paid much attention to these prison matters,' commented Wilfred Scawen Blunt in his Journals, in April 1910. *The Bigamist*, however, as the title suggests, is more concerned with an offender than with his punishment. It purports to give the reflections of a convicted criminal while serving his sentence. The point is certainly made that imprisonment for bigamy, far from remedying a social wrong, foolishly inflicts a greater wrong, but it is overshadowed by interest in the motives and psychology of the imagined criminal.

Entering into the mind and sensibility of his character, assuming his social background and speaking with his tongue, Barker excludes the possibility of objective critical comment; for there is no second character to right the balance as in a play. Instead of an argument, it is a plea for sympathy which is presented; yet not a mawkish one, as it is not based on present sufferings but on a revelation of the adventurousness, the natural protest against the futile-seeming monotony of respectable life, to which the legal offence is ultimately traced. Considering his home and the time he spent there, the 'I 'of the study concludes:

> ... it was as nice as could be *[homely and all that]*. But it grew that sometimes I'd sit there wishing the end of the world would come just for a change. *(Manuscript insertion in italics.)*

His way of escape is fantasy: he imagines himself to be somebody else; and the account turns into something very like a study of the histrionic impulse. The daydreams of Prunella, the poetry of State, the art of Jessica Madras have their simple counterpart here in the irresponsible make-believe that gives release from the sameness and narrowness of circumstances, the sameness and limitations of the self:

... you couldn't call it lying because it had nothing to do with facts at all.

Against the character's will ('I didn't ever want to get rid of the missus ... any more than I wanted to chuck my job in the factory'), and under new social pressures, the chosen fantasy begins to turn into another prison, curiously reminiscent of the first, before the Law and the custodians of its actual prisons arrive on the scene.

The relationship that leads to the bigamous marriage is presented as nothing out of the ordinary in degree or kind; the motives of easy-going affectionateness and compromising weakness, which determine it, are precisely those which make thousands of decent legal marriages. Evasion under cover of conformity is the way of the average man, who is the concern of the social reformer. This particular bigamist is extraordinary only in the extent to which he has let his imagination run away with him. The consciousness that has created him, and evoked the mixture of the grotesque and pathetic that is his imaginative life, is not far from that conveyed through Philip Madras: implicit in *The Bigamist*, as in *The Madras House*, is a sense of the inadequacy of idea and vision as substitutes for the creativeness that gives freedom.

*   *   *

Vote by Ballot is also concerned with fantasy as it operates in the lives of ordinary, apparently conventional people. This little play demonstrates Barker's idea of what the one-Act play might appropriately do. It is a product of the period which gave us those classics of the form, Hankin's *The Constant Lover* and Barrie's *The Twelve Pound Look*, and in its range and manner it shows likenesses to both. It is fundamentally a conversation-piece, an exposition of the main character's point-of-view, but it is diversified by being written for four voices. An actual social context is implied: the provincial English society that sees the success of the local manufacturer, puts him into Parliament and takes his eventual elevation to the peerage as a compliment to itself; it is a setting in which town and country, like plebs and squirearchy, graduate imperceptibly into each other.

Though the author's eye upon all this remains constantly ironic, it is very gently so. He is deliberately composing in the minor key, and there is just a hint of ambiguity, something a little deprecatory, about his careful delineation of this limited world and the modestly scaled, but likeable people in it. The style is precisely that which fitted Barker to translate the delicate naturalistic plays of Schnitzler. The note, hovering between appreciation and the faintest criticism, is struck in the stage directions:

> *Vivid colour the room does lack. Possibly to Mrs. Torpenhouse life itself is an affair of delicate half-tones, of grey and blue and mauve, and white that is not too white. Well, everything is spotlessly, chastely clean and well polished where polish should be.*

The play is social criticism only in the most general sense: a comic revelation of the foolishness of social assumptions, and especially the assumption that categories and conventions can express all the diversity of individual men. Mr. Torpenhouse has acted as Chairman of Committee to the Liberal candidate (regularly elected) for thirty years, only to reveal, when at last Lord Silverwell's son and successor loses the election by a single vote, that he has always salved his private conscience and kept his idealism bright by voting Tory; though he protests: 'Mine is hardly the official Tory mind. Why should it be?'

It is a faintly absurd and trivial form of dissent, and the character of Torpenhouse is in keeping. This part of 'the crooked man ... whose life's a crooked mile' calls for delicate handling and not quite naturalistic playing, poised as it is between hysteria and enthusiasm. From it the play mainly derives its slight whimsicality. Mrs. Torpenhouse, though younger, is reminiscent of old Mrs. Voysey: she is '*fragile*,' genuinely kindly; her understanding of people and personal relationships has some depths and subtleties; but her mind reaches to nothing outside the personal world; her identity seems to depend upon her love for her husband. Lord Silverwell and his son, Noel Wychway, are not, in conception, characters at all individual to Barker's work. What is individual is the precision with which they are drawn; indeed, Barker, writing a one-Act play, still relies greatly upon draughtsmanship to give continuous conviction.

The part-serious, part-playful tone is further preserved in the nature of the images and analogies used: the silver-gilt coronet, polished once a week along with the forks and spoons; or the boots on which Silverwell's prosperity is based, that Torpenhouse brings into the argument:

> Who wants to stand in a white sheet with his real and sham opinions hung round him? Confound it ... set me the example. Withdraw your poster that Wychway's boots are the best. Advertise what we really think of them *[...]* I've worn them for thirty years. And whenever the spring comes they hurt me ... not at other times.

The political allusion in the title and the context of local politics are strictly relevant to the human nature shown in this play: Torpenhouse is the modest hero appropriate to a democratic age, no weakling, but one who takes his tone from the moderation and compromise amid which he lives. His integrity is paradoxical, but it is also admirable; the comedy of it is inseparable from the limited sphere of its operation: the voting booth, which is the sole field of valour.

*   *   *

The double life had already provided one theme of 'Georgiana'. Barker's aim and the general plan of this tale are clear enough, though it must be admitted that it remains an anecdote without the fullness of life that compels belief. The story is told at two removes: the writer represents himself as listener to his father-in-law's narrative of an episode in his earlier life. The instinct of the dramatist-producer is at work in the setting of the narration: the two men walk through the shadows of a garden at night, while a lighted window makes them visible and also betrays the nearness of a third character, who is wife of the one, daughter of the other. Though the woman at no point enters directly, the three are truly a chorus to the inset tale and illuminate it by their attitudes and temperaments. The critical mind and the sympathetic imagination, which seem to have conflicted in the writing of *The Bigamist*, attempt in 'Georgiana' to strike a deliberate counterpoise.

Barker's heroine is once more the 'new woman', the free woman, who chooses her lover and her sexual fulfilment in a natural gesture, outside the law; but Georgiana is as far removed as Ann Leete from the assertive feminist, whose actions are dictated by the principle of her equality with men. It is the two men who discuss her who are concerned with abstractions, with the theory of women's rights. The irony of this tale, fundamental, but not very explicitly developed, lies in the male attempt to justify what is beyond justification: life itself, with which alone—and not the rights and wrongs of anything—Georgiana is concerned.

To an implicit recognition of this her former lover, telling the tale, has at last come. He fittingly prolongs his account of her from the foundering of their relationship upon deceit to her subsequent disastrous marriage and her old age: husbandless, childless, she has altogether lost the game, yet accepts all, serenely, good-humouredly. Her hunger for life, for its truth and its actuality, is fully exposed by the end of the story and recalls the character of Agnes Colander. In the full context of the story, Georgiana's response to life offers an unpointed criticism of the escape into a second life, a 'special' world apart, and the subsequent retreat from it, that was the sum of his adventure for the teller of the tale.

If Barker had the 'reformer's mind', he certainly did not let it go undisputed in 'Georgiana' any more than in his plays. His sympathetic attitude to fantasy, expressed in *The Bigamist*, is modified in this tale, as it is in *Vote by Ballot;* but the criticism is conveyed, in both instances, by subtler means than statement.

*   *   *

The later story, *Souls on Fifth*, bears marks of being a love-gift for Helen Huntington. It seems to have been written late in 1915 or early in 1916, during the time of waiting for his divorce, and partly, at least, in New England. The author seems to be playing with the facts of a personal situation for an intimate, sympathetic eye:

> 'I had an acquaintance on earth . . . who built up quite an elaborate theory of soul-affinities. But he ended by walking off with a married woman, which was, to say the least, a most immoral anticipation of God's purposes;'

and again:

'... they should be quite sufficiently happy.' 'That is about the height of one's ambition,' I said, 'in making a second marriage.'

The indulgent attitude of the 'I' of the story to his Little Soul, compounded as it is of humour, exasperation, mock sternness and tenderness, also suggests a reflection of an actual relationship. (In some respects, it anticipates the attitude of the King to Queen Rosamund, in *His Majesty*.) This origin of the tale would be justification enough of its fantasy form: it is a playful and graceful gesture, slight enough to preserve the personal message from being overwhelmed by larger concerns or too objective a manner; the compliment was completed by the publication of the story as a little volume with a frontispiece illustration by Norman Wilkinson.

But this was not the only fantasy that Barker wrote, and his liking for the form surely corresponds to the quality of his imagination and the idealism that he himself recognises as partly a retreat from life with its ineluctable conditions. To the prolific talent, of course, fantasy gives an opportunity for as full and rich an imaginative creation as it can compass; or it can be an effective vehicle for satire. But the satire on the souls whose 'own place' is Fifth Avenue is very general and rather superficial, driven by no force of anger or indignation; and the pure fantasy is hardly elaborate or vivid enough to claim acceptance for its own sake. It is possible that Granville Barker in New England had been reading Hawthorne's short fables. He himself takes the convention as the permissive condition for a day-dream that is also a slight moral tale.

There are signs of intensity in the piece: in its introspective emotional content and in touches of an uncompromising moral passion. The author's sense of life is most convincingly present in the evocation of loneliness, the undercurrent of bitterness and the mood of failure. To these elements the basic invention corresponds: the vision of the stranger wandering a deserted Fifth Avenue on inclement nights, catching at the shapes, like grey blotting-paper, of the souls of the recently dead that haunt the place. Among them he comes upon the Soul of a Fashionable Preacher, who interprets the scene, and then upon the Little Soul of a young woman. This one, alone of the host of souls, wishes to escape from this limbo, but is—and was in life—too weak in her desires to achieve the liberation she asks and that is gradually defined as liberation from self.

The moral core of the story is a direct challenge to the fantasy, a self-criticism, but also an assertion of the seriousness embodied in the fiction. The preacher points out:

> '. . . your faith is the one thing you do act up to. That's what we have discovered here. God makes no excuses. The pious opinions you hold have no more effect on the soul than a knowledge of the multiplication table;'

and the stranger, also a little satirically drawn, passes the teaching on to the Little Soul:

> 'It is the things you do that count, not all the petty beliefs and hopes, with which you decorate your heart and mind. The inexorable laws that God has made take no account of what you'd like to be and wish you were.'

There is an opposition between this vigorous, uncompromising logic and the death at the narrator's heart, the blank despair and bankruptcy of virtue that he feels.

The death-experience is briefly evoked, as the stranger and the Little Soul together face final isolation in the place of escape: the prairie, where the wind of annihilation blows:

> Shaking and shrieking and rumbling it came, in leaps of gusty anger with silence in between. I set my teeth or I must have cried out in fear . . . Then it was on us, brutal, vindictive.

At the last moment, the two find a refuge from this ultimate terror. Their egoism dissolves like ice, the barriers of their isolation break, as her soul passes utterly into his; and so the rebirth out of despair is achieved. The nightmare and the release take the commonest of symbolic forms in this illusion of the overcoming of death in the consummation of love. Yet fantasy it all remains, a surrender to the wish-fulfilling dream and an evasion of 'the inexorable laws that God has made'. A rueful awareness of the limitations of this make-believe pervades the tale and contributes to its half-humorous, half-melancholy irony.

Barker's style is rarely at its best in narrative or description. Indeed, inadequacy of language is the weakness that besets his work. It betrayed him most seriously in *A Miracle*, when he tried to write verse. He overcomes it in his major plays, when his writing is most completely appropriate to the stage and the actor. It may be that the fault is deep-rooted in *Souls on Fifth*. There is rather more indulgence of weakness here than art can afford. For the rest of his work, the piece has the value of revealing clearly that the instinct for domesticity that his heroes condemn and fight against was not foreign to his own nature, and that the dramatic conflict with the searching and inappeasable intellect had its source in a quarrel with himself.

*   *   *

The theme of escape from egoism is recurrent in his work. It emerges in *The Harlequinade* (1913) at the climax, when Eglantine, the eighteenth-century *beau*, dressed in his wedding finery, stares in the mirror and questions his valet:

> EGLANTINE. Quin. In the glass there . . . is that Eglantine?
> HARLEQUIN. Till this moment your lordship has been pleased to think so.

There is a pistol in Eglantine's hand. He deliberately fires it at the image that confronts him and smashes the glass.[8] Of the multitude of literary uses of the looking-glass symbol, it is likely that two in particular haunted Barker's imagination: the glass dashed to the ground by the deposed Richard II and the mirror in which the Lady of Shallot watched the 'shadows of the world'. (*A Miracle* testified to his response to Tennyson's mediaevalism as well as Maeterlinck's; Baptista's book sounds suspiciously like the *Idylls of the King*.) The symbol is organic in *Farewell to the Theatre*.

This play, written in 1916, has the form of a duologue between an actress-manager, Dorothy Taverner, and her solicitor and admirer, Edward. It is set in the lawyer's office, and its pretext is a discussion of Miss Taverner's financial position to decide whether she can continue in theatrical management. However, from allusions to the looking-glasses, before which the actress rehearses her parts, the play develops the poetic meanings of the mirror as a more fundamental theme.

This is another of Granville Barker's attempts at drama which all but excludes outer action and composes its inner action from the slight, yet constant shifts of mood and changes of attitude in the mutual response of the two characters. The play can be read as the actor-manager's apologia, the author's last bid for his public's understanding of what he had tried to achieve in the theatre: an appeal based especially on a discussion of the art of acting. It is also an obvious vehicle for a star actress. Dramatically, Edward is not quite a match for Miss Dorothy Taverner: he is there to set her off, admire, understand, be convinced; but he is distinctly less interesting, and this is a limitation upon the play, restricting action and conflict even within the terms that the dramatist has proposed for himself.

For the two characters represent antithetical principles: as Dorothy speaks for the wildness of the creative imagination, Edward is another of the figures of Law that appear in Barker's work, gently treated here, just suggestive of the human impulse to clamp down upon nature, regulate the activity of the spirit with a caution and calculation that seem to deny all trust and faith. Dorothy classes him with the profit-making rest and threatens him with the same heaven:

> ... bustling among the clouds ... making the best of things ... beating your harps into coin ... bargaining for eternity ...

The clash of temperaments may have been toned down to what the dramatist felt to be appropriate to the scale of the one-Act play. As it is, a thoughtful mood predominates; and a sympathy of feeling, that transcends differences of outlook, gives the necessary condition for the intimacy of the talk. But there has been no scaling down of the play's themes.

In his essay on John Marston, T. S. Eliot wrote:

> It is possible that what distinguishes poetic drama from prosaic drama is a kind of doubleness in the action, as if it took place on

two planes at once .. a certain apparent irrelevance may be the symptom of this doubleness; or the drama has an under-pattern, less manifest than the theatrical one.[9]

In this sense, Barker's drama generally approximates to the poetic, and *Farewell to the Theatre* is an illustration of how much greater may be the interest of the under-pattern than the surface concerns of the play; indeed, it is an extreme example of the subordination of outer dramatic pattern to the organic imagery that the dialogue contains. A token of how much is implicit in the scene is offered by the photograph of the child, Edward's daughter, which is on the mantelpiece.[10] She died nine years before, the dramatist tells us in his directions. She is not mentioned at all by the two characters; the photograph is just the lifeless, inadequate image of so much human experience, contained quiescent in the dramatic moment.

As in *Waste*, references to time are scattered throughout the text in casual-seeming, literal phrases: 'How punctual!', 'The rent's paid till Christmas,' '. . . the railway trains running on time,' 'Past one.' They accumulate and expand into simple, familiar metaphors and enforce the value of incidental symbols: the old Venetian mirror, or the crumbling wall. The static scene contains its dynamic images: the 'spinning earth' and the 'flying years' imply a whole universe with its perspective of distance. Through variation on the symbol of the mirror, in the actress's talk about her art, the traditional image of the *theatrum mundi* emerges as a major element in the design. The medium in which the dramatist works and the histrionic art, of which Dorothy speaks, are equated with the hidden theme of the play: the relation of the Self and the Other, explored by Calderon, Strindberg and Pirandello in terms of the same theatrical metaphor. Among the various Shakespearian uses of the figure that Barker may have had in mind, the most familiar is Prospero's closing of the revels.

'Say Egoist . . . say Actress,' mocks Dorothy at herself and at the world's verdict; and the central anecdote of the play concerns that crisis of her art when she turned face to the wall the mirrors, before which she used to rehearse. The motif of imprisonment, recurrent in the full-length plays, is here associated with fantasy:

What can we understand when we're all so prisoned in mirrors that whatever we see it's but ourselves . . . ourselves as heroes or slaves . . . suffering, triumphant . . . always ourselves.

And the climax of the play, marked by the snapping of the paper-knife, with which Dorothy has been playing, transforms the complex metaphor, now more covertly introduced, into a token of liberation from the self and the shattering of the fantasy by truth:

> Oh, my poor theatre! Keep it for a while then to patronise and play with. But one day it shall break you all in pieces.

The talk explores the motives—for money's sake, art's sake, Dorothy's sake—, which had led, or might yet lead, investors to back her ventures. The theme of profit and calculation reaches a climax in the mention of the gold that buys nothing at all, and which has been Dorothy's reward: 'my little scrap of gold,' she calls her discovery of reality in the human experience she shares with others; it is the mirror of truth, sharply distinguished from the empty mirror of self: 'From its brightness shines back all the vision I have.' Barker gradually associates the golden quality of sunlight with the character of the actress, as she visualises herself (an Ellen Terry in idyllic retirement at Smallhythe?) sitting among the marigolds in her garden, the setting sun upon it. The emblem of fire is a variation on the theme: Dorothy refers to 'my burning', and there are at least three variants on the phoenix image in the course of the dialogue, the name, 'Shelburne,' introduced at the beginning of the play, the title, *The Salamander,*' given to the last drama that Dorothy is to produce, and then the double value of the word, 'shell,' in one of the last speeches:

> How utterly right that I should end my days in a shanty built out of the stones of that great Abbey and buttressed up in its shell!

As he was to do with his last plays, Barker links *Farewell to the Theatre,* by slight, deft touches, with the world of a greater work, in this case, *Cymbeline.* A few phrases are enough: 'Milford Abbey is safe for you;' '. . . you never could have enjoyed my Imogen as you used to enjoy it;' 'I want to sit in the sun and spoil my complexion.' There comes echoing through: 'Fear no more the heat o' th' sun . . . ,' and with it the whole death-resurrection symbolism and a little of the mood of late Shakespearian tragi-comedy. The paradox of the 'first dead failure', which gave Dorothy her 'passion for failing', prepares the way for the final paradox of the acceptance of mortality as a release into the sense of infinite life. The claustrophobic nightmare is dispersed here, as it is not in *The Voysey Inheritance* and *The Madras House*. Even Edward, through his love of Dorothy, recognises that the familiar world, made and defined by men's minds, is itself an illusion, liable to vanish like the theatrical scene.

* * *

There survives, among Barker's manuscripts, a fragmentary record of the actual process of composing a long play. This includes, among other notes, three versions of the opening of a play to be called *The Village Carpenter*, together with two versions of the beginning of Act III. Associated with these are two completed Acts of *The Wicked Man* and various jottings relating to it. The notes for *The Village Carpenter*, of which there are thirty large sheets, seem to have been made in 1910; for among them appear a few notes for the article on Barrie, which was published in *The Bookman* in that year.[11] The scraps towards *The Wicked Man* are on notepaper with printed headings: '17 John Street, Adelphi,' whither the Barkers moved early in 1911, and 'Kingsway Theatre', the lease of which was taken at the end of 1911, as well as 'Court Lodge, Stansted', Barker's country home since 1908 and where he was known to be writing in 1911. Certain of the *dramatis personae* of *The Village Carpenter* appear in the two Acts of *The Wicked Man* and, despite considerable differences between them, the two plays reveal themselves, upon a closer study, to be one. By process of continual revision and re-thinking, *The Wicked Man* grew out of the earlier attempt. On the envelope containing the two completed Acts of this latest stage is written the date, 1914.

A fact immediately evident is that Barker's thoughts had gone back to his earliest published play; for first in the list of characters under the title, *The Village Carpenter*, is the name, 'John Baptist Abud,' and John Abud is retained among the chief characters in

The Wicked Man. A disconnected note identifies him as the grand-son of the earlier Abud, the youngest descendant of the large family come of Ann Leete's union with the gardener. Barker's first post-war play, *The Secret Life,* is in many respects more obviously related to *The Marrying of Ann Leete* than to the plays between. These manuscript fragments form a link between the two.

Progress from the first version to the second involved much modification of the theme and a sorting out, redistributing and discarding of many of the motifs that here, as in all Barker's drama, spring in great abundance from the central idea. The changes are in the direction of greater clarity and also closer unity; but the second version offers an interest in no way impoverished or shallower than that of the first.

It is not easy to be sure of the exact plan conceived for *The Village Carpenter,* or the precise inter-relationships of characters and themes that the dramatist intended. Something can be gathered from the notes on the characters. The chief figures seem to be four: Elisabeth, her husband and a younger man, Charles, all cultured, upper class characters, and, standing apart from them, Abud, the carpenter. None of the other characters that Barker originally intended to include appear in the 1914 form of Acts I and II, though it may be that the Alfred Morgan and Phila-delphia,[12] otherwise Mary, Morgan, to whom these early notes refer, but whose place in the action is left undefined, are represented in the Owen and Mary of the final text. The original title and the names, Elisabeth, Mary, John Baptist Abud, suggest that Barker had Christian, messianic symbolism in mind, and it does not seem to have been discarded when the later title, *The Wicked Man,* was chosen.

There are biblical echoes in that, too, and he left a list of them, not all accurately worded according to the Authorised Version, on one slip of paper. Its purpose can be conjectured: he may have brooded over the texts as he explored the implications of his theme, relating them and contrasting them in his mind, until he had de-fined the underlying argument of his play in their terms; and for the writing of his allusive style of dialogue some such constant background of reference must have been a useful aid. (The Author's Preface to *The Red Cross in France* mentions the Biblio-

mancy that he tried, before sitting down to start writing the book.)
This kind of meditation on his chosen subject is a likely origin for
the close-textured quality of his plays. It has sometimes been said
that his drama excludes religious experience altogether.[13] The
falseness of this judgment has already emerged during the course
of this study. This is an appropriate point at which to observe how
persistently Barker invoked Christian tradition and its values as
the context of his plays. His vision and sentiment were certainly
conditioned by Christianity and its paradoxes.

The general design that Barker had in mind for *The Wicked
Man* and the values that he intended his characters to express
can be deduced from the two complete Acts and the associated
notes. There was to be a double action: a main plot, involving
Elisabeth and Hugo Trelawney, Charles, brought up by Elisabeth
and youthfully in love with her, and Ottilia, whom he is expected
to marry; and an underplot, concerning John Abud and Mary,
the wife who left him for other men and, years later, returns to him
to die. In the relationship of Elisabeth and Charles can be traced
an anticipation of the bond between Joan Westbury and Oliver, in
The Secret Life; Elisabeth's sense of life at an end anticipates
Joan's;[14] Hugo, devoted to decency and propriety, pinning his
faith to successful activity, is the representative of the world which
Strowde rejects, in that later play. Ottilia does not emerge clearly
defined, but a jotting that compares her, in her beauty, to the Lady
of Shallot indicates that Barker was still finding meaning in an
image that he had drawn on before. Hugo is a politician, who returns from Westminster at week-ends to the house in the country
where Elisabeth, stubbornly refusing to accept his values and his
way of life, insists on living. Her outward life is a confession of the
emptiness of purpose that possesses her; yet her passivity is con-
templative.

Barker had made provision for the appearance, in Act III, of
Sir Frederick Skuse, father of Ottilia, another denizen of the
political society in which Hugo moves. But, as far as the play was
written, there is no direct presentation of that society and none of
the political dialogue that might be expected from Barker. In its
absence, the static and meditative quality of Acts I and II is oppressive; the drama lacks the tougher substance and more complex

fabric which characterise the plays that show the intimate movement of inner life directly interacting with the intrigue of public affairs. Yet the intended climax was to take the form of a disruptive violence, with the stabbing of Hugo by Abud.

The sub-plot was evidently to be a symbolic commentary on the other. Neither Abud nor Mary belongs to the ordinary world that is the true province of naturalism. He is a complex figure: a man of violence, challenging the stillness of Elisabeth, and something of the natural savage; he stands against the background of his tumble-down cottage in Trelawney's fields, or beside a hut within a wood—his workshop; 'Abud works savagely—furiously —he is a working animal,' is one of the dramatist's jottings, and another: 'He lived for a bit in a cave in the wood'; he has a kind of craziness that seems to mirror the despairs of Elisabeth and of Charles, to whom he voices his account of the world as he sees it:

> I know there's a god and I think he's a wicked one. Why? He's made right and wrong and that's his game you learn to play while he laughs to see it all come to the same thing in the end. But he didn't make us I don't believe, he don't behave like that. 'Long as you amuse yourself he lets you be ... But lift your heart above it and there's a jealous god ... Some souls, praps, he can chivvy to nothingness in this world, but us tougher ones we might be good for another time or two. Fine sport you know.

(It may be recalled that Barker was producing *The Dynasts* and considering a dramatised version of *Tess of the D'Urbervilles*, while working on this play.) Abud has served a prison sentence for assault and robbery, having been impelled by a murderous impulse to visit on the fortunate of society the misery of the unfortunate. The 'logic of deeds', he calls his action, his pursuit of justice, which was also a release from an intolerable pity. Looking back on it, he rejects it; and indeed it is one of a number of things in the play that contribute to the image of the God who is Judge and distributor of punishments, ruling the world of power whereby Hugo lives and that reflects his idea of order. Abud's former wife, Mary, has lived the life of a wanton. With the figure of the thief is linked the figure of the whore. Like their prototypes in the Christian Gospels, they challenge the conventions of virtue and vice and assert a reality beyond ethical judgments, a reality recognised by Elisabeth and Charles, the seekers after good.

Destruction is Abud's method of resisting the morality and order that corrupt. It is to death that he looks, not only for escape, but as an assertion of the truths life seems to deny. He continues to claim, on Mary's behalf, 'She's earned her right to die;' and his laconic challenge to Owen, the snivelling, half-educated townsman, a degraded creature, is: 'I take it as you don't believe in death.'

The morbidity in Granville Barker's work appears here again. It can be read as a casual symptom of an ineradicable lassitude in the man. It is certainly an incidental reflection of the age and tradition that formed his mind. However, his plays exploit what in life might be weakness, for in them the concept of death is given positive value: it corresponds to the desire for the impossible that can carry man beyond the limits of his nature, and it is the final revolutionary power that overturns life's values to reveal to man that the universe in which he lives is an uncharted wilderness, where he wanders as a stranger; 'the flowery wilderness,' Edward calls it, in *Farewell to the Theatre,* a place with no safe paths, and the condition of human freedom.

Civilisation elaborates its formalities about sex as about death, without altogether hiding the truth that only what men inwardly are will serve to answer the demands of either. Whether the character of Mary was intended to take a direct part in the action of *The Wicked Man* is not certain from what Barker wrote. What is clear is her value as a symbol of pristine sex, innocent and inviolable, and a sacrificial figure. Abud explains to the sympathetic Elisabeth:

> I loved her and I let her go . . . and put no doubt in her mind. She'd given herself before she married me . . . yes, once and again. I tell you, when she came close at nights it was like sunshine . . . she might have frightened a man if he'd understood. Mornings she'd seem no more than a child. So off she ran and on she went—I knew . . . ungrudging . . . not to be bargained with. They learnt how to buy and sell her . . . for all that's too free and fine for them they pull down to soil it. Only her spirit . . . and what a world we've made of it when we don't bow down to have such a spirit rest on us . . . that they've despised and left . . . .

This has its direct relevance to Elisabeth, for it is the true mean-

ing and value of her womanhood that she is seeking, feeling it to
have been despised and rejected by the world of Hugo's success.
She protests to him, as Dorothy Taverner does to Edward, of the
common life she shares with those society chooses to regard as the
worst of women. Like Amy O'Connell, Elisabeth and Mary
represent the fugitive values for which the dominant orthodoxy
has no use, which it tramples and casts out, or tames and regulates.
'All *love*,' runs one manuscript note for Charles, 'is illicit—secret.'

Taming is Hugo's business. It is against his ideal of having 'all
one's life under one's thumb' (a metaphor reminiscent of the possessive grasp of Carnaby Leete) that Charles rebels. To Elisabeth's
admonition, '. . . don't make a mess of your marriage,' Charles gives
the bitterly cynical retort: 'Decent people don't.' Abud admits
that, in the interests of Mary's own safety and ease, he could have
'tamed her'. The sense that man, in so far as he is a domesticated
animal, is by no means unquestionably higher than the brute and
is a very great deal lower than the angels, was clearly implied in the
farmyard imagery of *The Madras House* and is explicit in
Georgiana's contemptuous comments on farm and society alike.
Dorothy Taverner declares:

> . . . that your minds may be easy as you bustle through the world's
> work . . . so we must seem to choose the cat-like comfort of the
> fireside [. . .]. And perhaps I should have chosen that if I could
> have had my choice. [. . .] Had not some ruthless windy power
> from beyond me . . . blown me free.

Barker's fullest exploration of what tameness means was post-
poned until his last play, *His Majesty;* but the ideal of aristocracy
(in the classical sense, 'the rule of the best'), which all his later
writings pursue, even his non-fictional writings,[15] began much
earlier to be associated in his imagination with freedom from civilisation's laws. In democracy he came more and more to see social
man subdued to the mass, an evolutionary regression, in which the
quality that placed *homo sapiens* at the head of the hierarchy of
life-forms had been lost. It is a persistently romantic view, and
Barker's version of it had its contemporary parallels in the work of
Yeats and of Lawrence, among others. That generation's rediscovery of Blake had made accessible, in the intellectual air of the

time, concepts and images that certainly enriched the dramatist's work.

As far as it goes, *The Wicked Man* is an experiment in the writing of prose drama with a content of thoughtful emotion. In this, also, it is preliminary to *The Secret Life*, which deliberately alternates scenes of this nature with others of a more overt kind of drama. Intimacy and passiveness are germane to the themes of both plays, uncompleted and completed; but between suggestion and exact reproduction there lies, of course, a primary artistic distinction. The meditative conversation-piece was part of the territory which Barker set out to make especially his own as a dramatist. Poor dramatists are supposed to find it easier to write duologues than to handle a group of characters, and frequent recourse to duologues in the development of a play is assumed by some to be invariably a sign of technical inferiority. Reflection on the superbly orchestrated dialogue of Act I of *The Madras House*, Act I of the revised version of *Waste*, Act II, Scene III, of *The Secret Life* is enough to kill instantly any suspicion that Barker composed in duologue-form *faute de mieux*. In fact, any major dramatist learns to take account, in his plays, of the way that the life of human society reduces itself to communication between twos, until the pair gives place to the single individual and duologue to soliloquy, the dialogue with oneself.

Granville Barker undoubtedly studied the technique of Ibsen's retrospective conversation-pieces, but he may have learnt even more directly from Maeterlinck and Villiers de L'Isle Adam.[16] In August 1910, he had written a brief Introduction to three plays of Maeterlinck's, in translation, so renewing—if it needed renewing—his consideration of a dramatist who had influenced some of his earliest work. *Aglavaine and Sélysette*, produced at the Court Theatre in 1904, offered a precedent for the succession of duologues that makes up so much of *The Wicked Man;* of the three plays that his Introduction accompanied, *Interior*, his confessed favourite, might have served as a model for his own attempt to convert the material of meditation and suffering into the stuff of drama.

The introspective quality that *The Wicked Man* shares with *Aglavaine and Sélysette* has its effect on character presentation.

The *dramatis personae*, whose meditations are overheard, take shape in and through their sentiments. There is a danger that the author's sympathetic identification with his characters' inner life may blur the outlines, or dissolve them altogether. The barriers of individuality and bias, that define distinct personalities, tend to wear thin in *Aglavaine and Sélysette*. Dramatic effect gives way to more simply lyrical, in so far as the author's separation of his characters from himself is incomplete. In the critical attitude that he maintains to Philip Madras, Barker does succeed in so detaching himself. He has not, however, wholly succeeded in liberating Elisabeth Trelawney, by the stage at which *The Wicked Man* was abandoned. The difficulty unsolved here had to be struggled with again, in the meditative scenes of *The Secret Life*.

In reducing the number of characters on the stage to the minimum that the naturalistic convention in dialogue would permit, Barker was undoubtedly moving towards the nearest equivalent to the Shakespearian soliloquy (or Chekhovian disguised soliloquy) available to him, within the theatre at his disposal. He also turned to new rhythms and cadences to induce a quietly tense mood. Rhetoric is necessarily the language of the theatre, designed as it is to sway and direct the emotional response of a mass audience; a mass is accessible to appeal on more than one level, though, and crude rhetoric, which oversimplifies issues and clouds the mind with a violence of feeling, is not the only possible rhetoric. In his work on *The Wicked Man*, Barker developed a rhetoric that could address individual experience without disturbing the spell of the mass presence.

This style, used extensively in his last plays, is partly responsible for a slowing down of the pace. A single example from *The Wicked Man*, which recalls by its content a more vigorously rhetorical parallel in *The Madras House*,[17] will indicate the direction in which he was moving:

> . . . in a west wind I can hear these beeches . . . a deeper voice than all the other trees . . . and I've asked why our cleverness only begets cleverness and our riches and comforts more comforts still. Down below you'll be talking of thrift and the birthrate while I pray God to tell me why when Nature's had her crudest use of us our joy in life should no longer overflow . . . when our body has been fruitful

why should our souls 'be barren ... and deep as the voice of the
wind in the beeches my womanhood gives me the answer.

In that particular example there is nothing of language new-
minted; it is a tired style, perhaps too tired for poetic intensity,
for all that its languorous rhythms may have their ultimate source
in Pater. Much of the writing in *Souls on Fifth* is rather like it. Its
positive value is that it certainly induces the hush of intimacy.[18]
   The inspiration of Maeterlinck may be discerned in the content
of *The Wicked Man,* as well as in its form and lack of outer action,
except at the climax. The essential dramatic conflict in *Aglavaine
and Sélysette* is between vision and feeling, the ethical sense and
the poetic, those different principles which Barker seems to have
intended to play off against each other in 'Georgiana'. Taking the
hackneyed subject of the love-triangle, Maeterlinck removes it
completely from the realm of intrigue, in order to relate and contrast two kinds of love: the noble, idealistic love of Aglavaine and
Meléandre and the self-sacrificial love of Sélysette, that is fulfilled
in suffering without understanding. Intellectual assent goes to the
former, but it is the latter that he makes more poignantly beautiful.
This assertion of the supreme value of suffering, implicit in all
Maeterlinck's earlier plays, is to be read in Barker's work at least
from *The Marrying of Ann Leete.*
   The heroine of *The Wicked Man,* the character in whom suffering is articulate, appears rather closely related to the heroine of
another early document of the *théâtre de l'inexprimé: La Révolte*
by Villiers de L'Isle Adam. This play, which has only two characters throughout, was translated into English by Theresa Barclay in
1901, and the translation was re-issued in 1910, when it may well
have influenced the conception of *The Wicked Man.* The similarity
between the two heroines extends even to their names; and Villiers'
Elisabeth voices the protest of the soul against materialism, represented by her husband, Félix, in terms that Barker's manuscript
sometimes echoes closely.
   In Barker's work, the emphasis on suffering is usually balanced
by a complementary assertion: of the natural dependence of action
upon contemplation. The sacrifice of Mary, in *The Wicked Man,*
the deaths of Baptista (in *A Miracle*), of Amy O'Connell and—

looking forward to *The Secret Life*—of Joan Westbury, like the surrender of the Little Soul, all seem to offer a vicarious redemption and renewal of life for others. It is the failures, the defeated characters in the plays, that hold out a promise for the future. The world that they carry within them and the outer world seem to have broken connection, so that action seems to them unreal and futile; the same marks of an enchanted isolation are upon Elisabeth Trelawney as on Joan Westbury. Yet the plays which contain such characters are not simply expressive of that *acedia*, identifiable with the Freudian death-wish, which the twentieth-century has appropriated to itself. The passive figures are subordinate, in the completed plays, to others whose struggle back to wholeness constitutes the heroic action. It is probable that, even in *The Wicked Man*, the study of Elisabeth's despair was preparation for the regeneration of Charles.

Even so, the passivity and despair obviously dominated Barker's mind during his labours on that text; the intellectual energy, which makes for conflict and a wrestling with the conditions of the universe and men as they are, was subdued at that time, and so the play was discarded. It had been a rehearsal for the presentation, in the last two long plays, of the mood of an age that had suffered the final destruction, by the 1914-18 carnage, of its belief in progress as the nineteenth century conceived it. The difference of these last plays from Barker's earlier drama was quite certainly determined as much by a change in the world he saw about him as by his withdrawal from the theatre. It was now his concern to depict what had happened to the inner life of civilised man and relate it to an outer world in which chaos still triumphed. He does not portray the worldly success of his idealists in their struggle: the end of *The Secret Life* simply betokens that the struggle is not over; the end of *His Majesty* is an ironic retreat that is yet no surrender. It is only to the poet's eye that the intangible values shine brighter and more hopefully.

CHAPTER IX

The Secret Life

'What is great in man is that he is a bridge and not an end: what can be loved in man is that he is an *overture* and a *going under*.' (Nietzsche, *Thus Spake Zarathustra*, trans. Kaufmann.)

The war swept away the theatre in which Granville Barker had worked and the tradition of serious drama that he had done so much to build up. At the time when he was beginning *The Secret Life*, his old teacher, William Poel, was writing:

> · The condition of the English Theatre has moved steadily downward, and to-day it may be said to have touched its lowest level on record. . . . The plays of Shaw, Galsworthy, Barker, Masefield with those of all men who respect themselves and their calling, are put on one side as being impossible compositions, written by those who do not understand the needs of the public. . . .[1]

In this situation, when he was no longer in a position to produce his own plays and risk a heavy loss, Barker seems to have felt free to write for his ideal theatre. He made little effort to get his last plays produced. When Harcourt Williams, in 1933, proposed that *His Majesty* should be put on at the Old Vic, the dramatist replied:

> It would be pleasant to find myself working with you. Well done all round, and rather more than this in the parts which matter, the play might make its mark. But I have held it back, and shall, from every other rut of chance.[2]

He seems to have remembered Shaw's consistent advice to ambitious dramatists that they should publish their plays, and he may

210

have been prepared to wait patiently as long as Shaw waited for the producer and the company that could give a fair opportunity to his latest work.

The example of the Moscow Art Theatre was doubtless at the back of his mind, and so was the yet undefeated hope of an English National Theatre. William Archer, who divined that *The Secret Life* was 'written for next generation, if not for the next again', received the friendly protest:

> I never have—I cannot—write an unactable play; it would be against nature, against second nature anyhow: I act it as I write it ... there is no English company of actors so trained to interpret thought and the less crude emotions, nor, as a consequence—any selected audience interested in watching and listening to such things. But that, believe me, human fallibility apart,—mine to begin with —is the extent of the difficulty.[3]

Conscious of making very considerable demands on his performers, he did not do so irresponsibly. Although he had left the practical theatre, there is no relaxation of the effort to communicate in genuinely dramatic terms, in *The Secret Life* and *His Majesty*.

Barker seems more concerned with the potentialities of the physical stage in *The Secret Life* than in any of his earlier plays. Searching, apparently, for such a freedom and range of effects as the Elizabethan theatre offered to Shakespeare, he has experimented in the simultaneous and alternate use of different acting areas: in Act I, he provides for the division of the stage into two levels, a flight of steps leading up from the forestage to a balcony, five feet or so higher; in Act II, the forestage is intended to represent a first-floor gallery, behind and below which is a terrace, a backcloth of cypresses bordering it, visible through the gallery windows.

In place of the continuous Act structure which predominates in his earlier drama, the three Acts of this play contain eleven scenes, in which the playwright shifts the action about the stage, as well as from locality to locality in his imagined world, even from London to Massachusetts and back again. Now he demands the use of the entire width of the stage, but cuts off most of the depth; now he cramps his actors into a space representing no more than the corner of a room beside a window; in the first scene of all, he concentrates

visual attention on the vertical of the flight of steps, as the balcony
to which they lead is surrounded by a high parapet, and to these
steps the actors in the third scene are confined; two scenes in Act
III, set in a London room, could be staged in the most conventional of box-sets. It is most unlikely that Barker envisaged any
elaborate scene-shifting, necessitating breaks of any length. As a
producer, he distinctly favoured continuous playing, and by his
alternation of scenes in this play he has avoided major changes,
except between Acts. The modern method of continuous playing of
Shakespeare, largely Barker's own introduction, is the model for
what he intends.

In two scenes (I. i and II. iii) he makes the experiment of divorc-
ing sight from sound. In the first, the effect is to emphasise the
significance of both: a white, still figure, seated on the steps,
appears as a symbolic presence, a marble statue, into which life
enters during the course of the scene;[4] the talk and the music, which
proceed from the balcony, take on the force of a significant accompaniment, a first warning that Barker intends to exploit the
musical character of the dialogue throughout this play. In Act II,
Scene III, the sound of voices raised, and of footsteps walking or
running along the terrace, makes a background to the visible scene
in the gallery. The effect this time is quite different: a lively
counterpoint is achieved, and the nature of the scene between the
characters visible to the audience is considerably qualified. In both
instances, of course, Barker has invented variants on the relation
of chorus to protagonists.

The general æsthetic reason for so great a departure from his
earlier practice in the organisation of a play was certainly a desire
to bend all his resources to the communication of essential dramatic
effects: particular moods and contrasts of mood, changes in tension and the focusing of interest, and the over-riding rhythm. The
inner development of the play was to be reflected as faithfully as
possible in the physical scene, the theatre made as plastic as possible to the dramatist's shaping imagination.

Regarded more specifically, the division into Acts and scenes is
discovered to correspond to the musical form of the symphony.
The first and third Acts, with their three scenes each, suggest
sonata form: two distinct moods, one markedly lyrical, the other

more strongly dramatic, correspond to the tonic and dominant keys through which the themes are conducted; the alternating subjects are provided by the love story and the plot of political intrigue, the inner and the outer aspects of life, to which the recurrent motifs of moon and market-place are related; in each instance, the second scene is a modulatory development of both subjects. The second Act, with its five scenes, also moves between lyrical and dramatic episodes. The first subject, the political, predominates and the tempo is mostly brisk, except for the lyrical fourth scene, which is in effect a serenade; scenes iii and v are particularly long and complex, and the whole Act is considerably longer than the others. Through the whole play, the themes are interwoven in the dialogue without a break, one blending into another as in a continuous carpet-pattern.

* * *

None of Barker's other plays opens so strangely or so evocatively. The setting represents a house near the sea, and the stage should be all white and silver, as moonlight falls on white walls and salted turf. From over the parapet there sounds the end of a performance of *Tristan und Isolde*, half-sung, half-spoken, in a mixture of German and English, to a piano accompaniment. It is the very moment of Isolde's death; then the speaking voice adds: 'King Mark . . . raises his hand as if in benediction of the tragic lovers. The twilight deepens. The curtain falls.' So the note of tragic catastrophe is struck at the very beginning of the play. Admittedly, the mood is not of pure tragedy, for the performance has been grotesquely interrupted by gibing voices. But Wagner, Barker knows, is not so easily laughed off, and he brings back snatches of the music as background to the last minutes of the scene.

Chekhov's use of music as part of his complex dramatic vocabulary offers a close parallel to Granville Barker's here (and the English writer had had an opportunity to observe it in Stanislavsky's productions): in each case, the music not only contributes powerfully to the mood of the scene, it is a unifying element in the play as a whole; almost a symbol itself, it contains the emotions that the drama is set to explore. Here, in terms of music, is the first statement of the theme, more complete than in the still, white, visual symbol of the woman on the steps. Among the snatches from the music-drama that are heard at the close of the scene, the playwright specifies the melody of the *Liebestod* and, from Act II:

> Oh rest upon us ... night der Liebe. *[...]* Give forgetting ...
> That I live. Take me out ... in deinen Schoss ...

The *leitmotive* relating to the heroine and the inner life have been introduced. Through the rest of the play, the dialogue will recall them and interweave them in its symphonic texture; only in the mind will the actual music be heard again.

In the central part of the first scene, the figures on the balcony move to the top of the steps, or lean over the parapet, and the evening clothes of 1923 dispel the timeless, unlocalised atmosphere that the music and the stage picture have combined to evoke. The silent, listening figure of Joan Westbury moves and speaks and takes on the character of a living woman. The talk is mostly about government, party politics and the Civil Service, the Stock Exchange and official committees. The gathering sorts itself into its different members: the three middle-aged men, recalling their Oxford days, Salomons, the Permanent Official, Stephen Serocold, the indispensable organiser of his party, and Evan Strowde, the detached historian, whom Serocold is endeavouring to win back into political activity; the hostess is Strowde's sister, Eleanor, reminiscent of Frances Trebell, another spinster whose intellect, honesty and sense of duty have served a brother's career and incline her to social responsibility and political idealism.

But side-by-side with the exposition of the specific situation goes an exposition of universal themes. The sea, whose tides have been heard in the music, is brought into the dialogue, and references to the desert follow, the Egyptian desert. Lady Westbury's husband in Cairo is named Mark, a fact that confirms her identification with Isolde and prepares for the emergence, in scene iii, of Strowde as the Tristan in this version of the legend; but the first mention of Mark Westbury is immediately preceded by a passage that transforms this Egypt into a country of the imagination, breaking through the boundaries of time:

JOAN. You've never been to Karnak, Eleanor?
ELEANOR. No.
JOAN. We break our journey at Luxor whenever there's time. You should stand on the great gate and watch the moon rising over the Nile . . . and then think of all the armies that have marched . . .

For an audience in 1923, the marching armies of the first World War would not have been so far away; for an audience in the theatre, the Roman armies in Cleopatra's Egypt might well haunt the mind.

This, too, like *Antony and Cleopatra*, is to be a play of middle-aged lovers, set against the background of the great world, and presents a hero whose genius for government and heroic activity has lain idle beneath the enchantment of a woman. Barker may have had in mind the compacting feast aboard Pompey's galley, as he wrote his scene of the after-dinner drinking of his modern triumvirate, and the sensual metaphors of eating and drinking that run through the scene, most deliberately used by Salamons ('Tristan was the great dish,' 'gorged with emotion,' 'appetites turned to taste,') may have a connection with Shakespeare's use of such images and contain some memory of Mark Antony's 'Egyptian dish'.

But Granville Barker was certainly casting yet further back in time. In November, 1922, Howard Carter had uncovered the steps leading down to the tomb of Tutankhamen at Luxor. In February 1923, the tomb was opened and the sarcophagus discovered, with the trumpet of the young king that was to sound across the hundred generations from the eighteenth dynasty. Serocold improvises to the melody of the *Liebestod*:

Good night, Sir Geoffrey . . . Salamons K.C.B. flat . . . hidden handed bureaucrat . . . Beast in Revelations . . . your number will shortly be up.

With this note of an approaching end, the span is complete.

The first exchange between Strowde and Joan Westbury brings into the dialogue the *leitmotive* of the heroine:

STROWDE. Is that you, Joan?
JOAN. Yes.

STROWDE. Couldn't you endure it?
JOAN. I could hear perfectly. Look at the moon.
STROWDE. It might be a ship on fire.
JOAN. Burnt out.

The ship of the Tristan story, the Roman galley and Cleopatra's barge that 'burn'd on the water' are absorbed into the image of the Viking ship of death. A moon-boat is featured in legends of Khonsu, to whose temple the great gate at Karnak belongs; and the phoenix myth, of course, is Egyptian in origin.

Lady Westbury has been literally burnt out of her house. Her final words in the scene, 'Burnt out inside . . . the moon is. Gutted . . . such an ugly word,' hint of an inner life laid waste. Serocold's singing of the word, 'Schoss,' cuts across these lines, a secret comment on the fact that Joan has lost the fruit of her womb; for the sons she bore to Mark are dead, and there has been no physical consummation of her love for Evan. She stands to the latter, the hero, as a symbol 'of a sort of death in life'. This dramatic function and her appearance recall Irene in Ibsen's last play, *When We Dead Awaken*: a white figure, followed everywhere by her black shadow; another lady of the moon. In the name, Westbury, there is probably an allusion to Spengler's *Untergang des Abendlandes, Decline of the West*, published in 1918.

Two of Ibsen's plays seem to have been in Granville Barker's mind during the writing of *The Secret Life*, though he makes no direct allusions to either in the first scene and certainly does not require his audience to make the association. The last scene of the play, however, includes an obvious variation on the words of Irene and Rubek that come at the end of the second Act of *When We Dead Awaken*:

OLIVER. Love isn't all of that sort. Sometimes it brings Judgment Day.
SUSAN. But that's when the dead awake . . . isn't it?
OLIVER. Yes . . . to find this world's done with.

In Act I, Scene iii, Strowde says to Joan, using a metaphor prominent in the play: 'I'm not the first man who has found beliefs that he can't put in his pocket like so much small change.' A combination of this metaphor with that of burning is used by Ulrik

Brendel, when he walks out of the night to point the way to the catastrophe, in *Rosmersholm*: 'The last time I entered your doors I stood before you a man of substance, slapping a well-filled pocket ... And now as you see me to-night, I am a deposed monarch standing over the ashes of my burnt out palace ... Can you spare me an ideal or two?' (trans. F. Sharp.)

Rosmersholm and *When We Dead Awaken*, as well as *Antony and Cleopatra* and *Tristan*, have their *Liebestod*, the death which is the fulfilment and triumph of a supernatural love, and it is as a white figure that Rebecca goes with Rosmer to her death. Rebecca's symbolic white shawl seems to be remembered in the shawl placed round Joan's shoulders in the first scene, and perhaps also in the shawls that enwrap her, in her snowbound room, in Act III, scene ii.

But Joan makes a totally different direct impression from both those Ibsen heroines and, though she shares with Irene the symbolic attributes of inviolable chastity and death-in-life, Ibsen's obsession with guilt and innocence has no immediate relevance to her; Barker's fundamental concerns are related to what Ibsen calls 'the Rosmer way of life' and the freedom of soul that Rebecca stands for, but it is not Joan Westbury's part to work out the redemption of her past. The heroine and the theme of *The Secret Life* are the product of Barker's own experience as a thinking man.

One image reflecting the idea of death-in-life emerges in Act II. It is offered to Joan by the young man, Oliver, who completes the group of three chief characters in the play:

> A shell missed me outside Albert and did for my watch. I could shake it and it would tick for a bit ... but the spring was gone.

That is to him a token of his own inner life, that the war seems to have checked at the age of eighteen. In it is crystallised the notion of time at a stop (even in the midst of the long procession of human generations), implied in many forms in *The Secret Life*. Serocold, in the second scene of Act I, also expresses the sense of not ageing as other men do, and indeed he preserves the manner of the eternal undergraduate. There is energy in him, but no life-giving vision, no spring in the ticking watch. In Act I, scene iii, Strowde and Joan Westbury look back together on their lives arrested in the spell of an eighteen-year old love.

The first scene in its entirety has prepared for the revelation of this fairy-tale theme: appropriately planned and conducted by Serocold, the evening's performance has been a rehearsal of the past, 'Romantic youth . . . dragged from its grave and gibbeted'; a macabre travesty of resurrection (as also, from one point-of-view, was the raising of the sacred sarcophagus of the Egyptian King). On the scene looks down the dead planet, ceaselessly moving, that looked down on Ancient Egypt. The years to which the music carries back the group were those of Strowde's brilliant promise, left unfulfilled. The invitation that Serocold has now brought him to leave aside the writing of history and re-enter the political arena holds, in such a context, little assurance of real regeneration.[5]

Barker found the dynamic principle, which makes possible the hero's progress and the movement of the drama, in the experience of war: the same experience as gave him his source for portraying death-in-life. Though it shows a resemblance to *Waste* in characters and character-relations, *The Secret Life* is much more concerned with the depths of feeling. The poetry of *Waste* is essentially philosophical; this play is rooted in suffering, the suffering that the dramatist had seen during the war and the dread and hopelessness that the aftermath brought to many minds. Joan Westbury's thought of the marching armies gives the actress her first opportunity to suggest the profound, troubled sadness that possesses this mind. To so many in 1923 the talk in the bright sunlight of the second scene must have been almost unbearably poignant, as Serocold recalled his last meeting with Joan:

> SEROCOLD. Tea at the Military Tournament . . . nineteen thirteen. Your boy was with you.
> JOAN. Which?
> SEROCOLD. The one that was killed.
> JOAN. They were both killed.
> SEROCOLD. Both!
> JOAN. Within a month.

A dazed, unself-pitying acceptance has succeeded the first agony, but it leaves her mind free to ponder the images of a yet more widespread waste of life:

JOAN. . . . yesterday I was in camp again beyond Khartoum . . . watching the little black babies crawl about in the sand. I can remember one that died and didn't want to die . . . most of them, you know, come and go as easily . . . and he fought the air with his fists. (Act III, sc. ii)

The phrase from *Waste*, 'that balked scrap of being,' has been translated into terms that make a more direct impact. The image of the giant steam hammer cracking a nut is introduced into the text, just after that quoted passage of dialogue between Joan and Serocold, and it continues to be implied in the recurrence of the word, 'blow'. Armageddon is reduced, in this play, to the tiny fragments of individual experience, which seem so insignificant in the scale of universal calamity. Yet Joan is aware of a sense of loss and pain passing beyond the narrowly personal: 'One's capable,' she says to Strowde, 'of uncomprehended suffering,' and the acceptance of a universal law sounds in her rhetorical question, 'Why ask what an earthquake's for?'

When the line of thought reaches its climax, as she grips Kittredge's hand in the pain of her fatal illness, an extension of the earlier image implies an answer:

JOAN. Be stern with me . . . or I can't bear it, I'm afraid.
MR. KITTREDGE. I'm afraid you can. Headache or heart-ache or a harder thing . . . those that can suffer them must suffer them, it seems. You are the stuff, Joan, that forges well.

Seen in retrospect from the end of the play, all the pain that the drama contains takes on such meaning: it is the pain of change and growth, tempering instruments for a creative purpose. Within the experience of the hero, the agony of Joan's refusal to marry him and the later pain of the knowledge that she is dying are crises in his progress.

The mind wounded by life, or labouring in the agony of new stirrings, expresses itself in the antagonism and cruelty which supply as large an element as passive suffering in the emotional content of *The Secret Life* and contribute a vigour to the dramatic movement.

Oliver Gauntlett is Strowde's natural son. Though the illicit relationship is unacknowledged between them until Act III, its psychological ambivalence is present from the first introduction of

Oliver. Unconscious of the obvious implication, he explains to Joan Westbury the nature of his attitude to Strowde:

> Evan was picked out for me, you may say . . . I remember saying once, when I was eight, that I meant to grow up like him.

Though freed by the war from the 'greedy instinct to live', Oliver still has the younger generation's ruthlessness towards the old: 'He's in my way' is another comment on his unrecognised father; and most childishly revealing of all is his defiant boast:

> I can tell he's afraid of me. Why? Because he knows that I know he has failed. And he knows that I hate him for it.

Oliver obscurely feels that he has been cheated of his true inheritance, having to content himself with 'a beast of a world to have left on one's hands'; yet he still pins his hope to Strowde, while regarding him as the betrayer of faith.

The young man's desire to become the other's secretary is a modern version of the aspiration to be squire to his knight. (Serocold's reference to the Military Tournament is one example of the means used by Barker to maintain the parallel with the world of chivalry and the Arthurian context of the Tristan tale.) A critical passage in Act II, scene iii, presents the encounter, over a writing-table, in which Strowde tests his quality. The heaviest blow dealt by father to son is the revelation of a 'firm disbelief' that the time is ever ripe for idealism. Before it is through, Oliver issues his answering challenge:[6] 'Then why don't you shoot yourself?'—and it takes the rest of the play to meet it.

As Strowde and Oliver attack each other, so the latter taunts the young American girl, Susan Kittredge, who towards the end of the play promises him new hope; and Evan treats his sister, Eleanor, throughout Act II, with what seems a peculiarly wanton cruelty, until she turns from him at last in an outburst that makes part of the triple climax of the play. She begins by speaking of the History, which was the child of their 'marriage', nourished with her life; then she herself seems a child, grieving over rebukes to be endured in the course of learning its lessons:

> What does it mean to me to feel that if I burned every copy now, you'd hardly shrug your shoulders . . .[7] and to find this task of

mine ... which you've taught me, and thank you ... this report
spattered with your mockeries! I sat up last night crying over it
like a child over a copy-book [...] The curse is on you, it seems,
of coming at last to despise whatever you do and are. I'm sorry ...
but I must save myself ... my soul, if you like ... from despair.

It may seem to be the devil's work that Strowde is doing (he has
recently jested to the visiting politician, Heriot, of Eleanor's fear
'that I may corrupt your happy faith in life'), but in it is the cruel
violence of tearing the self away from the past, and the cruelty of
birth. In turning upon his sister, it is upon himself that he has
turned.

The forces of destruction that manifest themselves in the individual lives of the characters are also working blindly in the world
without. The play gives an objective view of a Europe laid waste,
in the memory that haunts Oliver of an East Galician town reduced
to a rubbish heap and preyed on by disease. He himself, an empty
sleeve the visible token of a maimed life, is a constant reminder
of the lost generation. Disgusted with the world in which he is
compelled to survive, he identifies faith and honour and right
order with the dead, the regiment of ghosts that he takes marching
with him in the darkness of every night, until he is too tired to
think. His desire for the 'fresh start' frames itself in terms of the
warfare amid which his mind still lives. With a display of youthful
defiance, he plays the anarchist:

> Grin through a mask and explode an idea on them ... and the
> Phillipses show the white scuts of their minds like rabbits.

He has, we learn, recently been arrested at an anarchist meeting,
and the imagery of gun and bomb and the lamp-post of summary
execution echoes in his talk. As his elders sit in the gallery at
Braxted Abbey and discuss the troubled times and the men who
offer themselves as leaders, the young voice of Dolly Gauntlett
interrupts with cheerful vigour:

> Vote for Brooke Bellingham ... our only bulwark against
> Bolshevism.

Strowde's comment is a measure of his contempt for the demagogue:

Think of it. A line of alliteration between us and the abyss,

and, like an echo of the thought, Oliver's voice with its habitually embittered tone floats up from the terrace:

A bas Belinjam! Conspuez Brooke.

He would tear the bulwarks down and let the abyss yawn, such is his disgust with life.

But Oliver, who has watched the same old kind of life crawl out again from the rubbish, knows the insufficiency of physical violence; it is to another kind of clean sweep and a truer Judgment Day that he looks forward. It is his father who teaches him how to set about his task, by embracing savagely the horror of a life without faith, in which the only value is success. In the first scene of Act III, Strowde admits to his own deliberate nihilism:

Are you still out to destroy? I'm showing you the sure way [...]
The reddest revolutionary is but a part of what he turns against
[...] Watch me succeed, Oliver. That will teach you how to down
me in turn.

Apprehension of the future overshadows the minds of most of the characters. To the healthy simplicity of Mildred, Lady Peckham, it takes the form of expectation of a social revolution, on which the American professor, Kittredge, gives his own gloss:

Why, we are living already, you may say, under a dictation of the
intellectual proletariat . . . .

To Joan, however, Kittredge reveals something of the more apocalyptic nightmare that haunts the depths of his mind:

I watch the new generations giving themselves to strange
tremendous forces to breed . . . what sort of a monster world.[8]

Strowde, talking with Eleanor, presents the future to her in the scientific language of 'the break up of the atom', that has become so much more of a commonplace of consciousness since.

As it stands in the play, the phrase picks up once more the theme of Joan's reference to the giant steam-hammer cracking the nut. Both ultimate physical destruction and the annihilation of human hope are meanings latent within the words. Perdition, the theological equivalent of the experience, is implied in the repetition of the terms, 'devil' and 'infernal', begun by Serocold in the first scene and continuing into the final scene, when Oliver suggests that Lord Clumbermere is a devil who beats the souls of men into pen nibs. Indeed, the evil that Strowde chooses, in Act II, is the choice of Faust.

The end of the world is at hand, most of the play seems to proclaim, as Serocold sings, 'Beast in Revelations . . . your number will shortly be up'; as Eleanor says when she brings the news of Mark's death for Joan, 'It'll seem like the end of the world'; but the external catastrophe only reflects individual choice. The sentiment of the end possesses Strowde and holds him idle, in the first Act, as it seems physically and spiritually to possess Joan; with it is identified all the imagery of barrenness found in the earlier plays and now more prominent than ever. In Act II, scene iii, Barker draws the analogy between the experience of the social being and that of the innermost man:

> STROWDE. . . . you have never found that the whole world's turmoil is but a reflection of the anarchy in your own heart?
> ELEANOR. No.
> STROWDE. That's where we differ then.

It is the difference that marks the hero.

*   *   *

Outwardly, Strowde's life takes two turns during the course of the play: the death of Mark Westbury, which frees Joan for him, precipitates his decision to emerge from retirement into open conspiracy for a return to Parliament and the Cabinet; when the news comes that Joan is dying, he abandons everything to journey across the Atlantic—a reversal of the voyage of Isolde to the dying Tristan—, though he does not expect to see her alive. The inner aspect of his progress is revealed in the course of his relationship with Joan and with Oliver.

In the third scene of Act I, the nature of the love that Evan and Joan know is explored by the two of them, as they sit on the steps of the cottage, in the moonlight. Looking back over his life, he declares to her:

> Well.... if we loved the unattainable in each other ... and if all we could easily have taken mattered so little besides that we let it go with hardly a murmur ... why, I've learnt to believe, I suppose, in what's unattainable from life and nothing else can content me or stir me now.

Joan finds Christian terms to express the experience:

> But seek first the kingdom of God ... and the desire of all things else shall be taken from you?

Granville Barker does not take Christian belief as his starting-point in any of his plays. When he employs Christian language, it conveys truth rediscovered, by a personal search, in the over-familiar phrases. Here, for instance, he directs that Joan should speak this line '*With an irony that is irony of the soul.*' For what she and Evan are confessing to is the terrible knowledge of futility and purposelessness in their temporal lives.

They share the bitter discovery that the vision which once ravished them has tricked them out of achievement and deceived them into letting go everything that the natural man holds of value, though they believe in no after-life and no compensating reward for self-denial and sacrifice. Though it holds them still, the vision itself has taken on for them the quality of an evil magic. Oliver's youthful unhappiness is to echo their disillusion:

> ... we're tricked so easily ... on from the time that we're tricked into getting born! This world's all tricks, isn't it?

'Oh, this has been a jealous devil, like all barren things,' exclaims Joan now to Strowde, 'Ask your heart ... and your own life ever since.' This, then, is what it means to find the kingdom of God: a sense of waste, and an unalleviable suffering.

The dramatist has brought his two characters to a crisis unlikely to be altogether outside the range of his audience's mature experience: a recognition of the failure of personal hopes, and the heart-break which is a usual episode in idealistic love; it is the clarity and intensity of consciousness that are extraordinary. The structure of his play identifies this experience with another— equally important to the destiny of man, but which theatre-goers are less generally aware of,—a crisis inherent in political experience: the confrontation of idealism by practical necessity and human imperfection.[9]

It is essential to the heroic action that Strowde should penetrate reality through an emotional antithesis (love and revulsion from love): it is the condition of his moral freedom, which in turn will make it possible for Susan Kittredge to see him as one who has power to transform the world, as he himself is transformed. The dream of love has been a spell of sleep upon his spirit, holding him aloof and indifferent towards the practical world. Joan's refusal to marry him, which challenges the dream, stirs his capacity for action into being once more; for, with this, he accepts the imperfect world as it is and his own kinship with it. But this is a flight from half-truth to half-truth, which have yet to be reconciled.

Joan offers the definition of love that eighteen years of it have revealed to her: 'Perhaps, Evan ... for a last meaning ... to love is to love the unattainable.' She can wish that she had never known it, but 'that was, and it is the truth of me. I'd unsay it if I could'; and Evan can fully understand the sincerity of that desire, though it is his way to try and make experience more endurable by turning it into abstractions:

> Yes. We live another life from the beasts only in this tiresome belief that beyond the tokens of our living something we call truth exists. Yet there's nothing near to truth that we learn, but when we've felt the burden we'd cast it away ... we'd unsay it if we could.

The temptation that faces him, and to which he succumbs, is one of doubt: whether there is any good to be got, any end to be served, in forsaking what Trebell calls 'the easier world'; whether the following of the dream is anything other than perverse stupidity. He makes his attempt at denial, when he reaches out for power and tries, Faust-like, to rid himself of the burden of his soul for 'a certain satisfaction' (Julia Farrant's phrase); but his final discovery is that he, too, cannot unsay the truth learnt through his love for Joan.

Thus he is brought to an acknowledgment that the pursuit of the unattainable and the impulse to action and achievement are complementary aspects of his nature. The moral being of man is determined by the participation of both good and evil in the scheme of creation, and Strowde has to experience both heaven and hell before he can creatively reconcile his idealism and his realistic sense of the imperfections of men and circumstances. With the acceptance of the complementary relation between desire and possibility, freedom and necessity, the power within him, that 'must spring from the secret life', can inform and master the empty power which men derive from things, and fulfil itself as the power of the ruler over the destiny of mankind.

There is nothing casual, then, about the course of the action in this play; it embodies the human being's progress to full self-consciousness and the political being's progress into full consciousness of the nature of politics as one of the universals of experience. It is a progress to what Kittredge calls 'the soul's place', the second paradise, which is of knowledge and contains the principles of evil and of growth through evil towards good:

> ... entering, we abandon everything but hope ... and hope is a lure.

*   *   *

Like a musical accompaniment to the journey of the hero's inner life, the terms of natural existence run in counterpoint through the dialogue. The many references to eating and drinking relate man to 'the beast that gluts and starves',[10] but also, in their metaphoric applications, suggest the hunger and thirst after righteousness. Mentions of sleep and generation are also persistent. The dramatist establishes a physiological basis for Joan's sense of life wasted and at an end. She is ill of a tumour on the brain, and her restlessness is a symptom of the disease; night after night she lies awake and cries at last desperately, 'Evan, has one to die to sleep?' The voice, raised in question, awakens an echo: 'To die, to sleep ...;' and that implies a continuation: 'To sleep, perchance to dream ....'

There will be nothing final about Joan's death; through it, the life-giving dream will be renewed.

The materially-minded Lady Peckham catches sight of the two lovers walking in the garden and remarks to Serocold: 'They'd better hurry up. They're not getting any younger. She'll want more children;' but already the sense of 'too late' is weighing on Joan's mind. Strowde voices his contempt of 'the unbelieving mob' with its greedy cry, 'Lord give us increase . . . .' The horror of the finite made perpetual, which troubles Philip Madras and Elizabeth Trelawney, is his also; but Kittredge has comfort for the dying Joan:

The generation of the spirit is not as the generation of the flesh. . . .

This double value of the common imagery asserts the oneness of man, against the dualism of flesh and spirit; and indeed the action traces the growth of the soul out of the body's life, a supernatural love out of sexual appetite, so that the natural man is changed at last to a spiritual being. So Evan passes from Mildred to Eleanor, to Joan (who escapes him, but takes with her the last of his selfish desires); so Oliver, born of the passing instinctual love for Mildred, is transformed into the son of the incorruptible love for Joan. This same imagery of natural existence has its political relevance, too, recalling the political theorists' notion of the Great Beast, or brute mob,[11] and pointing the way beyond it.

The idea of generation takes full dramatic form in the changing relation between Oliver and Joan and, more prominently, in the conflict and reconciliation of Oliver and Strowde. The boy's youth is a token of his father's youth, full of promise, but also a contrast to it, as Oliver is passing through a phase of disillusion that mirrors the other's present state. Oliver, too, loves Joan: his knight's lady is his lady, yet she is also at the heart of his rivalry with his father. At the climax of the last Act, Strowde's decision to throw up his chance of commonplace success to go to the dying Joan wins from Oliver an acknowledgment of their relationship. Strowde then passes out of the play, leaving his son to act out the last scene with Susan Kittredge and Lord Clumbermere. In the presence of the two young people on the stage, at the end, Barker realises concretely his theme of the passing away of the old life to make way for the new.

In Act III, scene ii, appears a metaphor whose ambiguity Barker had previously exploited in *The Voysey Inheritance*. 'I'd have been so content,' confesses Joan, 'to be nothing but a wife and a mother . . . a link in the chain.' That recalls the kind of contentment which Ann Leete chose. Then, a little later, the image occurs again with a more sinister overtone: 'To be so hustled in our chains down this road we call time.' The freedom with which the playwright is concerned, the freedom that Strowde finds and hands on to Oliver, is twofold: it gives an expansive vista to the individual life, that must accept death and the knowledge—to catch at one of the scriptural echoes in the dialogue—that the corruptible cannot inherit eternal life; it also transforms the chain of the generations ('the armies that have marched', Oliver's regiment of ghosts) from the grim bondage in which slaves and prisoners march into a pilgrimage, with an inheritance of faith that gives even in this world a hope of temporal progress.

To this world man belongs, as Susan says of Evan, 'He belongs here,' and expects him back . . . different. Barker reasserts his concern with it by setting his last scene in the commonplace atmosphere of Strowde's London office and giving to Oliver and Susan the company of the practical idealist, Clumbermere. Susan's halfarticulate confidence hints an analogy between Strowde's final loss of Joan, 'being cheated to the last,' and the pursuit of an ideal state, though it can never come; and in the willingness to die for an unattainable love she perceives an impulse that may be creative in the context of politics.

There is no such thing as 'short work', she warns Oliver. It is a repetition of her grandfather's discovery that 'No story ever ends' and that 'There are more ways than one of reading most epitaphs'. The span of time evoked in the play's persistent images—from Tutankhamen to the break up of the atom, and the light years of universal time, over which the apocalyptic Beast presides,—does not simply dwarf the individual life: it is itself framed in the hero's long journey through and beyond despair, through and beyond evil; and the growth of the natural man into the spiritual man is thus a mirror of hopeful possibility for the political society, too. The prison of the temporal world is wide open when the final curtain falls on *The Secret Life*.

*　　*　　*

In none of Granville Barker's plays is the character scheme simpler, or more easily detected, than here. The function of certain characters, Salamons, Serocold, Kittredge and Clumbermere, is for the most part recognisably choric. The first two, who appear in Act I, scene i, are also foils to Evan Strowde. Salamons, the Jew, in his secret moral detachment is a critical reflection of the 'nice-minded historian' who long ago withdrew from political life and the responsibilities of his age; as the Permanent Official, identified with the prevailing system, he is a contrast to the anarchist hidden in Strowde and to the anarchic, illicit quality of the love that will make creative change possible.

Serocold, the well-meaning man, caught helplessly in the machine and turned by it into a restlessly active mechanical doll, is without the hero's power for evil. Lady Peckham, his sister, tells him that he is 'good all through', but honesty compels him to translate that into: 'I'm harmless.' In Serocold's faithfulness to his love of a childless wife, now dead, is a minor reflection of the love of Strowde and Joan. The parallel throws into relief the truth Barker wishes to assert by his inclusion of Serocold in the play: that good lies beyond the dualism of right and wrong; as Clumbermere is to explain, in the last Act, 'Subtracting evil doesn't leave good . . . not as I was taught to do sums.'

The choric function is taken over by Kittredge when the play explores the issues in greater depth. In presentation, the elderly American shows the richest personality and maturest mind of these minor characters, and he is more subjectively drawn than Salamons and Clumbermere. Associated as much with Joan as with Strowde, he has to contribute to the rich emotional content of the scene of her dying. His detachment is that enforced by age and won through wisdom; though still passionate at heart, he has to admit that the warfare of his works is accomplished and his best part now is to sit and hold Joan's hand and shed his blood for her, when pain tightens her grip. Strowde is the active protagonist; the fullest consciousness of what the action involves belongs to Kittredge.

Clumbermere is a simpler creature, no intellectual, the common man come to truth by his own road:

> I was bred to the Baptist ministry, and I still think I'm a spiritually-minded man. And perhaps if I'd been blessed with three children instead of seven, I might be running a chapel now.

His fortune was founded on 'Ink for everybody' and it is *Everybody's Book of Short Poems* that he carries with him always, as his Testament. He brings to the play a relaxation of tension and a humour free from the sinister shadows of the earlier scenes. As he asserts, shrewdly and unpretentiously, the necessity of reconciling the ideal and the practical, so he brings the drama to the level of the plain man and his ordinary experience; he is a character to whom audiences warm.[12]

Mildred, Eleanor and Joan are superficially related as the three women in Strowde's life. Their very different temperaments mark them as a trinity of flesh, mind and spirit. Mildred and her daughter, Dolly, who intensifies the impression made by her mother, represent the life of the body, innocent in its frankness. 'I've more energy than brains,' Mildred admits, 'And I never could fuss about my immortal soul. I'm not sure that I have one.' The bespectacled Eleanor works in a fur coat all the year round; 'Intellectual passion, Eleanor ... chilling, but admirable,' is Serocold's comment. Her faith is that: 'The work of our minds lives on.' It is for Joan that Strowde reserves the gibe at setting up 'as spiritual ladies and gentlemen'.

Mildred, with her two children, throws into relief the solitary figure of Joan, and the two characters give the measure of the distance between the easy, instinctive love of the body and the difficult love of the heart. But Joan is Mary to Eleanor's Martha, too. 'Energetic Eleanor' is the description given to the latter. Strowde, considering his sister's preoccupation with Guilds and Institutes and social welfare, fears that such women would 'make a commonplace world of it' in their endeavour to tidy it up; their housekeeping they extend, indeed, to life. The world ruled by the best of women, even by 'dear, good Eleanor' (in this the female

counterpart of Serocold), would be a dull one, and the thanks they
receive may be double-edged:

> STROWDE. I ought to respect your confident sanity. It has been
> as a strong wall about my more domestic self these forty years.
> Father bequeathed it to you.
> ELEANOR. I think so.
> STROWDE. I'm not a bit like him?
> ELEANOR. Not very.
> STROWDE. *[Whimsically.]* Poor Mother!

—and, though he quickly withdraws the taunt, his rejection of her
limitations sounds clear in his protest that 'the angels in heaven,
you know, are not what we should call civilised' and that formulas
are no adequate substitute for the exploring life.

Eleanor is a character out of the same mould as Frances Trebell.
Each reflects the strongly marked intellectual nature of the hero,
in their respective plays, but not the passion that accompanies it.
The dramatist's judgment of the insufficiency of an ethical
righteousness is more plainly implied in the presentation of
Eleanor than it is in Frances, though something of it can be traced
in the earlier character. (Eleanor, standing confused between
Serocold's political morality and immorality, represents the idealist with insufficient grasp of the nature of the actual world, who
thinks the problem of ends and means simpler than it is.) Close
as each is to her brother, the nature of the heroic experience goes
quite beyond her. Each is capable of suffering, but not of creation.
Their values settled, their feet firmly on the earth, they stand for
the best that the natural virtues can reach to, by taking thought.
They are much more humane and sympathetic than Shaw's masculine women, though drawn from the same easily recognisable
social type.

'I see great beauty in her . . . It'll shine out in time,' says Joan of
Susan Kittredge and, as her observation, it has great effect.
Mildred is conscious of her as 'a strange, still girl', and the description serves to suggest a relationship with Joan herself that Susan's
words to Eleanor, in the third Act, confirm:

> . . . we were playing a childish game . . . I did once start to tell
> you . . . pretending we'd changed places. She has my rooms at

home *[. . .]* So she used to write me . . . such good letters . . . and sign them Susan.

With Joan's death, it is Susan who is left in the ascendant, the beauty shining out, the new power emerging. She is a believer in miracles, in the possibility of being raised from the dead, and her presence in the final scene, '*modest, confident—confident, it would seem merely in an honest mind and her unclouded youth*', after the failure, defeat and death and the overhanging bitter mood of much of the play, is the dramatic confirmation of the hopeful truth she asserts. 'I'm afraid of you,' says Oliver, 'You're so alive;' and again, 'Do you wonder I'm afraid of you, Susan?' But the magic of the girl has already been conveyed in the affection between her grandfather and herself. Told by Strowde to count a hundred while he goes to dress for dinner, Susan surprises Lady Peckham by the literalness of her obedience and so, as often seems to happen, finds herself the object of discussion in her own presence:

> LADY PECKHAM. Then she's both a very good girl and a very deceitful one.
> *The young woman in question now unobtrusively takes part.*
> MR. KITTREDGE. She smiles. I always think that I know what she means when she smiles . . . but perhaps it's only because I'm fond of her. However, in that at least I'm not deceived.

So, by keeping her shy and still and quiet, the dramatist can make her reflect for an audience the values that his dialogue invokes.

Through all the design, the literal truth of human relations is maintained. Except in her stillness, and in the lyrical duologues, there is little of the ideal figure about Joan Westbury. She bears the marks of the nineteen-twenties and of her class. She can be gay, even rather unsuitably girlish, takes a rather malicious delight in hardly-veiled rudeness to Sir Leslie Heriot and indulges in little jokes of no particular wit; her most serious occupation seems to be playing with the young people a game that they call Straighters on the terrace. Little skirmishes tell the tale of petty, but amused, feminine rivalries:

> LADY PECKHAM. How are you, Joan?
> JOAN'S VOICE. Do you want to know?
> LADY PECKHAM. I ask.

JOAN. I feel like flying.
SEROCOLD. Door's locked inside I'll open it.
  *He goes down the turret stair. The exchange of compliments
  proceeds.*
LADY PECKHAM. Hot?
JOAN. No.
LADY PECKHAM. Pretty frock.
JOAN. One I had dyed.
LADY PECKHAM. You're losing a comb.

The motifs of the airy spirit and the prison of life are there
absorbed into the general careless tone. Eleanor and Mildred are
at once more intimate and more openly critical of each other:

ELEANOR. You're worried about Oliver.
LADY PECKHAM. Not a bit.
ELEANOR. What took him to that meeting? Who encourages him
in this foolishness?
LADY PECKHAM. I think he spins it out of his own inside.
ELEANOR. Well, as long as he behaves himself! . . .
LADY PECKHAM. I hope he'll do more than that.
ELEANOR. *[With a will-not-be-exasperated sigh.]* We're at
odds, I'm afraid, Mildred.
LADY PECKHAM. *[Plumply.]* We always were.

If it is possible to hear in that the retort of the body to the mind,
it is still allegory at its most effective, the abstraction completely
identified with the actual.

The cheerfulness of Lady Peckham and Dolly makes an invaluable contribution to the mood of the play. Barker's intention is
not now to write a tragedy, and the hopeful quality of the end of
the play is the more convincing for the confidence with which they
have prepared for it. The dramatist is so much at his ease with
Mildred as to be able to remove her from the stage by a device
as casual as the famous pursuit by a bear. 'Mildred, come and see
the Alderney bull,'[13] calls Serocold, to whom she has not long before
been talking of the begetting of children as the obvious aim of
marriage.

One other character is, as it were, thrown up in the course of the
action: Sir Leslie Heriot, who appears only in Act II, scene v. He
is, in fact, more central to the design than Serocold, or Kittredge,

or Clumbermere, and it is significant that the play touches its climax when he is on the stage. 'I respect ideals. But I test them . . . as life tests them,' he is made to say. His personality lends no oracular weight to the words, yet he does truly represent the outer challenge that confronts Strowde: not positive evil, but complexity, made up of 'bits from the rag-bag', with which the idealist vision has to be reconciled. His single appearance provides the necessary condition for the longest and most exciting political scene in the play.

*   *   *

Any drama, of course, depends mainly upon its dialogue to give convincing force to a basic design. In no other play does Barker employ such a variety of styles as in this text. Like the breaking-up of the Act structure into scenes and the physical division of the stage, this achieves the effect of marking more strongly the shape of the drama as a progress through varying moods. It may be remembered that the revision of both *Waste* and *The Madras House* was later work than the writing of *The Secret Life*, and so it may be that the full elaboration of the contrapuntal style, already noted in the discussion of those plays, was first devised for this and followed from the decision to use the Wagnerian themes in the first scene. Certainly there is hardly a word in the text of *The Secret Life* that is not as organic to the verbal carpet-pattern as any single note to a musical score.

The idiom of commerce and calculation is employed more abundantly in this play than any of the motifs that thread their way through Barker's earlier dramatic texts. It supplies the *leitmotiv* of the hero: 'I have left the market-place' (a further covert allusion to Antony?) announces his situation, when the play begins; but it is also (as in *The Merchant of Venice*) a basic idiom that all the characters share and that reflects a common consciousness. 'We to-day, in our westward-looking world,' the dramatist wrote in his essay on Tolstoy, 'are made one with another rather in the bonds of commerce than of Christ, says the cynic.'[14] The uses of this staple language are graduated so as to prevent the monotony of repetition from jarring. In performance, only occasional, specially pointed instances would register on the audience's consciousness; the author may have relied upon the continuous undercurrent to make a subconscious impression analogous to that Eliot has claimed for his unobtrusive verse rhythms and to prepare in the same way for the incidental climaxes.

Salamons, in the first scene, speaks ironically in the rôle of the eternal usurer that he has adopted, and the idiom belongs to the disguise: 'my mentality is now a little like the money you let me learn to master . . . it's a currency . . . I'm for what's marketable;' 'never be carried off on crusades you can't finance . . . don't over-draw on your moral credit.' The answer to him comes in the last scene of the play, in Lord Clumbermere's 'creed of a business man': 'even the demand for simple goodness is greater than the supply;' 'Righteousness is profit, Mr. Gauntlett . . . and before we can have honest profit we must pay our way.' More inconspicuous are the clichés: 'the tricks of the trade,' 'a tithe of your dis-honesty;' and there is a trail of literal uses of the same vocabulary: 'you might now be worth three pounds a week as pianist in a cinema;' 'it is earmarked for income-tax'; 'Do you thrill at the sight of the red leather despatch box with First Lord of the Trea-sury on it . . .?'

The question of what a man is worth, the use of his life and the value of his suffering, recurs persistently in all its relevance to the bargain struck by Faust. One definition comes in Act I, scene ii:

ELEANOR. I want fifty thousand pounds out of him for the Insti-tute of Social Service.
SEROCOLD. Well . . . I daresay you'll get it.
ELEANOR. I'm told he's a good little man.
SEROCOLD. He's good for that much.[15]

An ironic echo of that rings out at the end of the Act when Eleanor, having returned with the news of Mark Westbury's sudden death, adds her own piece of news:

ELEANOR. Well . . . I'll go up now. Lord Clumbermere was very sound. I think he'll give us thirty thousand.
This last inappropriate remark by no means shows an un-sympathetic mind. The thought was there, and she found

> *some support in it.* STROWDE, *though, is not unconscious of
> the effect of its simple utterance.*
> STROWDE. Good . . . .

A skilful actor can make such echoes and their effect audible in the consciousness of his audience, and actors of Shakespeare often do so.

The counterpoint in Act II, scene iii, is altogether simpler. The voice of the irrepressible Dolly Gauntlett floats up from the terrace: 'I'd tuck Susan under my arm too for tuppence;' in the gallery, Eleanor, discussing with her brother the report of her Committee, suggests: 'Perhaps Part Two upon Wages of Young Persons will amuse you more.' Variety of tone in the use of the theme keeps the attention unjaded. It may provide a sly witticism:

> MR. KITTREDGE. . . . Heaven forbid, though, that I should quarrel with the bread and butter I still need to consume.
> LADY PECKHAM. But you're a professor?
> MR. KITTREDGE. Emeritus.
> LADY PECKHAM. Does that mean you don't earn any money by it?
> MR. KITTREDGE. That also is implied.

In gentle, affectionate courtesy, Kittredge and Joan play upon the motif:

> MR. KITTREDGE. Please do come and see us, Lady Westbury, sitting in blankets before our wigwams.
> JOAN. What must I bring to trade with?
> MR. KITTREDGE. Your heart.

For the criticism, to which this technique is liable, we can go to Barker's own *Preface to Cymbeline*, where he comments: '. . . both antithesis and this sort of mental punning make easy habits of thought; youth likes their display, and they are a refuge in fatigue.'[16] So they may be, but the mechanical aspect of this method of composition constantly yields, in *The Secret Life*, to the flow of feeling. It is unifying, and it enables Barker to say—as every dramatist and poet must try to—more than one thing at a time. In the charged atmosphere of Act I, scene iii, for instance, the dramatist is playing with words all the while, but they would

be poor actors who could not strike home to an audience with
such a passage as this:

> JOAN. One's capable, you know, of uncomprehended suffering.
> I watched women making a sort of emotional profit out of their
> loss. People called me stoical . . . but it was only that I didn't under-
> stand . . . or want to. Why ask what an earthquake's for? My bit-
> terest moment was when I came home to find their kit sent back
> from France. Burnt up with everything else now, I'm glad to think.
> The emptyings, poor dears, of their pockets . . . of a dead boy's
> pockets!
> STROWDE. [*Setting his teeth to this.*] Death leaves us that . . .
> and life breeds in us fantastic hopes.

The form of words, 'I watched women making a sort of emotional profit out of their loss,' could pass unregarded in the stress
of feeling; yet an audacious actress could afford to recognise the
'passionate pun' even as she spoke the line. Human consciousness
is not simple, and a brain fighting to keep control is quite capable
of setting itself to some trivial turn of wit; communication is the
more complete for acknowledging the fact. Similarly, the effect
is not weakened, but enriched, if the actor so delivers Strowde's
comment as to allow the equivocation to come through and go on
working in the audience's minds. (For the words present a logical
sequence, as well as an antithesis: it is but a bitter comfort that he
can offer; it sounds like a message of despair, yet in it is concealed
a difficult hope, an obscure sense of the rightness of things which
the conscious mind does not yet understand.)

Beyond the characters and the reality of their feeling, like 'the
inner parts of a piece of orchestral music',[17] lies a more distant
and general poetry: 'Burnt up—The emptyings—of a dead boy's
pockets' recalls the first scene: 'Burnt out inside . . . the moon is.
Gutted . . . ,' and the singing voice, 'Give forgetting . . . that I live.
Take me out . . . in deinen Schoss.' So now, in 'pockets', there
sounds not only the motif of currency but a hint of the marsupial
pouch, or womb, emerging unmistakably with Strowde's use of the
word, 'breeds'. These are the momentary harmonies that we may
listen for again and again, before the dramatic reconciliation is
near.

The rhetoric of the intimate scenes is certainly not empty and inflated. The words are to be brooded over, and it is an atmosphere of brooding that the playwright has contrived for their delivery. It slows down the pace, of course, but the absence of speed is compensated for by the emotional intensity. The abstract statements, in which these scenes abound, universalise without dissipating the content of experience dredged up from the depths. The simplest words are stamped with it and are perhaps only truly comprehensible at all, when the hearer translates them into the sense of his own life:

> Yet there's nothing near to truth that we learn, but when we've felt the burden we'd cast it away ... we'd unsay it if we could.

To submit to a play like this involves being oneself changed, by the end of it.

* * *

The orchestration of voices is found to best advantage in Act II, scene iii, with its six characters assembled in the gallery and Oliver outside. Apart from the effects achieved by the use of the two levels with their different sounding-boards, Barker employs another form of counterpoint between a formal dialogue, that relies upon the memorable phrase, and the terse, extremely informal exclamations that are Dolly Gauntlett's natural expression. The contrast is intrinsically interesting and sharpens the attention; it is easy to guess that the playwright's motive was to pass off a charged, poetic and metaphorical language within the prose context without inducing the hush of the soliloquy-type scenes.

The following example shows the degree of success achieved. Dolly is walking down the gallery away from the group engaged in desultorily philosophical talk, when Strowde calls to her:

> STROWDE. Dolly, I'll toss you for a pound.
> DOLLY. *[At this gleam of great hope.]* Oo! Suppose I lose.
> STROWDE. A month's credit.
> DOLLY. Oo!
>   *But, too fearful of the risk,* DOLLY *disappears.*
> STROWDE. The life of the mind is a prison in which we go melancholy mad. Better turn dangerous ... and be done away with.

DOLLY'S *voice is heard from the end of the gallery.*
DOLLY. Evan.
STROWDE. Hullo!
DOLLY. I'll risk it. Heads.
    STROWDE *takes out a coin and tosses it.*[18]
MR. KITTREDGE. There is, of course, that faculty we call the soul by which we may escape into uncharted regions.
STROWDE. Heads it is!
DOLLY. *[Her voice is fervent.]* Thank God.
MR. KITTREDGE. But the rulers of men seldom seek them.

Serocold's voice, calling from the wings, interrupts in rather the same way Strowde's recital of the political creed, in Act II, scene v. It is just a single interruption now, its modifying effect slighter, as it can afford to be, when it is a deliberately theatrical climax that the dramatist is aiming at. The audience is gathered round for Strowde's formal, public assumption of the rôle that he is adopting open-eyed:

> STROWDE. *[Adding, for reassurance, a touch of humour.]* I believe, for instance ... Heriot, when I've won that bet I'll open Cabinet meetings by having this repeated, all standing ... I believe that men cease to be fools to bccomc knaves, and that we must govern them by fear and with lies. They will work under threat of starvation. Greed makes them cunning. . . .
> SEROCOLD'S VOICE. Evan ... I shall be late back.
> STROWDE. Wait a minute! ... but desire makes them dangerous. If they rightly remembered yesterday, they wouldn't get out of their beds to-morrow. Sleep's the great ally of the rulers of this world ... for it rounds each day with oblivion.[19]

The Machiavellianism of this hardly needs the direction to indicate that the touch of humour is added to '*more than a little steel*' in the actor's voice. The emphatic rhythms prepare for the final cadence and help carry the reminder that Sleep is 'The death of each day's life . . ., great nature's second course, Chief nourisher in life's feast' and that Time carries 'alms for oblivion', truths very pertinent to the general imaginative conception of the play and its running imagery.

The whole passage is in effective contrast to the brisker polemic of the earlier part of the scene, which may be heard in Heriot's shrewdly prosaic portrait of the disappointed idealist:

You'll get back to the House and you won't have enough to do there. You'll grow depressed and dyspeptic and you'll take to making acid interruptions inaudible in the press gallery. You'll find yourself chief of a little group of righteous high-brows in passionate agreement upon abstract principles, without an interest in common and considering themselves insulted if you ask them to vote solid.

Cadence and vocabulary help in the identification of the source to which Barker went for the more intimate poetic language of the duologues between Evan and Joan, Joan and Oliver, Joan and Kittredge. Creed for creed, Kittredge's answer to Machiavelli, spoken in solace to the dying Joan, comes in the emotional key of parts of the Authorised Version. The Epistles to the Corinthians were undoubtedly in Barker's mind when he wrote this play:

This I can believe. The generation of the spirit is not as the generation of the flesh . . . for its virtue is diffused like light, generously, unpriced. Doing and suffering and the work of thought must take its toll of us. And all that life corrupts death can destroy [. . .] For comfort's sake we lead our busy lives. Who wouldn't want to forget sometimes this strange, new, useless burden of the soul? Left comfortless, we must bear it for a while as bravely as we may.

This is not an entire solution of the problem of forging a poetic prose for the theatre; but it can be justified in the context of these quiet scenes, for the style and the values asserted are interfused, an inheritance freshly apprehended.

* * *

The play's chief triumph may lie in its extension of the field of a religious experience from the personal life of the love story to the impersonal life of affairs. The manner in which the two are blended at the climax and subsequent resolution deserves particular examination. It reveals the unfaltering rhythmical shape of the drama. The critical scene proceeds *allegro vivace* in its first episode, then modulates through the triple climax to the duologue, acted out *andante cantabile* between Strowde and Joan.

The new character to appear in Act II, scene v, Sir Leslie Heriot, is Bellingham's right-hand man. His presence conditions the mood of the first section of the scene and evokes an aspect of Strowde barely hinted before: an untrammelled zest, sign of restless vitality. Heriot is himself full of energy, abundantly shrewd in everything that relates to the practice of politics, with a friendly humour and a touch of genuine modesty that seems to contradict, but perhaps explains, the bust of Napoleon that, we gather, used to be visible on his office mantelpiece. Heriot is basically an egoist, unaware of this central fact about himself; to opportunism he confesses readily enough, knowing it a kind of wisdom:

> Statesmanship ... so I phrase it ... *[and he enjoys phrasing it]* ... is the art of dealing with men as they most illogically are, and with the time as it nearly always most unfortunately is. We hope for a better ... we strive for a better. Never let us cease to proclaim that. But the day's work must be done.[20]

It is characteristic of Barker's method that the general theme which his play proclaims should be summed up in a speech of so broadly comic an effect: truth from the lips of one who cannot help but be a demagogue, even in private talk with another politician who knows all the tricks.

Heriot has come on a diplomatic errand, prepared to manœuvre adroitly, but hardly prepared to be out-manœuvred in a manner that is a satire on his own methods and motives. The satirist, Strowde, moves gradually into his stride. 'Let your office fellows pull the cart while you drive,' says Heriot, and Strowde's comment, 'That is undoubtedly the whole art of government,' is innocuous enough in its ambiguity of tone. Having listened to Heriot's proposal with no more betrayal of his attitude than is concealed in the quiet remark that the other will flatter him if he thinks fit, he opens his own play:

> STROWDE. Bellingham's getting a bit feeble, is he?
> HERIOT. *[Innocently pricking an ear.]* D'you hear people say that?
> STROWDE. If he'll take me at your dictation it'll show the Gang, won't it, that you've got a strangle hold on him? And it'll show you that he feels you've got the Party behind you.
> HERIOT. *[Playfully disapproving.]* That's very tortuous.
> STROWDE. Tortuous ... but not very tortuous.

From this attack on his motives Heriot takes refuge in protests of

loyalty that do no more than illustrate the obliquity, of which he
has been so obliquely accused:

> Bellingham is a leader to whom I have been consistently loyal . . .
> and to whom I shall be as consistently loyal as long as he is my
> leader. Does that imply that I am to sacrifice the interests of Party
> rather than . . . put pressure on him?

Strowde presses his advantage more boldly with his tart challenge
to a term that rolls smoothly off the other's tongue:

> What the devil, my dear Heriot, is a p o l i t i c a l fact?

(Eleanor to Serocold, in Act I, was naturally more straightforward: 'My objection to your respected chief is simply that he's
a liar'; but her brother's contempt is even more for the self-decep-
tion that Heriot's protests exemplify than for his public dis-
honesty.)
   Evan is enjoying himself. Having cornered his opponent in this
way, he leads into a diversion, criticising the Government's management of the problem of the Trusts, until Eleanor joins them.
Then he comes right into the open:

> The practical question is . . . could Heriot and I between us get
> rid of Bellingham the sooner? I might put that problem to the old
> gentleman if he sends for me.

At this Heriot can only boggle; a reaction that earns him the yet
harder hit of: 'That's your method. It isn't mine.' Before he can
recover, Strowde is unkindly imitating his earlier moral tone:

> But if we d i d n ' t get rid of him the sooner the intermediate
> friction would not, on the balance, be profitable to the country.
> *[Then, venturing rather far in irony.]* And we must think of our
> country, Heriot.

But they soon end the bout like two boys, laying their bets cheer-
fully—a set of the History in half-calf to the Premiership—on
which of them is likelier to end as the king pin in the continuing
game of political skittles.

At this point, Barker is again letting go the thread of the tension a little. The hits are more desultory and more friendly, as the two return to immediacies. 'Shall I sit below the gangway and snipe at you?' asks Strowde, the Gang, of course, being Bellingham's; and Heriot is now sufficiently master of the technique to manage a glance that surely swivels round at what has been happening since his arrival, as well as taking in the recent China meeting: 'You've been getting your eye in lately, I've noticed.' With his reference to the present opposition in the House, 'sitting like a row of turnips', is prepared a momentary dramatic concentration of another kind. 'We need intellectual spade-work,' Heriot had said to Eleanor, in his complimentary greetings, and now Strowde flings the phrase back at him with an equivocation, the deadliness of which Heriot seems not to detect: 'Or shall I stick to intellectual spade-work?' There is an echo here of Oliver's 'Digging potatoes might sweat all the nonsense out of me, d'you think?'[21] No doubt, to aim at anything higher than the fruits of office would be judged the grossest political nonsense by Heriot.

The scene is again dissolved with the arrival of Joan, and the talk becomes somewhat more general, as both she and Eleanor take rather unwilling part in it. Serocold's voice calls to Heriot, who prepares to take his departure. But the lull and the warning of the approaching exit are both preparatory to the climax. So far, Strowde's attack has been on the petty egoists and opportunists who manipulate a so-called democracy, and his mood has been appropriate to the triviality that is the most deadly quality in them. Now he turns to the evil vision of the world in which they are masters and the Machiavellian doctrine that they invoke to justify their rule.

The force held in reserve, while he played with Heriot, and that was detectable only in a rather enigmatic manner, now shows itself more clearly; and the interest of the particular is absorbed into a less personal emotion. There is more of deadly sincerity than amused satire in the voice that recites the creed which is Heriot's unacknowledged own, and with which Strowde is at this very moment identifying himself:

. . . I believe that men cease to be fools to become knaves . . . .

—It is the conviction that his treatment of Heriot has expressed.—

> . . . and that we must govern them by fear and with lies. They will work under threat of starvation. Greed makes them cunning . . .

This is the definition of man in terms of a brute nature that he cannot transcend and that is fit for contempt. The evil enters in the deliberate denial of power to become anything else, for:

> . . . desire makes them dangerous [. . .] Sleep's the great ally of the rulers of this world . . . for it rounds each day with oblivion.

'Can you think of a greater driving force for evil,' Evan had asked Joan in Act I, 'than a man who has seen a better way and accepts the worse . . .?' The anticipation contained in that question is now fulfilled. The stillness of the listeners about him confirm the deliberateness, and indeed solemnity, of this confession of despair.

When he stops speaking, there is a temporary return to the earlier mood of the scene, as Heriot recovers himself and goes out reasserting his orthodoxy loudly—a final satiric touch, for it sounds more hollow than ever by contrast with the truth of Strowde's vicious feeling:

> I have an almost unbounded faith in the ultimate perfectibility of man [. . .] But mind you . . . the freer the democracy the firmer must be the guiding hands . . . .

It is a partial restoration of the comic view, unreflected in the attitude of Eleanor and Joan.

When Heriot has gone, the mood of Strowde's declaration is continued and developed in the more personal climax of Eleanor's reaction. It is her reaction from Strowde's surrender to the world upon its own terms, but her final words speak—beyond the range of her understanding—of the restlessness and despair through which men may escape their limitations:

> Turn in your tracks and be the thing you despise. Does it matter? The curse is on you, it seems, of coming at last to despise whatever

you do and are. I'm sorry ... but I must save myself ... my soul, if you like ... from despair.

Her brother is left seemingly unmoved by her suffering, accepting what he cannot help; still the scene gathers emotional impetus by the outburst and is not now allowed to slacken its force. She goes, as Strowde is saying:

I shall now have to advertise ... Wanted, a political hostess ...

and his voice suspended, his sentence unfinished until he and Joan are alone, betokens the dramatic suspense until the triple climax is crowned:

> JOAN. Upright, downright Eleanor!
> STROWDE. [As if following out his uninterrupted thought] Or will you save me a sovereign's worth of Agony column, Joan, and take the job?
>> She does not answer at once, and when she does, it is as if some other woman, far away, were speaking.
> JOAN. No, I can't.

And now the scene which opened so vigorously begins to descend in a long, quiet passage to the end of the Act. Eleanor's angry hurt has provided the bridge of feeling to its introspective mood. Appropriately to the play's theme, it is this dying fall that contains the seed from which the life of the next Act will spring. It recalls the final scene of Act I, when external circumstances, and the habit they induce, held the two apart; now it is Joan's discovery of the nature of their love which does so:

We chose to dream. The empty beauty would vanish at a touch.

The expression of her weariness, with its echoes of 'sleep ... to die to sleep', '... if I could once go quite obliviously to sleep', links the passage into one movement with the earlier part of the scene, as it repeats the central theme in the minor key.

Now Strowde has to learn that, for all his efforts, he cannot touch her; the arts of power are useless here. Again he asks, in the tone a friend might use: 'Marry me' (it has the effect of a musical variation); and, though Joan accepts the tone, her reply is the same:

> Some other time! Oh, can't we pretend that there'll be some other possible time?

It was the possibility that sustained them for eighteen years and fails them now. Evan's uncompromising response again catches something of the ruthless tone of the first climax:

> None other but the time one wastes and comes to want;

but Joan knows, and reminds him of his knowledge, of another order of reality:

> And the eternity in which we met.

The dramatist has carried the argument of the scene to this point in a continuous progress from the philosophy of the time-servers. There is still power, another kind of power, in Joan's voice, as she contradicts their short-sighted view.

But the tension lapses again. A moment later, sadly conscious that his appeals and his more violent outbursts are equally in vain, and that he is merely exhausting his strength, Evan has nothing more to ask than: 'Where are you, Joan . . . where are you?' It is a cry that will be echoed by Kittredge, when Joan seems to him to be sinking into her final silence, out of all human reach: 'Joan . . . where are you?' But it is now that she begins to die to Evan, though the living woman returns for an instant to ask, 'What's the time?' before leaving him to his unbeliever's prayer:

> Most merciful God . . . who makest thy creatures to suffer without understanding . . .
> *But he leaves the prayer unfinished and goes on with his letters.*

*   *   *

Act III, scene i, opens with Oliver, Strowde's secretary now, an older and rather happier young man in the businesslike atmos-

phere of the office. As the two converse over the—symbolic!—
timetable, the harmony between them appears as the ground of
Oliver's more balanced mood. The earlier defensive barriers between them have vanished, and Evan speaks his mind as openly
to his son as before he has done only to Joan. The dramatic movement towards the climax of this scene is heralded with the quotation that Oliver is asked to check for the speech being prepared.
Evan gives his comment on it:

> 'Now, O Lord, take away my life, for I am not better than my
> fathers.' Very modern and progressive and disillusioned of Elijah!
> Why ever should he expect to be?

This is indeed the dead end of the belief in progress. Yet in the line
is a reverberation from that prayer at the end of Act II, as well as
an anticipation of the news of Joan and his own symbolic death
that are to come. Oliver is now putting away the manuscript chapters of the book that Evan will never write—another version of the
unfinished story—, the thoughts precious to him that he hid away.
The young man's thoughts connect the idea of fathers and sons
with the papers in his hand, and he voices a new wisdom:

> ... better inherit a failure, I suppose ... for there's something to
> be done with it ... than a success.

They return to a brisk discussion of election prospects and the
work that they are now engaged on:

> OLIVER. Heriot thought he was making a smart move when he
> had you handed the hardest job going ... this Clumbermere busi-
> ness.
> STROWDE. Do you think he wants me to fail at it?
> OLIVER. [*Answering acutely to this test.*] No ... I think he
> hopes that some sorry moment will give him a chance to wring your
> hand and say: Well, never mind, old man!
> STROWDE. [*Appreciatively.*] Yes, I can hear him.

This is still the mood of the day's work. The profounder seriousness, only glimpsed so far, emerges more certainly when Oliver
levels, with no personal anger, his accusation against Strowde:

'Every letter I write for you . . . it's like laying a snare.' The older man's first response is mildy ironical. 'What do you expect of me, Oliver?' he asks; and so the motif of inheritance returns.

But Oliver presses his case, until Strowde gives him the answer that, hidden behind the creed of the Act before, seems to express him more completely, since he has rejected the suffering 'without understanding' that Joan and life have brought him:

> Are you still out to destroy? I'm showing you the sure way. It's to fulfil. The reddest revolutionary is but a part of what he turns against [. . .] I lived half my life in the happiness . . . and unhappiness . . . of a vision. One fine day I find that the world I'm living in is nothing like the idea of the world I've been living by. It comes quite casually . . . conversion to disbelief [. . .]
> You cease to suffer . . . you cease to hope. You have no will to be other than you are. You are, therefore, extraordinarily efficient [. . .] Watch me succeed, Oliver. That will teach you how to down me in turn. It's the best service I can do you.

Not the 'well-meaning man who daren't stop', but the 'ill-meaning man' speaks in that. The personal relation to Oliver, grown suddenly very intimate, supplies the condition for the concentrated articulateness of the statement. In it are summed up the leading themes and different actions of the play: the love of Joan and Evan, the relation of father and son, and the conflict over political power. This explicit statement is the signal that the resolution of the situation, thus wound up to the full, is shortly to begin.

Oliver's comment is a measure of his own growth since the interview in Act II and the discussion of nihilism that Strowde's opening words have recalled. Echoing what he then said to a man who, still faithful at heart to his vision, taught him the inadequacy of a purely temporal creation, it is the merciful executioner rather than the anarchist who speaks in Oliver's voice now:

> Wouldn't you sooner I killed you now where you sit?

On the current of his compassion, he is carried into an admission of his knowledge that Strowde is his father.

The playwright allows the two only the briefest moment to confront together this link between them that both now acknowledge.

It is sufficient time to make plain the extent to which Strowde, for all his denial of faith, has in fact involved himself in life, how far he has come from the indifference and detachment that occupied him in the first Act. Oliver, a little fearful of strained emotion— as the dramatist might well be—, quickly puts in: 'We can't begin to be fond of each other', though he is willing to confess that the feeling that Strowde would like it has caused him to make his admission. Evan's reply contains humility as well as restraint: 'No . . . I could never find any way to begin. But lately . . . I've learnt to be rather fond of you.'

Barker has a better use for this development than to make it the occasion of a self-sufficing, grandly emotional episode; so he interrupts the mood with the entry of Serocold on official business, shown in by the maid. The pace speeds up again and a friendly wrangle infuses its energy into the scene, but for a brief space only, —until Susan and Eleanor bring in the letter that tells of Joan dying in Massachusetts.

Evan's silence, until he and Oliver are alone together once more at the end of the scene, is the dramatic equivalent of his death, too. For this is the order for his release, the letter that he holds; and the cheque that he hands to Oliver is his own *quietus* as well as the true inheritance that can, now that they have found each other, be handed over. The intersection of lines in which there is no direct logical sequence is again significant here:

> STROWDE. *[Suddenly, straight at him.]* You'd go.
> OLIVER. I can't tell. I'd forgotten her lately. Yes, I'd start swimming there.
> STROWDE. Here's the cheque.

No-one else will acquiesce in Strowde's going; but Oliver takes after the spirit of this love.

The likeably sententious Clumbermere, among the other pieces of common wisdom that he will propound to Oliver and Susan, is to quote from his favourite *Everybody's Book of Short Poems*: ' "It's the little bit extra that counts for God." A good thought. Righteousness is profit, Mr. Gauntlett . . . and before we can have honest profit we must pay our way.' Strowde has now paid his way. Not only will he return, as Susan struggles to explain, a man born again; it is a new man who goes even now to the waiting ship. The corpse that he has done with (the Pauline phrase, 'the body of this death,' is appropriate) he leaves behind for Oliver to dispose of, through his political agent:

> If he thinks he can get my photograph and the gramophone records elected, he's welcome to try.

Strowde does not appear again in the play; the realisation of what comes after judgment passes beyond its bounds. The promise of a continuation is heard, however, in the final lines of the scene:

> OLIVER. I'm glad I've found you.
> STROWDE. I claim no rights in you. But I'm glad.
> OLIVER. It's something to go on with.
> *As he goes,* STROWDE *echoes him as if the words were—they are!—the very last he wanted to feel the meaning of.*
> STROWDE. To go on with!

'No story ever ends'; but even hope is a burden to be sustained.

* * *

In *The Secret Life*, Granville Barker gave fullest expression to all that the experience of decline meant to him. Awareness of it had obsessed him and his generation since the eighteen-nineties. The very prose of some scenes in this play has a *fin de siècle* languor. It is the *fin de siècle* consciousness that Joan Westbury represents; and the obsessional love between her and Evan Strowde conveys the inwardness of the Conradian words, with which Francis Thompson illuminated the gutter-tragedies of his time:

> Once step aside from the ways of comfortable men and you cannot regain them. You will live and die under the law of the intolerable thing called romance.

This 'romance', the dream which possesses the subjective life, is represented in some degree in nearly all, perhaps all, of Barker's plays; it is a leading element in his last play, *His Majesty;* but nowhere else does it dominate the drama as powerfully as in *The*

Secret Life. There is a very marked contrast between the emotional richness, with which it is treated in this play, and the hesitant delicacy of *The Marrying of Ann Leete;* Ann herself is a shadow beside Evan.

Through his probing of the images of death and the morbid element in his own consciousness, the dramatist had won his way out of the *impasse,* in which Philip Madras is fixed, to a perception of the nature of creative living: a strenuously won poise between the secret world of self and the objective world that men share. The artist does not here, as he seems at times to do in *The Madras House,* lose his identity and turn moralist. To moralist and social reformer, human errors, failures and disasters appear as undesirable accidents to be banished from life (the method of subtracting evil in the hope of leaving good); this play conveys the profounder perception that failure and disaster are but forms taken by necessity, an ineradicable element in the scheme of things, which is part of the expression of what man is and part of the process through which he changes. Strowde's 'ill-meaning' part in the struggle for power carries him forward as surely as does his love for Joan. Beyond the contradictions on which life is based, he moves towards the Hegelian unity that embraces them.

Beyond the dying civilisation, the play looks hopefully to new life stirring in individual heart and mind. The whole of Barker's dramatic writings are concerned with faith. None goes further than *The Secret Life* in defining what faith is, as a human experience,—and what it costs.

CHAPTER X

Arms and the Man I Sing

MR. KITTREDGE. We're all driven to talk nonsense at times . . .
when no other weapon is left us against the masters of the world . . .
who have made language and logic, you see, to suit their own
purposes.

Since he wrote his first play with Berte Thomas and entitled it *A
Comedy of Fools*, Granville Barker had continued to explore in his
drama the meanings of the antic figure of clown, Pierrot, masquera-
der, adopted by the artists of the eighteen-nineties as one of their
emblems. Foolishness—nonsense—fantasy, the three seem to have
been aspects of one concept for him, implying the inversion of the
world of common sense by the often absurd impulses of the
imagination. Through Dorothy Taverner he had spoken openly
in its defence:

Edward, would I cast for a king or a judge or a duchess actors that
couldn't believe more in reigning or judging or duchessing than
you wretched amateurs do? [. . .] I've fancied sometimes that poor
actors, playing parts . . . but with real faith in their unreal . . . yet
live those lives of yours more truly.

To the reality within the unreality of the naïve images of King and
Queen Barker comes in his last play, *His Majesty*, written between
1923 and 1928. The *theatrum mundi* is evoked now as a circus,
now as a puppet booth; the performance is opera, or comic opera;
and *homo sapiens* appears in many disguises from 'crossbowman'
to 'flying man', the God in the machine.

The play's story is of a throne at stake. The characters are the

252

persons of Ruritanian romance: a King returned from exile to seek his own, the brave Queen who insists on accompanying him into danger, the young Colonel who adores her, the faithful Lady-in-Waiting and her son, who is the gallant leader of the small loyalist band, marching on the capital like Garibaldi's Thousand. The setting is a Middle-European country, Carpathia, whose boundaries are not marked on any map. From *The Prisoner of Zenda* to King Henry, the prisoner of Zimony, seems no great distance. Throughout the play, Carpathia remains, in the eyes of Queen Rosamund, the land of romance.

But Carpathia is no country of escape. It has its place in an historically authentic world. The Austria-Hungary of Franz Josef is not difficult to recognise through the talk of old days, and his successor, exiled in 1918, is remembered in the name, Karlsburg, given to the Carpathian capital, where 'Comic Operas and stock-exchange scandals are the chief crops'. King Henry's country has suffered defeat in the War and the disastrous armistice convention afterwards. Red Terror and White Terror have raged. Now the trams are running once more and the moderates, led by Dr. Madrassy, hold precarious control. Political corruption is the only thing that thrives in the midst of an economic crisis. Neustria, on the frontier, is alert to stir up civil war among her neighbours and profit from it. American political journalists and Paris banking-houses, as well as free-lance Englishmen, looking for excitement, are concerned to watch the development of events. The images of chaos abound: the President of the Assembly has been assassinated; there is shooting in the streets; the peasants start digging up their guns again; the Château Czernyak has been looted; the price on Stephen Czernyak's head has been placarded before his mother's windows; a well-known Karlsburg restaurant is papered with bank notes bearing the King's head.

This capital could as well be Berlin as Vienna or Budapest. The early days of the Weimar Republic were not so different from the background that the play implies. When Barker was beginning his work on *His Majesty*, Adolf Hitler was writing *Mein Kampf* in his fortress prison at Landsberg, after the fiasco of the Munich *Putsch*. The play, too, has its man of destiny, awaiting his time. 'There's one way to govern a country . . . just one,' says Bruckner,

'Find where its real power is . . . and give that play. It's in me for the moment . . . and the men of my mind.' He has purged his own party and is gathering his young bullies about him. He tells the King the history of his fortunes: from boot-blacking to the university, 'and a bit later, when the war came, to prison. And when peace came . . . into exile.' King Henry is interested:

> THE KING. Were we fellow-exiles?
> BRUCKNER. I came back when you left.
> THE KING. What did you go to prison for?
> BRUCKNER. Optimism. Belief in the millenium . . . in the brotherhood of man and the rest of it. I'm quite cured.

As the disappointed idealist looks back to the time when 'the red flag was flying over Karlsburg', so the political methods he advocates look forward to the tactics of the Reichstag Fire, the mass arrests and the rigged plebiscites. Not until two years after *His Majesty* was published did Hitler and his S.S. guards become at all prominent, but the fictitious world of this play shares the spirit of the world that brought them forth. Karlsburg is the seething hell into which the whole of Europe might so easily slip,— and did slip.

The Secret Life traced back the anarchy of the time to its source at the roots of individual experience. The lyrical element of that play is more subdued in *His Majesty*. In his last play, Barker chooses instead to reach out and take the measure of the whole political world in which twentieth-century man is perforce a citizen. The prevailing style in which he now writes is an extension of the equivocal prose that he used for the conversation between Heriot and Strowde. It reflects his recognition of the nature of orthodox political communication: the diplomatic method of saying a thing and meaning not quite the thing said, but expecting to be understood and being understood; a tortuous method, 'but not very tortuous'. His political expression, as well as his political activity, is made to illuminate the nature of man. The impersonal movements of world history are part, in this view, of the individual's personal fate, and the responsibility of world order is an individual burden. The ultimate choice for political man, *homo sapiens*, the governor, is revealed now to lie between the rôle of the King and the rôle of Bruckner.

Perhaps the most frequently recurring verbal motif in the play, implying a unifying image, comes in the form of allusions to the body and its members: head and feet, arms and legs, the natural man stripped to his bare skin, 'bare fists', 'bare-back'. Implicit in it, as in *Coriolanus*, which may be the immediate source of this feature, is the notion of the body politic. Barker has further enlarged the range of the image by assimilating to it the various uses of the Pauline metaphor of the body of Christ and the concept of the *Logos* become flesh. A variant of the motif suggests the opposing sham: the puppet, or dummy, represented among the characters by Captain Papp, the son of General Horvath's tailor; and this in turn, of course, unites it with the theatrical theme.

The town of Zimony (Simony) makes an appropriate setting for the political bargaining of King Henry and Bruckner; for the power at stake in their conflict is not material, though giving mastery over material forces. (Gratz, where the Cardinal Archbishop is in residence, is another of the places significantly named in the text.) The identification of the state as Man writ large is accompanied by a dramatic demonstration of the political value of integrity, the condition of grace.

Not Bach, Chopin, or Wagner, provides the thematic statement in musical terms as key to this play's action; instead, the Polovtsian dances from *Prince Igor* lend their barbaric excitement to the drama. Through all its talk, *His Majesty* shows the lineaments of a play of war: the Château Czernyak is a camp on the march; the battle is fought at Zimony; the King and Stephen Czernyak are hero and anti-hero, not only in the sense of their farcical counterparts, Bluntschli and Saranoff, but as *anima* and *persona* of a single figure: the epic protagonist. Besides *Coriolanus*, the Shakespearian plays that Barker seems to have had most in his mind are *Henry IV* and *Henry V*, and Czernyak is his Hotspur.

* * *

The play opens in Switzerland, neutral, democratic, while the issue is as yet unjoined. Henry, King of Carpathia, in the villa of his exile, grants an interview to the American journalist, Henry Osgood. It is a democratic age: even 'the Press man is human',

Osgood declares to Guastalla, the *aide* who shows him in, and may talk to a king as 'man to man', in his 'intellectual shirtsleeves'. The American has come from Eisenthal, where Stephen Czernyak and his insurgent royalists have set up their headquarters. The interview is at Osgood's request, but it is the King's opportunity to make his public declaration:

> I shall not re-enter Carpathia like a thief or as a conqueror.

America, Paris, Neustria, Karlsburg and Eisenthal can make of that what they will; it is as non-committal as may be, a public washing of his hands. As a man, when he says to Count Zapolya, 'I want no more bloodshed,' he seems to mean it sincerely; but the official statement is a political weapon—for himself or his enemies.

So much conveyed, the two can relax again, the King can question the journalist and discover their other common interest, the breeding of poultry. Thus the dramatist introduces a serio-comic motif:

> THE KING. But prize birds pay *[. . .]* (*He takes from his writing-table a triple photograph frame.*[1]) My Bourbourgs. Mark me now ... they've a future as a dominant. Louis Quatorze ... Louis Quinze ... Louis Seize! A family joke.

In Act II, King Henry does return to Carpathia, but not as a thief or a conqueror; he keeps his word. The end of the play presents him leaving once more, with his Queen, for another exile. As their train starts off, they turn to the newspapers that have been brought to them and read Osgood's retrospective account of his interview. As they argue over his description of the study, a recurrence of the same motif emphasises the correspondence between the play's beginning and its end:

> THE KING. Louis Seize furniture is not rococo *[. . .]*
> *Suddenly they are shaken in their chairs: almost out of them.*
> THE QUEEN. Are we stopping?
> THE KING. No ... this is where the line was cut.

It may be that cocks in Carpathia cry 'Rococo!' The idea of a constitutional monarch as a prize bird with his wings clipped is frequently suggested by the dialogue. 'We wretched kings, though,' King Henry's complaint goes further, '. . . prisoners of custom . . . when we're not exiles!' Even the etiquette, by which Queen Rosamund sets such store, hedges kingship about. The 'line' obliquely suggests the dynasty, and 'cut' is a token of the guillotine. *His Majesty* is a tragi-comedy, and the discord of the theme of regicide with the theme of the farmyard fowl signals the clash of moods and the dramatist's latest paradox.

Under the King's skilful treatment, Osgood is brought round to giving his personal view on the Carpathian—and European—situation. His sophisticated culture laid aside, there speaks out the descendant of pioneers: 'What's wrong with an axe and a spade and a bit of land to clear, said my grand-dad when he went West . . . .' An axe is the republican's weapon, as well as a farmer's tool; a spade—though a politician will not call it that, if he can help it, —is used by the Carpathian peasant to dig up his gun. The metaphor of dragons' teeth lurks, in this context, even in the American farmer's allusion to the second sight he saw in Europe, 'a battlefield two days old'. The ironic contrast of cultivation and destruction, swords and ploughshares, will be a continual undercurrent of the text, emerging in the material symbol of King Henry's sword and the symbolic value of the figure of Jakab, the farmer. ('Yesterday,' says the distraught Queen, presenting the latter with an order no longer valid, 'you would have been a Knight of St. Andrew'; and the antitheses are reconciled.)

Meanwhile, Osgood's straight simplicity passes judgment:

> I don't know now which rile me more . . . the men that fool their
> fellow-men and call it government or the fellows behind that they
> let fool t h e m . . . that stir the mud and fish their dirty profit
> from it. But if for five short minutes I could be God Almighty I'd
> make a handful of the lot and drop them in the cold Atlantic . . .
> and we'd hear the joy-bells ring [. . .] And what's wrong with
> exile from a world like this? That's the question . . . man to man
> . . . I'd like to have been asking you.

The difference between this and the severely guarded tones of the formal interview is very marked. The King, even now, though he manages to be charming and friendly, sympathetic and even a little confidential, maintains his restraint. It distinguishes already a temperament that cannot indulge in such crudely simple day-dreams, or believe at all in that kind of sweeping solution. But it is more than a personal characteristic; it implies the truth that even the courtesy of kings has its political value and a king's smile is a political action. When Osgood is gone, King Henry acknowledges as much in reply to the Queen's impatient demand, 'Why do you waste time with such people?':

> My dear Rosamund! The Press! Besides ... one must be extra civil to America.

For the governor, prince or democrat, there is no escape from politics.

Queen Rosamund, however, is contemptuously sceptical. 'Why?' she asks of this again, and is answered: 'That is a searching question. We always are. I don't know why.' A direction to the actor indicates, however, that he may find some meaning in it. No doubt the clue lies in the picture Osgood has involuntarily given of himself: the man from far away on a short visit, secure in his neutrality, come among men like God Almighty, the country-folk crowding round him, as he 'sat in (his) machine by roadsides'. The image of the descent of the God is directly preparatory for the second half of the Act and the King's decision to return to his people and save them if he can.[2]

To be above it all, or away from it all, even in exile, is certainly an advantage. Roger Dod, the young Englishman who is to fly the King back to Carpathia and drop propaganda leaflets from his aeroplane, will preserve such detachment in the thick of things, regarding civil war as a superior kind of sport, in which it is his function to 'run the team'. The possibility of another kind of detachment, at once uncommitted and responsive, guarding faith even in an act of betrayal, is what King Henry puts to the test.

The decision is precipitated by the audience given to Count Zapolya. The 'old fox', one of the diplomats who made the Peace of Versailles, now makes his second appearance in the Act. (The first was very brief, just opportunity enough for him to show his double face, as Osgood was received:

OSGOOD. Paris . . . 1919 *[. . .]* we all thought when they presented you with the treaty you played them off the stage. You had our sympathy.
ZAPOLYA. Thank you. It was a melancholy occasion. But . . . like a true tragedian . . . I ate a good lunch afterwards.

A character who wears his mask so consciously is fitting exponent of the lessons of political duplicity. In the scene which follows, his significance is reinforced by the interruptions of Colonel Guastalla, a reluctant quick-change artist, who has to shed his uniform for civilian clothes, whenever he goes out, and civilian clothes for uniform to appear in the Queen's presence. Both characters belong by nature to this house of open secrets, where the defence against spying is to ensure that the head housemaid, an agent shared by three foreign powers, overhears everything of political importance. After a lifetime in the practice of his profession, the normal movement of Zapolya's mind seems to be oblique. It makes him an able interpreter of affairs.

The discussion runs on Dr. Madrassy, present head of the government at Karlsburg. 'Why didn't your Majesties go back when he gave you the chance?' the old man asks; and his answer to Queen Rosamund's objection invokes the first rule of the game:

THE QUEEN. He made conditions *[. . .]* He never meant us to accept them.
ZAPOLYA. What better reason could you want, Ma'am, for doing so?

Take a statesman at his word and you have him at a disadvantage; it is of little value, and yet his power may depend on its not being publicly betrayed. So much the well-meaning politician accepts, and Zapolya is himself an honest man, hating the tactics of the knaves. The Carpathian situation itself illustrates *their* method:

ZAPOLYA. . . . I grasp its principles . . . so called. You look for trouble . . . or discreetly foster it. Securities go down and you buy. When the trouble's over they go up and you sell. And there's a profit.
THE KING. They may not go up. Then you're ruined.
ZAPOLYA. Not if you've been reckless enough . . . for then your rivals step in to save you. High finance has its altruism. It desires

not the bankruptcy of a sinner . . . of a sufficiently spectacular sinner. Bankruptcy is catching . . . .

The crudest material interests cannot survive without evolving a morality, it seems;[3] though it is surely an infernal morality that supports the practice of letting hell loose for so many months of anarchy to serve your ends. Yet, caught in such toils, the victim may find his innocence a defensive weapon:

> THE KING. How could Stephen let himself be tricked like this?
> ZAPOLYA. Has he been tricked, Sir? He always meant to fight. He has had their money. They leave him in the lurch. He's free of them . . . and so would you be.

A bribe is not a bribe, when what it pays for is freely given; and treachery betrays the traitor's advantage. From equivocation Zapolya—and the dramatist—is moving on to paradox.

Having thus prepared his listeners' minds, the elder statesman can proceed to give his advice:

> I venture to hope he'll disobey you, Sir. But write the letter. Five thousand men facing such odds for you . . . shows you are still to be counted with. The letter will free you from blame for the folly of it. And if by chance he should win . . . success never needs much explaining away.

Barker seems to be punning again. It is certainly the letter of the law (which Voysey explicitly rejected) that the statesman would use as his excuse.

When Zapolya has gone, the effectiveness of his lesson in political thinking is evident; even the Queen has caught the trick of it:

> THE QUEEN. He'll have you murdered . . . if he gets the chance [. . .].
> THE KING. No . . . it wouldn't do.
> THE QUEEN. He could hang the man that did it.

If justice is seen to be done, it does not much matter politically, perhaps, if it is a mockery of justice; order of a kind is preserved. 'Rosamund . . . don't be so tortuous,' protests the King at her apparently directest of truisms. His words sound like an echo of the remonstrance she was making to him, a few moments before: 'Don't be paradoxical.'

In effect, the scene has exposed the split in human consciousness between private and public morality, which necessitates what Orwell called Doublethink: the equivocation, which is its natural expression, testifies to the false morality of material interests. Paradox, the language of faith, is radically different and opposes itself to duplicity, as it unites truth and counter-truth in the single statement. The dialogue has not been merely working a trick of style to death, but using it to propound the principles between which the dramatic conflict is to be fought out. Just before the scene ends, the theme reaches its climax in Queen Rosamund's account of the King's nature:

> You're not a coward ... and you won't fight. You argue like a lawyer ... and let anyone get the better of you. You ask everyone's advice and agree with all they say ... and now you do this foolhardy thing.

The hero, though he may have mastered admirably the diplomatic game, appears to be on the side of paradox, and his relation to the antithesis established between the letter and the *Logos* will but be confirmed in his later refusal to be 'the dumb sign of a faith made tame and ridiculous'.

* * *

Barker employs several means of relieving the strain of all this finessing with words and ideas. The 'breeze' of Osgood's outburst is one; the element of domestic comedy, in which Red Terror and White Terror appear in the guise of Rhode Island Reds and Wyandottes and the royal children are in quarantine for chicken-pox, supplies another; the character of the Queen is a third. In all, the effect of dramatic contrast is combined with a serious significance that contributes to the play's total statement; even the reference to chicken-pox is a first sideways glance at the diseases of the body politic.

Most important of the three to the total dramatic structure, and the concept it embodies, is the figure of Queen Rosamund. 'No man is safe from his supporters,' the King reflects, 'that's the first lesson every leader has to learn.' Czernyak and the Queen between them will embarrass him most in the struggle that he is to undertake; and the conflict with Bruckner will reflect a no less fierce, though more intimate, conflict with the Queen: confident of her own divine sovereignty, she is prepared to be the most rebellious of his subjects.

She is essentially a tragi-comic creation. On her first appearance in the play, while Osgood is still on the stage, she does not attract sympathy. Magnificence is the first quality that the dramatist associates with her, and it now takes a form that, compared with the King's easy courtesy, is very like snobbery. She regards etiquette as of the greatest importance and accepts flattery as the merest tribute due to her rank. In the moments when she is alone on the stage with the King, at the end of the first scene, it is her impatience that is most in evidence, and a directness that brushes aside doubts and qualifications as of small account:

> When you know what you want all problems are simple.

In the second scene, with Zapolya (there is no break in the playing, but the structural divisions are clear and, as in the first Act of the previous play, there is an approximation to sonata form), this impression of the character is maintained; but gradually the absurd aspect of the figure becomes clearer, and with this shift there goes a slight veering of sympathy towards the woman—who happens to be the Queen. For all her insistence on being practical, Queen Rosamund cannot even pull the right string, when she wants to lower a map. When the *aide* comes in, she states as a self-evident fact, '. . . you would like to resume your uniform, Colonel Guastalla'. It is certainly evident that the Colonel adores her and will do anything for her, and the King's mild protest on his behalf accepts the foolish situation as inevitable. The Queen is what she is, the one factor that will never change, never deviate in its vision of order: royalty at the centre, its authority unquestioned. 'To pander to a Swiss Government and its dignity,' is the reason she gives for poor Guastalla's fate, 'They'd make us dress like grocers

within doors if they could.' Such an unswerving assumption of
her own rightness even compels admiration; it has an absolute
value.

With Count Zapolya's departure, the King's patience with her
shows its source in an affection to which she softens. Treated as a
woman, she responds with a ready humanity, and the real warmth
of this creature of feeling begins to make itself felt, together with
her undoubted, unassuming courage:

> THE KING. I'll take Guastalla. It'll be a risky journey . . . what-
> ever happens when I get there.
> THE QUEEN. Do you expect me to sit here and w a i t ? I'm
> your wife, Henry . . . even if I might be a better one.
> THE KING. My dear . . . if we both came to grief the children
> would be left pretty helpless.
> THE QUEEN. I'm sorry . . . I'm not that sort of a mother.

When Barker discussed with Harcourt Williams the possibility
of a production of *His Majesty,* it was the problem of casting the
part of the Queen that exercised him most.[4] (He suggested for
the King, Nicholas Hannen, who had played Philip Madras in
1925, and Charles Laughton for Bruckner.) He insisted that the
rôle needed to be tackled emotionally, 'from inside out, not with
that tight cleverness which tries to work from outside in'. Fay
Compton he was inclined to reject on the grounds that she had
'finally resolved into the minor key', whereas the part required a
melodramatic quality, combined with absolute sincerity.

For the irrationality, the passionateness, even the childishness,
of Queen Rosamund are not rejected out-of-hand. King Henry,
though he pursues his own course against her, maintains connection with her in a personal affection and the forgiveness that recognises nothing to forgive. Head and heart, though they drive at times
chaotically against each other, are finally reconciled in a scene
where the balance of comedy is restored, as they are reconciled in
the domestic harmony that is the closing note of Act I.

The absurdity of the Queen, and her Ruritanian quality, is too
fundamental to allow her to be a purely tragic figure, yet the playwright's conception of her embraces tragic experience: she will
have her 'moment' of absolute suffering; she will know failure;
she will betray the King, find herself in conspiracy with men she

despises, and have to carry responsibility for the death of the champion of her cause; she will repay the Countess, her oldest friend, by sending her son to be murdered, and will win her triumph at the price of a child's life. At the end of it all, she recognises herself that she is not changed, not 'a better woman', for all the suffering and humiliation she has gone through and caused.

Her integrity is guarded by the figures gathered about her: Countess Czernyak, whose love is unwavering, despite the cost; Guastalla, whose completely unselfish admiration for her preserves a kind of innocence in him, even while leading him to deceive the King; old Colonel Hadik, who is 'goodness itself'; and Stephen Czernyak, who achieves martyrdom because of her folly. The tragedy implicit in the character of the Queen is, indeed, preserved and isolated through its reflection in the figure of Czernyak. At one point in the play's development, an echo makes audible the dramatic relation between the two characters. 'She's not very wise,' says Countess Czernyak of her mistress. 'What does that matter?' replies Stephen, who wants a cause to fight for. A little later, when King Henry in sudden cold anger turns on the Queen, 'Please try not to make a fool of yourself,' the impersonal greatness that is in her emerges with her passionate retort, when so much is at stake: 'What does t h a t matter?' Czernyak's nobility answers to the quality of her vision.

After politely asking Osgood where in America he came from, the King responded: 'Iowa City, Iowa! You can have found nothing more romantic in Europe, Mr. Osgood, than I find that.' So Barker introduced the double view, at once realistic and romantic, to be maintained throughout the play. In Act I, the romantic images are mostly the Queen's contribution, naïve images of the King on horse-back, leading his troops into battle, or—more solemn— 'standing that day before the altar . . . crowned, with your sword stretched out, taking your oath to save Carpathia in her need'. Her longing for beauty and greatness is a genuine thing. Her romantic vision has a validity that corresponds to the counter-truth of paradox. In it, the romantic figure of Czernyak and the actual figure of the King, wise, practical, realistic, yet steadfast for truth, are imaginatively fused.

*   *   *

Though the mood of comedy predominates in Act I, the dramatist introduced a slight shift in atmosphere, even as he induced a more intimate quality of feeling, by setting the second scene in a growing dusk. The map of Carpathia, unrolled, was the focal point, preparing the way for Act II and the movement into the field of action. The transition towards tragedy continues from this, but is not completed until the close of the second Act is reached.

Within a few minutes of the new raising of the curtain, the alarm of danger is given. The Queen has entered the salon of the Château Czernyak through the long windows that overlook the terrace. The King and Guastalla are not in view. A shot rings out:

> THE QUEEN. What's that? What has happened?
> COUNTESS CZERNYAK. We'd better wait here now ... till we know.
> *But the* QUEEN *realises what it might mean.*
> THE QUEEN. Oh, Ja-ja ... that couldn't happen ... Yes ... it could!

The suspense, the sharpest moment yet, is quickly relaxed. The shot was Guastalla's and he missed by an inch the old man, Colonel Hadik, who had the King covered but recognised him before he could fire. It *could* happen is the note that the dramatist has sounded for the whole play to follow; and if there is no regicide and no general conflagration, it is just so narrowly averted.

The audience has already had an opportunity to take in the appearance of the room: the uncurtained windows and the proportions, reminders of a graciousness that has been; the chandelier smashed; the candle, stuck in a wine bottle, standing on the grand piano; great patches on the walls that have been stripped of their pictures (the Velasquez, explains the Countess, is hidden in the laundry); it is a room that has been looted; and the rest of its furnishings, a kitchen table and a couple of not very comfortable chairs, seem less incongruous there than the piano. Such a room is 'a roof over our heads', as the Queen says, a welcome refuge to the party forced to land in a fog and then walk ten miles to get there, though it betokens only a precarious hold on the material world and its peace is what follows devastation.

As the Queen sits and gossips to the Countess, Guastalla and the

King move briskly about their preparations: Dr. Madrassy, having been summoned there, grew tired of waiting, has left and must be recalled; a message must 'be conveyed to Czernyak; telephones and codes and currency are in question. The *aide-de-camp* goes out, and the King's movements sustain the impression of restlessness and the anticipation of crisis through the remainder of the scene. At the back of the set, at right angles to the windows, are double doors opening on a second *salon,* and from room to room he goes, looking for notepaper and blotting-paper,. a fountain pen, coming out to fetch the candle, to get a cigarette, returning to read to the Queen the letter he has written. Notepaper, a fountain pen, these are the weapons of his kind of warfare; but the playwright also uses such commonplace trivialities, the Queen's news about the children, the Countess's details about old friends in Karlsburg, to preserve a continuity of naturalism in a scene that verges ever closer to symbolism.

A duskier light filters gradually through the windows, and in it the barriers between past and present, and between seen and unseen realities, are dissolved. The memories of the two women take shape and mirror the nature of their consciousness. 'I find myself here among the wreckage,' says the Countess, 'For my life's like this, Ma'am.' For her the room is peopled:

> I stood [...] and saw it wrecked round me by men and women I'd known, some of them, as children [...] and one of them snatched back a little silver Madonna they'd taken ... I suppose he thought I valued it. They killed him ... there by that window. His own brother helped to kill him. ...

The peace she has found there contains the sense of a debt paid: 'We lucky ones have been borrowing prosperity for these few hundred years.'

The Queen's vision is strangely opposed to this image of anarchy:

> I dreamt last night ... I woke with such a jump and the moon was shining on me ... about that last Birthday ball [...] the men in their uniforms and all those pretty girls kissing my hand ....

Perhaps it was moonshine, for she knows that it has vanished

and wonders whether that world was ever real. But the dramatist
is making the atmosphere the most substantial thing in this scene.
It absorbs retrospectively the effect of a brief passage in the last
part of Act I, when the King spoke of his memories, and so gave
the truth of his consciousness of royalty's isolation:

> What made my grandfather build that great stucco barracks of a
> palace? Dreary and draughty! Put less than twenty at table and
> the private dining-room's a desert. And one winter when I was a
> boy . . . and the city electricians had struck and it was foggy . . . I
> lay in bed there by candlelight and I could not see the ceiling!

That image blends with the present scene, as, in the dreariness
and dusk of the Château Czernyak, a candle is lit for him.

The little flames spurt up again, when first the Queen, then the
King light their cigarettes, and there is a tiny glow as they draw
upon them. *Firefly* will be the name of the boat that, in the last Act,
waits to take them to their second exile; like fireflies are the little
illuminations that appear among the ruins. This is the inner world,
the secret aspect of post-war Europe, tenuously evoked. And the
flames may be the first beginnings of a blaze; the *ignis fatuus* of the
romantic imagination may lure to destruction. Light-fire-burning,
the three related concepts have begun to weave their way through
the dialogue. Gloom and fog imply the mystery in which Man
exists.

When it is nearly dark and the candle is flickering from the inner
room through the half-open doors, the scene reaches its climax
with the appearance of Colonel Hadik before the Queen, now sitting alone. He is a very old man, and his age, the queer shadows
about him, and the reminiscences which have been bringing the
past to the brink of the visible, combine to make an audience receptive to the strange nature of his rambling talk:

> I study mathematics still. In the higher mathematics lies knowledge
> that has hardly yet been cursed by man's use of it. I can still work
> in the garden. I need only bread besides . . . and a little wine. I'll
> kill a man in self-defence if I must. I do not justify that. But such
> is the nakedness of our nature . . . of which I am no longer ashamed.

He is speaking as much to himself as to the Queen, and the earlier
incident, when he so nearly shot the King, is certainly in his

thoughts as much as the Queen's questions, 'But how can you manage? What do you do?' He is an aristocrat and a scholar who has learnt simplicity and, as the directions have it, *'by sheer devotion to his simple duties'* he becomes *'the perfect butler'*. But the simple diet which contents his needs is sacramental; and the knowledge on which his mind is set contains within it a promise of absolute integrity.

The character, and the whole style of the scene, have their counterparts in Chekhovian drama. A gloss upon Hadik's words will come in another mode, in lines spoken by the King to Czernyak, in Act III:

> You don't believe in my divine right, Stephen. But the fact is . . . if I haven't that, I've no other. Nor has any man.

This, the divinity that every man needs to seek in himself, is the play's pivotal theme.[5]

A moment of complete darkness, and the lights go up again, bright enough this time, for *'a new and very brassy oil lamp'* has been brought from the village. Countess Czernyak is revealed asleep in the chair that was occupied by the Queen, and the first lines—recalling in this the opening of *The Secret Life*—come from the inner room, where the King and Queen are arguing with Dr. Madrassy. 'Nonsense,' 'foolish' are the weighted words to be caught, before the actors, Madrassy first, then the others, move to the forestage.

The new character has a moment to introduce himself, in his words to the Countess, as a not unsympathetic figure: 'I always liked him,' he says of the King, 'Broken loyalties lie heavy on a man.' The scene that follows reveals, in fact, two men who talk the same language, are at ease with each other's mode of thought, and respect each other's quality enough to be keyed up for the encounter. (We have already been told that Madrassy was once the King's tutor in classics.) Unlike Zapolya, the present head of the Carpathian state was not bred to politics, and the view he has to offer is a new contribution.

A climax comes with the entry of Hadik to announce, 'The kitchen stove is lit,' meaning, it seems, in the terms of the secret code established by the Queen and Guastalla, that Czernyak, 'with eight motor cars,' is through the trenched and wired section of the road, on his way to capture Madrassy. The absurd form of the statement serves to comment obliquely on the news, which just before was broken to the King, that the insurgents have begun to advance from Eisenthal towards the capital; and Madrassy's 'head this rabble from Eisenthal ... blaze your way to Karlsburg' confirms the metaphor. (The mention of 'the kitchen stove' also carries on the domestic images that thread their way through the play.) For the King, Hadik's message is one of a succession of incidents that speak of deceptions practised on him by his most partisan adherents; and appropriately, even a little ominously, it is now that he remembers his sword, as he protests to Madrassy:

> ... if I were the fool or the trickster you seem to take me for, I'd surrender my sword [...]. By the bye, Guastalla, I must have a sword. Why was mine left behind?

and he speaks of it as an object of commonest use.

In the mood of urgency that the news has introduced (and from now on a sense of happenings elsewhere—the movement of cars, aeroplanes, men, the engagements of troops—will continue to add to the dramatic dimensions of scene after scene), Dr. Madrassy, drinking the malted milk he just has time for without greatly jeopardising his safety, relaxes from official opposition into personal frankness. He tells of the revolution as he experienced it; and his pride in work soundly done, that is his virtue, links him with the King and with Colonel Hadik:

> My staff stuck to me [...] and the work went on somehow. And through Red Terror and White Terror not a school in the country was closed.

The quality of the man who does his best in spite of disillusionment is not mean:

> MADRASSY. So I found myself my country's saviour. And really ... considering ... I've not done so badly.
> THE QUEEN. You're an opportunist, Dr. Madrassy.
> MADRASSY. That is the word, Ma'am.

The audience has already received the clue to its interpretation in Zapolya's vocabulary of politics:

> THE QUEEN. A time-server!
> ZAPOLYA. If a politician can serve his moment of time to any purpose, Ma'am ... that may not be a reproach.

By conveniently contracting rheumatic fever and then shingles, Madrassy has preserved a front of detachment, a formal innocence of the blood spilt in two waves of violence; the detachment and innocence that the King has to offer are here most unromantically weighed and found to count for something. Both men now appear as honest moderates on the side of the angels, with no inflated ideas of their own dignity:

> THE KING. You're not jealous of my coming back to make peace? [. . .].
> MADRASSY. A little jealous. I'm human.
> THE KING. Not afraid for your job?
> MADRASSY. I've a wife and children to keep.

So Hadik's reminder that man's nature contains an element of the divine is supplemented by this assertion that authority does not annul the common humanity of kings or ministers. These two know the necessities of men and circumstances and the use of patient negotiation; they recognise that to be 'too thorough-going' is in effect to 'give up politics' as surely as did that Bruckner who shot the President of the Assembly.

At his departure, however, Dr. Madrassy gives a glimpse of what politics has cost him, the bitterness of knowledge and the sternness it has produced. His words to the King are spoken out of his own darkness:

> MADRASSY. I'm the slippery politician, Sir ... I don't fight. I hope you won't. But it may be your task to fight ... if not to fight and win to fight and fail. To fight ... knowing you'll fail ... hating to fight and with no faith in fighting.
> THE KING. Pretty damnable doctrine!
> MADRASSY. Is it? We must not be egoists ... even in virtue.

In his irony the note of purely tragic feeling is struck for the first time. What is to happen will not take quite the form that his words suggest, but will be similarly paradoxical: betrayal after betrayal as a way of keeping faith. Madrassy's parting comment to Countess Czernyak, on the pamphlet on rickets that she returns to him, is equally applicable to his own political wisdom: 'We do wring a little knowledge from the God above our warring gods. A bitter fruit . . . but sound.' Such fighting as the King will do will be in Madrassy's cause.

From the debate the scene returns at the end to a more symbolistic presentation. The group breaks up, the talk becomes more casual, and the Queen's fiery longing for action finds expression when she seats herself at the piano and starts to play some of the ballet music from Borodin's *Prince Igor*. The last dance lends its militancy to the plans that the King and Guastalla are making. The lamp has now been brought to the table, where its light is concentrated on the map spread out there. Countess Czernyak, her daughter, Dominica, Colonel Hadik and the Queen herself are now only dim figures in the shadows. The walls of the room are dissolved in blackness. Guastalla and the King are both in uniform. This is the camp on the eve of battle, and it is to a camp-bed, in the state apartments, that the Queen will presently go.

As she plays, changing soon to the slow movement, the Queen talks also, and with her mention of Snowjacket, the State charger, she catches King Henry's attention. The allusion implies the view of monarchy as an old-fashioned pageant, a circus for the entertainment of the mob, but fuses it with the image of the King riding his white charger into battle and with the idea of royal infallibility that is the innocence of princes.

The dramatist employs a casual word from the King to bring Colonel Hadik to his side. The old man is trembling:

> Would your Majesty perhaps give me some less responsible appointment? I was proud of my guns once . . . but I am not very wise now. I could still fight . . . but you never know who guns kill . . . and I think now it may not be right to . . . .

That also harks back to what might have happened at the beginning of the Act. So a mood of doubt is introduced. Queen Rosamund's playing stops; her promises echo emptily: 'Your poor beautiful home, Ja-ja! But we'll build it up.' The King, drafting a proclamation, searches his mind in vain for new and meaningful phrases; from the piano there now come '*a few last, desolate, single notes*'; and so the curtain falls. This is no prelude to victory, but an evocation of forlorn hopes and weariness of the struggle.

*   *   *

But Act III opens in daylight and at the end of Armistice talks at Zimony railway station.[6] It seems as though the dramatist has once again cheated his audience of the excitement of action. Something of the mood of the last moments before the curtain fell is carried over into the new scene; there is an air of depressing futility over all. The setting is the shoddiest of structures, marked out by a pair of engineless coaches and two wooden hoardings, raised on the station platform. The King finds himself without a pen that will write; Czernyak's field-glasses are broken; soon it emerges that there has been no battle, only the strain of three weeks' negotiation. There is a sign of how far Barker had travelled from the dominance of Shaw's influence, and from his own *Madras House*, in his rejection of the conference as an opportunity for debate round a table. When the audience has had time to observe the new figures on the scene, the picture breaks up, and the signatories of the treaty go their various ways.

Czernyak's mettle is evident enough; he is every inch a soldier, with the hardness and authority of a leader of men that count for more than maturity in years. His quality is shown up the more clearly in contrast to the enemy's General Horvath, the old soldier gone soft, rotted from within by a self-flattering sentimentality, and the voiceless lay-figure of the *aide*, Captain Papp, who attends him. The other new character is Bruckner, enigmatic in his stillness and silence.

When the King has gone to one of the coaches and Horvath to the Ladies Waiting Room, converted into an office, Guastalla calls in the Englishman, Dod, and introduces him to Madrassy. With a manner cooler, if possible, than Czernyak's has been, Roger Dod seems to be the 'typical' Englishman, fair-minded, unsubtle, with little interest in the depths beneath the surface of things. In presentation, he is a severely limited figure; but his significance is not simple and the resemblance to Czernyak will be brought out again. For the present, the ambiguity of the figure is hinted, even through his apparent obtuseness, in the conversation with Madrassy:

> DOD. No ... politics aren't my pigeon [...] Nor is journalism.
> MADRASSY. You have a gift for it. You have added appreciably to the confusion of the public mind.
> *Why waste these delicacies of sarcasm?*
> DOD. But your King's a good fellow [...] Couldn't you have censored that caricature of the two of them ... riding bareback into Karlsburg? [...] introduce me to the fellow that did it I'll have pleasure in horsewhipping him.
> MADRASSY. The world looks like that to him [...] Your view of life is a prettier one, I'm sure. But is it any truer?
> DOD. I don't see what that has to do with it.

The retort anticipates the Queen's passionate 'What does t h a t matter?' and yet the character of Dod takes the mind back to the anti-romantic Ferguson, in *The Weather-Hen*, and his declaration, 'I'm not troubled with honour'. There is a sense in which King Henry is not troubled with honour, either; and in the thematic relation between the Queen, Czernyak and the King, Dod makes an essential link.

The Act seems rather slow in getting into its stride: the different groups of characters talk among themselves and give way to others, and no single movement seems to be emerging; but this is calculated preparation for the crescendo that is to sweep through the second half. It is soon enough apparent that the terms of the armistice are not finally settled. Certain questions have been left open, and the two parties have their own ideas of how they should be solved. One question is what is to become of the King; the other, who is to occupy the town. Before either is pressed to the point of danger, the dramatist takes his opportunity of drawing a parallel between them and explaining the dramatic issues at stake, in a simple exemplary form.

The turn of the King comes first. For the first time he seems inclined, as he talks to Madrassy and Bruckner, to make a bid for a constitutional sovereignty. The phrases, 'if I found I wasn't wanted', 'if you're sure I'm not wanted', creep into his talk and have a questioning accent. Bruckner takes him up: 'Who wants you, Sir . . . and what for?' For answer, King Henry picks up the blotting pad, on which he has been drawing:

> Here we have him complete . . . head, body, two arms, two legs! *[. . .]* You gentlemen that govern him . . . and there are so many of you nowadays . . . despise him, don't you? He knows that. You flatter him . . . because you're afraid of him . . . and you come at last to hate him *[. . .]* it's a sort of comfort to him . . . tussling with life . . . to feel that there's one fellow-creature, at least, free enough from the tussle to want nothing from him . . . not even his vote *[. . .]* it might be a real job still. However . . . I gave you my word.

That has the effect of forcing Madrassy's hand: they have the King physically in their power, and the condition for letting him go is abdication.

The King understands the significance of Bruckner's presence well enough, though he is not yet angered, as he will be shortly, into declaring to Madrassy: '. . . your loyal colleagues will be saying that I've bribed or cajoled you. Mr. Bruckner's witness I don't try to. Isn't that what he's here for? Or will he be suspect now?' He is less concerned, at this point, with the rule of perfidy than with the powerlessness that Madrassy's threat reveals:

> MADRASSY Does it follow, Sir, because nothing could be sillier than to make a martyr of you . . . that we shan't do it . . . shan't have to do it whether we like it or not?
> THE KING. *[. . .]* Are you really so helpless? Is this what democracy has come to?

And he concludes by asking again: 'Are you sure that I'm not wanted here . . . are you quite sure?' It seems to be some liberation from necessity that he has to offer.

The slowly mounting tension is further increased by Czernyak's angry interruption to announce disagreement with Horvath over the occupation of the town; and he has to stand impatiently by, while the Mayor of Zimony, Mr. Nagy, seizes this as his opportunity. Down-to-earth, harrassed by the necessity to placate everybody, the Mayor, who sees himself as a minor replica of the King, is *homo sapiens* in person, conjured up from the mannikin that the King has drawn and come as in a morality to speak for himself. The character counts for so much, yet dramatically for no more: he has, in effect, his one speech, and then he is dismissed.

Before he goes, he makes it clear enough that at Zimony everything has a price, possibly even what a King could give:

> ... we did hope your Majesty's coming back meant that you'd just say the word [...] People come quarrelling to me ... I listen ... I've got to. I let them talk till they're tired ... there's not much else I can do [...] And I say to myself: Now there ought to be some word ... !

But he does not know what it is, and his appeal resolves itself into: 'For the dear Lord's sake leave us in peace,' the meaning Osgood found so plain in the language he did not know. After Mr. Nagy's serio-comic 'turn' before his eminent audience has provided this interlude, there is to be little relaxation until the Act is finished.

After the restraint that the Mayor's presence has imposed, tempers flame out, and even the King's affability is no longer so evident, as the danger in the situation that Czernyak has announced becomes clearer. On a point of honour the King will not give way and he drives Madrassy to put his crucial question:

> Do you mean to make us fight you ... after all?

The King takes up the challenge, though he still makes it clear enough that he wants no bloodshed:

> Give me choice of weapons ... yes, I'll fight you and beat you! And you'd thank me.

Fearing the turn that events may take, Madrassy and Horvath hurry out to consult with the Commander of their troops. There is at least an excuse for suspecting their good faith. It seems to be Czernyak's moment, and he urges:

> Sir ... Sir ... break off with them! They've given us the chance [...] Give me my head now and I'll have you in Karlsburg in a week.

(There is a price on that head, we may remember, and the King would save it if he could.)

The argument is interrupted by Lieutenant Vida with news for his General of the insubordinate Sergeant Bakay. The reminder touches off Czernyak's own explosion against the discipline imposed on him, though how precisely relevant the case of Bakay is we must wait to hear. The manner in which the King continues to refuse the chance of action recalls his earlier statement that he has known Czernyak from childhood. 'We must wage a war for you some day . . . against the heathen,' he says, with a touch of compassion for the young man's ardent simplicity, a spirit to which— he will recognise—a brave martyrdom is not the hardest of fates. He cares for Stephen sufficiently to try and explain what he himself has learnt: that his real power lies in the refusal of advantages. In words that recall Louis Philippe (as do other details in the play), he declares: '. . . when next I open Parliament I shall walk down the hill from the Castle . . . frock coat, top hat, with an umbrella if it's raining [. . .]. Will it be very unkingly?' 'Not if you do it, Sir,' is the reply. 'Worth trying . . . d'you think?' asks the patient master again, but this time his pupil's answer is: 'I don't believe in miracles, I fear.' Yet it is no hazy mysticism that the King is talking, but the soundest, plainest sense, and he knows it:

> Nor I. And I don't know the Mayor's magic word. It would be the natural thing to do. You don't believe in my divine right, Stephen. But the fact is . . . if I haven't that, I've no other. Nor has any man. This time I must put it to the proof.

But Czernyak's temperament will not let him be persuaded of the power of simple integrity, or that the divinity of kingship—if it exists at all—is a product of the sanctified heart of man: the potential best that is in him. King Henry himself is more of a democrat, aware that the dignity of every common man consists in his being, in this sense, a king. He goes off for his evening walk, content to let the situation develop: 'If they don't knuckle under . . . those three . . . you can send for me. But I fancy they will.' The truth is that Czernyak hardly wants them to.

To his mother also this leader of men appears touchingly vulnerable as, too proud for self-pity, he falls back on a cold bitterness and stubbornness of will. Sympathy and judgment live separately in the Countess's mind, so dictating the stillness that is hers throughout the play. She is faithful; she accepts; but she cannot actively participate. Her watchful presence and awareness of the issues give an undercurrent of sadness to her son's more volatile emotion. The tragedy contained within the tragi-comedy is to be Stephen Czernyak's, and to it she is the chorus. An omen of the crisis of the Act comes now, in this quiet moment:

> COUNTESS CZERNYAK. ... This is a bitter business for you, my dear. *[...]*
> CZERNYAK. I'd not have asked him to thank me, even! I wish she were the man.
> COUNTESS CZERNYAK. She's not very wise.
> CZERNYAK. What does that matter?

Now Bakay is brought before his General, and Czernyak's battle with himself is externalised and his sense of betrayal avenged. The disciplinary action is all the harsher for being in fact self-discipline; and there can be little doubt that, as he lashes the man with his tongue, he is aware of him as the reflection of what he regards as his own disgrace:

> CZERNYAK. ... Pleasant for his regiment ... won't it be ... to see their senior sergeant-major chained to a gun-carriage! *[...]*.
> BAKAY. I'd rather be shot, General.
> CZERNYAK. Who asked you what you'd rather be?

The blistering self-contempt pours out in insult: 'You'll fight or not as you're ordered. And you won't ask why. You're fed ... you get your pay.' Bakay's reply to this contains a not so covert reference to the King: 'let the traitors go home again ... whoever they are'; it is uncomfortably close to the treacherous meditations that Czernyak himself half-voiced to the Countess and now drives him to a savagely ironical climax:

Cut off his stripes. Cut them off with that pen-knife here and now.[7]

The weapon is indeed appropriate, as to it his own sword seems

19

to be surrendered. The loyalty of Bakay to Czernyak is only the fiercer, though, for the high temper he recognises in all this:

> I'd follow you to hell, General . . . which I set out to . . . and you know it!

The sarcasm in the other's final 'Much obliged!' is particularly acid; for does he not value the insubordination more than the obedience?

The row over, Dod, venturing within range, receives for his coolness the backwash of Czernyak's irritability:

> We've managed to give you a sporting time, I hope.

But the Englishman has sufficient understanding of the other and of the true nature of the little scene just acted out, before its gathered audience, to be able to comment:

> Providence can beat you . . . and the rest of us . . . when it comes to irony, General.

The absence of any break at this point intensifies the strain, registered even in an unexpected outburst by Guastalla, directed at Countess Czernyak of all people:

> I'm not asked to think. I'm a shorthand typist with good table manners, warranted to look well in uniform.

(In this instance, the character in his costume seems to be less, not more, than the natural man; appearance is substituted for the reality of the symbol.) Barker is using his group of minor characters, Dod, Guastalla, Countess Czernyak, Colonel Hadik, who stands listening on the steps of the carriage, to key up anticipation of the end of the adventure, whatever it may be. Hadik's question, 'Did you hear gunfire?' is a warning, dismissed at first. Dod goes on lecturing the others until, aptly upon his words, '. . . someone says Shoot . . . and you hit the wrong people' (an echo from Hadik in Act II), the guns make themselves heard in the theatre.

The sound is a summons to the Queen, who now appears, for

the first time in the Act, raised up on the steps of the other carriage, dominating the stage-picture. *'She looks a tragic figure as she stands there, a long wrap thrown round her,'* the dramatist directs. The light has already begun to change to the dusk of the end of Act II, and to the mind's ear Borodin's music is audible again. The battle has begun, and Colonel Hadik's words enforce the impression of its actuality: 'Our twenty-pounder with the faulty primer [. . .] It's a mile away and more . . . coming into the wind [. . .]. That makes the full battery [. . .] I hope they won't fire Number Four again too soon [. . .] Machine guns, Ma'am.' They go to climb the signal box, all contributing their personal reactions to a mood in which rising excitement and consternation are blended.

Nowhere else in his drama does Barker so reap the benefit of continuous playing. The lights go down, his control of the audience is relaxed for a moment only, then the action is resumed at the very pitch where it broke off. Now the Queen, in a fur cloak (her costumes in this Act are the traditional ones of tragedy), occupies the centre of the stage, under the light of high-swinging arc lamps. There can be no staging of this Act behind a proscenium, of course. If the mood were different, the likeness to the circus arena might be consciously recognised. As it is, the flimsiness of the hoardings, that hold back the darkness without, is more evident than before.

Almost at once the King comes on, aweing them all by his grimness. At first, the only response to his call for a sword is Queen Rosamund's hysterical fantasy:

> Henry . . . you're going to lead them! Oh, at last! You'll draw your sword and lead them!

In the sharpest clash of feeling, he repulses the absurd dream, his harshness closer to cruelty than anything yet seen in him:

> THE KING. Please try not to make a fool of yourself.
> *The* QUEEN *cries out in despair.*
> THE QUEEN. What does t h a t matter?

And she seems, emotionally, to have the right of it; he will acknowledge as much to the British Minister, when the crisis is past.

Czernyak has been summoned, and there follows a tense little episode that is an ironic counterpart both to the earlier interview between King and General and to the public shaming of Bakay. There is no sense of the contrived performance about this, however; the restraint speaks of an agony of mind in both that is less easily relieved. The facts come out: the spontaneous advance of men who did not know that the armistice was signed, followed by a battalion that did know; the firing opened in a town empty of enemy troops. The defence that Czernyak has to make for his men is ignominious, no defence by his own standards: 'They did not shoot,' he says, 'at first. They warned all the women to stand clear. These tradesmen have been cheating them for weeks [...]. They're human. They want their own back.' Beside himself, he turns to accusation: 'So did you, Sir.'

A signed treaty violated, a word of honour betrayed, the troops —even Czernyak's own Eisenthalers—stubbornly refusing orders, the situation signifies the rout of the men of integrity and the breaking of Czernyak's pride. He can try—like Bakay—to salvage his personal honour by demonstrating a personal fidelity:

> They've been talking to m e . . . some of them! I'd no answer. Give me my orders, please.

But King Henry will not consent to a pretence of authority, when the only kind he cares for has been destroyed, and he refuses the appeal:

> I've no orders.

It is a baffling statement, which may have a private meaning, too: a hint that there is no Authority, in his own philosophy, except what a man may find within.

At this, the conflict of hero and anti-hero reaches its crisis in words of submission that are also a call for the punishment which wipes out dishonour:

> CZERNYAK. I wish to God I were with them, then . . . waiting to be shot! You've broken me, Sir . . . you've broken me!

The divine right that he denied has been put to the proof and has brought him to surrender. Though in a further irony, his appeal for the absolution of blood will be answered.

It is Ella, the Countess's maid, who at last brings the sword— as if it were an umbrella; and it is quickly put to such practical use as the King can still make of it, when General Horvath arrives; for His Majesty's surrender to the enemy must follow Czernyak's to him. But accepting the King's sword is more than Horvath, lover of compromise and evader of responsibility, has the courage to do; rather any means of settlement that will not bring principles into it, and there *are* four inns in the town square, where the rebels are congregated. '*The* KING *can stand no more of it; he throws the sword on the ground with a grand clatter and vanishes into the railway carriage.*' For the rest of the Act the symbol draws all eyes.

The distracted Horvath turns upon his *aide-de-camp*, 'Don't stand there like a tailor's dummy. Tongue-tied fool!' Then, with the triple bow prescribed by court etiquette, he retreats. The Queen is near to breakdown, but the challenge of Bruckner's presence temporarily steels her will. He now takes the centre of the stage and declares himself openly for the first time. There is a direct thrust about all he says. He comes straight to the point now: 'If you still want to win you've a chance left;' though the King has earlier told Czernyak that he wants more than that. Bruckner is not too nice for the trade he lives by and, in words that are an echo of Zapolya, but have been given a more sinister meaning by events, he asserts the logic of an obsession with ends:

> . . . if you win you'll be whitewashed. And if you're not . . . you'll have won.

There is no smiling irony about that utterance, and Bruckner does not trouble to disguise the inevitable consequence of that kind of victory:

> You can let him loose and stick a crown on him once you've landed him there.

Indeed, Captain Papp on Snowjacket would then do as well. (The image of the puppet thus joins those of the state charger in his horse-box, hens in the coop, sailors 'cooped up' in modern ships —a metaphor that still lies ahead—, man imprisoned in the machine.)

Czernyak's honour is still a real enough thing for him to repudiate this suggestion, but the Queen's stupidity—the unkind term is hers—is yet to be reckoned with: her belief that kingship establishes right, rather than right, kingship. Her resolution seems to compel both Guastalla and Czernyak against their will. (Bruckner's remark, 'You seem to believe in yourself [. . .]. People with nothing better to believe in will believe in y o u,' serves as comment on the fact.) For is not this the 'word', however late, even too late, for which the young man has been waiting? None of them, it seems, can read the riddle of Bruckner who, like the King himself, is capable of saying exactly what he means in full awareness of what the meaning implies; whereas the Queen and Stephen Czernyak even talk as in a dream, unable to seize the truth of the words that come to them. 'Do you want us to win?' challenges the Queen. 'There are things I want less,' comes the answer of the man whose own infernal mastery depends on the acceptance of success as the world's ultimate value.

With an unexpected gesture, Queen Rosamund takes off her pearls. Apparently unconscious that the one who gives a bribe sells honour as surely as the one who takes it (though Zapolya had taught this lesson, also), she offers them to Bruckner: token of a bargain that would make them fellow-conspirators. Knowing that honour is useless to his cause, he can afford to be amused. But this is too easy a victory; more needs to be at stake than the Queen can offer, more blood shed in sacrifice, it may be, before the country will feel the need for his medicine. He recognises, for the moment, what he and she have in common: the contempt for the tool, together with the readiness to use it for one's own purpose; handing back the necklace, '*with what is very nearly a bow,*' he says:

> I respect you, Madam, for the attempt. I am not above bribes. But you haven't my price in your pocket for the moment [. . .] Besides . . . once a man has taken his bribe he's no longer worth it, remember! No . . . I must fight you for a bit . . . and beat you if I can. Thank me for that, at least.

Let her keep her honour, and owe it to her enemy.

Perhaps it is this that spurs Czernyak to desperation, perhaps the obscurer impulse that drives the tragic hero to choose his fate. There is a further step downwards to be taken in his confusion of honour with spiritual pride. To dash for the enemy's guns, while Horvath is kept talking—and with that sword lying there for all to see!—is 'not a pretty trick'; but he will do it, and hope to wipe out the double treachery with courage, the sacrifice of the last of the virtue that is in him. But the Queen, for all that he, Guastalla and even Bruckner, can do between them to stop her, will take this, too, upon herself:

> CZERNYAK. I don't ask your Majesty's approval.
> THE QUEEN. You have it.
> GUASTALLA. For God's sake don't say that, Ma'am.
> THE QUEEN. You have it.
> CZERNYAK, *with her clarion note to hearten him, has gone.*

With matters so settled, the Queen herself leaves the scene, and the republican goes to join his colleagues. By this time, Roger Dod has returned. With the neatest of touches, he rounds off the Act. Seeing a sword where the others can only see a symbol, he picks up the silly thing out of the way. True, his arm is bound up and, in more than one sense, he is out of it all; but the King, one feels sure, would agree with him in his refusal to give the object any superstitious reverence, knowing that the power of the symbol is intangible. And it may be that there is more to the treachery of Czernyak and Queen Rosamund than respect for the symbolic puppet, some further value in their selling of their personal honour for a dream.

*   *   *

The curtain goes up for the fourth Act to reveal the inside of a railway carriage, furnished as a sitting-room. It is a cramped scene, the line of windows admitting the dreary daylight of an autumn afternoon and as dreary a view of the further side of the station. In actual fact, this is a prison. Colonel Hadik's mention of a funeral, as he shows in Sir Charles Cruwys, the British Minister, does little to lighten the mood; and Sir Charles finds it cold, too.

The only touch of warmth and brightness that the scene has to offer is given by the bunch of red and yellow chrysanthemums that Guastalla is carrying, as he comes in, and that he later gives to the Queen:

> GUASTALLA. A woman ran out of a shop and asked me to bring your Majesty these.
> THE QUEEN. Oh! Did you thank her for me? I hope you thanked her.

Her response to the anonymous little gesture of human kindness is testimony to an inner desolation and indicates how far she has come since the first Act of the play and her imperiousness towards Osgood. As she sits, aside from the King and Sir Charles, '*she holds that simple gift of the flowers as if it were a friend's hand*'. When the main business between the two men is concluded, they talk casually of other matters and the King asks Guastalla about the funeral which he, it seems, has attended on the King's behalf:

> GUASTALLA. I walked behind the bier. Your Majesty's wreath was a very pretty one.
> THE KING. In the country here, did you know, a child's body's carried by children. There's no coffin ... they cover it with flowers.

That suggests a further meaning in the flowers that light up the visible scene. The child was accidentally shot on the day of the mutiny, we learn. 'Her father kept the toll-gate' sounds the passing-bell in its grim pun (a double pun, inasmuch as her death was the price paid for the rebellion, '. . . our one casualty, I'd hoped,' says the King).

For these *facts* the audience is kept waiting, however, until the scene is nearly over; the dramatist is now preparing his symbols for developments later in the Act: for the news of the death of Czernyak and, beyond that, for the Queen's cry:

> I can't die fighting ... but they could have found some way to kill me.

It is the King who, in the dialogue of the first scene, raises the question, 'And what happens next?' to which Sir Charles has no direct answer. Its echo will arrive with the crisis of the Act, in Bruckner's '... what next?' The other warning of what dramatically is in store comes in the words of Sir Charles:

> We can't afford to have this affair of yours turn tragedy. Europe's nerves aren't braced to it for the moment.

But not until the third scene will that anticipation be fulfilled and the Queen's wish for a tragic catastrophe be cheated.

The character of Sir Charles has the effect of steadying passions. He belongs to the same world as Count Zapolya, though he is a younger, more vigorous and, to that extent, more confident man. He and the King have been facing each other across one of the tables for only a few seconds, when the subtleties of the first scene of the play are recalled. Sir Charles makes his official announcement, its main point slipped diplomatically into the participial phrase:

> Upon your Majesty's abdicating I am authorised by my government to offer you a suitable asylum.

Exile, asylum, prison, even quarantine, they come to much the same thing, and the King will not consent so easily to be locked in. His appreciation of the Minister's point, and of the manner in which it is made, is itself an acceptance of the challenge: 'That's very civil of them,' he comments, twirling the official-looking letter that he brought in with him, 'And this that you've brought me . . . is the form I fill up?' But Sir Charles cannot allow to pass the suggestion that his Government is intervening in the internal affairs of Carpathia to put pressure on either Dr. Madrassy or the King. He sticks to 'the correct thing':

> I believe so, Sir. I did not bring it. It came with me.

King Henry response has an edge: 'A nice distinction.' It is clear enough, in fact, that here is another adversary come to bargain over the prisoner's ransom.

Sir Charles is drawn on to give his account of the current situation: Madrassy still in office, but more helpless than ever and more insecure; 'In the country the bottom's dropping out of things. The mark's going to glory ... the towns can't buy food ... the peasants are digging up their guns again.' Matters have worsened since the end of the last Act, it seems, but only in one respect have they altogether changed: Czernyak, still with a couple of thousand men, is within a day's march of Karlsburg, advancing still. For whatever is going to happen just that much time, one day, is left. There has been gunfire and some casualties, but Madrassy has continued to stave off civil war—no mean feat for a helpless politician, if an unspectacular one,—by the expedient of ordering Horvath to retreat always out of reach of the insurgents. That Madrassy has reached the limit of his power of restraint Sir Charles makes clearer before he leaves: 'Bruckner's nominee took over Horvath's command this morning.' There seems no alternative to abdication for the well-meaning man who sees the gain that would come of it:

> A respectable republic in being! Stocks and shares mounting again!
> And their only excuse for letting hell loose spirited away.

Yet the King appears inclined to savour his freedom to the last possible moment:

> Shall I sign now, Rosamund ... or wait till to-morrow?

For her, that would mean waiting to the last for the miracle. But he is sceptical of magic words and miracles alike. Barker seizes the opportunity to remind his audience that he has taken the conditions of the actual world for his dramatic situation and man as he is for his hero; in a world where miracles happen, 'Carpathia would be asking for another sort of king;' King Henry's kind of heroism is the only kind that truly answers to the nature of the situation.

Yet, when there is no other outward course to be followed, the King can choose to declare himself inwardly on the side of those whose loyalty to him has taken the form of disobedience. Turning inward to find their reflection in himself, he supplies the formal statement of the play's dominant theme that, as in the third Act of *The Secret Life*, makes way for the dramatic resolution.

Sir Charles has asked bluntly: 'D'you want them massacred? Do you, Sir?' The only reply he gets might be their own:

> They know they can't win. They must know that. But they'd sooner be killed to a man than give in [...] What if they've the right of it? [...] I almost wish I had my sword again [...] so that I could be foolish too.

The British Minister admits: 'I don't say we'd not have welcomed your success. But what less could you expect us to welcome?' So the thesis and antithesis are stated. From that point the King continues in a disguised soliloquy (he 'seems to speak from far away'), his opening words an unimpassioned recollection of Henry Osgood's disgust at the profiteers:

> There are two ways of looking at this world, aren't there? As a chaos that you fish in for your profit . . . and you can always pull something up. Then there's the world of your idea . . . and some of us would sooner go on to the end, hoping that may come true.

The practical question is implied in that: Is he to betray that same faith in Czernyak's men and leave them, as the Queen has put it, with 'nothing left to fight for'? Before the play is over, he will have to do so, he, too, betraying faith to keep faith. 'Have you ever been possessed by an idea, Sir Charles?' he asks now, and is answered, 'In my youth I believed I was a poet.' So he goes on:

> I came back set not to fight . . . and with nothing I wanted to win. But I did come to think for a little that there was something for me to do here. I shall never do it. Who wants it done? Yet I've never felt so much a king as I do now. As a poet . . . you'll understand that.

So to the reckoning in terms of success is opposed the tenacious faith in 'the battle that's worth losing', the battle that can't be won, in a world where to live is to sell oneself and one's values daily and hourly.

*   *   *

After this semi-lyrical suspension of the action, the form that the new crisis takes is unexpected. It is early the next morning, the light greyer and more wintry than ever. The King and Queen are not yet up. Countess Czernyak, Hadik, Guastalla and the maid, Ella, open the scene in a little flurry. The news is exchanged: Bruckner has arrived. He is on the stage, '*glum and bodeful,*' and the King appears in his dressing-gown. Bruckner has just time to enquire, 'Was that Countess Czernyak?' and so make the audience alert for the private knowledge that prompts this new interest.

He wastes no time with the King:

> If you'll do as I tell you I'll have you in Karlsburg within the week.

The King's response sounds agains that motif from the earlier part of the Act:

> In my coffin?

In another moment, following upon that cue, Bruckner's second hammer-blow falls:

> Czernyak's dead.

And, for the flowers on the bier, Bruckner has soon a sufficient epitaph to offer:

> . . . half measures were no use with him.

The threads of comedy and tragedy are being drawn together again; for there is a sense in which Czernyak's idealism represents the King's unswerving integrity, and the coffin and the epitaph symbolically anticipate the final sacrifice that he has yet to make.

Colonel Hadik brings in a tray, and over the domestic coffee cups —reminiscent of Madrassy, in Act II, drinking his malted milk, —the talk develops:

> BRUCKNER. The two of us can stop things here stampeding to perdition. If we don't . . . and pretty quickly . . . I don't know now what else can.
> THE KING. We make . . . politically . . . an odd pair, Mr. Bruckner.
> BRUCKNER. Does that matter?

It is Czernyak's question and the Queen's, coming for the third time with a repetition of the offer that they tried to press upon the King and that he refused; but the form of words no longer expresses the idealist's protest: this is the realistic view. Bruckner is a desperate man now. 'I've been wondering all this week if the very legend of you locked up here mightn't beat us,' he admits, and the force of that has been driven home by the events of the night. His account of them and of his plans has the frankness of *realpolitik* brutality:

> I've the troops in hand . . . I can wipe out these men Czernyak has left stranded. I've purged my own party and I can turn out Madrassy if I want to [. . .]. Count Czernyak wasn't over civil . . . he meant me no good . . . I don't blame him [. . .]. I sent two young hopefuls of mine to see him through the lines. They picked a quarrel with him and shot him [. . .]. It took me ten minutes to find out that I daren't punish them for it. Daren't! I've not pushed my way and other men out of it without knowing what that means!

Even the Queen would know, if she remembered Zapolya's instruction in the correct forms. Bruckner drives to his conclusion:

> I lay down an hour to think things over . . . then I started here to you. I won't be hustled to the devil if I can help it.

So he has discovered that Czernyak's death is his price, that the Queen in Act III could not yet pay him; and the taking of it has bound him. Over the coffee cups, man to man—it is men who do such things—, he outlines his 'practical plan':

> . . . I shall let things go hang for a week till everyone's pretty frightened . . . for that'd mean stiff reprisals. Then I'll march in the troops for a day's shooting. Then I'll risk it . . . I'll proclaim you [. . .]. We'll work a plebiscite [. . .]. Then we must govern and stand no nonsense [. . .]. We've to get this country to work again . . . and to fight again, maybe. Men are children mostly, and . . . give them a chance . . . wicked children . . . and as lazy as they're let be. Put tools and guns in their hands . . . you must! But take care the ideas in their heads aren't dangerous toys to play with.

That is essentially the same statement as Strowde made in his infernal creed; but the King is content to take up the last words:

> The sight of me with a crown on occasionally would keep them
> amused, you think.

It hardly seems likely that he will consent to become this sort of
toy, abrogate all power, accept Bruckner's invitation to give his
political sanction to murder and sell his integrity now to deceive
and enslave his people, when he refused Czernyak and would defy
Sir Charles's well-meaning blackmail as far as he could. An audience might well be puzzled, if the mood of the scene were less
compelling, to know the playwright's reason for staging yet another refusal, thus prolonging the play, as if his power of invention
or resolution were failing him and driving him to repeat his effects.

By this time, the visitor has placed on the table a packet taken
from the corpse and, when he has failed to strike from the King by
prettier means a response favourable to his purpose, he opens it
and shows the contents:

> Czernyak tried to bribe me with silly promises. But here's his list
> ... and a pretty full one ... of my underlings. These (*the bank-
> notes*), I dare say, were for paying a couple of them to cut
> my throat. And these, I think, are her Majesty's.
> *The tissue paper, untwisted, shows the Queen's pearls.*

Suddenly, almost ludicrously, the play seems to be veering away
from tragedy towards melodrama. But of this, too, Barker had
warned in the casual talk before Sir Charles went out:

> SIR CHARLES ... The opera's crowded. I dropped in last night
> ... to show I'd nothing on my mind.
> THE KING. What were they giving?
> SIR CHARLES. Tosca.
> THE KING. Terrible stuff. Cats on the tiles!

Now Bruckner seems to be turning into the villainous Scarpia.
Tosca, the actress, of course, is represented by the Queen: perhaps
only a tragedy-queen after all, the half-childish make-believe of a
common woman. The motifs, bargain, treachery, murder, counter-
treachery, are the same as Sardou and Puccini deal with. Here in
the domestic interior, the play offers in terms of dramatic style a
more direct and forceful version of the King's remark:

I could hardly tell you, Mr. Bruckner, how fantastically unreal all you've been saying has seemed to me.

What else but fantastic opera does the bloody violence of war, revolution and reprisals seem to the rational man, practising his domestic morality, offering hospitality, acknowledging a common human nature whose tokens, beginning with that bunch of flowers, have been scattered like gages of reality and sanity throughout the Act?

Even after listening to Bruckner's murderous plans, the King can be a little drawn to him, when he recalls him from the old days:

> You were famous as a boot-black. And always reading! [...] I used to bring you books. You kept a little stack of them under a duster in the corner . . . .

Similarly, with no political purpose, Bruckner can say, before he goes, 'I trust the news won't upset Her Majesty.' The two men have drunk coffee together 'over Czernyak's dead body', though King Henry will make no political compact on such conditions. (Private and public morality, as they are usually recognised, seem here to be reversed.) The King can even envisage the villain's redemption:

> I could hardly tell you, Mr. Bruckner, how fantastically unreal all you've been saying has seemed to me. If ill-luck ever sends you abroad again . . . look me up. I'd much like to know if it doesn't come to seem so to you.

For men are not born villains, or heroes; these are the disguises that they assume and may discard, and the way to one may be through the other.

By this time the document of abdication is signed, and witnessed by Guastalla, who has been summoned by a bell that also signalled the climax of the Act. This is King Henry's way, not only of dissociating himself from Bruckner, but of acting to prevent Bruckner's 'remedy' from being applied. No act could be less spectacular, yet it is the most effective that the King has made since the play began: the fulfilment of his kingly responsibility, not the washing of the hands that seemed to concern him in the play's first scene.

'That's useful,' says Bruckner, for the need of something to say. The pen has accomplished what the sword could not. As Guastalla hands the document to Bruckner for return to Madrassy, the King's comment admits the price of this usefulness and of the victory he has gained:

> How much belief in me was to be left when we'd shaken hands over Czernyak's dead body? Enough for your purpose! I could serve that well enough, no doubt ... as the dumb sign of a faith made tame and ridiculous ... its loyalties turned to the breeding of snobs. No, I'll betray my cause in my own way.

He too, with this 'desertion' of the men who want to fight for him and who will be left to feel fools, perhaps bitter and resentful fools, has now joined Czernyak, Guastalla, the Queen, as a traitor to men, in his loyalty to the idea.

When the guilt has thus been willingly incurred, there follows almost at once a token of redemption. Now that the bank-notes and the pearls have no more political value for him, Bruckner relinquishes them without any further consideration, as if they were '*a mislaid umbrella brought back*'; and, as such, the pearls, symbolic no longer, can go back into the property box, alongside the sword. The whole scene may be regarded as the redemptive counterpart of the end of Act III, and now all parties are released; even Bruckner 'will be fighting (Madrassy) in the open soon'. It seems that honour, though betrayed over and over again, is 'the cause that can't be lost',—so long as it is not betrayed at heart. The King formulates the paradox once more:

> You may beat him. With the best intentions he betrays his beliefs. But the belief that has been betrayed may then beat you.

The resolution now proceeds more swiftly, and its progress is more certainly marked through the musical character of the development. The symphonic form has been sustained, all along: after the slow movement of the second Act, Act III provided a highly dramatic and elaborate scherzo; with Act IV, Barker returned to sonata form; the circular movement, through which all the themes introduced in Act I are gradually gathered in, is already evident, and will become more so, as we move towards the final harmonies.

The purging of the symbols, and burning away of shams, is continued with the 'death' of the Queen into the woman. It comes in the third scene, precipitated by a little thing: the thought of King Henry inspecting their naval escort in an ill-fitting, ready-made suit. Then Sir Charles Cruwys finds her weeping in a chair, and she does not seem to mind so much being found. The transition back to the key of comedy is begun before that, however. On Bruckner's departure, King Henry has called her in—he has scarcely spoken to her since Czernyak joined the mutineers—, returned the pearls and told her of the young General's death. Then he glanced at the notes:

> THE KING. But what was he to do with t h e s e ?
> THE QUEEN. Bribe people.
> *He gives an exasperated sigh.*
> THE KING. How many more times am I to tell you that this old note with my head on it is worthless?

They were in no mood for jesting then, but the atmosphere was a little lightened for the forestalling of Guastalla's 'surrender', with which the scene ended:

> THE KING. Now, Guastalla ... don't apologise. I knew you were up to something. You can't keep a secret to save your life. And don't try and resign. That does no good. We must clear up these papers. They may pack us off at any moment now.

A mixed light, given by the shining of the station arc-lamps in through the windows of the rapidly darkening carriage, prepares the final scene again for the blending of opposed moods. Dominica and Countess Czernyak, whom the Queen has not brought herself to tell of Stephen's death, but who has somehow known of it since morning, ensure by their presence a continuity of tragic feeling, though softened now to grief. At first, the Queen and Dominica are alone. It is now that the presence of the young woman in the play is artistically justified, as she takes her place in the gallery of portraits of faithfulness, to which even Ella, the maid, belongs. Countess Czernyak is to leave with the King and Queen. Dominica has come from Karlsburg to say good-bye, but refuses to accompany her mother. Queen Rosamund takes her to task, but the girl has the final answer:

> The worse things were, I think, the more I should have to stay *[. . .].* It's my country, you see.

That has similar force to Susan Kittredge's words, 'He belongs here;' but the mood is rather darker. The effect on the Queen is complex, and the moment recalls the end of Act II when, at the piano, she had remembered the loneliness of their exile and so given a deeper emotional value to the King's introduction of his proclamation, 'To my people. . .'.

Dominica goes, and Hadik shows in the old farmer, Jakab. At first, the episode has its own kind of desolateness, as the old man stands staring from the doorway and neither he nor the Queen finds anything to say. He has only come to look at her, anyway, 'as my wife . . . and His Majesty . . . said I ought . . . it being the last chance there'll be'. It is the last time, too, that she will stand there, a symbol of royalty. The entrance of the King puts Jakab more at his ease; and now begins an interplay of conflicting emotions as the lines of conversation cross. The old man keeps happily on with his own topic, drawing the King's good-humoured response ever and again, grumbling out his pleasure at being given Snowjacket:

> JAKAB. Not that he'll earn his keep.
> *The* KING *is jovial but firm.*
> THE KING. Now . . . not one penny do you bluff out of me by that tale!
> JAKAB. He's no use for ploughing. He'll go in the small muck-waggon. But how often do I have that out?
> THE KING. You'll ride him to market every Friday.
> JAKAB. I won't. My son's got a motor car.

The Queen is still equal to registering a romantic protest:

> Snowjacket should be shot, Henry.

That will come echoing back: 'why haven't they killed us?'— 'they could have found some way to kill me.' It is in the presence of the old farmer that Countess Czernyak crosses the stage and the Queen breaks out with: 'Henry . . . she knows.' The King goes out to inspect the parade and Jakab, with no-one but the audience to listen to him—for what ears have the Queen and Guastalla for this?—, seizes his chance to deliver a speech.

The little interlude is a counterpart to that provided by the Mayor of Zimony; for this keeper of flocks and herds is *homo sapiens*, the common man, too, but recalling this time, in his imprecation on politics, the pioneering American grandfather of Henry Osgood:

> JAKAB. . . . Governments! I've seen 'em come and I've seen 'em go [. . .]. There's nothing I ask of 'em but to let me alone. Politics! My son's for politics . . . my wife'd be if she got about [. . .]. Will politics grow corn . . . or raise beef? Jacks-in-office come round badgering me! Will I plant this . . . will I sow that? Why won't I pay taxes? I won't pay no taxes. I'll feed you or starve you . . . take your choice . . . according as you worrit me or let me alone . . . .[8]

That is the comic answer to the question, Guns or butter? 'Jacks-in-office' is the comic cue for the collapse of the house of cards and the ending of the puppet-show.

Still the old man lingers, and the Queen is beside herself. At last he says, 'I did understand there was something to give me [. . .] I'd thought of an order.' It takes the Queen some minutes and the interpretation of Guastalla to understand what he means. Then for the last of the symbols she finds a use, those 'Two Grand Crosses of St. Anne and five Second Class St. Andrews', which she amused the King, in Act II, by bringing from his bedroom cupboard, because 'they might be useful'. Now she makes the presentation: 'Mr. Jakab! Yesterday you would have been a Knight of St. Andrew.' The farmer is delighted and understands perhaps better than she does:

> Of course if it's not valid it don't do you any good. But you mean it kindly.

The words bring back the vision of the red and yellow chrysanthemums in the Queen's hand.

The dramatist has one more turn of the screw for the Queen: Jakab is shown out, Countess Czernyak appears with a message, then—a well-tried comic trick—Jakab and Guastalla are back again, their way blocked by the parade, and they go out by the other door. The Queen gives the Countess her answer (it is a matter of paying for a hat-box), and at last there is nothing to keep her strained nerves taut any longer. The storm of weeping breaks. To Sir Charles, whom she now treats quite familiarly, she pours out her distracted thoughts. They are jumbled, like Alice's. She takes in that they are going to Bermuda and that it is a small island with an excellent climate:

> I've never been across the sea [...]. One of my bad dreams when I was a child was that I was left on a piece of land no bigger than a dinner plate ... for the lesson-books never said it need be any bigger ... surrounded entirely by sea. And I'd wake up screaming.

There again is the imprisonment motif, though the King on his return sounds a more cheerful modulation: 'Charming place. Houses built of coral [...]. No mosquitoes to speak of.' Monsieur Ferdinand, of whom Zapolya spoke, the Director of the Crédit Ponthyon, is recalled, not only in talk of the New World, whose discovery another Ferdinand financed, but in the hint of another place of exile and enchantment, another coral island in the 'still-vex'd Bermoothes'. The mention of the dream heralds the fading of the 'insubstantial pageant', a more poetic version, pregnant of more, than the discovery that 'You're nothing but a pack of cards';[9] but *The Tempest* and Lewis Carroll both contribute to this resolution.

The Queen goes on, and now the thought of Dominica Czernyak obliquely modifies the theme of 'a great Prince in prison lies':

> Oh this wicked country! Thank God it's not mine ... not really mine! Better have none!

The motif of the aloofness of the God sounds in that, though still muffled. She breaks out again, after a brief pause, and the little flames in the dusk of Act II (the King is now talking to the officers of the *Firefly*) blaze up, recall the phoenix-imagery of *The Secret*

Life, blend with the motif of death, and lead back into the theme of the vanishing symbols:

> We've been putting petrol on the ponds here because of the mosquitoes *[. . .]*. I can't die fighting . . . but they could have found some way to kill me. Tell me about Bermuda.

The King, joking with Sir Charles, completes the transition to the comic mode in terms of the political themes: democracy and revolution and constitutional kings; they interweave with the theme of the bargain ('I'm a pauper,' '. . .bring in the New World to redress the bank-balances of the Old,' 'I put a pile of money into it'); and so on to the farm and poultry and—from Sir Charles—the broadest of puns, unconsciously made, a schoolboy pun sounding the general note of farce:

> Something comes from Bermuda. Potatoes! I'll ask about poultry. We shall be in touch with you till you leave Toulon.

The producer has to decide at what point the lights go on in the carriage. When the play ends, the King and Queen are reading the newspapers and there is darkness outside the windows; that much is clear, but the directions do not mention the precise moment of the change in the quality of the lighting. 'Toulon' itself, and Sir Charles's departure, would seem the most probable signal. Certainly the King notices, at the next moment: 'We're off.' But it is a false start; the train, which has jerked them nearly out of their seats, stops again. 'Something went wrong with the connecting rod,' says the King; and the lights would go off again. (The Queen can still see her letter from the flare of the arc-lamps.) For the tragic melody is now re-introduced for the last time, with the appearance of Colonel Hadik at the carriage door:

> THE KING. You're coming to the frontier.
> HADIK. That's countermanded. God keep your Majesties.

They are on their feet for the farewells, the King's: 'You've been goodness itself . . . ever since you wanted to shoot me! God bless you'; and the Queen's:

> Dear Colonel Hadik . . . dear, dear Colonel Hadik! You knew we'd
> fail . . . you never minded. Oh, such a strength to me!

In Hadik's words, as he makes his triple bow, there rings clearly
at last the theme of the resurrection of the supernatural king
(which has occurred in muted form many times before, even in
Bruckner's word, 'legend'):

> Out of my grave, Ma'am . . . to be your servant! Back to it! Back
> to it! But your Majesty's most humble servant . . . to the end . . .
> to the end!

Having come to his people in their need, the divine figure dies,
or migrates, once more. For a moment the symbol has been invoked, and the mood of the invocation remains while the Queen is
shaken:

> No . . . he did that to mock me! He did! God forgive me . . . I'm
> wicked. But I think my heart's broken.

But the King's simple line, 'We've our lives to live,' with the accent
and the truth of Dominica's 'It's my country, you see', restores the
tragi-comic vision yet again.

The lights go up, the train re-starts, and nothing remains but
the ordinary world. There is a swift glance back at the action. 'I've
done what I came to do. I have won,' says the King; and indeed
he has stopped bloodshed. But, 'Don't be paradoxical, Henry,' retorts the Queen, carrying the play back to Act I, when she last
said the same thing, and so rounding off the defeat of equivocation.
The reading of Osgood's newspaper report sustains this impression of the circle complete, and complete in every respect. The
comic opera vulgarity of the style ('. . . spite of the smooth démenti
His Majesty's eye flashed, I thought, towards the map of Carpathia behind the rococo writing-table and he fingered the hilt of
his sword') lights up satirically the romantic theme, the sham, of
which the play has shown the inner truth; and the curtain falls on
the Queen—the woman!—seizing the paper to read about herself:

> . . . A stately blonde, a woman in whom mothercraft goes hand in
> hand with high political intelligence. . . .

*   *   *

In the years after the first World War, European consciousness found its most acceptable dramatic reflection in the mode of Expressionism. *His Majesty* is untouched by Expressionist mannerisms, but the same spectres haunt it as haunt the plays of Kaiser and Toller, the Čapek brothers and Brecht: anarchy and carnage and the machine as God; Carpathia, with its province of Eisenthal ('Iron Vale'), is certainly the land of Juggernaut.[10] The political awareness that the Expressionists cultivated deliberately was no new thing to Barker, though the range of affairs to which he now turned it was new; and he was never naïvely *engagé*. The impression of epic scope that the play gives may owe something to the influence of the epic film, the new art-form that contributed so decisively to Expressionist technique. For parallels to the setting of Act III, it is to Kaiser and Brecht that we can most fittingly go.

As we have seen, Barker had put the old theatrical metaphor into service in *Farewell to the Theatre*, but it is probable that his much more dynamic use of it in *His Majesty* bears some relation to Pirandello's *Six Characters in Search of an Author* and *Henry IV* (the first performed for the Stage Society in 1922, and both seen in Paris in Pitoëff's famous productions[11]) and to Yeats's *Player Queen* (produced by the Stage Society in 1919). Here were major illustrations of the tragi-comic potentialities of the *theatrum mundi* theme; and Pirandello, especially, had employed it to assert dynamically the interpenetration of art and life.

The reversal of a romantic plot and romantic values had, of course, been effected by Shaw much earlier, in *Arms and the Man*. The parallel between Shaw's hero and anti-hero and Barker's, in *His Majesty*, has already been drawn. It corresponds to a similar founding of the structure of both plays on paradox. Shaw's reaction from romance appears quite as much a theatrical pose as the attitude it mocks; Barker, however, gropes for the subjective truth within both attitudes. This difference gives rise to another, in the reflection of the outer world that the two plays offer. There are tragic meanings in *Arms and the Man*, but almost submerged in farce; and, in its social application, the paradox works largely as an intellectual formula. Barker, looking out upon the modern world, in which we live, perceived a spilling over of tragic implications that tragedy itself could not contain, but he preserves them as part of the inner life of his characters. 'We have our lives to live,' says the King of Carpathia; and the conflict between the actual world and the world of his desire troubled his author in the midst of his imaginative creation. The harsh contradictions of comedy and tragedy had, therefore, to be preserved, in order to convey the force of that conflict. There is no evading the demand of art for resolution, and so the symphonic technique, perfected in *The Secret Life*, becomes the necessary solvent, as music is in the tragi-comedy of Chekhov.

The firmness of structure of Barker's last play was anticipated as far back as *The Voysey Inheritance* and, as there, springs largely from a dialectical scheme and the interrelation of characters. The whole group of figures has issued directly from the single imaginative core of the play. The man of peace and compromise had but to call to his own opposite, and the rest seems by a happy inevitability to have followed.

CHAPTER XI

Does it Work in the Theatre?

The question that this chapter raises cannot be satisfactorily answered between the covers of a book, but only through the scrupulous testing of theatrical production which recognises the nature of the work with which it is dealing and the conditions of preparation it requires. Even then there may be no final answer, though much incidental profit.

Granville Barker's plays have in fact had little of such testing. *The Marrying of Ann Leete* has not been performed professionally since the original (private) Stage Society production in 1902. *The Secret Life* and *His Majesty* have not been seen at all on the professional stage, although they have been broadcast.[1] *The Voysey Inheritance* was revived in 1934 and again, at the Arts Theatre, in 1952. *The Madras House* was last seen in the West End theatre in 1925 and *Waste* in Michael MacOwan's 1936 production, the first after the lifting of the Censor's ban. Repertory and amateur companies have paid rather more attention to this drama, but under inevitable limitations that are hardly fair to the plays. Barker's polished dialogue has been recognised as natural material for radio, but broadcasting in fact wastes much of the power in work so carefully designed for a visual medium. Certain qualities, especially the psychological detail and intimate emotion of the plays, might be successfully conveyed by television.

Neglect breeds more neglect and encourages dismissal of these plays as out-of-date. (The mood of *The Secret Life* is sufficiently that of to-day to have struck a response from Mr. Colin Wilson, however.[2]) A close study has revealed that there is more in all of

301

them than a merely topical interest, and that they exist in their own self-consistent and autonomous worlds. The causes of the initial neglect are, perhaps, what most need to be considered.

To begin with, there are obvious practical difficulties in the way of commercial production. Large casts are required, and even the smaller parts call out for skilled and perceptive acting. Barker admitted that he had held back *His Majesty* from every 'rut of chance', and after the 1934 revival of *The Voysey Inheritance* he wrote to Harcourt Williams:

> Things have not changed in 40 years. For our sort of play and our sort of attitude to the theatre—yours and mine—*real* repertory and a permanent company are the only solution.[3]

These were, indeed, the conditions for which he had written. Shaw's work was transplanted relatively happily from the 'advanced' repertory theatre to the ordinary commercial stage; but Shaw always wrote for a traditional type of actor, Barker for a new type.

Apart from the expense of engaging all-star casts and the difficulty of finding a producer to control them, a lengthy period of rehearsal is necessary. The organic rhythmical development, which Barker substitutes for the dramatic action that proceeds by obvious leaps and bounds, requires superb discipline from the company. Following the example of Molière and of Goldoni, he looks for the unbroken movement and precision of the dance from his performers. Furthermore, his dialogue has to be mastered, not delivered straight into the auditorium. It calls for a technique of delivery equally removed from that appropriate to rhetorical drama and from the throw-away style of simple naturalism.

His prose is essentially poetic; the individual words are meaningful; euphony is one of his most frequent considerations; the actors are provided with memorable phrases to convey a passion of thought. Yet these very qualities represent a peril to be escaped. It is only too easy for the actor to be carried away on the current of a lengthy passage, or to fall into the error of reciting sentiments, beautifully turned. (Michael MacOwan's story, referred to earlier, is a demonstration of this.[4]) In fact, the characteristic power of Barker's plays is generated by a clash of contrary movements: in the conflict of the over-riding rhythm with the shifting awareness of the character, the 'little pieces' of thought and feeling; and in the tension between abstract statement and the personal experience that informs it. (This last effect has to be achieved constantly by the actors of Trebell and Strowde, for instance.)

The aim is a drama which is impressionistically alive all the time, 'continually sparks, great or small, struck between one actor and another'.[5] But the process is tiring for the players and may even become tiring for the audience, asked to concentrate on detail without respite. Mr. Alec Clunes comments:

> At their best there is in the plays something akin to the joy of a Torquemada cross-word, at their worst something akin to sewing little beads meticulously on to embroidery. He asks you to squint at something close to.[6]

It would be an artistic mistake to try and secure constant recognition of the verbal themes that echo through the dialogue; the result would be comparable to the early productions of Louis Jouvet, of which Norman Marshall has written: '. . . he made every line sound equally important until the meaning of the play was smothered in its own words.'[7] It would be a singularly insignificant production, in which none of the echoes, puns and implied images were conveyed to the audience; but the abundance of the text, and the richness of experience implied, gives individual producers and actors room to manœuvre. The interpreter has a responsibility for selection, to give point and emotional resonance where his personal understanding of rôle or play decrees. It is a very considerable responsibility, which only the creative interpreter is fit to take.

So it is not enough to leave this drama to amateurs for its testing and preservation. Alec Clunes is emphatic on this point:

> This particular kind of producing and acting call for the very best professional to bring it off . . . because of the degree of precision in technique involved.[6]

Such is the vulnerability of the plays, but it is not necessarily their poverty. Anyone who has seen (or heard) a poor production of one of Chekhov's plays cannot fail to recognise that his drama likewise is no vehicle to carry incompetence to a measure of success.

It is not only in the relation between the play and the actor that

Barker's work is similar to Chekhov's. James Bridie's response to 'the hack critics' chant that Barker's plays had no plot' is said to have been: 'These fools think that a play has no plot unless they can see the bones sticking through the flesh.'[8] On early acquaintance, Chekhov's plays may baffle in the same way, as the characters seem to talk purposelessly and inconsequently through the most commonplace hours of shiftless lives. Only in exceptional circumstances (perhaps the availability of a Stanislavsky, or Michel Saint-Denis, may count as such), does a theatrical revelation convert popular audiences to the acceptance of such plays.

Against the richness of interest that Barker's drama may yield, moment by moment, has to be balanced the length of his plays and the slow, lyrical movement of many of his scenes. It takes great ingenuity to say so much without disrupting the naturalistic fabric. From the 'static' drama of symbolism Barker had learnt the art of significant pauses and repetitions, lingering over incidentals and exploring their subtleties. Muted emotion, with a poignancy denied to unrestrained passion, answers only to the lightest of touches from the dramatist. His fully elaborated system of symphonic composition was the culmination of Barker's technical experiments, and it does not make for plays tailored to fit comfortably between dinner and the suburban trains. Audiences prepared to sit through Eugene O'Neill's play-cycles are not likely to protest at length alone; but it is a factor that seriously discourages many managements and amateur companies, especially when there is no further unfolding of story to give obvious justification for the dragging on of the performance.

Cutting, which seems to be the practical answer, is only too likely to be artistically disastrous. The rhythm and balance of the Act and, beyond it, of the entire play, were disturbed by the shortening of the scene in the Moorish Room, in a recent production of *The Madras House* by the Royal Academy of Dramatic Art; even the scale of the character-drawing was affected. Perhaps more serious was the sacrifice of dramatic tension, and confusion of the psychological movement, in a Third Programme broadcast of *Waste*, when the business of opening and discussing the letters, just before Trebell's suicide, was almost entirely omitted. The subtle modulations and variations of tempo, which contribute greatly to the pleasure Barker's plays can give, are only too easily destroyed. Unskilful cutting will make nonsense of the inner dramatic movement, as the excision of passages of the music would obscure the whole conception of a Beethoven symphony.

It may be argued that a drama that cannot face up to the rough handling of the commercial theatre and is also little adapted to the shoe-string economy of the average 'artistic' theatre, does not deserve to survive. There are many critics of the idea of a National Theatre, to which Barker was dedicated. Some claim that only academic virtues can live in the sanctified atmosphere of such an over-protected institution; they might unkindly add that his plays show just the emotional anaemia and exaggerated care for style, which mark the theatre dying of respectability. The argument must be weighed.

Yet it will not do to forget that it is the argument of a theatre which has for a long time been remarkable for its paucity of good drama, and in which 'a sheer inability to realise or compass the hard planning and austere practice of the dramatic form'[9] has been only too generally evident among 'serious' playwrights. We may wonder whether an adequate style for the performance of Chekhov could have been developed, except in such special, protected conditions as the Moscow Art Theatre could offer, and count our loss if such conditions had not been available.

Galsworthy, writing to Edward Garnett in defence of his own work, expressed one of the commonest English assumptions about the theatre:

> *The Fugitive* has in it barely enough drama for the stage. I get more and more to see how we literary folk misjudge that medium. It all has to be very strong, rather coarse, meat to get across those blankety footlights.[10]

Such an attitude must be held responsible for keeping the theatre so generally a place of rather simple indulgence, where the thoughtful relax their mental standards and no more than a rough artistry is expected, in return for a short respite of self-forgetfulness. Incidental faults in Granville Barker's work do not weaken its general significance as a challenge to this prevailing view: he experimented in the refinement of dramatic methods, so as to make possible the treatment of matter neither obvious nor crude, and he did not write down to the probable obtuseness of audiences or go half-way to meet the anticipated imperfections of actors. The carelessness of great genius is admirable as a sign of abundance; Barker attacks the lurking assumption that carelessness has any virtue in itself.

All great drama certainly contains an anarchic element, as the essential dramatic experience is of disruption, after which the elements settle down again in a new order. Those predecessors of Barker, who contrived to write great drama in a predominantly naturalistic mode, prevent the spectator's mind from passing smoothly over a glossy surface of photographic quality. *The Master-Builder, Rosmersholm* and Strindberg's *The Father* are profoundly disturbing plays, because incomprehensible to a mind that cannot, or will not, leap from one order of reality to another; and the leap, if judged from the standpoint of sanity, is into madness and nightmare. In this they are not different from the major plays of other ages and styles, including both *Œdipus Tyrannus* and *King Lear*.

Now one effect of Barker's artistry, most evident in the revised form of his plays, is a certain glossiness. (Perhaps the Edwardian cultivation of 'style' is chiefly responsible.) The illusion of 'normal' actuality is preserved throughout;[11] not even in *His Majesty* does the familiar world entirely disintegrate about us. This marks a limitation in the power of his drama, which seems to be closely related to the kind of society it presents. The progress from *The Family of the Oldroyds* to *His Majesty* shows some resemblance, in a simple view, to the social climbing of which their author has occasionally been accused. (Shaw's progress from *Widowers' Houses* and *Mrs. Warren's Profession* to *The Millionairess* and *Buoyant Billions* is open to equally unfavourable interpretation.) But Granville Barker is never content to write the comedy of manners. His choice of the intellectual man, in the ruling class, as his hero can be regarded as a sign of the reach of his imagination more than of its poverty; for here was the centre of consciousness in which the complexity of the modern world might be most fully mirrored. He was possibly rather afraid of primitive feeling, as he was shocked and frightened by the violence of the first World War. Yet there are depths under the gloss of his work, and an awareness of primitive human nature, submerged and smothered, is at the root of his heroes' self-torment.

What is personal to the man acquires another significance in the context of his art, as the childless man's obsession with the unborn child gathers to it his general reflections on the spiritual condition of civilisation. The relative power of intellect and emotion in the man constituted a strength for the particular dramatic task that concerned him. If his plays have not always the emotional power to involve audiences passionately (and the last two are hardly open to this criticism), yet they have another power: to make the impersonal aspect of human life, politics, comprehensible in terms of the common currency of human feeling and as an extension of self-knowledge.

The antithesis between man and society has often been regarded as intrinsic to naturalism. In Barker's drama, however, the false dichotomies of man and state, idealism and pragmatism, imprisonment in the circle of the brain and in the bonds of society, are exposed and resolved, as the social and political issues are worked out in terms of the individual's discovery of the interpenetration of good and evil.

Barker may have been right in considering such a comprehension of the nature of politics as necessary to the survival of a democratic society. He certainly regarded the theatre as an instrument of collective salvation; his plays make an effort to restore it to the true political function that, of all artistic media, it is best adapted to fulfil. Perhaps their most important political contribution is their heroic element: the reminder that man need never be only a pawn in the historical process, but has the responsibility for his own destiny.[12]

The English theatre of to-day may have by-passed his plays in some respects; but the individual and valuable vision they offer has no substitute, and they are ahead of us still in their re-discovery of the abundant resources that drama may command. Creative imagination has been cramped and fettered in English dramatic convention since the Jacobean age; an understanding of Granville Barker's work brings a realisation of how little this need be so. If his plays are to remain among the classics that we bury, the loss to our native dramatic tradition will be difficult to make good.

NOTES

(CHAPTER I)

1 (p. 1). Doris Arthur Jones, *Life and Letters of Henry Arthur Jones* (Gollancz, 1930), p. 211.

2 (p. 1). *The Bookman*, vol. xxxv, No. 210 (March 1909), p. 244.

3 (p. 1). Bernard Shaw, " Granville-Barker", *Drama*, New Series No. 3 (Winter 1946), p. 14.

4 (p. 2). William Archer, *The Old Drama and the New* (Dodd, Mead & Co., New York, 1929).

5 (p. 2). The peremptory dismissal of Barker's plays in John Gassner's *Masters of the Drama* (Dover Publications, New York, 3rd ed. 1954), pp. 619-20, is fairly typical of our day. Raymond Williams, *Drama from Ibsen to Eliot* (Chatto, 1952), pp. 24-5, makes *Waste* the text of an argument on the limitations of naturalism, but does not discuss Barker's work directly at all. C. B. Purdom, *Harley Granville Barker* (Rockliff, 1955), esp. pp. 204-14, makes numerous incidental remarks on Barker's plays, but is mainly concerned with them as reflections of the character of the man. However, a notable plea for reconsideration of Barker's plays was recently made by Gerald Weales, "The Edwardian Theater and the Shadow of Shaw", *Edwardians and Late Victorians*. English Institute Essays, 1959 (Columbia University Press, 1960), pp. 160-187.

6 (p. 3). On the relation of *Misalliance* and *The Apple Cart* to Barker's plays, see (forthcoming) articles by the present writer, " Bernard Shaw on the Tightrope", *Modern Drama* (University of Kansas), 1961, and " Two Varieties of Political Drama," *The Shavian*, 1961/2

7 (p. 4). Frank Vernon, *The Twentieth Century Theatre* (Harrap, 1924), pp. 50-52 *et passim*, discusses Barker's achievement as actor, producer and author.

8 (p. 4). Many of the following generalisations are based on three deservedly well-known books: Holbrook Jackson, *The Eighteen-Nineties* (Grant Richards, 1913); William Gaunt, *The Aesthetic Adventure* (Cape, 1945); Graham Hough, *The Last Romantics* (Duckworth, 1949).

9 (p. 6). Hannah Arendt, *The Human Condition* (University of Chicago Press, 1958), esp. pp. 22-58.

10 (p. 6). *ibid.*, p. 29.

11 (p. 7). Chekhov may be primarily interested in human emotions (a private world), but the passivity of his characters within a historical process that works anonymously is instructive in the present context.

12 (p. 7). *Human Nature in Politics* (Constable, 1908), p. 12.

13 (p. 7). Cf. the definition given by Simone Weil, *The Need for Roots*, trans. by Arthur Wills (Routledge & Kegan Paul, 1952), p. 8 and Arendt, *op. cit.*, p. 55, on the public realm.

310 *A Drama of Political Man*

14 (p. 9). A Preface to *Macbeth*, which Barker was working on before the fall of France, has not been traced since his death. See Purdom, *op. cit.*, pp. 267 and 277, which contains the remark: "Most of the manuscripts he left of partly finished works have disappeared."

15 (p. 9). There are three editions, items 3 (i), (ii) and (iii) in Appendix III to Purdom, *op. cit.* ("A List of Writings", compiled by Frederick May and the present author); but the one published in 1913 differs from the first in a few details only.

16 (p. 10). On this tradition and Maeterlinck's place in it, see May Daniels, *The French Theatre of the Unspoken* (Edinburgh University Press, 1953). It is difficult to determine when Barker first became acquainted with Musset's work.
—He alludes to it in *The Exemplary Theatre* (Chatto & Windus, 1922), p. 282.
—Sarah Bernhardt appeared in *Lorenzaccio* at the Adelphi Theatre in 1897. Gordon Craig's earliest production was of *On ne Badine pas avec l'Amour* at Uxbridge in 1893. George Meredith's novels may have been a channel for the indirect transmission of the methods of this drama to Barker.

17 (p. 10). See William Archer, "A Pessimist Playwright", *Fortnightly Review*, N.S. vol. 50 (Sept. 1891), pp. 346-54. His translation of *Intérieur* is included in the little volume of *Three Plays* by Maurice Maeterlinck (Gowans & Gray, 1911), for which Barker supplied an Introduction.

18 (p. 10). His mother's répertoire included recitations from Shakespeare, as well as bird imitations. A recital given by her at the Steinway Hall was reviewed in *The Era*, 27 Feb. 1892, p. 9.

19 (p. 11). e.g. "The Heritage of the Actor", *Quarterly Review*, ccxl, No. 476 (July 1923), p. 61: "If this is the dramatist's day, he will be wise to consider the actor, not as a mere appendage to his work, but as its very life-giver. Let him realise that the more he can learn to ask of the actor the more will he gain for his play. But asking is giving. He must give opportunity." But the same point is made in nearly every critical book and article that Barker wrote.

20 (p. 12). *Prefaces to Shakespeare*. First Series (Sidgwick & Jackson, 1927), pp. 136-7; not in the Batsford edition (1958).

21 (p. 13). Quoted by Robert Speaight, *William Poel and the Elizabethan Revival* (Heinemann for the Society for Theatre Research, 1954), p. 149.

22 (p. 13). e.g. by Norman Marshall, *The Producer and the Play* (Macdonald & Co., 1957), p. 153.

23 (p. 13). *The Tragic Muse*. The whole novel is an interesting commentary on the French and English theatres of the late nineteenth century.

24 (p. 14). See *Dictionary of National Biography* and A. B. Granville, *Autobiography* (London, 1874), incomplete and published posthumously. A collection of essays, *Critical Observations on Mr. Kemble's Performances at the Theatre Royal Manchester* (n.d.) has been attributed to Bozzi-Granville.

25 (p. 14). According to the late Herbert Thomas; cf. Sir Lewis Casson's excellent account of Barker in the *Dictionary of National Biography*.

26 (p. 15). That Granville Barker was paid thirty shillings a week during Miss Horniman's first theatrical venture was 'a familiar theme of hers in private conversation when she was totting up the score of her "fruitful failure".' (A private letter from Mr. Rex Pogson to the present author). Cf. Purdom, *op. cit.*, p. 5.

27 (p. 16). See text of a speech by Barker at a complimentary dinner to Dr. Wheeler, published in *The British Homoeopathic Journal*, vol. xxix, no. 1 (Jan. 1939), pp. 65-66. Schnitzler's *Das Märchen*, in an English version by Granville Barker and Wheeler, was produced by Maurice Elvey for the Adelphi Play Society, 28 Jan. 1912. The text was not published. Although Wheeler's name did not appear on the title-page of Barker's free version of *Anatol* (Sidgwick & Jackson, 1911), it is probable that the author, who confessed to knowing hardly any German, was helped by him in that work also.

28 (p. 16). Perhaps when Barker took part in the first production of *Caesar*

and Cleopatra by Mrs. Partick Campbell's Company at Newcastle-on-Tyne, in 1899.

29 (p. 18). Wilfred Scawen Blunt, *My Diaries*, Part II (Martin Secker, 1920), p. 101, entry for 30 May 1904.

30 (p. 18). Desmond MacCarthy, *The Court Theatre*, 1904-1907 (A. H. Bullen, 1907).

31 (p. 19). Insight into this period is offered by *The Letters of George S. Gordon*, ed. Mary C. Gordon (O.U.P., 1943), pp. 223, 224, *et passim*.

(CHAPTER II)

1 (p. 21). In *The Eighteen-Eighties*. Essays by Fellows of the Royal Society of Literature, ed. Walter de la Mare (C.U.P., 1932), pp. 159-196.

2 (p. 22). *On Poetry in Drama* (Sidgwick & Jackson, 1937), p. 31.

3 (p. 23). Produced in a single programme for the Stage Society on 29 April 1900.

4 (p. 23). Three performances were given: on 26, 27 and 28 June 1904, at the Royal Court Theatre. The history of earlier plans for the production of the play is conveyed in *The Letters of W. B. Yeats*, ed. by A. Wade (Hart-Davis, 1954), pp. 382-4 *et passim*.

5 (p. 23). See D. C. Calthrop's autobiography, *My Own Trumpet* (Hutchinson, 1935), pp. 32 and 210-212.

6 (p. 24). "The Heritage of the Actor", *loc. cit.*, p. 73. Barker worked, as producer, with actors who were thoroughly trained in the art of speech, as modern actors commonly are not, and he exploited their ability to the full.

7 (p. 25). In "La Tragique Quotidien", *Le Trésor des Humbles* (Mercure de France, 1910), pp. 168-9.

8 (p. 25). "Discoveries", *The Cutting of an Agate*, included in *Essays* (Macmillan, 1924), p. 339.

9 (p. 26). e.g. "From *Henry V* to *Hamlet*", *Aspects of Shakespeare*, ed. J. W. Mackail (O.U.P., 1933), p. 73: ... did Shakespeare . . . then and thereafter take the wrong road ? ... much critical authority—though it will not quite say Yes—is still apt to imply it, *etc.*'; and *ibid.*, p. 75: 'Without doubt Shakespeare imagined effects which never were fully achieved in his theatre. But there is a great gulf fixed between this admission and saying that he imagined effects that never *could* be achieved, saying, in fact, that he ceased altogether to write in the terms of the art he had mastered'; cf. *Prefaces to Shakespeare* (Batsford, 1958), II, p. 157.

10 (p. 26). W. Bridges-Adams, *The Lost Leader* (Sidgwick & Jackson, 1945), p. 4.

11 (p. 26). Bound in with a proof-copy of *The Exemplary Theatre* which passed from Barker's own library to the Meyer-Sassoon Library of the British Institute in Paris. One of the cartoons is reproduced in Purdom, *op. cit.*, facing p. 194.

12 (p. 26). I am much indebted to Sir Lewis Casson's conversation, as well as his published comments, for information about Barker's methods. He recognised, says Sir Lewis, that most actors' imaginations only work freely when they are able to move about.

13 (p. 27). *Prefaces to Shakespeare*. (Batsford), II, pp. 106-7

14 (p. 28). *The Study of Drama* (C.U.P., 1934), p. 66.

15 (p. 28). Extract from a lecture on "Co-operation in the Theatre", reported in *The Manchester Guardian*. (An undated cutting, in the present writer's possession, seems to belong to the 'twenties.)

16 (p. 28). A collection of ninety photographs and eight programmes of Moscow Art Theatre productions was brought back by Barker in 1914 and

recently figured in a catalogue issued by Ifan Kyrle Fletcher: *The History of Entertainment*, no. 190, item 158.

17 (p. 29). *The Exemplary Theatre*, p. 246.

18 (p. 29). *ibid.*, note on pp. 246-7.

19 (p. 29). Principal among these have been: Sir Lewis Casson, in "G.B.S. and the Court Theatre", *The Listener*, 12 July 1951, pp. 53-4, and his article on Harley Granville Barker in the *Dictionary of National Biography*; W. Bridges-Adams, *op. cit.*; and Hesketh Pearson, *Modern Men and Mummers* (Allen & Unwin, 1921), pp. 176-80, *The Last Actor-Managers* (Methuen, 1950), pp. 71-9, and "The Origin of 'Androcles and the Lion' ", *The Listener*, 13 November 1952, pp. 803-4.

20 (p. 31). See Bridges-Adams, *op. cit.*, p. 6, and compare Pearson, *The Last Actor-Managers*, p. 75.

21 (p. 31). Barker, like Shaw, added these directions for the benefit of a public for whom the appearance of plays on publishers' lists was a striking novelty. (See St. John Ervine, *Bernard Shaw* (Constable, 1956), p. 328.) Misunderstanding of their purpose is astonishingly long-lived.

22 (p. 32). *On Poetry in Drama*, pp. 33-34.

23 (p. 33). *The Exemplary Theatre*, p. 245.

24 (p. 33). Purdom, *op. cit.*, p. 256. Quoted here with Sir John's permission.

25 (p. 33). "The Theatre in Berlin ", *The Times*, 19 Nov. 1910, p. 6.

26 (p. 33). Michael MacOwan, "Working with a Genius", *Plays and Players*, July 1954, p. 7.

27 (p. 33). The dramatic punctuation used in the printed texts of his plays breaks up the dialogue into just such fragments.

28 (p. 34). Quoted by Purdom, *op. cit.*, p. 255.

29 (p. 35). Poel's method, described by Sir Lewis Casson ("William Poel and the Modern Theatre", *The Listener*, 10 Jan. 1952, pp. 56-8), involved a severe subordination of the actor's power to an imposed pattern. Yet Speaight, *op. cit.*, p. 123, quotes Ernest Milton as saying, 'rather surprisingly': '. . . in interpretation he seemed to guide or imperceptibly influence, never dictate'.

30 (p. 35). See Casson, "G.B.S. and the Court Theatre", *loc. cit.*, p. 53.

31 (p. 35). After his famous Shakespeare productions, Barker told Casson that he regretted the lavishness of their staging, which had distracted attention from the spoken word.

32 (p. 36). "William Poel and the Modern Theatre", *loc. cit.*, p. 58. The quotation in the next sentence is from an unprinted portion of Sir Lewis's talk, the text of which is in the Enthoven Collection.

33 (p. 37). See p. 60 of this book and corresponding note 2.

34 (p. 38). *Men and Memories* (Faber & Faber, 1932), pp. 202-3.

35 (p. 38). See (e.g.) Speaight, *op. cit.*, p. 200.

36 (p. 38). St. John Ervine, *op. cit.*, pp. 342-3.

37 (p. 38). P. P. Howe, *The Repertory Theatre* (Martin Secker, 1910), pp. 189-90.

38 (p. 38). *ibid.*, p. 145.

39 (p. 38). *ibid.*, p. 159.

(CHAPTER III)

1 (p. 41). Much of the information on which this chapter is based was supplied, or confirmed, by Mr. Thomas. On his own, independent career as playwright and actor, see Frederick May and Margery M. Morgan, "The Early Plays of Harley Granville Barker", *Modern Language Review*, vol. li (1956), pp. 324-38.

2 (p. 42). On 15 March of this year, Thomas played Apollodorus, with Barker

as Lucius Septimius, in the Newcastle first performance of *Caesar and Cleopatra*.
3 (p. 44). Duse and Bernhardt had alternated in *Heimat*, in London in 1895.
Mrs. Patrick Campbell played in the English version, *Magda*, in 1896.
    4 (p. 44). The probability of some Meredithean influence on this character is
confirmed by independent testimony to Barker's admiration for the novelist.
See pp. 49-50 of this book and corresponding note 7.
    5 (p. 46). A passage from one of these scenes is examined in *MLR* li, pp. 332-3.
    6 (p. 49). The whole passage containing this line is analysed *ibid.*, p. 336.
    7 (p. 50). *The Repertory Theatre*, pp. 112-113. Cf. *Bernard Shaw's Letters to
Granville Barker* (afterwards to be called *The Shaw-Barker Letters*), ed. C. B.
Purdom (Phoenix House Ltd., 1956), pp. 35-7, including the words: 'Ada
Rehan is obsessed with the notion of playing Diana of the Crossways. I told her
I might get someone to adapt it for her. Now you are the only playwright with
anything of the quality of Meredith's style.' (Letter of 23 Sept. 1904).
    8 (p. 55). The producer was Robert Farquharson. Charles Ricketts' account
of the Society comes in *Self-Portrait*, letters and diaries collected and compiled
by T. Sturge Moore, ed. by Cecil Lewis (Peter Davies, 1939), *passim*. The text
of *A Miracle* (unpublished) is in the Lord Chamberlain's Office; the date of
licence is: 21-3-07.
    9 (p. 55). *Saturday Review*, 30 March 1907, pp. 390-91 (not reprinted in
Around Theatres); cf. *The Stage*, 28 March 1907, p. 15. Yeats, in the best of his
short dramas, has precisely the power of language that is missing from *A Miracle*.

(CHAPTER IV)

1 (p. 58). See (e.g.) Archibald Henderson, *European Dramatists* (D. Appleton
& Co., New York & London, 1926), p. 389: '. . . this eugenic, but unnatural
solution'.
    2 (p. 60). Translated by C. D. Locock, in August Strindberg, *Lucky Peter's
Travels and Other Plays* (Cape, 1930), pp. 177-8. A lengthy extract from
this Preface (not including the present passage) was given by Justin Huntley
McCarthy in *The Gentleman's Magazine*, 1892. An article by McCarthy on
Strindberg appeared in the same year in *The Fortnightly Review*. At the same
period, J. T. Grein was considering the inclusion of *The Father* in the programme
of the Independent Theatre. See Michael Orme, *J. T. Grein* (Murray, 1936),
p. 127.
    3 (p. 63). On a possible further significance in the reiterated 'bet', see below,
p. 81.
    4 (p. 65). See also p. 91 of the present book on Barker's possible indebted-
ness to Ruskin for the metaphor of the game, as it is used in *The Voysey
Inheritance*. Mr. Tatton's question, 'What were we playing . . . cricket ?' (*Ann
Leete*, Act I) may be interpreted in the light of Ruskin's lecture on "Work",
in *The Crown of Wild Olive*: 'You play, as you call it, at cricket, for instance . . .
whatever we do to please ourselves, and only for the sake of the pleasure, not
for an ultimate object, is "play", the "pleasant thing", not the useful thing . . .'
The 'useful thing', in *Ann Leete*, is honour.
    5 (p. 65). Barker's choice of names is often worth pondering. Only rarely as
in Wychway (*Vote by Ballot*) does he use the obvious punning nomenclature of
the comedy of humours. The significance of Abud, or Osgood (the democrat in
His Majesty) is concealed by a stress that clashes with the pun on 'a bud',
'as good'. Amy (*aimée*) and Rosamund (in *Waste* and *His Majesty*) indicate the
symbolic value of the two heroines, which is not fully revealed until the action
of the play is complete. Other instances of names which may confirm the
critic's interpretations are: Constantine Madras, the far from constant Moham-

medan and Imperialist who has retreated eastwards from the barbarian hordes;
Jessica, who thinks she can be a Christian and still enjoy the Jew's fortune;
Tozer, addressed as 'you dog' by Sir George Leete and representing the brute
in man; Bakay (back + aye), a paradoxically loyal rebel, in *His Majesty*; and the
—sham names, denoting false imitations: Cottesham, Horsham (whore),
Windlesham (windle = spindle). The repetition of 'cant' (Kant), in *Waste*,
works on the same level as a reminder of Trebell's 'idealist philosophy'.

6 (p. 67). See p. 28 of this book and corresponding note 15.

7 (p. 67). *Plays, Acting and Music* (Duckworth, 1903), pp. 146-8.

8 (p. 67). *The Fantasticks*, George Fleming's version of *Les Romanesques*, was
produced by Mrs. Patrick Campbell's Company in June 1900. The part of the
heroine was played by Winifred Fraser, who was the Ann Leete of the Stage
Society production of Barker's play.

9 (p. 75). Was any of the submerged force of the fable due to the legend of
Queen Victoria's proposal to Prince Albert and Victorian feeling for the Queen?
Barker diverges from Strindberg in his attitude to the aristocratic woman who
takes the initiative; the Swedish dramatist regards Julie as a usurper, engaged
in a futile stuggle against nature.

10 (p. 75). *Plays*, by Leo Tolstoy (O.U.P. for Tolstoy Society, 1928), p. xiv.

11 (p. 76). The images of disorder are less concealed in *His Majesty* (cf.
first quotation on p. 226 of this book).

12 (p. 80). Cf. Ecclesiastes 1. 18: 'For in much wisdom is much grief: and he
that increaseth knowledge increaseth sorrow.'

13 (p. 81). F. A. C. Wilson, *W. B. Yeats and Tradition* (Gollancz, 1958), p. 94.

14 (p. 81). See D. M. Eastwood, *The Revival of Pascal* (Oxford, 1936),
esp. Chapter VI. A definition of the Pari given on p. 85 is especially applicable
to Ann's proposal to Abud: '. . . the Pari stands for a decisive step rather than
a permanent philosophy; it is the symbol of a crisis.'

15 (p. 81). *The Will to Believe* (Longmans, Green & Co., edition of 1907), p. 6.

(CHAPTER V)

1 (p. 82). The suggestion was made with the success of *The Fantasticks* in
mind. See *Bernard Shaw and Mrs. Patrick Campbell: their Correspondence*,
ed. Alan Dent (Gollancz, 1952), pp. 12-13.

2 (p. 82). Addressed to the present writer.

3 (p. 83). *The Court Theatre*, p. 29.

4 (p. 84). See item 12 (ii), Appendix III, in Purdom, *op. cit.*, p. 296. The
additional Act was written to make a play of more usual length for professional
production.

5 (p. 84). *On Poetry in Drama*, p. 38.

6 (p. 86). Charles Archer, *William Archer* (Allen & Unwin, 1931), pp. 272-4.

7 (p. 87). *The Exemplary Theatre*, p. 123.

8 (p. 87). See *The Complete Plays of Henry James*, ed. Leon Edel (Hart-Davis,
1949), pp. 678-9, 761-5.

9 (p. 89). *The Voysey Inheritance* was first performed 7 Nov. 1905, while
Shaw was finishing *Major Barbara*.

10 (p. 89). These exclude a basis in the youthful Barker's knowledge of a
(perfectly honest) solicitor's family very like the Voyseys, even to the matri-
monial affairs of the artist-son. Indeed, two of the sons, George Foss (Hugh)
and Charles Fulton, *né* Foss (Booth), impersonated themselves in the original
production.

11 (p. 94). 'Granville Barker, when will you understand that what has
ruined you as a manager is your love for people who are "a little weak perhaps,

but just the right tone." The right tone is never a little weak perhaps: it is always devastatingly strong. Keep your worms for your own plays; and leave me the drunken, stagey, brassbowelled barnstormers my plays are written for.' (Letter from Shaw on problems of casting, 19 Jan. 1908, *The Shaw-Barker Letters*, p. 115.) In fact, Edward's weakness is a superficial condition, and no actor who could not create the impression of strength under a quiet exterior would be capable of acting the rôle as the play demands.

12 (p. 94). This is the 1934 version; originally his demand was for a machine-gun.

13 (p. 94). The revision was undertaken for Harcourt Williams's production at Sadler's Wells, in which Barker had a considerable hand. His production copy (typescript), differing in some respects from the published text, is at the British Museum.

14 (p. 96). *The Observer*, 3 Aug. 1952, commenting on a Third Programme broadcast.

15 (p. 97). Cf. Ruskin, *Unto This Last:* '. . . it may be discovered that the true veins of wealth are purple—and not in Rock, but in Flesh . . .'; and also: 'There is no Wealth but Life.'

16 (p. 97). See p. 106 of this book; cf. *The Secret Life*, III. iii: 'OLIVER. . . . Ever ready to indicate the practical ideal.'

17 (p. 100). Cf. quotation from *The Republic*, p. 90 of this book.

18 (p. 100). Contrast State's doctrine in *The Madras House* (quoted below, p. 178) and Ruskin, *The Crown of Wild Olive:* '. . . if you can fix some conception of a true human state of life to be striven for . . . then, and so sanctifying wealth into "commonwealth", all your art, your literature, your daily labours, your domestic affection, and your citizen's duty, will join and increase into one magnificent harmony.'

19 (p. 101). This line may have been cut from the text because too easily recognisable as a re-statement of Ruskin's 'celebrated theory of value' which, as Shaw put it in a lecture given in 1919 on "Ruskin's Politics", 'is now a celebrated blunder'.

20 (p. 103). The most famous example is Captain Alving in *Ghosts*.

21 (p. 103). The first idea for this piece of 'business' was supplied by an actor, and Shaw suggested that more might be made of it. (See *The Shaw-Barker Letters*, p. 57.)

22 (p. 104). *The Court Theatre*, p. 27. The 'four Acts' are those following Act I.

23 (p. 105). This is the 1934 text, showing verbal alteration of the original.

24 (p. 107). Quoted in Purdom, *op. cit.*, pp. 151-2.

(CHAPTER VI)

1 (p. 109). Cf. Shaw, *The Quintessence of Ibsenism* (second edition onwards) in *Major Critical Essays* (Constable, 1932), p. 153: '. . . the suicide (in *Waste*) is unhistorical; for neither Parnell nor Dilke, who were the actual cases in point of the waste which was the subject of the play, killed himself'; cf. p. 143 of the present study. The Dilke story has been reconsidered by Roy Jenkins, *Sir Charles Dilke: a Victorian Tragedy* (Collins, 1958).

2 (p. 109). Trebell is a cross-bench politician in a metaphorical sense, too: he straddles the gulf between two phases of human consciousness. See pp. 143-4 of this book.

3 (p. 110). Barker made the minor change of replacing Horsham's temporary manservant, in Act III, by Saumarez, the secretary.

4 (p. 112). Cf. Graham Wallas's concern, in *Human Nature in Politics*, with the question, 'whether those forms of political thought which correspond to the complexity of nature are teachable'.

5 (p. 112). *loc. cit.*, p. 74.

6 (p. 113). See Purdom, *op. cit.*, pp. 71 and 72.

7 (p. 117). Sir Lewis Casson speaks of Barker's love for the music of Bach: he used to play Bach records on the pianola; when he was recovering from typhoid fever during an Irish tour, Sybil Thorndike spent hours playing Bach to him on the piano.

8 (p. 119). The play's early emphasis on education is partly explained by the classical view of education as the *raison d'être* of the state, the ultimate aim of which is the moral perfection of its members. (See *The Politics of Aristotle*, translated with an Introduction by Ernest Barker (O.U.P., second edition, 1948), pp. xlix-lii.) Cf. p. 144 of the present book.

9 (p. 121). The vocabulary he uses betrays that Barker had the First Epistle to the Corinthians in mind, esp. ch. I, vv. 25-28.

10 (p. 128). See p. 320, note 11, in this book.

11 (p. 128). Here and in *The Secret Life* the writing-table appears to be a symbolic property: it is the true battle-ground, the *tabula rasa* on which the philosopher-statesman, according to Socrates, designs the perfect state, bringing together into a harmony his observations of men's moral natures and his contemplation of ideal forms. (*Republic*, Book VI.)

12 (p. 131). The idea of time is thus visually focused. The many reminders of time in the dialogue comment insistently on the tragic situation. Barker repeatedly plays on the themes of past, present and future, e.g. in Act I:

> TREBELL. It ought not to . . . at the moment.
> AMY. Why not?
> TREBELL. The past has no place in love-making . . . nor the future . . .;

in Act II, as part of the discussion of time and eternity:

> TREBELL . . . Save me from Mr. Facing-both-ways. The present may be his . . . but never the future;

the original version of Act II invites speculation:

> WEDGECROFT. Religious education won't do now-a-days.
> TREBELL. What's Now-a-days? You're very dull, Gilbert.

The first example is quickly followed by the phrase, 'moonlit moments', used by Trebell, and this strengthens a suspicion that Zarathustra's vision of the moonlit gateway may have contributed to *Waste*: ' "Behold this gateway, dwarf!" I continued. "It has two faces. Two paths meet here: . . . This long lane stretches back for an eternity. And the long lane out there, that is another eternity. They contradict each other these paths . . . The name of the gateway is inscribed above: 'Moment' . . ." ' (Nietzsche, *Thus Spake Zarathustra*, Part III, trans. Kaufmann.) Certainly Barker identifies Mr. Facing-both-ways with Janus. The great gate at Karnak, in *The Secret Life*, Act I, also seems to have the value of the Nietzschean image.

13 (p. 132). *Preface to Julius Caesar* (Benn, 1926), p. xvii; cf. *Prefaces to Shakespeare*. (Batsford) II p. 371.

14 (p. 139). Browning's formative influence on Barker's imagination (already noted in *Our Visitor*) may be traced here; cf. esp. "Rabbi ben Ezra": 'For thence,—a paradox/Which comforts while it mocks,—/Shall life succeed in that it seems to fail:/What I aspired to be,/And was not, comforts me . . .'

15 (p. 139). The dramatist comments on this whistled signal: '*all ardent Wagnerians used it in the eighteen-nineties*'. As a token of triumphant prophesy, it was certainly allied to the ideas of the millenium and the coming of the Superman.

16 (p. 141). This is not to say that it is not a profound and complete conversion, for thought is life to him and absorbs all his emotions. The abstractions draw him on, until nothing but the philosophical absolute will satisfy him. Cf. Ibsen's *Brand*, with its allied tragic theme. Trebell and Brand alike sacrifice

all human relationships to an idea, and sacrifice themselves also, at first in their living and then—when no other form of sacrifice remains—in their death. Of course, Brand's death does not appear to be suicide, though it is undoubtedly sought.

17 (p. 143). *Play-making* (Chapman & Hall, 1912), p. 275. Archer's inform-ant was Barker himself. There are grounds for supposing that *Waste* contained an autobiographical element.

18 (p. 143). See *Dictionary of National Biography*.

19 (p. 143). Quoted in Purdom, *op. cit.*, p. 95.

20 (p. 144). Cf. Ibsen's *Emperor and Galilean*, in which Julian the Apostate is accredited with the dream of a Hegelian Third Empire to combine Christian spirituality with the spirit of Greek philosophy. The 'liberator who came too soon' is also the tragic hero of Strindberg's *Master Olof*.

21 (p. 144). Basil Willey, "How 'Robert Elsmere' Struck Some Contem-poraries", *Essays and Studies*, New Series vol. x (1957), pp. 53-68, states that, forty years ago, Mrs. Humphry Ward's novel of the clergyman who lost his faith was known to 'everyone who had read anything at all'.

22 (p. 145). These are also marks of the Nietzschean hero. See Eric Bentley, *The Cult of the Superman* (Robert Hale, 1947), p. 74.

23 (p. 145). These are two of the three elements which clash and are recon-ciled in the dialectical structure of *Major Barbara*.

24 (p. 146). Barker's connection with the Fabian Society gave him a detailed background to the Education dispute, especially as presented in the first version of *Waste*. Sidney Webb's support of the London Education Act of 1903 (a Tory measure), which brought schools of all denominations, including Anglican and Catholic, under the control of the L.C.C. and on the rates, offended the Liberals, members of the young Labour Party and many fellow Fabians. See Beatrice Webb, *Our Partnership*, ed. by Barbara Drake and Margaret I. Cole (Longmans, Green & Co., 1948), pp. 252-7 *et passim*. A more general view of the debate among the Fabians is given by Edward R. Pease, *The History of the Fabian Society* (A. C. Fifield, 1916), pp. 142-8. See also Shaw, *Doctors' Delusions, Crude Criminology, Sham Education* (Constable, 1932), pp. 353-73.

25 (p. 146). One such occasion, a supper on 3 July, 1914, is described by Charles Ricketts, *Self-Portrait*, p. 202.

26 (p. 146). See Wilfred Scawen Blunt, *My Diaries*, Part II, pp. 296-8.

27 (p. 146). Is there an allusion here to the anecdotes current about the appointment of Alfred Austin as Poet-Laureate in succession to Tennyson ? See N. B. Crowell, *Alfred Austin: Victorian* (Weidenfeld & Nicolson, 1955).

28 (p. 147). Archibald Henderson's exaggerated disaste for Trebell (*European Dramatists*, p. 391) betrays a misapprehension of the attitude of the dramatist to his hero. One of Barker's own critical comments is apposite here: 'A hero, let us be clear, is the character of which a dramatist, not morally, but artistically, most approves.' (*Prefaces to Shakespeare* (Batsford) II p. 351.) C. B. Purdom, *op. cit.* pp. 205-7, provides a recent instance of the close identification of Trebell with his author's personality.

29 (p. 147). Beatrice Webb, *op. cit.*, p. 352.

(CHAPTER VII)

1 (p. 149). See Ruskin's lines, quoted above, note 18 (p. 100). They may be a source of the design of *The Madras House*, which does indeed combine the themes of art, daily labours, domestic affection and citizen's duty into one harmony.

2 (p. 152). In the original text of 1909, published in 1911, it is an agapanthus that blooms in the conservatory. On the significance of that first choice see pp

178-9 of this book. The revised version of *The Madras House* was made and published in 1925.

3 (p. 155). *The Eighteen-Sixties*. Essays by Fellows of the Royal Society of Literature. Edited by John Drinkwater (C.U.P., 1932), pp. 102-48.

4 (p. 155). From Robert Reece, *The Stranger: stranger than ever* (1868), quoted in *The Eighteen-Sixties*, p. 105.

5 (p. 155). *The Sleeping Beauty*, quoted *ibid.*, p. 117.

6 (p. 156). This is the revised version. The original has: 'most important things' in place of 'master tests'. Through the change, Barker is able to introduce, as he had done in *The Voysey Inheritance* and *Waste*, the theme of power in general and, in particular, the struggle between the sexes for dominance.

7 (p. 157). See Purdom, *op. cit.*, pp. 102-3. Shaw's Tarleton shares certain features with Constantine Madras, although the two characters are totally different in their general effect. St. John Ervine, *op. cit.*, p. 428, mentions the superficial relation of Tarleton to three actual men: Carnegie, Whitely and Selfridge. See also the present writer's article, "Bernard Shaw on the Tightrope".

8 (p. 158). *History of the Fabian Society*, pp. 163-84. Another Fabian whom Barker may possibly have had in mind in drawing Constantine Madras was Hubert Bland (see St. John Ervine, *op. cit.*, p. 123), who later provided Shaw with a model for Hector Hushabye.

9 (p. 158). According to Archibald Henderson, *op. cit.*, p. 388, Barker had become a socialist in 1901.

10 (p. 158). See Hesketh Pearson, *G.B.S. A Postscript* (Collins, 1951), pp. 157-8.

11 (p. 165). The phrase is assigned to State, but his interpretation of it, which is the chief object of Barker's satire, may be regarded as a travesty of the 'gospel of beauty' associated with Ruskin, in which aesthetics and ethics were reconciled.

12 (p. 167). Note the *pocket—womb* antithesis again: commercial profit *versus* creation.

13 (p. 176). See (e.g.) Archer, *The Old Drama and the New*, p. 362. James Agate's protests at the 1925 revival are recorded in *The Contemporary Theatre* (Chapman & Hall, 1926), pp. 235-9; but a reversal of his verdict is implied in the praise of the Philip-Jessica scenes expressed by the reviewer of a recent broadcast of the play (*The Listener*, 17th Nov. 1960, p. 909). Radio is undoubtedly an appropriate medium for the intimate naturalism of Act IV; it can also be argued that present day theatrical fashion makes audiences more receptive to Barker's method here.

14 (p. 178). *Modern Painters*, vol. 3, Part 4.

15 (p. 179). The figures of murderer and whore are central in the design of the unfinished play, *The Wicked Man*, discussed in Chapter VIII.

16 (p. 182). In the first version, the town is Manchester. Canning Town recalls State, the apostle of mass-production, whose fortunes were founded on canned peaches.

17 (p. 182). This is a further theme picked up in Shaw's *Misalliance* (cf. Lina's outburst near the end of that play: '. . . this Englishman! this linendraper! he dares to ask me to come and live with him in this rrrrrrrabbit hutch, and take my bread from his hand . . .'). The imagery of the farmyard will be encountered again in the short story, "Georgiana", discussed in Chapter VIII, and in *His Majesty*. Both Shaw and Barker doubtless owed much in this critique of society to Edward Carpenter, *Civilisation, Its Cause and Cure* (1889).

18 (p. 183). R. H. P. Curle, *Aspects of George Meredith* (Routledge, 1910), p. 9, wrote: 'Humanity, in the midway between nature and civilization, has lost the centre of control. It is his work to regain it, and to make the balance surer than before.' This comment might have been written with reference to the passage from *The Madras House* quoted above, p. 183. On Meredith's

concept of Nature and its relation to moral virtue, see Curle, *op. cit.*, pp. 56-80 and G. M. Trevelyan, *The Poetry and Philosophy of George Meredith* (Constable, 1907), esp. pp. 119-26.

(CHAPTER VIII)

1 (p. 185). See A. Sutro, *Celebrities and Simple Souls* (Duckworth, 1933), p. 115.

2 (p. 185). See Hesketh Pearson, *Bernard Shaw* (Collins, 1942), p. 244.

3 (p. 186). The present author is greatly indebted to the late Lady Keeble (Lillah McCarthy) for much of the information in this chapter.

4 (p. 187). The letter is in the possession of the present writer.

5 (p. 187). On this version, which survives in manuscript, see Calthrop, *op. cit.*, pp. 210-12.

6 (p. 188). A typescript copy is in the New York Public Library.

7 (p. 188). See item 123 in Appendix III, Purdom, *op. cit.*, pp. 307-8.

8 (p. 196). Cf. Ruskin, *Modern Painters*, vol 5, Part ix, on the broken mirror.

9 (p. 198). T. S. Eliot, *Selected Essays* (Faber & Faber, third edition, 1951), p. 229. Originally included in *Elizabethan Essays*.

10 (p. 198). See above, p. 31.

11 (p. 200). *The Bookman*, xxxix, no. 229 (October 1910), pp. 13-21.

12 (p. 201). Is the notion of a city of brotherly love implied? The same idea seems to have been in Barker's mind as when he mentioned the agapanthus in *The Madras House*.

13 (p. 202). See (e.g.) Purdom, *op. cit.*, p. 282.

14 (p. 202). Elizabeth speaks of her sons as lost to her, now that they are away at school and claimed by Hugo's world with its ideal of 'getting on'. Joan's sons have been killed in the war. So both look on themselves as finally barren.

15 (p. 205). His Presidential Address to the English Association, *Quality* (Humphrey Milford for the English Association, 1938) and the concluding sections of *The Use of the Drama* (Sidgwick & Jackson, 1946), pp. 76-8, are among his writings that touch on the theme.

16 (p. 206). Shakespeare's lyrical scenes also taught Barker much. The duologue between Lorenzo and Jessica, for instance, is recalled in the moonlight interludes of *The Secret Life*.

17 (p. 207). *The Madras House* (1925), Act IV, especially Jessica's speech '.... The way men allow Nature to befool them into swinging the pendulum . . . they've no other notion . . . between getting babies born and starting wars to destroy the surplus! . . .'

18 (p. 208). Cf. Bridges-Adams, *op. cit.*, p. 6 on the 'holy hush' which characterised some scenes in Barker's productions.

(CHAPTER IX)

1 (p. 210). William Poel, *What is Wrong with the Stage* (Allen & Unwin, 1920), pp. 9-10.

2 (p. 210). Extract from a letter quoted by Purdom, *op. cit.*, p. 240.

3 (p. 211). From a letter printed by Charles Archer in *William Archer*, p. 397.

4 (p. 212). Cf. the symbolic value of the statue of the woman in *When We Dead Awaken*. (See pp. 216, 217 of the present book.) The division of visual

from aural aspects is practised in several of Maeterlinck's little plays (e.g. *Intérieur, Les Sept Princesses*) and, doubtless on the model of those plays, in Yeats's *Purgatory*.

5 (p. 218). There is a parallel here to the pressure put on Rosmer by Kroll and by Rebecca (in Act I of Ibsen's play) to emerge from his scholarly retirement and take sides in the current political struggle.

6 (p. 220). "A Roland for an Oliver."

7 (p. 220). The parallel with Hedda Gabler burning the 'child 'of Thea and Lövborg is obvious.

8 (p. 222). Cf. Yeats's "The Second Coming" (1921): '. . . a vast image out of *Spiritus Mundi*/Troubles my sight. . . . And what rough beast, its hour come round at last,/ Slouches towards Bethlehem to be born?' Kittredge's words take up Serocold's allusion to the Beast in Revelations (Act I, sc. i) and Oliver's complaint about the 'beast of a world to have left on one's hands' (Act II, sc. iv) and link them with the motif of generation, in a way suggestive of a cyclic view of history.

9 (p. 225). Cf. Graham Wallas, *Human Nature in Politics*, pp. 153-5, on the usual disastrous progress of the political idealists:

. . . after a time a sense of unreality grows upon them. Knowledge of the complex and difficult world forces itself into their minds . . . . Most men, after the first disappointment, fall back on habit or party spirit for their political opinions and actions. . . .

Wordsworth's *Prelude* describes with pathetic clearness a mental history, which must have been that of many thousands of men who could not write great poetry, and whose moral and intellectual forces have been blunted and wasted by political disillusionment. He tells us that the 'man' whom he loved in 1792 . . . was seen in 1789 to be merely 'the composition of the brain.' After agonies of despair and baffled affection, he saw 'the individual man . . . the man whom we behold with our own eyes.' (*The Prelude*, Bk. xiii, 11. 81-84.) But in the change from a false simplification of the whole to the mere contemplation of the individual, Wordsworth's power of estimating political forces or helping in political progress was gone for ever.

10 (p. 226). Cf. *The Republic*, Book IX: '. . . when the rest of the soul—the reasoning and human and ruling power—is asleep; then the wild beast within us, gorged with meat or drink, starts up and having shaken off sleep goes forth to satisfy his desires.' See next note.

11 (p. 227). It is doubtful if Barker uses any word of more complex significance than *beast* (or the variants, *brute*, or *animal*), as it is employed in *The Secret Life*. A reminiscence of Aristotle's definition of man as *zoon politikon* is basic. The association with the simple instinctual life, present in Miss Chancellor's reference to 'the beasts of the field' (see above, p. 165), is still included in the word; so are the general connotations of Meredith's 'Nature', present in the phrase, 'toiling animals', in *Ann Leete*, which Carnaby identifies with the entry into 'Nature's cloister'. The association of the motif of the beast with the motif of breeding, observable in Kittredge's lines, quoted above, p. 222, and maintained throughout *The Secret Life*, was anticipated in the idea of the labour of birth, the burden of the beast, contained in Ann Leete's choice of the simple life. Abud, in the notes for *The Wicked Man*, is described as "a working animal', a definition of man which recalls Hobbes's famous account of human life in a state of nature: 'solitary, poor, nasty, brutish, and short', and also Marx's definition of Labour as the metabolism between man and nature. On the other hand, the great Beast, or monster, is at once an apocalyptic image, the creature of the Platonic myth (*Republic*, Book VI) and the sovereign political power of Hobbes's metaphor of the leviathan. Machiavelli's fable of the ruler who must be prepared to act as a beast, fox or lion, may also be relevant. The various inherited meanings of the word, *beast*, are not, of course, simply latent

in the dialogue of *The Secret Life*, but are invoked to full power through the operation of the dramatic context.

12 (p. 230). This was most noticeable in the only performance seen (at the University of Leeds in 1953), despite the fact that the play had already run for a considerable time when he appeared on the stage. This quality in Clumbermere should be taken into account when the question of the length and possibly unnecessary protraction of *The Secret Life* is under discussion.

13 (p. 233). One of the comic variations on the theme of the beast. Another is audible in Kittredge's: '. . . my works [. . .] repose in the half-calf of a definitive edition. . . .'

14 (p. 234). *Plays*, by Tolstoy, p. xii. Carlyle's 'cash nexus' was certainly in Barker's mind.

15 (p. 235). Cf. Shylock: 'My meaning in saying that he is a good man, is to have you understand me that he is sufficient' (*Merchant of Venice*, I. iii).

16 (p. 236). Original Preface to *The Tragedie of Cymbeline* (The Players' Shakespeare, Benn, 1923), p. xiii.

17 (p. 237). *Prefaces to Shakespeare* (Batsford) II, p. 76.

18 (p. 239). This again recalls Pascal's Wager ; indeed it is probably Barker's most immediately forceful application of the symbol. The counterpoint thus underlines the significance of the conversation in the gallery, even while lightening its tone. The theme returns in the scene between Strowde and Heriot.

19 (p. 239). The power of these two speeches is partly determined by the rhythm, but more fundamentally by the concentration of meaning in its multiple echoes (e.g. 'fools'—'knaves' may be traced back to *King Lear*, but have here the eighteenth-century virulence of their re-iteration by Swift, especially in *A Serious and Useful Scheme*). Machiavelli, advocate of force and fraud, is a general source of the whole (cf. especially *Discourses* I. 3:

> . . . it must needs be taken for granted that all men are wicked and that they will always give vent to the malignity that is in their minds when opportunity offers . . . . men never do good unless necessity drives them to it . . . . it is said that hunger and poverty make men industrious, and that laws make them good);

but Hobbes's doctrine of Fear as the universal social motive, discussed by Graham Wallas in *The Great Society* (Macmillan, 1914), pp. 89-98, is also reflected in the passage. Both derive ultimately from Aristotle's observation: 'Man, when perfected, is the best of animals; but if he be isolated from law and justice, he is the worst of all.' (*Politics*, I. ii. 15.) Graham Wallas, *Human Nature in Politics*, pp. 173-4, can be read as a commentary on the whole sentiment and attitude expressed:

> After a time the politician may cease even to desire to reason with his constituents, and may come to regard them as purely irrational creatures of feeling and opinion, and himself as the purely rational 'overman' who controls them. It is at this point that a resolute and able statesman may become most efficient and most dangerous. Bolingbroke . . . spoke in a haunting phrase of 'that staring timid creature man'. A century before Darwin he, like Swift and Plato, was able by sheer intellectual detachment to see his fellow-men as animals.

20 (p. 241). Cf. Blackborough's words, quoted above, p. 123.

21 (p. 243). In Act II, scene iii. Strowde, seated behind his writing-table, sets about testing the young man's quality and the seriousness of his intentions:

STROWDE. What's wrong with the city?
OLIVER. What's wrong with a mine that's on a map and a cotton-field on a balance-sheet?
STROWDE. Not primitive enough?

OLIVER. Maybe. Digging potatoes might sweat all the nonsense out of me d'you think?

Oliver is mature enough to distinguish between the insufficiency of a return to simplicities and the necessity of getting beyond abstractions to individual realities.

(CHAPTER X)

1 (p. 256). An audience would see a small triptych, subconscious preparation for the emergence of the theme of the *logos*, the icon of divine sovereignty.

2 (p. 258). Cf. Aristotle. *Politics*, I. ii. 14: 'The man who is isolated . . . is no part of the polis, and must therefore be either a beast or a god.' The image of royalty as 'a God on earth' is developed in the Shakespearian contribution to *Sir Thomas More*.

3 (p. 260). Cf. Joseph Conrad's treatment of this idea in *Nostromo*.

4 (p. 263). See letter quoted in Purdom, *op. cit.*, pp. 240-41.

5 (p. 268). This appears to have given Shaw his central theme for *The Apple Cart*.

6 (p. 272). It is likely that this setting was suggested by the circumstances of the German capitulation in 1918.

7 (p. 277). This recalls the ceremonial degradation of Dreyfus. Shaw discusses the effectiveness of a theatrical representation of this in *Our Theatre in the Nineties* (Constable, 1932), I, pp. 283-6.

8 (p. 295). Barker's decision to include Jakab in the play reflects his appreciation of the importance of the peasantry in the Central European countries after the 1914-18 war. One wonders whether he had read an article by (Sir) Lewis Namier on "The Peasant and the State", *The Spectator*, 27 June 1925, reprinted in *Skyscrapers and Other Essays* (Macmillan, 1931), pp. 156-62. Namier remarks of the peasant that: '. . . "democracy" has made him dominant in all the agrarian countries of Europe'. He characterises him in terms that are closely parallelled in Jakab's monologue:

> All other classes are to the peasant mere parasites living on his labour, and he would gladly do without them . . . . we . . . in England . . . do not understand their immense, passive strength and their tragic, though natural, incapacity for government . . . . The interest of the peasant in the State is too remote to make him an active, positive element in it. . . . Their hours of work are regulated by the sun and the weather, and the returns of their labour are determined by the soil and the seasons. The benefits they possibly derive from the State they hardly perceive, but they know it as tax-collector and recruiting-sergeant . . . . the peasant alone . . . is anterior to the State; he could, if need be, revert to self-sufficiency, and can therefore afford to be an anarchist.

Jakab is thus the a-political natural man balancing that 'mortal God', the sovereign; and, significantly, it is to Jakab that the symbolic royal charger is finally entrusted: the new responsibility.

9 (p. 296). Cf. the staging of a scene in Pitoëff's production of Pirandello's *Henry IV* (see p. 299 of the present book), which earned the author's approval: the man known as 'Henry IV', when the world of his illusion was collapsing about him, rushed about the stage in an attempt to prop up the cardboard walls of the set, as they threatened to fall upon him. (Described by Norman Marshall, *op. cit.*, p. 76.)

10 (p. 299). As Barker certainly had Anthony Hope's *Prisoner of Zenda* in mind, when writing this play, he may also have been aware at least of the title

and imagery (including the railway symbol) of another of Hope's novels, *The God in the Car* (1894), concerned with the ruthlessness of the Empire-Builder. (This serious theme is overshadowed by a conventional society love-story.) Another probable source is Laurence Housman's *John of Jingalo* (1912). 11 (p. 299). *Six Characters* was produced in April 1923 and *Henry IV* in Feb. 1925 (after opening in Monte Carlo, the previous month). Though Barker did not make his home in Paris until 1930, he was a frequent visitor there and a friend of Jacques Copeau.

(CHAPTER XI)

1 (p. 301). *The Secret Life* in Jan. 1948 and *His Majesty* in Nov. 1950.
2 (p. 301). *The Outsider* (Gollancz, 1956), pp. 39-46.
3 (p. 302). Quoted by Purdom, *op. cit.*, p. 243.
4 (p. 302). See above, p. 33.
5 (p. 303). Michael MacOwan, *loc. cit.*
6 (p. 303). Mr. Clunes's professional estimate of Granville Barker's plays was communicated to the present writer privately. For its interest, it merits quotation at greater length:

"Actable"? Yes, of course, they [*the plays*] have been—and are—acted with great success. G.B.'s knowledge of the sheer craftmanship of writing plays was enormous—perhaps too great . . . . And this is what I am hinting might be "wrong" with the Barker plays. I am sure that my major pleasure watching them is in admiring the delicacy of the craftmanship. The hardest task that producer and actors will have, though, is in compelling my involvement and sympathies with the characters. And this despite the fact that I am personally generally in sympathy with the play's moral, or total gesture . . . . Perhaps the most satisfactory evenings in a theatre are those which cause one to be involved in the play. But there should be no law against being invited to watch an expert carpenter juggling with the most delicate tools of his trade. But one must expect a cooler atmosphere—and far less people . . . .

7 (p. 303). Norman Marshall, *op. cit.*, p. 77.
8 (p. 304). Related by Mr. Clunes.
9 (p. 305). *The Exemplary Theatre*, p. 117.
10 (p. 305). *Letters to Edward Garnett* (Cape, 1934), p. 208.
11 (p. 306) The illusion is precariously maintained in *Rosmersholm* too. Indeed the challenge to comprehension offered by Barker's work at its most introspective, as in the last Act of *Waste* and *The Secret Life*, is essentially the same kind as *Rosmersholm* presents.
12 (p. 307). Cf. Richard Ellmann's comment, in "The Two Faces of Edward", *Edwardians and Late Victorians*, p. 198: 'Granville Barker brings Edward Voysey to sudden maturity when, like the hero of that neo-Edwardian novel *By Love Possessed*, he discovers the world is contaminated and that he may nonetheless act in it.'

INDEX

325